EAGLE MINDS

EAGLE MINDS

Selected Correspondence of Istvan Anhalt and George Rochberg (1961–2005)

ALAN M. GILLMOR, EDITOR

Wilfrid Laurier University Press

This book has been published with the help of a grant from the Canadian Federation for the Humanities and Social Sciences, through the Aid to Scholarly Publications Programme, using funds provided by the Social Sciences and Humanities Research Council of Canada. We acknowledge the support of the Canada Council for the Arts for our publishing program. We acknowledge the financial support of the Government of Canada through the Book Publishing Industry Development Program for our publishing activities.

Library and Archives Canada Cataloguing in Publication

Anhalt, István, 1919–
Eagle minds : selected correspondence of Istvan Anhalt and George Rochberg / edited by Alan M. Gillmor.

Includes bibliographical references and index.
ISBN 978-1-55458-018-7

1. Anhalt, István, 1919– —Correspondence. 2. Rochberg, George—Correspondence. 3. Composers—Correspondence. I. Gillmor, Alan M. II. Rochberg, George III. Title.

ML410.A59A4 2007 780.92'2 C2007-902763-6

Cover photo and frontispiece: Istvan Anhalt and George Rochberg, Kingston, Ontario, August 1985. Photo by Beate Anhalt. Library and Archives Canada. Cover design by Sandra Friesen. Text design by Catharine Bonas-Taylor.

Waterloo, Ontario, Canada
www.wlupress.wlu.ca

for Willis

CONTENTS

LIST OF ILLUSTRATIONS

ACKNOWLEDGMENTS

My profound gratitude must be offered first, of course, to Istvan Anhalt and George Rochberg, who cooperated in this enterprise with uncommon generosity, clarifying countless points of fact and obscure calligraphy. Moreover, both took the time to proofread their respective letters in a draft version, catching as a consequence numerous typographical errors which one is tempted to blame on the computer voice recognition software but which, more honestly, must be attributed to the lazy eyes of the editor. I would also like to offer my deep appreciation to Gene Rochberg, who, since her husband's death, has taken over the onerous task of proofreading and editorial advising.

I would like to thank Dr. S. Timothy Maloney, the former Director of the Music Division of Library and Archives Canada, for taking a strong personal interest in this project from the beginning and assisting me in numerous ways, and to Jeannine Barriault, Maureen Nevins, and the staff of the Music Division of Library and Archives Canada I record my appreciation for their splendid assistance and consummate professionalism. Dr. Felix Meyer, Johanna Blask, and Petra Kupfer of the Paul Sacher Foundation in Basel, Switzerland, as well as the Music Division of the New York Public Library, have kindly placed at my disposal letters of Anhalt to Rochberg held in their respective George Rochberg Collections. I would also like to single out Zoltán Bartos (Museum of Fine Arts, Budapest), Paul Landau (Director, Israel Music Institute), Nancy M. Shawcross (Curator of Manuscripts, Rare Book and Manuscript Library, University of Pennsylvania), and Christine Taylor (Interlibrary Loans Department, Carleton University).

To my colleagues, Professors Paul Attallah, Donald Beecher, Bryan Gillingham, Elaine Keillor, Gregory MacIsaac, Steven Wilson, and James

Wright, all of Carleton University, I extend my gratitude for their assistance on a number of points great and small.

A bald list does not adequately reflect my deep gratitude to those—many of them subjects of this correspondence—who generously responded to my inquiries: the late Roger Beare, Glenn Black, Arnold Broido, Curt Cacioppo, Ivan Chan, David Clunie, Lowell Cross, Brenda Dalen, Morris Eaves, Robin Elliott, Alfred Fisher, Donald Gillmor, Joseph Graham, Arlene Greenberg, Beverly Holmes, Fr. Giancarlo Isoardi, Peter Laki, Gord McFee, Helen Mirkil, Monte Keene Pishny-Floyd, Winston Purdy, Michael Roeder, Gordon Smith, Melvin Strauss, Joel Thome, and John Thomson.

This book has been published with the help of a grant from the Canadian Federation for the Humanities and Social Sciences, through the Aid to Scholarly Publications Programme, using funds provided by the Social Sciences and Humanities Research Council of Canada.

INTRODUCTION

In the late summer of 1960, an International Conference of Composers was held in the southwestern Ontario town of Stratford, since July 1953 the home of the renowned Stratford Festival. Under the leadership of Canadian composer Louis Applebaum, who in 1955 became the first music director of the festival, an eight-day series of panels, discussions, and concerts opened on 7 August. In attendance were fifty-five composers from twenty countries, more than half of them from the United States and Canada, as well as a number of music critics and administrators. Among the participants were the composers Luciano Berio, Karl-Birger Blomdahl, Henri Dutilleux, Iain Hamilton, Vagn Holmboe, Elizabeth Maconchy, Otar Taktakishvili, and Joseph Tal. The American contingent included Roy Harris, Ernst Krenek, Otto Luening, Gunther Schuller, Edgard Varèse, and George Rochberg, and among the Canadian representatives were Violet Archer, John Beckwith, Claude Champagne, Udo Kasemets, Oskar Morawetz, Jean Papineau-Couture, Harry Somers, John Weinzweig, and Istvan Anhalt. Rochberg appeared on a panel entitled "Serialism" alongside his countryman Ernst Krenek and the Briton Iain Hamilton. Both Rochberg and Anhalt had music performed during the conference, the former represented by his *Duo Concertante* for violin and cello, the latter by his first Symphony.[1] Thus began a lifelong friendship between Anhalt and Rochberg. Shortly thereafter began a correspondence, which continued until the spring of 2005; sadly, Rochberg died, on 29 May 2005, as this book was in its final stages.

I first met Istvan Anhalt in the fall of 1970. He had joined the Faculty of Music of McGill University soon after his arrival in Montreal in 1949. In August 1970, I arrived at McGill as a young assistant professor.

Anhalt almost immediately befriended me, smoothing my entrée into a large and many-faceted department. Much to my regret, I did not meet George Rochberg, although we communicated by letter and telephone on a number of occasions. I had long known of him through his music and recall vividly the "culture wars" that he precipitated with the first performances of the string quartets (nos. 3–6) commissioned by the Concord Quartet in the 1970s. I had long treasured a grievously worn copy of the original LP recordings of these works.

In 1985, the Music Division of the National Library of Canada (since 21 May 2004 Library and Archives Canada) received the first instalment of Anhalt materials—scores, drafts, letters, photographs, and so forth—that would form the István Anhalt Fonds.[2] The composer asked me if I would act on his behalf as an external appraiser of the collection, as required by the Archives. This I agreed to do, acting again in that capacity on four other occasions, in 1993, 1997, 1998, and 2000. It was while examining the archive that I discovered the correspondence between Anhalt and Rochberg, a large cache of handwritten letters, an increasingly rare instance of the pen superseding the computer as a major means of communication. So taken was I with the richness and the sheer intellectual range of this correspondence that it very nearly diverted me from the business at hand, as I sat in the Archives for some days absorbed in the letters. Accordingly, I approached Anhalt with the suggestion that the correspondence be edited with an eye to publication. He seemed open to the idea and approached Rochberg late in 1991 for his reaction; his response was swift, unequivocal, and, to put it mildly, forceful:

> In re this business of our correspondence: my feelings & thoughts are quite strong and definite <u>against</u> anyone—no matter their qualifications—bringing it out in a book while I'm alive. Isn't that your view too? That's what I got from your last letter where you bring up Allan [*sic*] Gillmor (unknown to me) and the call you got from the librarian of the Nat[iona]l Libr[ary] of Can[ada] Music Div[ision]. I don't know about you, Isty, but I'm not even "flattered" by such "interest." Either people are running out of ideas—on that score I think that already happened long ago!—or levels of "curiosity" have risen lately so that knowledge or what used to pass for knowledge is now being replaced by high-class gossiping <u>by</u> intellectuals <u>about</u> intellectuals (and artists, composers, poets, et al.) for intellectualism in whatever "form" seems appropriate. (25 August 1991)

Much to my regret, Anhalt concurred: "We completely see eye to eye about this. No poking around in this as long as we are alive. What happens after is not my concern" (1 September 1991). There the matter would rest for six years.

At the time of my third appraisal of materials for the Anhalt Fonds, in 1997, I again raised the question with Anhalt, who suggested that I contact Rochberg directly. Shortly before I did so, and unknown to me at the time, it is evident that he had had a change of heart, for on 31 October 1997 he wrote to Anhalt:

> I'm writing to tell you I've changed my mind from the former rejecting no, *nyet, non* to a genuinely accepting *oui*, yes, of course, why not? I never dreamed that a correspondence such as ours had greater "significance" than a purely personal one; but if Gillmor, who is a scholar, and scholars view everything differently from us strange birds, maybe because they have better close-up and far-distant vision of the "meaning" of things than we do, thinks there's something there of larger value to music & musicians and those who live at least part-time in the exotic world of musical culture, why then I guess we should, each in our own way, encourage him to go ahead. Of course, I'm very interested in his approach and all that. So let's see how it develops.

The arduous task of transcribing nearly four hundred handwritten letters—of which approximately two-thirds are offered here—began early in 1999. To facilitate this monumental task, the Music Division of Library and Archives Canada, then under the direction of Dr. S. Timothy Maloney, placed at my disposal its newly acquired computer voice recognition program Dragon Naturally Speaking. Considering that this was a pilot project, the Archives also generously provided me with photocopies of the entire correspondence. In exchange, I was required to maintain a log of my "learning curve" with the software and present my findings to the Library and Archives staff and interested members of the public as part of their speakers series "Savoir Faire." The first stage of the enterprise was completed by the spring of 1999; subsequent letters (to 2005) were transcribed by hand. No doubt the technology has improved substantially in the intervening years. As good as the 1999 version was, its limited vocabulary, dyslexic tendencies, and occasional bizarre homonymic substitutions (e.g., "Socrates" = "soccer keys") often proved annoying and frustrating, but without the availability of this technology, the project would almost certainly never have gotten off the ground.[3] I can only hope that this book will not only amply repay and honour the trust placed in me by two men who allowed me to enter into their private intellectual, creative, and personal worlds over a period of more than four decades but indeed prove to be "of larger value to music & musicians and those who live at least part-time in the exotic world of musical culture."

Composers have written about music for centuries—Monteverdi, Rameau, and Wagner, to cite but three obvious examples—but the phenomenon has grown exponentially over the last hundred years or so, as the *locus* for musical composition, beginning most markedly in the post–Second World War era, moved increasingly into the rarified atmosphere of academia, particularly in North America. Thus Anhalt and Rochberg belong to an increasingly common group of composer/scholars who, had they not written a note of music, would still command attention for their musical scholarship. While the music of Wagner, for example, continues to override his extensive polemical prose, it is arguable that other, more contemporary, polemicists—Milton Babbitt comes readily to mind—might in time be remembered almost exclusively for their contributions to the literature of music theory and aesthetics. It is too early to hazard a guess as to whether that will be the fate of Anhalt and Rochberg. Of course, it is entirely possible that both aspects of their creative lives will remain relevant for future generations.

There are a number of interesting parallels in the careers of both men. They were born less than a year apart, Rochberg on 5 July 1918 in Paterson, New Jersey, Anhalt on 12 April 1919 in Budapest. Both men are of Jewish background, a factor that informs both their musical and intellectual lives to some extent. They were both caught up in the Second World War, Anhalt as a conscript in a forced labour battalion in fascist Hungary, Rochberg as an infantry lieutenant who saw action in Europe and was wounded in September 1944 at Mons, France. Both enjoyed long and successful marriages (Rochberg in August 1941 to Gene Rosenfeld, Anhalt in January 1952 to Beate Frankenberg) and both fathered two children: Anhalt two daughters, Helen (b. 1953) and Carol (b. 1955); Rochberg a son Paul (1944–64), a poet and short-story writer of precocious talent who died tragically in his twentieth year, and a daughter Francesca (Chessie) (b. 1952). Like many composers of their generation, both men explored atonality and serialism after the war and both broadened their aural experience in the 1960s and 1970s to embrace traditional elements, including collage and tonality. Both Anhalt and Rochberg chaired major university music departments (McGill/Queen's and Pennsylvania, respectively). Anhalt's monograph *Alternative Voices* and Rochberg's *Aesthetics of Survival* appeared nearly simultaneously in 1984. And finally, both men maintained active creative lives into their eighties.

Over the course of more than four decades, the correspondence traces an interesting trajectory. The early letters are concerned mostly with the creative work of both men, their musical compositions and their scholarly publications. While this discourse continues, more or less, throughout, the discussion gradually expands to include literature and philosophy as well as questions of Jewish identity and heritage. Beginning tentatively around 1969, Anhalt begins to document his extensive readings in Judaica—Jewish history and mystical traditions—while Rochberg responds over the ensuing years with increasing skepticism to religious orthodoxies as he develops what can only be called a kind of pantheistic spiritual sense. Finally, from the mid-1980s to the late 1990s the correspondence builds to a strident crescendo as both men respond critically and passionately to what they perceive to be the brutalization and spiritual emptiness of a consumer society careening out of control.

There can be no denying the necessity for experimentation in the arts, for the spirit of adventure must never be suppressed, as the checkered and distressing saga of music in totalitarian regimes makes abundantly clear. As Anhalt writes in the "Epilogue" to *Alternative Voices*:

> The innovative surge of music and art never ends, because man's need to create, to redefine, is unceasing. Every generation that sees the world in a different light than earlier generations will demand a mirror to reflect, clearly and sharply, that very new perception (which can, and at times does, contain very old elements freshly rediscovered). To provide that mirror is a task for poets, artists, and composers, along with scholars and scientists and creative thinkers in other domains. Each generation is likely to have its own artists, poets, and composers.[4]

It is axiomatic that a great deal of the most powerful and enduring music of the last century is unimaginable without the example of the Schoenbergian ethos and the Second Viennese School. With hindsight we can see that the drift into atonalism was as inevitable as it was necessary, a response to rapidly changing concepts of time and space that informed all of the arts in the period of early modernism, resulting in a wholesale rejection of, among other things, linear narrative in literature, traditional perspective in painting (and, in a different sense, music), as well as, in some quarters, the very idea of transcendence and the notion of the art work as a static and fixed artistic document, valid ideally for all time. As the underlying principles of tonality came under attack, the system, like the very society that created it, began to break down under the stress of expansion, beginning most forcefully with Wagner and gaining momentum with Mahler and others, including a young Schoenberg. Clearly, new musical languages and techniques arise in response to the need for expanded expressive means, and a post-Freudian "age of anxiety" found its ideal voice in the fluid sound-world of atonalism, which for a time seemed to offer an almost limitless realm of possibilities. However, rather like a living organism, it eventually ran its course, or, perhaps more precisely, lost its way.

As a student of Nadia Boulanger in the late 1940s, Anhalt was initially steered clear of the Schoenberg school, but he recalls the profound impression made upon him by a Paris performance of the Austrian composer's Piano Concerto, Op. 42, and soon after his arrival in Canada he was delving into René Leibowitz's treatise on twelve-tone composition.[5] Thus Anhalt's atonal journey began only after his arrival in Montreal, with the 1953 Piano Trio, and his first foray into serialism was the *Fantasia* for piano of the following year. The Violin Sonata of the same year, dedicated to the composer's father Arnold, is built on a single row divided into two hexachords, the second of which is a transposed inversion of the first. The largest of Anhalt's works to be informed by twelve-tone principles is the Symphony of 1958. Although this composition would be the last to be based on anything close to what might be called Schoenbergian orthodoxy, a free atonality would inform Anhalt's works for years to come, often coexisting with tonal gestures and collage-like techniques.

It is important to note that Anhalt maintained a modernist stance long after Rochberg's rejection of neophilia in the early 1960s. Beginning in 1959 with the *Electronic Composition No. 1*, the Canadian composer entered into the heady new world of electronic sound production, aspects of which would resonate in a number of works of the 1960s, most notably *Cento* (1967), with its stereophonic tape collage, and *Foci* (1969), a multimedia work calling for slide projectors, enhanced lighting, and taped sounds emanating from six discrete channels located around the performance space. As late as 1975 synthesized materials would make an appearance in his opera *La Tourangelle*.

While Anhalt was exploring the expressive possibilities of electronic music and collage techniques in the 1960s, Rochberg was moving rapidly back to the future in his search for a language that would free him from what he increasingly began to see as the limited expressive range of serialism. Interestingly, much of the original attraction of serialism for Rochberg was what he perceived to be its power to penetrate deeply into the realm of the unconscious, to reveal the darker side of the psyche, rather like a kind of sonic depth psychology. Now he began to see the over-rationalized, systematized dissonance of the neo-Schoenbergians as emotionally restricted and one-dimensional, a kind of "musical esperanto,"[6] incapable of expressing the larger dimensions of life. The result was a series of works—most famously (or infamously, perhaps) the Third String Quartet—that would provoke a stormy reaction among the composer's peers. Clearly, a collective nerve had been hit, for few American composers of Rochberg's generation have produced such a violent reaction and response, both pro and con, but mostly—at least initially—the latter. The gloves, as it were, came off as Rochberg was accused, either directly or by implication, of being a scurrilous traitor to the cause, a coward, a master forger and shameless *pasticheur*, a parasite, a skillful mimic, and, most luridly, a kind of cultural grave robber.[7]

Symbolic of the widening aesthetic gap between the two men are the monographs they both published within months of one another in 1984. While Rochberg's *Aesthetics of Survival* is a collection of essays which defend in one way or another what many perceived at the time to be his reactionary position, Anhalt's *Alternative Voices* is a wide-ranging study of the metaphorical power of speech-sounds in the post-1945 era, centred upon the music of Berio, Ligeti, and Lutosławski, three of the then-reigning giants of high modernism. What is most interesting, however, is not the apparent aesthetic differences between the two composers at this time but rather their common quest for the mythopoeic roots of human experience, for both Anhalt and Rochberg, as both their books and their correspondence amply reveal, had long shared similar and compelling interests in concepts of time and space, cosmology, psycholinguistics, semiotics, poetry, and philosophy both ancient and modern, eastern and western, as well as a belief in the efficacious power of artistic creation, its unique capacity to "present holistic and graspable pictures of complex chunks of reality."[8]

Although Rochberg's last strictly twelve-tone work was the First Piano Trio (1962–63), it is evident that his disillusionment with serialism—in particular total serialism—had been incubating for several years before that. As early as 1957, in a review of Pierre Boulez's two-piano work *Structures* (Book I), he touched on a theme that would haunt many of his later public (and private) statements when he charged the French composer with disregarding the nonrational side of the human spirit, with substituting a "remarkable cerebration" for "a deeply felt creative necessity."[9] Fifteen years later, Boulez would become the target of one of Rochberg's most celebrated aphorisms: "The past refuses to be erased. Unlike Boulez, I will not praise amnesia."[10]

In a 1959 essay Rochberg argued that a completely rationalized system of composition ("total organization") is incapable of mirroring subjective experience, for it tends to divorce the composer from the composition while impairing the equilibrium between musical structure and its perception.[11] He refined the argument in his presentation at Stratford in 1960, one of the first essays to explore his longstanding fascination with the concepts of time and space in music: the relationship between duration and existence and the roles of memory, identity, intuition, and perception in the shaping of human experience. Commenting on the two dominant approaches to high-culture music in the first two decades of the post-1945 era, Rochberg identified a problem common to both. Although seemingly polar opposites in their approaches to the organization (or nonorganization) of sound, both total serialism and chance music, in Rochberg's view, are inherently incapable of projecting the three-dimensionality of time perception—past, present, and future—in artistically meaningful ways. Chance music, associated in particular with John Cage and his disciples, seems content to accept a continuous Zen-like present as sufficient in itself, to which might be added Stanley Cavell's observation that "speaking through chance foregoes a voice altogether—there is nothing to say."[12] Total serialism, on the other hand, by objectifying duration, is similarly restricted by allowing its form-giving properties to be compromised. In short, it fails to provide an organic three-dimensional model of duration as experienced through the human perception of time: past (memory) and future (anticipation) become conflated into a continuous present, and the crucial balance between information and redundancy has malfunctioned. As Rochberg explained:

> The suprarationalism of total serial music defeats the durational process in the end; that is to say, it does not engage the listener in his most profound intuitive relation to life and experience, through his grasp of duration by means of which he creates and recreates the order of his personal identity and therein finds his being.[13]

Thus, both composers moved beyond what might be called orthodox serialism rather early in their careers, Anhalt quietly and without fanfare, Rochberg quite vocally and publicly.

In an essay published just over a decade ago, I wrote what at the time I considered, perhaps naively, to be this rather innocuous paragraph:

> Even though Schoenberg, with barely forgivable arrogance, declared in the early 1920s that he had discovered a principle that would assure the supremacy of German music for the next hundred years, not long

> after his death in 1951 the pendulum began to shift dramatically away from serialism as an organizing principle. We can now see the Schoenbergian language, particularly in its earliest Expressionist phase, as a symptom of a society in crisis—a kind of nervous breakdown in the consciousness of art. Later, in the period between the wars, serialism courted neoclassicism and the resulting union spawned a depressingly large body of works written in what the less charitable critics have dubbed 'the international academic style.' Once again in the long chronicle of Western music manner had triumphed over substance. What has died, of course, is not atonality per se, but rather orthodox serialism in its purest most abstract form, and we can now see atonality, whether free or serialized, as yet another expressive tool, a powerful one to be sure, most effective (as in Berg, for example) when used in conjunction with other gestures, such as tonal stability, to suggest contrasting mental states and varied psychic orientations. It is, in short, a language of instability, and therefore, in psychological terms, of abnormality.[14]

In a letter to Rochberg of 1 March 1999, I quoted most of the above paragraph, pointing out that, somewhat to my surprise, it generated strong negative reaction in certain quarters, to which he replied:

> Of course you were bound to stir up a hornets' nest with a statement like the one you sent me. They are a nasty lot of zealots still nesting in the cracks & niches of academia. Thomas Kuhn pointed out a long time ago [in *The Structure of Scientific Revolutions*] that it is the believers in an outworn, superceded paradigm who keep it shuffling along, even if it's half-dead; and the no-longer-valid-paradigm will only die with the physical death of the last believer. (letter to the editor, 6 March 1999)

Now that the rout of serialism, at least in its most rigid and doctrinaire form, appears to be more or less complete—despite pockets of resistance here and there—the entire debate is less compelling. Schoenberg's "democracy of tones" had, in less imaginative hands, degenerated into a "dictatorship of the proletariat." The orthodox serialist vision of the future now seems a mirage. Stylistic uniformity has given way to a kind of "polystylism," or a "multilingual" art, to use Rochberg's term. Atonality and tonality are no longer seen as mutually exclusive, and serialism, long absorbed into the fabric of much contemporary music, is but one of many compositional procedures. It is the inherent tension between atonality and tonality, chromaticism and diatonicism, asymmetry and symmetry, the modern and the pre-modern—what Rochberg calls "The Dance of Polar

Opposites"[15]—that provides much of the vitality of the best contemporary music, including that of Anhalt and Rochberg.

One of the most important subtexts of this correspondence is the role of religion and Judaism in the creative and intellectual lives of both men. It is a vexing and slippery problem for, far more than other major religions, Judaism is closely wedded to notions of ethnicity, culture, and nationhood, in such a way as to perpetuate a sense of psychological and social separateness. It is quite clear from the correspondence that both men recognize the time-honoured distinction between spirituality and religion and see no contradiction in accepting the former while rejecting the latter. As a kind of corollary to this, they also would have no difficulty endorsing Dietrich Bonhoeffer's claim that stupidity is far more dangerous and difficult to confront than evil.

It is helpful to point out that, in attempting to interpret and balance the opinions of both men on a range of topics, it is necessary to take into account their markedly different prose styles and personalities. Rochberg's views are often expressed with an extraordinary directness and passion, at times bordering on exasperation, even despair, as he observes the seemingly fathomless capacity of humankind (*homo chaoticus*, as he was wont to say) for folly and self-delusion. Though no less profoundly disturbed by many of the same issues, Anhalt tends, with some notable exceptions, toward a calmer, more measured and nuanced response in his prose while subsuming a number of his deep social and philosophical concerns quite directly into his music.

Shortly after 17 August 1962 Anhalt writes, partly in response to news of Paul Rochberg's grave illness: "What is the 'hope' of the person, like me who has no religion, and whose relationship to God is ... amorphous, to say the least?" Rochberg says much the same thing some years later when he declares that he is "a lapsed Jew" who cannot accept "the narrow, exclusionary doctrines of orthodoxies," preferring "to acknowledge instead a grander vision of spirit in enveloping man and the world of nature" (7 December 1984). Eventually Rochberg came even closer to a kind of pantheistic world-view, in the process telling us a great deal about himself and his uneasy relationship to his fellow travellers:

> Have I ever mentioned my abhorrence of the religion of Judaism, its narrow-chested, nationalistic legalisms, rituals, tribal echoes—none of which I can identify with in the least? Of course, this is only part of my general distaste for <u>all</u> orthodox religions of whatever stripe. Yet I am religious, my life is dominated by a sense of the awesomeness of whatever powers fashioned this incredible universe & maintains it. I

> think more than anything I relate very directly & strongly to the American poet Robinson Jeffers's view: that "God" is unconcerned with man, & that man is only a small part of what is—though in his fevered mind sees himself as the major part & as God's favorite "son." Jeffers loved mountains, the sea, plants, animals, the stars—the whole creation but kept his distance from man. (17 February 1988)

For Rochberg one of the fundamental flaws in the Judeo-Christian tradition is its insistence upon the dual nature of reality, the separation of the exterior and interior worlds, of the practical and the visionary, of humans from nature, of self from world. This form of Cartesian dualism, in Rochberg's view, is at the root of a contemporary confusion of values as "we rush, pell-mell, from one 'saving' cult or religion to another, all the while hungering to grasp reality and hold it fast."[16] Just as our distant ancestors, we postulate, melded the notion of "inside" and "outside" unselfconsciously into a more seamless unity (mythical time, or "dream-time," for the Australian aborigine), so must we replace our perception of piecemealness with a grander vision of a vast unity. For Rochberg, art is not a separate reality, for "art is not only an expression of man's consciousness, it is also a form of World-Consciousness reflecting back on itself. However distant man may be from the source of his creation, that source is built into him."[17]

Rochberg's position on doctrinaire religion continued to harden in later years—"all the God-oriented & determined religions are empty of meaning to me" (24 December 1992)—so it comes as no surprise that he should have expressed a certain bewilderment upon learning (from a letter of 1 July 1996) that the Anhalts had attended, from around the time of his mother Katalin's final illness (she died on 27 October 1985), a small Reform synagogue in Kingston, although in a much later letter (16 April 1997) Anhalt emphatically insists that "I don't pray with them" (emphasis in original). It is reasonably clear that Anhalt's fascination with what he calls "the syncretistic richness" of his Jewish heritage (8 January 1987) is deeply rooted, not in religious orthodoxy, but rather in his search for identity and for answers to the eternal existential questions, a theme that underlies, in one way or another, a number of his musical works (*Thisness*, *Simulacrum*, *SparkskrapS*, *Traces (Tikkun)*, for example). Whereas Rochberg was the American-born son of Ukrainian-Jewish immigrants, Anhalt experienced a savage dislocation during the darkest years of the Second World War, and although he has long expressed his gratitude to his adopted country, he has experienced a disorienting sense of being "thrice homeless" in a way that Rochberg could not. Consequently,

Rochberg's search for meaning and identity was not nearly as powerfully connected to his own Jewish heritage. Nevertheless, it is interesting to note that a few of his musical works have, either implicitly or explicitly, a Jewish theme or subtext (*David, the Psalmist*, *Passions [According to the Twentieth Century]*, *Sacred Song of Reconciliation*, for example). When Anhalt tells Rochberg that "I share your distancing from 'religion' if that word means dogma, observance, liturgy, prayer, etc." (21 January 1993), one can accept the statement very much at face value, for Anhalt clearly shares Rochberg's aversion to the narrowness of vision and the rule-bound trappings of "organized religion." Rather, Anhalt's intense interest in the rich Jewish intellectual tradition (which of course is intertwined with Jewish religious thought on many levels) is but one facet—an important one to be sure—of that complex web of experiences that provides each of us with at least an illusion of who we are. In a letter of 9 February 1988, Anhalt states: "Instead of wanting to learn to become a better articulated Jew, in his Jewishness, I want to do something else. I want [to] understand my very specific reality, which includes my Jewishness and being at peace with my entire past, even if that part includes a great disconcern for Jewishness." Some eight years later he spelled it out quite directly:

> As far as my interests in things Jewish are concerned this is a totally different story and it has almost no relationship whatever to our congregational affiliation. The roots of this 'interest' 'feed' from these sources: (1) personal memory of a life which was lived with a series of changes in the awareness of 'being Jewish' (what kind of Jew!? was a question which took a very long time to surface in my consciousness) from those 'traces' acquired in childhood through (2) the Hitler-years, then (3) as a D[isplaced] P[erson] (Jewish!) living/studying in Paris who benefited from (4) a small (but vitally important) stipend from 'L'Union des Étudiants Juifs' in Paris, and 'rescued' from that 'bottleneck' by (5) a H[ebrew I[mmigrant] A[id] S[ociety] worker (Lottie Levinson) who helped me to apply for a Lady Davis Fellowship, tenable in Montreal, which also came with a (temporary) appointment to McGill. In gratitude (& for practical reasons) I dedicated my 1st Symphony (1958) to the Bicentenary of Canadian Jewry, a critical event in my professional life. (23 July 1996)

Elsewhere Anhalt reveals his familiarity with the esoteric teachings of Judaism (kabbalistic thought in particular) with a statement such as the following:

> But 'religion' is only a word. What does matter [is] what one thinks about one's fleeting presence in a tiny corner of the universe & what happens after one's 'ego-integrity' is at an end and the 'bits and pieces' get ready to falling apart & merging, once again, with the 'rest of the stuff' of the universe. […] We leave behind 'traces' in the process and 'looking back' we see 'lines' and x-dimensional patterns formed by what we did, didn't do, but thought of doing, etc., etc. all in a wonderfully complex whirl. (16 April 1997)

Again we see a direct relationship between Anhalt's intellectual and creative lives as similar themes inform his musical works, most notably *SparkskrapS* and *Traces (Tikkun)*.

Thus, the differences between the two men vis-à-vis religious orthodoxy and Judaism are more a matter of degree than substance, and I suspect that Anhalt might have little difficulty with Rochberg's assertion that "the time has come for redemptive religion to disappear, Judaism, Christianity, Islamic. People have to cleanse their minds and souls" (1 May 1999).

More so than Anhalt, throughout much of his creative life Rochberg manifested more than a passing interest in the philosophy, literature, and music of the Far East. This is reflected in his scholarly writing ("The Bells and Drums of Confucius: Exploring Cross-Cultural Ways," for example), his music (*Between Two Worlds*, *Imago Mundi*, *Slow Fires of Autumn*, *Songs in Praise of Krishna*), and in his readings: among the books he strongly recommends to Anhalt over the years, mention might be made of *The Tibetan Book of the Dead*, *Japanese Death Poems*, several novels by Shusako Endo, and *The Complete Works of Chuang-Tzu*. With reference to the latter, it is interesting to note this passage from a letter of 13 December 1997: "I am & have always been drawn to the non-salvational doctrinal notions of Hinduism (their 'Agni,' god of universal fire closely resembles Kabbalah 'sparks'), Buddhism & feel more at home with Taoist ideas than anything else."

Both Anhalt and Rochberg visited Israel, Anhalt once (in 1992), Rochberg three times (1963, 1970–71, and 1982). Anhalt was "very touched by the people of Israel" (17 March 1992) and noted that his residence half a world away in Canada did not in any way diminish his deeply felt concern for the safety of the Israeli people and his belief in the legitimacy of the Israeli state. And although Rochberg could speak of Israel as, paradoxically, "both wonderful and unnerving at the same time" (19 July 1983), after his final visit he wrote that he and Gene had found it "terribly depressing," concluding that he had no wish to return: "I don't think I could bear it." The very image of three or four million Jews "trying to stay afloat in a sea of 122 million Arabs" was for Rochberg a terrifying image: "I hardly know the answer myself but feel the desperateness of the people who escaped from one hell or another only to end up in still a new form of hell" (17 February 1988).

In a letter to me of 3 December 1997 Rochberg suggested that I might be interested in reading Geoffrey Wheatcroft's *The Controversy of Zion.* Curiously, no mention of this monograph appears in the correspondence. Wheatcroft's is an interesting thesis and one with which Rochberg, presumably, concurred, although I suspect he would not have embraced Wheatcroft's position with the same degree of jingoistic zeal. The author, a former literary editor of *The Spectator* (London), provides a thoughtful analysis of some of the historical constitutional conflicts which faced (and continue to face) the creation of a Jewish state. If Israel were to become a theocracy (a situation, not surprisingly, vociferously opposed by Rochberg) citizenship would depend primarily on faith and therefore, technically, would exclude others, even nonreligious Jews or Jewish converts to other religions. If, on the other hand, it became a secular democracy it would be inclusive and embrace all religious faiths, thereby ceasing in a sense to be a Jewish state. It would appear that contemporary Israel attempts, with debatable success, to chart a course somewhere down the middle. As North American Jews, Rochberg and Anhalt have not had, of course, direct experience with either scenario, for as Wheatcroft states, when he unfolds his main thesis, they have found their Zion, and it is the New World. To summarize very briefly, Wheatcroft documents the astonishing success of North American Jewry in many fields of endeavour, not least of which is music, both classical and popular, and the Hollywood film-making establishment, which, between them, became the chief mythologizers of a new people in a new world. Wheatcroft, borrowing from the American diplomat and businessman Henry Morgenthau Sr., titled one of his chapters, "America is our Zion":

> They had made their decision, that heroic generation, voted with their feet, two million of them, in crossing the Atlantic to a land founded on the very principles of life, liberty, and the pursuit of happiness. They had no need of any other way to pursue it. They had found in America much prejudice and hardship, but they had also found something unknown to them before: a land where a poor Jew could live freely and without fear, and a rich Jew could live openly without evasion. They had solved their own Jewish Question by becoming Americans. From the bottom of their hearts, they spoke the same words: 'America is our Zion.'[18]

Despite the fact that the United States honoured him in numerous ways and provided him with security and considerable freedom to practise his art, Rochberg did not disguise his deep concern for his homeland and what he perceived to be its decline, its tarnished image abroad, and its diminished claim to moral authority. His later letters, especially, reveal an increasingly dark analysis of a country that, he felt, was in grave danger of losing its way. Rochberg saw clearly, some years before the World Trade Center tragedy, that much of what ails present-day America can be traced to a convergence of right-wing politics and fundamentalist religion, forces that have never been very far beneath the surface of American life but which have merged in recent years into a powerful ideological alliance, what he called the "growing tide of theo-politics":

> More signs all the time of the growing tide of theo-politics, i.e., politics dominated by theology, God-talk, God-fear, God-propitiation gestures. The American variety practiced & put forward by right-wingers & Republican conservatives is pale next to Islamic & Hassidic fundamentalisms, but shares some of the same motivations: reversion to God-dominated, doctrinal religions & theological ways of conducting LIFE. Naturally the same impulse, depending on strength of inner need & compulsion, surfaces & takes on the coloration of each external culture & the history connected w[ith] it. I'm glad to be closer than farther away from the end; that way I will not live and see the coming-into-existence of thoroly hateful forms of living taking over the USA. (10 October 1998)

We are always curious to know something of a composer's musical and literary tastes, for such knowledge acts like a mirror of the mind, helping us to situate creative figures within a finite number of aesthetic frameworks, thereby facilitating a deeper understanding of the changing profile of their work as it responds to the expansion and layering of experience.

Apart from a half-dozen or so chamber works composed during an eight-year period between 1946 and 1954 (among them an early string quartet and piano sonata, a piano trio, the *Fantasia* for piano, and a violin sonata) which at least have the appearance of "absolute" music, the bulk of Anhalt's music is programmatic, usually not in the overtly pictorial nineteenth-century manner but rather in a more abstract sense in which the extra-musical impulse is often hidden (or partially hidden) behind multiple layers of "deep themes" (the term is Anhalt's), which are often buried, like "frames framing frames ... forms and structures all containing a multiplicity of substances."[19] Indeed, so subtle, abstract, and multi-layered does the process become on occasion that R. Murray Schafer was compelled to write: "Istvan is probably our most ratiocinative composer & I love everything he writes except when it becomes too hermetic—which is I believe a word he once used to describe my work (or at least some of it)."[20] Although these "deep themes" address many of the sociological, psychological, and philosophical concerns of the composer, it would seem that the overriding thematic stimuli have to do with the experience of memory and the search for identity and, more recently, the fluctuating dynamics of, in particular, a North American consumer society that seems increasingly to celebrate banality under the banner of cultural democracy and freedom of expression.

Although Rochberg was preoccupied with many of the same themes—political, sociological, philosophical, religious—his music, especially his considerable body of purely instrumental works, to a greater extent than Anhalt's oeuvre, tends to exist in a world set apart from his often powerfully felt beliefs as articulated in his extensive prose. Once again we see a fundamental difference in the personalities of the two men: Anhalt, for the most part, more cautious and controlled in his critical responses and therefore less revealing of himself, Rochberg more passionate, forceful, and forthcoming; it is impossible to resist a threadbare cliché and consider Anhalt the "classicist" to Rochberg's "romanticist," although I have little doubt that both men would have grave difficulty with such vague terminology and such a simplistic dichotomy. Let each, then, speak for himself. As noted above, Anhalt's monograph *Alternative Voices* and Rochberg's *Aesthetics of Survival* both appeared in 1984, and both writers provided a detailed critique of the other's work. In a letter of 27 May 1984, Anhalt wrote:

> As to substance: yes on the surface we would seem to represent differing viewpoints on some aspects of contemporary music and art, and these appear to be rather far from each other on an imaginary fan of aesthetic choices. But, I must say, that I have trouble with a metaphor such as this, because it does not begin to reflect the true depth of the issues involved, nor the complexity of the context one has to cope with. So let us allow that, yes, there are differences between our respective outlooks. But why should one find this to be surprising or troublesome? I not only can live at peace with this notion but feel very positive about it. Difference or no difference, I have a tremendous feel[ing] of closeness, of affinity, for your kind of commitment and an admiration for the sharpness of your apperception, the courage with which you are appealing to the sense of responsibility of the artist, for your eloquence, and for the clarity and poetry of your language. But

> there is something else besides. I hear in your prose a familiar cadence and intonation: that of a latter-day prophet who saw the monster and rose to do battle with it, whatever the consequences may be. Perhaps prophets have no choice. Perhaps you and I had no choice either but to go along our respective paths that, in retrospect, are shown by our footsteps. There might come along a third person one day who would declare us to be similar, despite certain obvious divergences between us. Perhaps one of the common elements so identified would be our Jewishness, which I have had much trouble to define since a long time. But, lo, here it echoes in certain sentences in these two books. Has this Jewishness something to do with the circumstance that we are the champion survivors among all nations? Or/and with a self-imposed obligation to periodically—occasionally ill-received—emit warning calls (prophecies) for all—Jew and Gentile alike—to hear and heed? Tell me, what do you think of this?

On 15 January 1985, Rochberg responded:

> Our "differences" I see as differences of, call it, personal proclivities, tendencies of mind and nature; and as I see it we share in too many things for those differences to matter that much. *Au contraire*, they forge an even closer link between us because I see them as complementing each other; i.e., it's as though your more "rational" initiating tendency all the while you are completely sensitive to and reaching over to the more feeling side of things forms the complementary polarity to my more "non-rational" initiating tendency while I strive to make my intuitive understanding of things clear and lucid, more "rational." Taken all together we—or our different starting points—form an approach to a totality. Not unlike old musings of mine where I have tried to imagine what it would be like to combine <u>in one violinist</u> the qualities and capacities of a Heifetz and a Stern. Imagine the lofty purity of the one together with the gutsy, earthy passion of the other—both available when needed to the same performer.

Here one can see the influence of Jacques Maritain on Rochberg's thinking, for, like the French philosopher, Rochberg was fond of "fiery" metaphors and often speaks, both in the letters and in his published writings, of the spark or fire of creative intuition:

> The composer's ears are like anyone else's; only his sensibilities are more intense. That's why he composes; he "catches fire" as J. Maritain says about the poet. Well, that's only a metaphor for saying his brain is bursting hot with ideas because anyhow the brain is hot; it's an energy system. And music is its corona. (25 May 1965)

In other words, the starting point of poetic intuition is not reason but what Maritain calls the "spiritual or musical unconscious"; but, he cautions, reason and calculation are necessary to handle or control the fire.[21]

Repeatedly in the letters, Rochberg unfurls his essentially romantic colours. In responding to a 1961 New York concert of works by Elliott Carter, Leon Kirchner, and Milton Babbitt he concluded:

> In short the burning intensity of a Beethoven or Mahler or the dark somber intensity of a Brahms or the bite of a Schoenberg or Varèse are not there because the engagement with life & reality which produces suffering is not there. […] Even the gentler Webern has a kind of white heat, a concentration of condensation which cuts its way into the soul & enriches the heart. (9 September 1961)

Rochberg went on to plead for the artist as a visionary. In his opinion, composers of the stature of Telemann and Rimsky-Korsakov were competent, polished craftsmen, but little more:

> Give me the awkwardness of Mussorgsky with its wild passion; or the occasionally clumsy ways of Charles Ives with its ability to overcome its own inadequacy. Music today is more than sounds and sound manipulations, at least for me. It is a way of reaching the ineffable or exorcising the Devil. It is *duende*, the black sounds of human blood as Garcia Lorca says. We have to dip ourselves back into life. We have to get behind the external facade of phenomena. (ibid.)

Of a younger generation of composers, it is interesting to note that Rochberg championed the Americans Stephen Albert and William Bolcom many years before they became widely known. Albert, a student of Rochberg and a 1985 Pulitzer Prize winner who died tragically in a car accident at fifty-one, was "a true artist, one of the few of his generation," who wrote "with great passion," exerting "remarkable control over his means" (11 April 1965). As for Bolcom, Rochberg saw him as a "powerful musician" and foresaw that he would in all likelihood emerge as a "real composer" (emphases in original) (24 March 1968).

As early as 1961, in the very first extant letter to Anhalt, Rochberg recorded his rejection of Varèse's notion of music as "organized sound" (11 February 1961), and more than a quarter-century later, in a critique of music by the Australian Richard Meale, the American George Tsontakis, and the Dane Hans Abrahamsen, he wrote about the continuing contemporary obsession with sound *qua* sound, with colour and texture, which more often than not resulted in an absence of form-defining line and temporal organization:

> Astonishing how much talent per square inch they have. But no clear emotional signals came through their ingenious "designs." Do they feel? In their private lives I'm sure they do. Why not in their music? Are they afraid or inhibited or even perhaps embarrassed to speak with passion, to declare their personal pain or joy (if they're lucky enough to have joyous moments in life)? (3 May 1987)

He concluded in one concise but dramatic sentence that could stand as a kind of Rochbergian credo: "Art is for 'warriors,' not gentlemen" (ibid.).

Anhalt's letters reveal very little of his musical prejudices and preferences except to note that he remains remarkably open to new musical experiences. As noted above, he seemed eager to explore the zigzag movements of musical modernism in a constant search to expand the expressive range of his own music. Thus he was among the very first in Canada to explore both neo-Schoenbergian techniques and electronic music, taking as little or as much as he needed before moving on. For Anhalt there is no inherent contradiction in, for example, admiring certain aspects of John Cage's still-controversial aesthetic position and embracing the music of a traditionalist such as Dmitri Shostakovich:

> Last week we saw in Toronto Shostakovich's opera *Lady Macbeth of Mtsensk*. Very powerful stuff. Its drive, power, and inventiveness kept us in a spell during most of its 3 hours duration. It is also orchestrally right for that sordid tale, which he splendidly manages to universalize. And to think that it is the work of a 24–26 year old! Staggering. (9 February 1988)

Anhalt found much to admire in a generation of composers which included such iconic figures of what might be called high modernism as Berio, Kagel, Ligeti, Lutosławski, Nono, Stockhausen, and his countryman Schafer. Even here, however, his aesthetic judgments are measured and unpredictable. For example, in one sentence he can dismiss, with, alas, no further commentary, György Ligeti's *Requiem* as "a gimmicky piece" while praising the same composer's *Nouvelles Aventures* as "an important work" (30 September 1970).

It is reasonable to assume that composers generally appropriate literature for musical purposes only when it resonates on some level with them. Rochberg's literary sources were wide-ranging, from the Old Testament (Genesis, Psalms, Song of Solomon, Isaiah, Hosea) to Bengali poetry and Sumerian liturgical texts, from Shakespeare, Blake, Shelley, Byron, Burns, Christina Rossetti, and Housman to Heine, Rilke, Melville, Joyce, de la Mare, Arnold Stein, and, of course, his son Paul.

Judging from the correspondence alone, there are several major literary figures that stand out in the Rochberg lexicon: Blake and Yeats most vividly and, from a more contemporary era, Jorge Luis Borges, Milan Kundera, and the American poet Robinson Jeffers. If there is a single writer who takes pride of place with both Rochberg and Anhalt, it would have to be Robert Musil, in particular his unfinished magnum opus *The Man without Qualities*, that prolix tale of an empire lurching to the edge of the abyss, an epic journey that begins its narrative precisely twelve months before the "guns of August" in the capital city of the Imperial and Royal (*kaiserlich und königlich*) Austro-Hungarian monarchy ("Kakania") on "a fine day in August 1913." Rochberg alerted Anhalt to Musil's masterpiece in 1995, and the latter reacted with enthusiasm: a "great writer, Musil. I think his impact on me is almost that of Kafka" (22 September 1995). Five years later Anhalt is still reminding his friend of the book's impact on him when he writes of "that master of plumbing the soul" who "has assumed a major significance for me, as you know ... I am & will remain grateful to you for this" (23 June 2000).

As early as 1968, Rochberg announced to Anhalt that he was "a thorogoing Blakean by now" (24 March 1968), and the English visionary retained a place of central importance to him until the end of his life. But (again judging solely from the correspondence) it was another visionary, William Butler Yeats, who seemed to inspire Rochberg's greatest admiration. Although he never set the Irishman's poetry to music (if we discount an early aborted opera on Yeats's 1904 play *The King's Threshold*), Rochberg wrote almost rhapsodically of this "amazing man" who

> railed & raged from his 20s on against Death & Time, lived half in and half out of "reality" because of his powerfully driven intuitions of former lives, the mystical, the occult. More than any other great artist of the 20th cent[ury], our time, he sculpted himself, quite literally, shaped & hammered and pounded his feelings/thoughts/visions/sufferings into his poetry. A real phenomenon. Yeats insisted on the supremacy of the artist's imagination over any "temporal" power such as state & church. (31 October 1997)

Although Rochberg confessed that Yeats's *A Vision* was "a crazy, mixed-up piece of occultism with brilliant moments of insight" (30 June 1997), he could also write that he was not

> surprised that scholars who value his poetry might turn a blind eye to his *A Vision*—or glaze over when it's mentioned. It's a very strange, if not downright weird, piece of work. Yet just as theosophy & spiritu-

> alism fed Kandinsky with no visible loss to his real work, ideas of reincarnation, karma, personality-formations based on conflicting tendencies seemed to sharpen Yeats's view (vision) of existence, people, events with no loss that I can see to his work. He's the poet who reaching I would guess roughly our present age & stage said: "Grant me an old man's frenzy, / Myself must I remake / Till I am Timon and Lear / Or that William Blake / Who beat upon the wall / Till Truth obeyed his call; / A mind Michael Angelo knew / That can pierce the clouds, / Or inspired by frenzy / Shake the dead in their shrouds; / Forgotten else by mankind, / An old man's eagle mind." Great, isn't it? But not easy to reach for: An old man's eagle mind. (31 March 1994)

With Anhalt we have less evidence of his literary tastes judging from the music alone, for he was his own librettist for all his dramatic works, beginning with *Foci* in 1969 and ending with *Millennial Mall* in 1999. A survey of the early vocal works (1942–67) reveals an eclectic range of literary sources, among them his Hungarian contemporaries Gábor Devecseri and Sándor Weöres; Homer and the Bible; William Davenant and Robert Herrick; Whitman, Eliot, de la Mare, and Hopkins; the French Holocaust survivor André Verdet; and the Canadian Eldon Grier. With the later works—beginning tentatively with the polyglot word-collage of *Foci* (1969) and most significantly with *La Tourangelle* (1975)—the sources of Anhalt's extra-musical inspiration, for the most part, must be sought beyond the literary canon. Whereas Rochberg's literary tastes reveal a great deal about his aesthetic posture as a composer (his fascination with "mystics" such as Blake and Yeats, for example), with Anhalt we must direct the search inward, to an interior realm wherein the creator becomes poet, psychologist, ethicist, and social critic all in one, in an ongoing search for meaning and identity. The composer became his own poet, words and notes but two closely related facets of his creative thought process. In the memorable words of Charles Ives, "the fabric of existence weaves itself whole,"[22] a sentiment that Anhalt would surely endorse, for he views his life as an artist and as an intellectual along a continuum, just as Ives saw no separation of his life as a composer and writer from his career as a businessman.

Anhalt tends to approach a new musical work quite literally as a research project. His four large-scale dramatic works are cases in point. *La Tourangelle*, for example, brought him to the Ursuline convent in Quebec City as well as to a number of scholarly sources on the history of the religious order in New France and its founder Marie de l'Incarnation. Similarly *Winthrop* saw him spending time in Boston in the library of the Massachusetts Historical Society as well as in the Cambridge University rare book room, immersed in everything from the *Bay Psalm Book* and the *Roxburghe Ballads* to the writings of John Bunyan and Cotton Mather. Moreover, when not touring East Anglia (particularly John Winthrop's native Suffolk), Anhalt attended lectures at Cambridge and conferred with scholars at other British universities. (Tellingly, much of the research for his monograph *Alternative Voices* and for his "historical pageant" *Winthrop* was carried out concurrently.) If there is any one dominant source behind the creation of *Traces (Tikkun)*, it is Gershom Scholem, particularly his various works on Jewish mysticism and the Kabbalah. However, there are other, more hidden, sources behind this "pluri-drama," as Anhalt revealed in a letter to Rochberg:

> Now this 'other,' all the 'others' in relation to each 'other' (I'm just starting to glean the vastness of this literature, encompassing Buber, Bakhtin, Heidegger—the scoundrel/genius, yet another—Sartre, Husserl, etc. etc.) was on the top of my conscious mind during the past 4–5 months, as I was probing *Tikkun* (now called *Traces (Tikkun)*) towards the last double-bar (which it reached as no. 654, if I recall it correctly, a few days ago) … In fact: the whole piece's one (there are several) core theme is the dialogical relationship between people, as distinct from, &/or complementary to, the monological one. (20 January 1994)

Finally, *Millennial Mall (Lady Diotima's Walk)*, "a voice-drama for the imagination," although calling upon literary sources as disparate as Plato's *Symposium* and Musil's *Man without Qualities*, is perhaps the composer's most sustained musico-dramatic analysis of contemporary post-industrial capitalist society, an attempt "to get at the essence of contemporary North American society through certain kinds of probings, enactments, and the like."[23] Conservative political factions in Western societies frequently reiterate the slogan "social engineering" in an attempt to discredit "liberals" and frighten anxious citizens with the spectre of Big Government. In section 7 of *Millennial Mall*, "Advertising Unlimited (Lesson in Magic)," Anhalt makes it clear that Orwell's "Big Brother," at least in the West, is not invasive and repressive government but rather the monolithic advertising industry, which manipulates our psyches from cradle to grave with ever more insidious tactics, promising eternal youth, glamour, and a fantasy for all pocketbooks. Indeed, the mall has become the prime contemporary symbol of alienation, a kind of urban dystopia which leaves fractured and dysfunctional communities in its wake, with numbed consumers left sleepwalking in a sterile fantasyland, a crazy-quilt of garish, competing sounds and images, "The Global Carnival," as Anhalt has it, "The Millennial Carnival," "Our Carnival."

Much of Anhalt's work is informed by his quite extensive knowledge of critical theory and contemporary philosophy:

> I seem to be in a word-phase now. I am reading Michel Foucault's *The Order of Things*, a little by Derrida (*Dissemination*) and Ricoeur's lucid *Interpretation Theory*. I find these French thinkers writing in terms of a different (several different) metalanguages than those anchored in the English, North American, positivist, empiricist tradition. We dig (normally) Popper, Russell, and in a daring moment go even for Wittgenstein. But these Frenchmen (all spiritual heirs to Mallarmé, directly, or by the intermediary of a Barthes—if this is the correct genealogy) think/speak/write differently, using ellipsis, metaphor, and other artifices of poetical/rhetorical discourse much freer than those closer to our turf. (31 October 1984)

It might be suggested that the discourse of critical theory is, in certain ways, analogous to music, especially contemporary high-culture music, with its inherent ambiguity, its alternative ways of saying, its challenge to institutionalized forms of thought. Music's capacity to mirror abstraction in seemingly limitless ways gives it the status of a privileged language, operating in a sphere removed from more earthbound language systems, with their linear ordering of thought processes—one sound at a time—for music is the language par excellence that operates with a degree of simultaneity, like a maze of moving mirrors within mirrors, on multiple levels of time perception, a language, moreover, that reinvents itself with every new composition. On 1 November 1988, Anhalt wrote to Rochberg:

> Our pathways may seem, and are, different, but the end point, trying to understand a little bit more of what makes a human human, is probably the same. I do it by relating music to the world and the world to music, in an infinite regress of interacting mirror-images.

Although Rochberg's harsh critique of American society in particular began, not surprisingly, with the Vietnam era and continued through the eras of Reagan and Bush Jr., it is not until the mid-1980s that Anhalt began to reveal in a major way a number of deep-seated sociopolitical concerns which would run like a leitmotif throughout the correspondence very nearly to the end some two decades later. Thus, both composers joined a growing chorus of intellectuals who leave a powerful and disturbing impression that "the world's night is spreading its darkness,"[24] that we are witnessing the degradation of a culture. It is clear that the main target is a Western capitalist consumer society, headquartered in America, where millions of deracinated people remain anaesthetized and kept largely quiescent by an endless stream of unsavoury trivia, inane babble, and senseless imagery. It is, in a sense, what Plato feared: degraded souls appealing to our lowest instincts. On 13 April 1985 Anhalt wrote:

> But there are other things I am worried about that are a bit closer to my own customary field of action. I am referring to the vulgarization, commercialization, manipulation, etc. that shouts with ever greater force in the pages of the 'entertainment' (not art, mind you) sections of our newspapers, out of the frame of the 'tube,' etc. The din is enormous and the mass-magic is supported by an ever more heinous application of the democratic/elitist pseudo-dichotomy used as a poorly disguised curse.

A decade later Anhalt consolidated his discontent in a series of long letters, couched in a language of searing and damning intensity, in which he chronicles his responses to—among other things—globalization, the electronic revolution, and mass culture, all of which, of course, are inextricably intertwined in one way or another. With uncharacteristic vehemence, Anhalt rails against the "mega-profit corporate machine economy" which "turns out a steady sewer full of brutal, mindless, sexually exploitative flood of image and sound, which works its insidious black magic on the young, and on those who never grew up" (7 September 1995). He goes on to note that

> children, probably, ingest this horror, dished out by giant financial interests, corporations, in the guise of 'entertainment,' and 'freedom of information,' 'democratic environment of communication.' Here the potential victimhood of inexperience, normal physical/psychic development (sexual), brutalized/commercialized art(?) and big business merge in a complex interactive mush which pulsates with ferment as a swamp populated by noxious biological organisms from the micro-ones to toothy giant predators, the like of super-reptiles. (ibid.)

As if merely warming up to his topic, Anhalt continues to point up the negative side of the electronic superhighway, a potential drug that regurgitates an unrelenting and "ever increasing bulk of undigested, unasked for, not-sought-out information, all thrown at the viewer, who gets mesmerized, hypnotized" (ibid.), reduced to a zombie-like state of mindless consumption, rather like so many Pavlovian dogs. As a result, individuals are dehumanized into mere programmable human resource units, robot-like automata left with an inchoate feeling of fear, emptiness, and loneliness. We end up living in a continuous state of pseudoreality, a sham world.

As one acquainted with the ideas of Heidegger, Anhalt knows well that language is the shaper and master of humankind, not the other way around. In a long letter of 27 November 1996, he vents against the creeping degradation of language which now threatens to invade the very academy which once stood as one of the last bastions of informed criticism of the dominant society but which increasingly has succumbed to the homogenizing and neo-Orwellian will of a monolithic mass media and a multinational corporate agenda:

> The hirelings of the so-called 'chattering' classes cooperate effectively, and with the help of promoters of a new class of linguistic mutations, our conceptual landscape was, and continues to be, subjected to a subtle yet brutal, near subliminal (for those who do not 'deconstruct' these new linguistic horrors) brain washing. Examples: the semantic ballooning of words like: consumer, (human) resource, resource-management, globalization, accountability (who constructs the scales, assigns rank ordering, etc.?) as if it can be taken as proven that the 'thing' lends itself to counting!

Responding to this last *cri de coeur*, Rochberg wrote to his old friend a week later, on 4 December 1996:

> [Y]ou were/are splendid in your rage against all the offal the world is producing & wallowing about in—not least starting w[ith] the stink of the human ego. I have always been in a rage vs. the world. Never have I seen a good reason to reconcile myself to the stupidities through which we slog our way in this life. At the same time—mostly, but never 100%, I feel great compassion for my fellow travellers who trod the "dirty streets of London," work in the "satanic mills" (be they institutions, whatever). But you really called the shots. I don't apologize for not being an "expert." In life there are none—we enter the mystery, live it, leave it, never quite knowing what it is or why, whether or whence. The brain/reason is only a tiny light in the vast dark. We live by feel. Unhappily, we mostly guess wrong about almost everything. *C'est la guerre*.

The vast majority of these letters are in the István Anhalt Fonds (MUS 164) in the Music Division of Library and Archives Canada. These consist of

Rochberg's originals and Xerox copies only of Anhalt's letters, although the latter did not begin making copies of his letters to Rochberg until the early 1980s. Therefore, many of his letters from the first two decades of this correspondence no longer seem to be extant. (Anhalt has informed me that he quite faithfully answered Rochberg's letters so that when two or three of the latter's letters appear in direct sequence, it likely signifies that an Anhalt letter is missing.) Fortunately, we do have a few of Anhalt's letters from this early period consisting of carbon copies, some of them on McGill University or Queen's University letterhead (nos. 12, 69, and 71), and recently a number of his letters have surfaced in the George Rochberg Collection of the Paul Sacher Foundation in Basel, Switzerland (nos. 23, 39, 45, 48, 52, 55, 57, 63, 134, and 154–55), and in the New York Public Library for the Performing Arts (nos. 8–9). Nevertheless, the correspondence is seriously lopsided in Rochberg's favour until the early 1980s. Despite this unsatisfactory situation, the decision has been made to retain most of Rochberg's letters from this early period because of their valuable insights and intrinsic worth.

Shortly after Rochberg's death, Gene Rochberg forwarded to me the originals of three letters of Anhalt (nos. 220, 236, and 240) and one by her husband (no. 239), copies of which had not found their way into the Anhalt Fonds, as well as the originals of thirty-four letters of Anhalt, copies of which are in the Anhalt Fonds. In accordance with the rules of archival protocol, all of these will join the Rochberg Collection in Basel.

There is a large gap in the correspondence between February 1976 and January 1981. Both correspondents claimed extraordinarily heavy work and travel schedules during that period which left little time for reflection and private correspondence. Of course this may be all there is to it, for both men were in full flight, as it were. From 1971 to 1981 Anhalt was involved in administration as Chair of the Music Department at Queen's University and soon after the premiere of *La Tourangelle* in July 1975 had begun work on his second opera *Winthrop*; concurrently with his work on the opera, he began the research for his monograph *Alternative Voices*, continuing with both projects while on sabbatical leave in 1976–77 at Cambridge University. During the same period, Rochberg produced a very large number of compositions, among them his Fourth Symphony, four of his seven string quartets, the Octet, the *Partita Variations*, and the monodrama *Phaedra*, travelled widely in the United States to attend premieres of his works, and had begun work on his opera *The Confidence Man*. Yet, one wonders if the reasons for the silence run deeper. After all, considering the strong bond between these two men, five years is a rather long absence, and when Anhalt writes, "It is a day to be happy and celebrate: I got back a friend. You! Or, to put it better we proved it to each other that we have never lost our mutual friendship, which just slumbered during all these years while we went on in our separate trajectories" (7 February 1982), one is left wondering if there were deeper reasons for the hiatus. Anhalt provides a clue when he speaks of "separate trajectories," for this was the period that saw the consolidation of Rochberg's "postmodernist"[25] style as he turned to the past as a way of reinventing himself as a composer while Anhalt continued to explore the contemporary themes and issues that provide a rich and multi-layered subtext to his music to this day.

Perhaps the chief thing that attracted me to this correspondence initially is its intellectual range and richness. These "conversations" traverse a considerable intellectual territory, and although this volume will be of interest to students of the two composers in particular as well as to chroniclers of contemporary North American culture in general, such is its broad sweep that it should prove to be of value to anyone curious about many of the key issues—cultural, political, philosophical—of our time. Accordingly, the first editorial decision to be made concerns the documentation. More than five hundred endnotes might be considered excessive, but the decision was arrived at early on to risk erring on the side of over-documentation. For reasons sketched above, the working assumption was that this book will find an audience beyond the musicological establishment. Therefore, it seemed not unreasonable to assume that names familiar to most musicologists—Henry Brant and Joseph Tal, for example—are not necessarily known to nonmusicians; conversely, it seemed safe to assume that musicians are not necessarily familiar with the work of, for example, social scientists, such as Dwight Bolinger and Abraham Moles, or that general readers would necessarily be familiar with the large cast of characters inhabiting the scholarly and historical world of Judaica. For these reasons, no apology is deemed necessary; besides, endnotes can be—and often are—ignored!

Such is the intellectual "density" of this correspondence that relatively little has been deleted. Early on, the decision was made to excise all material that, in the judgment of the editor, had little or no bearing on the subjects' creative lives. Hence, standard closing formulas and salutations, lengthy descriptions of foreign travel, and routine passages involving family matters and health concerns have, for the most part, been removed. (An exception has been made for the passages recording Paul Rochberg's decline in the early 1960s, considering that Paul's premature death, as well as his poetry and short stories, had a bearing on his father's musical evolution.)

It should also be recorded that Anhalt is writing in his fourth language—after Hungarian, German, and French—and although his command of the English language is fluent and for the most part idiomatic, the occasional slight awkwardness of expression has been retained so as not to reduce his writing style to some characterless, generic "house style." Here it is necessary to point out one of the idiosyncrasies of his writing style. Like the musician he is, Anhalt is given to lacing his sentences with ellipsis points, rather like musical rests, breathing places, or phrase endings, most of which have been retained as an essential characteristic of his prose. His own ellipsis points are identified by three periods, thus ..., whereas the usual editorial use of ellipsis points to signify deletion of text is indicated by three periods encased in square brackets, thus [...]; this is an idiosyncrasy of Anhalt's prose style that gradually seemed to rub off on Rochberg, for it begins to intrude to a small extent in his later letters. Whereas Anhalt has adopted standard Canadian English practice in matters of spelling, which—like much of the English-Canadian character itself—is an uneasy cross between British and American traditions, Rochberg, of course, uses standard American spellings; this is particularly noticeable in words such as "color/colour," "program/programme," "center/centre," and "theater/theatre." Contrary to standard North American practice, and unlike Rochberg, Anhalt tends towards the British convention of single quotation marks around titles and direct quotations. In this regard, it is interesting to note that he makes frequent use of quotation marks, often around single words or short phrases, a result, perhaps, of his longstanding interest in psycholinguistics and semiology and, more particularly, his familiarity with certain aspects of current critical theory, for one is tempted to attribute this stylistic quirk to a kind of "postmodern" sense of the inherent ambiguity of language, the subtle semantic nuances of even plain words. It should be noted that Rochberg often makes use of such linguistic Americanisms as the abbreviations "thru," "nite," "tho," "thoroly," and "@" (for "about"); all of these personal idiosyncrasies have been retained. In order to minimize editorial clutter with ubiquitous use of [*sic*], minor errors of spelling and grammar have been silently corrected. For ease of reading, dates of letters have been modified to conform to the pattern "day/month/year." Both writers occasionally use single (occasionally double) underlining of words or phrases for emphasis; this has been retained, although titles (of musical works, books, etc.) have been changed to italics where appropriate. Until 1976, Anhalt spelled his given name in the Hungarian fashion, with the accent (István); by the time his side of the correspondence resumed in 1982, he had dropped the accent. For the sake of uniformity, the latter convention has been adopted here throughout.

NOTES

1 See John Beckwith and Udo Kasemets, eds., *The Modern Composer and His World* (Toronto: University of Toronto Press, 1961); see also Rochberg, "Current Chronicle: Canada," *The Musical Quarterly* 47/1 (January 1961): 103–5.
2 See Stéphane Jean, *The István Anhalt Fonds* (Ottawa: Library and Archives Canada, 2004).
3 See Alan Gillmor, "Taming the Dragon: Using a Voice Recognition Program"/"Apprivoiser le dragon à l'aide d'un programme de reconnaissance de la voix," *National Library News/Nouvelles de la Bibliothèque nationale* 31/10 (October 1999): 9–10.
4 Istvan Anhalt, *Alternative Voices: Essays on Contemporary Vocal and Choral Composition* (Toronto: University of Toronto Press, 1984), 267.
5 René Leibowitz, *Introduction à la musique de douze sons* (Paris: L'Arche, 1949).
6 Quoted in Joan DeVee Dixon, *George Rochberg: A Bio-Bibliographic Guide to His Life and Works* (Stuyvesant, NY: Pendragon Press, 1992), 139.
7 See, for example, Steven D. Block, "George Rochberg: Progressive or Master Forger?" *Perspectives of New Music* 21/1–2 (Fall–Winter 1982/Spring–Summer 1983): 407–9; Lance W. Brunner, "George Rochberg: 'The Concord Quartets,'" *Notes: The Quarterly Journal of the Music Library Association* 38/2 (December 1981): 423–26; Andrew Porter, "Musical Events: Questions," *The New Yorker*, 12 February 1979, 109–15; and Hugh Wood, "Thoughts on a Modern Quartet," *Tempo* 111 (December 1974): 23–26.
8 Anhalt, *Alternative Voices*, 267.
9 George Rochberg, "Pierre Boulez: *Structures*," *Notes: The Quarterly Journal of the Music Library Association* 14/2 (March 1957): 197. It is interesting to note that Boulez would write, some thirty years after the composition of *Structures*, that great art was "a mixture of the rational and the irrational; the two are like a knot that is impossible to untie." "The Composer and Creativity," *Journal of the Arnold Schoenberg Institute* 11/2 (November 1988): 122.
10 Rochberg, "Reflections on the Renewal of Music, *Current Musicology* 13 (1972): 76; reprinted in Rochberg, *The Aesthetics of Survival: A Composer's View of Twentieth-Century Music*, ed. with an introduction by William Bolcom (Ann Arbor: University of Michigan Press, 1984), 233.
11 See Rochberg, "Indeterminacy in the New Music," *The Score* 26 (January 1960): 9–19 reprinted in Rochberg, *Aesthetics of Survival*, 3–15; rev. and expanded ed. (2004), 3–15.
12 Stanley Cavell, "Music Discomposed," in *Art, Mind, and Religion: Proceedings of the 1965 Oberlin Colloquium in Philosophy*, ed. W.H. Capitan and D.D. Merrill (Pittsburgh: University of Pittsburgh Press, 1967), 88–89.
13 Rochberg, "Duration in Music," in *Modern Composer and His World*, ed. Beckwith and Kasemets, 64; reprinted in Rochberg, *Aesthetics of Survival*, 77; rev. and

enlarged ed. (2004), 67. Here it may be helpful to recall Rose Rosengard Subotnik's observation concerning the social failure of a great deal of modernist music, namely that the musical significance of much contemporary high-culture music is located literally and exclusively in the individualized and often cryptic structure of the work, "to the point where it is protected against even the simple social activity of comprehending"; and she traces this attitude back to Schoenberg, for whom "'the *idea*,' as prior to sound and style, generates and indeed *is* 'the totality of a piece.'" "The Challenge of Contemporary Music," in Subotnik, *Developing Variations: Style and Ideology in Western Music* (Minneapolis: University of Minnesota Press, 1991), 270–71, 275 (italics in original).

14 Gillmor, "Echoes of Time and the River," in *Taking a Stand: Essays in Honour of John Beckwith*, ed. Timothy J. McGee (Toronto: University of Toronto Press, 1995), 24.

15 Rochberg, "Polarity in Music: Symmetry and Asymmetry and Their Consequences," *Proceedings of the American Philosophical Society* 141/2 (June 1997): 174; reprinted in Rochberg, *Aesthetics of Survival*, rev. and expanded ed. (2004), 250.

16 Rochberg, "Fiddlers and Fribbles, or, Is Art a Separate Reality?" *New Literary History: A Journal of Theory and Interpretation* 18/2 (1987): 258; reprinted in Rochberg, *Aesthetics of Survival*, rev. and expanded ed. (2004), 145.

17 Ibid., 278/162.

18 Geoffrey Wheatcroft, *The Controversy of Zion: Jewish Nationalism, the Jewish State, and the Unresolved Jewish Dilemma* (Reading, MA: Addison-Wesley, 1996), 129.

19 Anhalt, "*Thisness*: Marks and Remarks," in *Musical Canada: Words and Music Honouring Helmut Kallmann*, ed. John Beckwith and Frederick A. Hall (Toronto: University of Toronto Press, 1988), 211.

20 R. Murray Schafer, letter to the editor, 12 December 1997.

21 See Jacques Maritain, *Creative Intuition in Art and Poetry* (New York: Pantheon Books, 1953), 90ff.

22 Quoted in Henry Bellamann, "Charles Ives: The Man and His Music," *The Musical Quarterly* 19/1 (January 1933): 48.

23 Anhalt, "About the Libretto of *Millennial Mall (Lady Diotima's Walk)*," in *Istvan Anhalt: Pathways and Memory*, ed. Robin Elliott and Gordon E. Smith (Montreal and Kingston: McGill-Queen's University Press, 2001), 457.

24 Martin Heidegger, *Poetry, Language, Thought*, trans. with an introduction by Albert Hofstadter (New York: Harper & Row, 1971), 91.

25 Although the term "postmodernism" often appears in reference to Rochberg's post-serial music, it should be noted that the composer rejected the validity of the label: "a term I have no personal use for" (20 May 1984). For him, the search for a more balanced culture required a more profound solution than the scattered pluralism and relativism offered by the postmodernists. Rochberg's objections aside, it is indeed regrettable that such an oxymoronic and polysemous term has become firmly entrenched in the discourse of critical theory. To be sure, all attempts at labelling complex cultural movements are fraught with difficulties, but "postmodernism" seems to occupy a special niche in the lexicon as one of the most elusive and imprecise of such terms. It will be understood in this context in the general sense of a sociocultural attitude rather than in the narrower sense of a specific artistic trend or style. Just as Gertrude Stein memorably referred to the First World War as the first Cubist war, one could suggest that what might be called a "postmodern con-

sciousness" is a chronic condition in the global village, a kind of Cubist vision writ large of a technology-saturated world in which we attempt to negotiate a path through a multiplicity of polarities—fragmentation and homogeneity, eclecticism and innovation, unity and disunity, continuity and simultaneity, local community and globalization, order and freedom, faith and reason, high culture and low—a jangle of sounds and images flooding cyberspace, not to speak of urban space, in an unrelenting bombardment of the senses, a world in which mass advertising has become the capitalist art form par excellence. Little wonder that a single label should be incapable of encapsulating such a fractured and disoriented society as ours, a "moronic inferno," in Saul Bellow's tragicomic metaphor (borrowed from Wyndham Lewis), an endless carnival of crassness and banality that induces cultural amnesia. Postmodernism, in this sense, can perhaps best be seen as a symptom of a technocratic society, of cultural pathology, a pessimistic expression of a generation's sense of uncertainty and foreboding.

PART ONE

A NEW FRIENDSHIP (1961–1964)

Most important to me is the fact that we share a common feeling for each other and a healthy respect for what each of us is trying to accomplish. On such bases, friendship in the old classical sense becomes a reality. For me there is little in life but music and love.

— Rochberg (September 1961)

George Rochberg, Newtown Square, Pennsylvania, 2000. Photo by Fred Jervis.

1961

I

11 FEBRUARY 1961

Dear Istvan,

I hope this finds you & yours well. Things are not as good here as we would like. [Our son] Paul's condition remains only poor to fair and new complex developments keep arising. Perhaps we are too impatient but it seems like a long time for him to remain this way without the assurance of better days ahead.

Last Thursday I went to Yale to attend the opening of their electronic studio. Much of the proceedings—lecture demonstrations by Luening, Ussachevsky, Mel Powell (director of Yale Electronic Music Studio), Bülent Arel, Babbitt, Berio[1]—same old stuff. Most of the works (few played in totality) also "old," except for Arel's *Stereo Piece* and *Church Music.*[2] One begins to discern the craftsmen: Arel & Babbitt. So far though I have heard too little "music" & I must confess am growing tired of hearing music defined as Varèse defines it—though I admire him greatly—as "organized sound."[3] That's like saying that the world is "organized matter" or some such nonsense. Ives is supposed to have said "sound has nothing to do with music."[4] If you take him at face value, he's wrong of course. But if you understand him to mean the sound is merely the property, the carrier by means of which the music gets through to the head or the heart then it's a good statement. Also note Mahler who said: "The music is not in the notes."[5] In any case, I was struck 2 days later after much reflection that none of these people, even the better craftsmen like Babbitt, know how to orchestrate their sounds. So far I remain unconvinced until I shall hear something first rate which I expect from you. My new quartet[6] is in rehearsal for March 30th. It is almost too damned complex. I long for simplicity. I'm currently revising *Time-Span* in odd hours available after the press of other things.[7] Thinking of a new orchestra piece along new lines—probably with voice or voices. […]

George

2

2 MARCH 1961

Dear Istvan,

Forgive the belated acknowledgment of the *Journal* & your note—both most welcome. I read your reviews with much pleasure & interest, particularly, the Varèse.[8] It came in the middle of working on the first part of an analytic study of what I am now calling "space-form";[9] couldn't have come at a more appropriate time. If I may, I'd like to work in some of your review as direct quotes.

There are plans brewing to take us to Canada again this summer—depending on whether Paul, our son, is admitted to the special summer session at [Université] Laval. In any case chances are good that we will see each other either in Montreal or in N[ew] Y[ork]. […]

George

3

9 SEPTEMBER 1961

Dear Istvan,

Your letter was joyously received, especially the news that you completed No. 4.[10] I hope to hear it. While I never read or saw *On the Beach*[11] I know its import. In my own way I feel "grim" anyhow about the prospects that face us. But never mind that now. Most important to me is the fact that we share a common feeling for each other and a healthy respect for what each of us is trying to accomplish. On such bases, friendship in the old classical sense becomes a reality. For me there is little in life but music and love. My capacity for both is very great even if in the course of a whole lifetime not always fully realized. I appreciate your remark about the unlikelihood of friendship past 30. But life is full of miracles and spring does come again.

Your report of your activities was fascinating, literally. You are one of those who searches and meets reality head on. I admire this. I do it in my own way, perhaps not as directly. I tend to resist the pull of a new current until I feel its inevitability. Then I can give myself to it. We differ too in that you are really much kinder than I. I am referring to your remarks about Cage, Feldman et al. I think you're much too kind, giving them more credit than they truly deserve.[12] However, I will not deny you may be right ultimately.

Gene & I drove to N[ew] Y[ork] last Wednesday to hear the works sponsored by the Fromm Foundation for the Int[ernationa]l Congress: *Vision and Prayer* [1961] of Babbitt for voice & RCA synthesizer, a work of Elliott Carter for harpsichord, piano, large ensemble & a work by Kirchner for violin, 'cello & large ensemble.[13] I remain thoroughly & totally unconvinced of both the synthesizer (as Babbitt employs it) and of Babbitt as composer. The work was tepid, lacking in thrust, scope & range of ideas. Again an electronic analogue of an instrumental conception which to my mind would not improve, however, even if projected "live." There were moments where I felt positive embarrassment, so badly conceived was the work & so poorly realized. The Carter was the best work but left me unsatisfied. He went over the edge with this one. It's a pastiche of timbre, leaning heavily on the Webernites, Varèse & Carter ("old" Carter). Its chief feature was ambiguity. Nor did I respond to the obvious formal disposition—two cadenzas, one each for the keyboard instruments. At least when there is a cadenza in a Mozart or Beethoven concerto it acts as a commentary on what has already occurred. One can take a certain pleasure in this. But to gesture & posture, to offer cadenzas which have no evident relationship to what has transpired—not for me. Still, there was much I liked: fantasy, flexibility, sense of exploration. Kirchner's piece was fluent, stylish but grew weaker & weaker after the opening statement. The fact that he has harbored his ship safely in the by-now quiet waters first discovered by Bartók & Schoenberg renders the experience of hearing his music merely pleasant. His effort to achieve climax came to nothing. The attempt to be momentarily dramatic the same. I came away from the concert feeling one overpowering dissatisfaction: namely, the inability of any of the three composers to make a passionate statement, to produce vibrant music that catches you up & does not let go until it has said all it intends to. In short the burning intensity of a Beethoven or Mahler or the dark somber intensity of a Brahms or the bite of a Schoenberg or Varèse are not there because the engagement with life & reality which produces suffering is not there. If music is merely the writing of the "pieces" I withdraw my criticism. But that is the least of what music is. I do not care if the technical aspects of Carter's or Kirchner's music, each in its own peculiar way, are more than competent, polished, sure. Rimsky-Korsakov was a damned good craftsman; so was Dvořák; also Telemann & a host of others. But they were not visionaries. Give me the awkwardness of Mussorgsky with its wild passion; or the occasionally clumsy ways of Charles Ives with its ability to overcome its own inadequacy. Music today is more than sounds and sound manipulations, at least for me. It is a way of reaching the ineffable or exorcising the Devil. It is *duende*, the black sounds of human blood as Garcia Lorca says.[14] We have to dip ourselves back into life. We have to get behind the external façade of phenomena. Neither Babbitt, Carter nor Kirchner is capable of this & consequently their music ultimately remains stylistic effort which will be washed away with the next new wave whatever it may be. Schoenberg has no real value as far as I'm concerned merely as the basis of the 12-tone method. He means something because he speaks with the intensity & rasping tone of the prophet crying out in the wilderness. Even the gentler Webern has a kind of white heat, a concentration of condensation which cuts its way into the soul & enriches the heart. Well, never mind my raving & ranting. I simply can't take my music calmly—objectively.

I finished the quartet as I told you. Whatever its faults may be & I sense it has them although at this point I can't put my finger on them precisely, it has passion and a kind of concentrated intensity which finds its way into my best music. The voice will enlarge its sonorous scope & its emotional structure. If I ever get a decent tape of its performance, tentatively scheduled for Feb. 25,[15] I'll send you a copy.

There's not much to say by way of details re the 2nd Symphony. It will be conducted by Werner Torkanowsky who I understand is very good. Let us hope this is actually the case. […]

George

4

11 OCTOBER 1961

Dear Istvan,

I finished copying the quartet last Thursday, delivered it to the printer Friday morning on my way to N[ew] Y[ork] for the performance of my *Blake Songs*.[16] They were beautifully sung and played (chamber ensemble) by Shirley Sudock & Hartt Players on ISCM [International Society for Contemporary Music] program—which will be repeated at the U[niversity] of P[ennsylvania] this Friday. There are some works which give one lots of trouble & my *Blake Songs* never seemed to be what I wanted them to be—it was one of those things I worried over & never let out of my hand. At last I feel free of them & must finally reconcile myself to their imperfections.

When I have a copy of the quartet not in use I'll send it to you—right now whatever copies are being prepared are going somewhere, mostly to the people who are supposed to give the first performance (Feb. 1962), if they can learn it, that is. […]

George

5

18 NOVEMBER 1961

Dear Istvan,

I have had your last very much in mind but in the suddenly unhappy circumstances which struck our family recently I have not been able to reply—or to locate the letter itself. Our son Paul underwent brain surgery 3 weeks ago yesterday. There is little point in relating everything that led up to this crisis. He is making a good recovery & should be home fairly soon, by Thanksgiving, God and the doctors willing. A concomitant of the growth in the brain which is now being treated by radiation is the malfunctioning of the hormone system brought on by pressure on the pituitary. The doctors have been working very hard to reestablish his metabolic balance. How long it will be before Paul will be able to resume normal activity is very hard to predict—no one is able to say. We have lived through these weeks as in a nightmare, waking each morning with that sharp stab of incredulity. Gene has been truly remarkable through the whole thing & Paul himself has been brave, uncomplaining & the soul of patience. Usually (meaning each of the past Saturdays since he has been in the hospital) Gene & I spend the day with Paul together, having alternated times of day during the week—but today I have a bad cold & dare not carry viruses to him—so that gives me a chance to write some letters—it is quite impossible to do anything demanding more effort. […]

George

6

26 DECEMBER 1961

Dear Istvan,

[…] Your letter of the 18th arrived today—possibly delayed by the Christmas mail. It warmed us. We had just come back from the hospital where Paul had his 3rd from the last of radiation treatments. […] The tension & pressure is beginning to tell. But she [Gene] is holding up remarkably—with the assistance of tranquilizers which she ordinarily abominates. Paul himself has been literally astonishing—the very soul of quiet patience—an inner fortitude seems to have supported him through this whole time. It's too early to know just what the effects of treatment will be but the doctors seem to feel encouraged so far. It has been apparent that Paul will not go back to school this year. All things considered, this is a small sacrifice. He is beginning to read again though unable to sustain it for long stretches of time. I'm sure he will be grateful for whatever you send. It's very thoughtful of you. Two more days & we can begin to breathe more easily.

I should be going to N[ew] Y[ork] Thursday for rehearsals of the 2nd Symphony which is being performed Dec. 30 by the N[ew] Y[ork] Philharmonic with Werner Torkanowsky conducting. This is a special Naumberg concert, Jan. 2. The work will be recorded by Columbia.[17] Meanwhile I have been trying to keep up with my duties & teaching at the Un[iversity]. I must confess it has been remote from me but I go through the motions. The only thing I've done which "brought me to" was writing a paper I will give at the Un[iversity] Jan. 25 & use for other places later. We are surely working along similar lines. I call mine "The New Image of Music"[18] & have tried the impossible task of describing <u>what</u> has happened, <u>why</u> it happened and <u>what it means</u>. It was the hardest thing I've ever tried. I'll send you a carbon once it's typed. Before the holiday is over I plan to knock together another paper based on a chapter of the "book" I had started but am now giving up mainly because I can't sustain the effort under present circumstances & because the ideas can still be used for separate papers to be written as they jell. This one will be called "Duration in Music"[19] & deals with the problem of perceptibility of structure. Anyhow the most important thing is to get back to writing music.

I was awfully shocked to learn about the separatist movement in Quebec. These people must be motivated by strange forces. Frankly I don't think the U.S. gov[ernmen]t. will be particularly happy to have a "socialist" state to the north of them! I wish I understood better what was going on in the world—does anyone? There are moments when I think I see it all very clearly—a huge convulsive movement to shake off the old world, Europe, & America—to shake off the white man—a realignment of power—a new culture (but what kind?) dawning—it's all very vague. But all the café bombings in Algeria, uprisings in Africa, in S[outh] America—this all means something profound for the direction of mankind. But who can say if it's good or bad. My sympathy is always with the underdog—the have-nots—there are plenty of them in the world. Maybe this is all leading to a new Barbarism. Whatever it is, it is damned hard to go on writing music & harder to make it good. But this is what we're here for it seems to me. I'm sorry you have so little time for yourself—it's a crime. You must get them to give you more time. [...]

George

NOTES

1 Otto Luening (1900–96), American composer, teacher, conductor, and flutist, best remembered for his experiments with electronic music after 1952; along with Ussachevsky founder of the electronic music centre at Columbia University, the forerunner of the renowned Columbia–Princeton Electronic Music Center in New York. Vladimir Ussachevsky (1911–90), Manchurian-born American composer, close associate of Luening at Columbia University, one of the first Americans to experiment with the electronic medium. Mel Powell (1923–98), American composer and teacher, noted jazz pianist, and big-band arranger as well as composer of atonal and electronically synthesized music; between 1957 and 1969 he taught at Yale University, where he became chairman of the composition faculty and director of the electronic music studio. Bülent Arel (1919–90), Turkish-born American composer, known for his electronic music, particularly works that combine tape and instruments as well as audio and video tape. Milton Babbitt (b. 1916), American composer, who taught mainly at Princeton University; co-founder (with Luening, Ussachevsky, and Roger Sessions) of the Columbia–Princeton Electronic Music Center. Luciano Berio (1925–2003), one of the leading figures of the international avant-garde in the 1970s and 1980s.

2 Presumably *Stereo Electronic Music No. 1* (1961) and *Music for a Sacred Service: Prelude and Postlude* (1961).

3 Edgard Varèse (1883–1965). "Even before World War I," Paul Griffiths notes, "he [Varèse] saw the necessity of new means to realize his conceptions of 'organized sound' (the term he preferred to 'music')." *The New Grove Dictionary of American Music*, ed. H. Wiley Hitchcock and Stanley Sadie (London and New York: Macmillan Press, 1986), 4: 447.

4 The precise quotation is: "My God! What has sound got to do with music!" Charles Ives, *Essays before a Sonata, The Majority, and Other Writings*, ed. Howard Boatwright (New York: W.W. Norton, 1970), 84. Also relevant in this context is the composer's much-quoted retelling of his father George's response to the off-key singing of the stonemason John Bell: "Watch him closely and reverently, look into his face and hear the music of the ages. Don't pay too much attention to the sounds—for if you do, you may miss the music. You won't get a wild, heroic ride to heaven on pretty little sounds." Charles E. Ives, *Memos*, ed. John Kirkpatrick (New York: W.W. Norton, 1972), 132.

5 The precise quotation is: "What is best in music is not to be found in the notes."

6 String Quartet No. 2 with Soprano (1959–61).

7 *Time-Span II* for orchestra (1962), a major revision of *Time-Span I* for orchestra (1960), which was withdrawn by the composer, although it had been premiered by the St. Louis Symphony Orchestra, which commissioned the work, at St. Louis on 22 October 1960.

8 Istvan Anhalt, "New Records," *The Canadian Music Journal* 5/2 (Winter 1961): 34–39 (a review of two recordings of music by Varèse); and review of *Experimental Music: Composition with an Electronic Computer* by Lejaren A. Hiller, Jr., and Leonard M. Isaacson (New York, Toronto, London: McGraw-Hill, 1959) in ibid.: 61–67.

9 George Rochberg, "The Concepts of Musical Time and Space" (1963), in Rochberg, *Aesthetics of Survival* (1984), 78–136; see especially Part III: "Speech-Form and Space-Form," 117–36; rev. and expanded ed. (2004), 68–126; 107–26.

10 *Electronic Composition No. 4* ("On the Beach") (1961).

11 Nevil Shute, *On the Beach* (1957). Shute's novel about the global devastation of nuclear fall-out was the basis of Stanley Kramer's eponymous 1959 film.

12 Although aesthetically far removed from both John Cage (1912–92) and Morton Feldman (1926–87), who were among the leading lights of American experimental music in the 1960s, Anhalt treats them with a mixture of sympathy and ambivalence. In his paper "Music: Mode of Human Communication," which was read at McGill University in March 1962 (see "1962," note 6), he writes: "sometimes I find their music beautiful; sometimes just interesting, and at times tedious to listen to" (22).

13 Elliott Carter (b. 1908), Double Concerto for Harpsichord, Piano and Two Chamber Orchestras (1961). Leon Kirchner (b. 1919), Concerto for Violin, Violoncello, Ten Winds, and Percussion (1960).

14 *Duende* literally means "imp," "goblin," or "demon"; for Lorca *duende* is the "mysterious power" of great art: "'All that has dark sounds has *duende*.' And there is no greater truth. These dark sounds are the mystery, the roots pushing into the soil which we all know, which we all ignore, but from which comes what is real in art.... Angel and muse come from outside; the angel gives light and the muse gives shape.... The *duende*, though, must be awakened in the deepest dwellings of blood." From the text of a lecture the poet gave in Havana and Buenos Aires in 1933, "Theory and Function of the *Duende*," in Federico Garcia Lorca, *Selected Poems*, trans. Merryn Williams (Newcastle upon Tyne: Bloodaxe Books, 1992), 219–30.

15 The String Quartet No. 2 was premiered, in a private performance, in Philadelphia on 23 March 1962; the first public performance took place a week later, 30 March 1962, at the University of Pennsylvania; both performances by Janice Harsanyi, soprano, and the Philadelphia String Quartet.

16 *Blake Songs* for Soprano and Chamber Ensemble (1959–61; revised 1961–62) premiered 6 October 1961 in New York, Shirley Sudock, soprano, and the Hartt Chamber Players, Ralph Shapey, conductor.

17 Symphony No. 2 (1959), New York Philharmonic, Werner Torkanowsky, conductor, Columbia ML 5779 and Columbia MS 6379 (1962).

18 "The New Image of Music," *Perspectives of New Music* 2/1 (Fall–Winter 1963): 1–10; reprinted in Rochberg, *Aesthetics of Survival* (1984), 16–25; rev. and expanded ed. (2004), 16–25.

19 "Duration in Music" (1960) was first published in Beckwith and Kasemets, eds., *Modern Composer and His World* (1961), 56–64, and later reprinted in Rochberg, *Aesthetics of Survival* (1984), 71–77; rev. and expanded ed. (2004), 61–67.

1962

7

10 JANUARY 1962

Dear Istvan,

[...] The week in N[ew] Y[ork] took its toll. I'm battling a cold but will survive I'm sure. The performance was poor but the recording session went very well so things tended to achieve a balance.[1] You are perfectly right in pointing out the lack of insight into the true nature of the work. But what should we expect in a thoughtless, jaded world where enthusiasm & the ability to marvel are rarities?

Paul is improving week by week. He is reading more & starting to think of school. While it won't be possible for him to attend school on a regular basis we are thinking of a tutor arrangement or part-time attendance, whichever turns out to be more practical.

I'm sorry your paper goes slowly but I'm certain once inside it you will succeed very well.[2] Needless to say I'm eagerly looking forward to it—to compare "notes." My own effort is done after much sweat & rewriting.[3] But it still may not escape your "composer's dilettantism." I know your feelings & groan inwardly every time I strike on the hard rocks of philosophy or psychology. Still I don't think we must proceed by means of "scientific method" since we <u>are</u> dealing with art & art is not susceptible to a methodological ideology which derives from totally foreign fields & subject matter. In N[ew] Y[ork] I had dinner with a mathematician who pointed out—"music to my ears"—that there is no such thing as an abstract scientific method—that it is a false theology even for the scientist; that there are <u>methodologies</u> which are valid only in relation to the fields they attempt to organize—hence there are as many methods as there are definably different areas of scientific investigation. Here I stop since I cannot take this much further & especially because I do not want to throw you any curves.

When I can I will begin to work at a revision of *Time-Span*—it is hard work to revise but I feel the need to take the work one step further before leaving it alone forever. […]

George

8

16 FEBRUARY 1962

Dear George

I was sorry to read that you and your family have to prolong the time of uncertainty and anxiety … We very much feel with you and wait anxiously for news about Paul! Have patience … (a thing easier to write about than to master). […]

During this period of anxiety I did work on the preparation of the concert, the programme of which I include here. (We only put up such [a] concert if there is worthwhile material for it. That does not happen every year.) This was the second time that the local union helped us in this manner. This of course removes the handicap: student composers' works played by student players. I told my students: go ahead write for professionals. Of the four student composers one is a well above average talent, Alan Heard.[4] His present leading lights include Varèse and Berg. He is twenty, intelligent, tough (meaning that he is willing to fight out a solution) and possesses a composer's imagination. […]

BMI Canada showed recently an interest in publishing the score of my symphony as a study-score. They plan to reprint it from the original transparencies, but in case this wouldn't work they seem to be willing to have the work recopied. That would be my first publication.[5] Perhaps it's time … Another good news: I found the title for my March 5th lecture: "Music: Mode of Human Communication."[6] As you well guess I did not start writing the damn thing, as yet. I kept on reading and reading, but now I am ready to call it a halt and start writing during this weekend. I am afraid that I may have only a rough copy for the lecture and so won't be able to send you a copy on or about the 5th of March, but it won't be delayed much. (I am much too curious to find out what you think about it. This prompts me to ask: how did your lecture go?[7] Please send me a copy of it, but don't mail it before the 4th of March. I don't want to start discussion with you before my lecture is over.)

I am so happy that you are thinking of composing again and that the preparations for the premiere of your quartet are progressing. Please keep me posted on these; what you do is among the very best music com- | 13
posed today [that] I know of directly! […]

Istvan

PS: I met Powell[8] last summer at Columbia. It was a meeting without opportunity for more than a brief "feeling out."

9

17 MARCH 1962

My dear George,

We are so happy that Paul is better, and we can well imagine what that must mean to you and Gene. We are with you, with all our heart, throughout this process of recovery …

Your "New Image" is a beautifully thought through, constructed and written paper. It is like a musical composition: one which could have been composed by George Rochberg … Your diagnosis of our musical present is penetrating and I almost totally agree with it. Your description of the employment of the principle of planned indeterminacy is nothing short of masterly. Your emphasis on what you term the "sound-object" and "motion" establishes the right foci. With regard to "musical motion," however, I must register a slight dissent with what I understand to be your position. As I see it: there is a continuum of attitudes towards musical motion throughout the recorded history of western music. These attitudes seem to reflect, in my view at least, the composer's *Weltanschauung*, conscious or otherwise. I cannot prove it, but feel it that the mind of Newton is behind Bach, as well as Beethoven in the same way as Einstein and Schoenberg are behind Cage and Stockhausen.[9] Viewed in this light Cage ceases to be a freak, and his no-continuity, as well as indeterminacy, assume a "normal" role in the historical process. I loved to read what you said about the "spatial images" of music. But I cannot say whether I agree with it or not. I just don't have the faculty of <u>thinking logically</u> about space and time, that is, of time being a dimension of space. This however does not prevent me from being deeply moved by your eloquent description of the condition of the present-day composer. I am referring especially to the last two pages of your paper. This section is truly a most personal testimony, and the question of agreement or disagreement with it recedes into the irrelevant. […]

I am dissatisfied and disturbed by the present state of my paper: "Music: Mode of Human Communication." As you will undoubtedly see: it is badly worded, diffusely constructed, lacking foci and proportion. I don't recall having ever had so much trouble with writing. I simply was not ready for writing before it got late and then I had to hurry to meet the March 5th deadline. I was debating with myself during the whole day, today, whether or not to show you a copy. I decided to send it to you anyhow with the commentary. As work stands now I will not be able to rewrite it before May. So please consider it what it is: a crude draft, which shows the plan, the approach, the main lines of argument, and the conclusion but deficient in everything else. Since I consider it a draft only, please do not show it to anyone, and when you will get the "final version" destroy it. […]

Istvan

10

25 MARCH 1962

Dear Istvan,

A veritable bonanza package, your letter & your paper! How pleased I am that you liked my effort. But honesty on my part requires that I register my own dissatisfactions with it: over-generalized, too sweeping in scope, and particularly not sufficient penetration into the area of the spatial idea which leads for me to what I am now thinking of as "meta-music." But I can't cope with it mainly because it's beyond my rational powers to grasp or to catch long enough to pin down; besides it cost me so much effort & energy to write that I'm off words & verbalization in a strictly formal sense for a long time from now on. In any case, it means a great deal to me that it meant so much to you.

I respect your remarks about your "mode of communication" and will wait for the final version. But in the meantime, may I throw out a few thoughts? First, I am forcibly struck by the sheer mental power you display to handle the concepts you work with. To me they are of so abstract a nature that to succeed as you do in building up your analogy between music & language is a feat in itself. I wish I were more familiar with & could think more readily & immediately, i.e., directly, in the terms you employ. I confess it's tough going for me. While some details may escape me—additional readings will correct that I hope—the overall structure is crystal clear; that is, what you build up as premises & the conclusions you draw from them. I'm not sure I agree with the rationale of your approach but I see its logic. I wonder how necessary it is to build so completely on the analogy between music & language. Isn't it possible to derive the structure of communication per se from music itself without resorting to the language of linguistic analysis? I see we are rather far apart on Cage but I want to read your paper again (& especially the section where you deal with Cage) before expanding my comments.

Today I finished sketching the revisions of *Time-Span* which will become *Time-Span II*, leaving the first version intact. I must say I'm exhausted. Part of this comes from Friday night when my String Quartet No. 2 (with voice) was given a private performance at a "patron's" home. It went much better than I had hoped for & had to be repeated. (This Friday, March 30, is its first public performance at the Univ[ersity].)[10] It is 30 minutes long & builds its own special world, a world of intensity and sadness. I was overcome with emotion as were apparently many others. Janice Harsanyi who sang the soprano part (2nd half of the work, roughly) was truly magnificent. If the tape that was made is any good I'll send a copy. […]

George

11

17 AUGUST 1962

Dear Istvan,

It's very difficult to write but I feel if I don't the silence between us will lengthen and you will not know why I have not been able to write till now. As had been arranged, Paul went into the hospital early in July for a series of tests and was then discharged, everything apparently fine. Ten days went by, since he was home, and during that time peculiar symptoms began to show themselves until by the 1st week of Aug. it was clear to us something was wrong again. On Aug. 7 he was operated on again, this time on his spine, to prevent paralysis of his lower limbs. We now know that his life is severely endangered, in fact the situation is virtually hopeless. We may be able to bring him home in a few weeks but in what condition no one will or can predict. It is not likely he will walk again. What the future course of his illness will take no one knows. We are almost broken by this blow but we are trying hard to keep going, to keep our daughter from the knowledge, to keep the house from falling apart, to help our Paul keep up his courage. He has been through so much and it is cruel and senseless. I understand nothing any longer. […]

George

12

16 | [a draft with Anhalt's changes and corrections; undated, but clearly shortly after 17 August 1962]

My dear George,

Your letter of the 17th ~~got~~ got here this morning and ever since having read it you did not ~~go out of~~ leave my mind. What a trial you and Gene must go through we can only dimly sense, but this is more than ~~sufficient~~ enough to bring one close to the feeling of helplessness, close to being choked up. This evening Beate and I after having finished the meal kept on sitting at the table ~~silently~~ without a word. I knew what she was thinking and she knew also what was on my mind … ~~We wish we could give you now an effective friendly hand. We even thought of going down to visit you. But how? You are so right in thinking that~~ During the day we repeatedly kept on asking each other what we could do which could ~~express~~ demonstrate our ~~love~~ affection and friendship ~~to you~~ which we feel for you both; ~~and which I should add that~~ to do something which could contribute to the magnificent courage and strength you are showing in this ~~circumstance~~ situation. Would you have a suggestion? Please do tell us if you have an idea in which way we could be of any use to you now!

~~I feel exactly the same way as you do about wanting with to talk with you to each other. It is really a pity that a whole year went by without getting together …~~ I am ~~afraid of~~ reluctant calling you on the phone ~~(I don't know when to call you for one thing)~~, and in the same time wishing to speak with you. ~~But please~~ However I wish you would call me, if the thought occurs to you; and if so, please call me collect, it is my turn now. […]

We mailed you today a small parcel. ~~The contents~~ We brought the contents for you and Gene from Mexico. Perhaps you will want to give the cufflinks to Paul. ~~It was~~ Tell him that without having met him we have a deep affection for him. ~~Speaking about Paul a thought comes to mind, that how simple it would be for me if I would be a "believer"~~

There is another thing I ~~want to write to you~~ was thinking about today; it is "hope." What is the "hope" of the person, like me who has no religion, and whose relationship to God is … ~~such that~~ amorphous, to say the least. When things seem "out of one's control" seeking "hope" is natural, at least it appears so to me. Perhaps "hope" is the belief that there are relationships at work in the processes of the organism of the individual as well as in that of a group of individuals, or even in "unorganic" matter, which can and do produce eventually states which experts (and their expertise is based often ~~on insufficient~~ on statistical evidence) considered unlikely, judged from the vantage point of statistics. ~~There are a hundred thousand and one intangibles in a sickness in a situation~~ So my dear George keep up your courage, keep up your hope, because acting on the strength derived from "hope" you may contribute that small "intangible" which may mean miraculous improvement ... In the idea of "hope" is ~~embedded all the ignorance we ourselves are covered with~~ embodied ~~we express~~ our burning desire ~~to see through that veil of ignorance which stands between our desire for holistic understanding of man and our pitiful experiments about man~~ to understand. [...]

[Istvan Anhalt]

NOTES

1 That is, the recording sessions for the Symphony No. 2 (see "1961," note 17).
2 See note 6 below.
3 See "1961," note 18.
4 Alan Heard (b. 1942), composer and teacher, a student of Anhalt at McGill University (B.Mus. 1962), where he taught for a time (1967–71).
5 Anhalt's Symphony (1958) was published in 1963 (Toronto: BMI Canada).
6 "Music: Mode of Human Communication," paper read at the invitation of the Faculty of Music, McGill University, on 5 March 1962 (unpublished), Anhalt Fonds 164/F1,5.
7 See "1961," note 18.
8 See "1961," note 1.
9 Karlheinz Stockhausen (b. 1928), one of the leading figures of the international avant-garde in the 1960s and 1970s.
10 See "1961," note 15.

1963

13

11 MARCH 1963

Dear Istvan,

[...] I have ordered the two books you brought to my attention & am eagerly awaiting their arrival. The Whitrow book[1] especially sounds "meaty." At the present time all these matters seem so remote mainly because I have been so deeply involved myself in family & the university that the little time left to myself has had to go into specific tasks; for one, I've just completed the first draft of a paper I'm to read in Israel this summer at the East–West in Music Conference in Jerusalem, Aug. 5–12. The reason for having to do it so early is that they want all papers in advance to print & distribute so everyone can familiarize themselves with the ideas before attending panel discussions. I was supposed to write a 20-minute paper on "Ethical & Aesthetic Values in Contemporary Music"[2] but wound up instead with at least 2 or 3 times more. It is impossible to treat such a subject briefly. As it was, I had a devil of a time discovering what I believed & and then finding a way to say it. Writing prose has become a trial. I approach it as though it were music & and then I'm in deep trouble. The paper may interest you & if so I'll send you a copy once it's ready. I discussed the general confusion in the area of values, the Soviet situation vis-à-vis Socialist Realism (Khrushchev recently made a statement which bears out everything negative I said—one cannot be in favor of art as ideology), then the fundamental relations between moral & aesthetic values—or what I think they are. The major part of the paper is taken up with commenting on statements by Cage, Krenek & Babbitt in order to determine whether contemporary music as seen through the eyes of some of the more prominent composers writing on music today bears any relation to these values, etc. I hinge my whole argument on what I call the "withdrawal of the subjective self" from the act of composing & come up with a basically negative picture: Cage denies moral-aesthetic values, Krenek does too by inference[3] & for Babbitt these would appear to be irrelevant. I conclude the paper with a statement of what I feel must obtain between the composer & the work he is engaged in if some semblance of art is to be achieved.

Before I took up my work on the paper I was trying to make headway with a trio for violin, cello & piano—old-fashion combination!—which I am writing for an ensemble in N[ew] Y[ork].[4] It is devilish hard to write. I know what I want—or think I do—it continues to elude me. […]

I was happy to hear you got the recording of the Symphony [No. 2]. I honestly couldn't tell you what the technical details of recording were. You can imagine I would have much preferred Szell to record it[5] but from a certain point of view Torkanowsky did a good job despite my reservations. Now I'm waiting for the recording of my 2nd quartet to come out. It was promised for Feb. but now it looks like it won't be out until the end of this month & maybe early April.[6] The Louisville Symphony will record my 1st Symphony soon.[7] All this is very nice but I am more interested in getting back to work & writing new music. […]

George

14

1 JULY 1963

Dear Istvan and Bea, Bea and Istvan!

Your letters still spread their glow and warmth—it is truly impossible to tell you how they made us feel—but surely you could not have been writing about us! But since I know you will insist you were, we must accept your wonderful words at face value & know that they convey your love & friendship which we respond to completely. For on our end the days following your too early departure were filled with talk of both of you & how in some strange way we felt that we were very much the same kind of people despite obvious external differences. It is rare indeed to find oneself—ourselves—at this late date (despite the much-vaunted longevity of our modern generations) finding true friendship & love based on mysterious essences & capabilities. Paul was apparently as much taken by both of you as you were by him. He literally glowed when he spoke to you! Those were two memorable days indeed and we hope we can repeat them often either under the same roof or yours.

Paul came home from the hospital last Thursday after 10 days. The operation itself was brief as these things go, about 45 minutes, & Paul was up & strolling around 3 hours later!! Evidently his back is healing well, if slowly which was expected, & we are now taking him in 3 times a week to have the dressing changed. The process will continue until the wound is completely healed & there is absolutely no sign of any danger. Once past this, it may well be possible to put aside the whole 2 years previous (since Oct. 1961) as a very bad dream, an existence which seemed utterly impossible to survive but, like all such times, through which we emerge somehow, marked but not destroyed. We hope fervently for this. […]

I think I understand what you must be going through, Istvan, in your "situation" & I can only hope for your sake that it will soon be resolved positively. In any case I am not forgetting our talk the last evening you were here when we finally gave you your opportunity to "complain" & I shall do all I can when the circumstances are right to wean you away from Montreal & Canada. It gave me especial pleasure to know that you were already at work on your orchestra music. This despite the external pressures! Isn't this the way it seems to happen in life for the creative spirit? "Damn the torpedoes, full speed etc." The illusion of necessity, the necessity of bringing something new into the world is the most beautiful, to me, of all illusions & one without which it would appear to be impossible to live at all. It's for this that we bear so much or so it seems. I found a few hours to begin a more direct acquaintance with your *Symphony [of Modules]* & am all the more eager to hear the tape. The work is wonderfully innovative, genuinely orchestral in conception, beautifully articulated. It would be the height of presumption for me to tell you, or try to tell you to put it more accurately, what I think a phrase is! Your score is a living demonstration of the reality of the musical phrase. I wonder if ultimately this is not really the secret of composition & when all is said & done no amount of "new techniques" which do not somehow embody this secret or continue to live through its manifestation can validate composition as music. To shape & articulate "the phrase" is perhaps a greater challenge than to compose a new texture, etc.; well, you know my prejudices full well so I won't continue in this vein especially since I know from your music that we believe in the same thing fundamentally. I am especially eager now to see the new work when you are ready to show it.

The trio [No. 1] is a little more advanced than when you were here. I managed somehow with Paul's exhortations as a goad to continue working even while he was in the hospital. If this damned heat wave will let up (we've had, as you've probably read, 5–6 days successively of 90 to 97 with humidity. Utterly impossible to function properly) perhaps I can return to real work. In any case, whenever it's printed, I know that this is the last piece I will write in this particular way. I want to get on to do something else that is brewing, i.e., a different point of view, a different angle of approach. How tired I'm getting of complex surfaces. I long for the ability to make simple, direct statements & bury the complexities below the surface where only I will know they exist or perhaps a few sympathetic souls will care to burrow for nuggets, if any exist, that is! […]

George

NOTES

1 G[erald] J[ames] Whitrow, *The Natural Philosophy of Time* (London: T. Nelson, 1961).
2 Unpublished paper originally delivered at "East–West in Music" Conference, Jerusalem (August 1963).
3 See, for example, Ernst Krenek, *Music Here and Now*, trans. Barthold Fles (New York: W.W. Norton, 1939).
4 Trio No. 1 for Violin, Cello, and Piano (1962–63), commissioned by the Nieuw Amsterdam Trio.
5 The Symphony No. 2 was premiered by George Szell and the Cleveland Orchestra in Severance Hall on 26 February 1959.
6 Philadelphia String Quartet, Janice Harsanyi, soprano, CRI 164 (1963).
7 Louisville Orchestra, Robert Whitney, conductor, LOU 634 (ca. 1963).

1964

15

22 MARCH 1964

Dear Istvan,

[...] I have been back & forth between here & home a number of times since Jan. Several reasons necessitated this, among them not only Paul's situation which remains about the same—he's just had a second series of drug treatments which we hope will help—but my own inability to stick it out here alone for too long a stretch—2 to 2½ weeks is about my limit—nevertheless being here has provided us with time to write & I'm deep in a work which is a new departure for me from practically every point of view. There will be 6 "choral passions" (as I call them now) based on the text collages (many languages, different periods of culture).[1] I see the work staged but not as conventional theater or musical theater—don't quite know yet. [...]

George

16

13 DECEMBER 1964

Dear Isti & Beate,

[...] Today is 3 weeks, 3 aeons, 3 thousand years since Paul left us. We are trying to recover our balance—it is difficult. I am not in touch with what I must do but I keep up the habit of the routine. Gene is wonderful as she always has been. She has with Chessie kept up the activities of the domestic side of our lives & Chessie has missed only one dancing lesson. We don't really know about the future of things. That will have to come to us as we go on. Perhaps during Christmas I can finish the score of my *Zodiac*[2]—just copying is required & it is the kind of activity which helps since I can't do any real work.

Mostly we have been preoccupied with plans for publication of Paul's poetry & stories. Before he died there were three acceptances: his story "The Silver Talons of Piero Kostrov," was accepted by *Chelsea Review*,[3] one of the good quarterlies in N[ew] Y[ork] we're told; a poem, "J'ai embrassé l'aube d'été," was accepted by a small mag[azine] called *Input*—they have agreed to print a notice that the publication is posthumous & have asked for another poem which I'm sending off today;[4] the editor of *Dimension Cincinnati*, a slick mag[azine], an old friend of ours, liked Paul's work & was planning to publish; now he plans a memorial, probably an article on Paul as a writer.[5] These are the immediate things but we want to publish all the poetry & the 3 stories in one volume.[6] A number of writer friends who were close to Paul & admired his work have offered their help. Perhaps someday Paul's spirit will, through his words & the clear, sweet images he formed out of them, reach far & wide. As his physical being gave way to the disintegrating forces of his illness his spirit grew more calm and luminous. He said in "Piero Kostrov": "It is growing dark. And I do not wish to lose the sweetness of the day." […]

George

NOTES

1 *Passions [According to the Twentieth Century] for Singers, Jazz Quintet, Brass Ensemble, Percussion, Piano, and Tape* (1964–67).

2 *Zodiac* (1964), a transcription for large orchestra of the *Twelve Bagatelles for Piano Solo* (1952).

3 The little magazine *Chelsea*, no. 17 (August 1965), contains the following items pertaining to Paul: a short appreciation, "Paul Rochberg," by Paul's friend and mentor, playwright and novelist Christopher Davis (3–5); Paul's short story, "The Silver Talons of Piero Kostrov" (6–24); and three of his poems: "The Strangest Thing" (25), "A Rusty Hermit Crab" (25), and "Cavalry" (26–27).

4 "J'ai embrassé l'aube d'été," *Input* 2/1, issue 5 (Spring 1965): 16; the other poem submitted by Rochberg appeared as "(untitled)" and begins: "There is a world / That is only dreamed / In nights / When your eyes / Are a thousand stars" (ibid., 10).

5 *Dimension: Cincinnati* 2/12 (May 1965) published nine of Paul's poems: "I am baffled by this wall," "There is something lost / In loving," "My heart is wet of wanting," and six *Fantasies*, as well as the following note by Arthur Darack, the magazine's editor: "Paul Rochberg died at the age of 20, and with him ended rich hopes. He was an enchanting youth, full of intellectual and physical grace. But he was also one of the most talented members of his generation. 'Of his generation'—how terrible to say this of one whose last two years were spent in agony, undergoing a

fruitless series of desperate operations for an illness that he must have known would tolerate no recovery. Despite it all, he went on writing poetry, of beauty, of an almost painful insight, and of an astonishing verbal resource. He wrote prose too, and he had skill in parody and wit that would have distinguished him in any mature company. Grillparzer's epitaph for Franz Schubert surely applies: 'here intombed a rich treasure but still fairer hopes'" (24).

6 A collection of Paul Rochberg's poems and stories, with an introduction by George Rochberg, eventually appeared as *Paul Rochberg: Poems and Stories* (Newtown Square, PA: Muse of Fire Press, 1990).

PART TWO

MUSICAL COMPOSITION (1965–1976)

From your letter I sense that you have stepped up the level of intensity and concentration of your work. This is what really matters, apart from one's family.

— Anhalt (February 1976)

Istvan Anhalt, Kingston, Ontario, 2005. Photo by Beate Anhalt.

1965

17

11 APRIL 1965

My dear Istvan,

[…] Needless to say I am touched that you continue to plague your colleagues with the plan for a lecture. The policy you outline seems "conservative" only on the side of the date-limit. Other than that I myself feel that the intelligent lay audience needs the general overview, the insight, the assistance through the labyrinth without which they would surely get lost & fall prey to the clutches of the minotaur. The title I offered, "Music: Aural Fact or Fiction?,"[1] is intended to do this—whether I will succeed is another thing. In any case I'm trying to get it together now because on May 3 I must give a lecture in Cincinnati. The greatest need I feel is to try, if possible, to clarify the inner contradictions & rending tensions of our cultural life vis-à-vis music. I'm still open however to suggestions if McGill does want me to come. I like very much the way you outline the "seminar" session—that is the way I am most comfortable anyhow—let's do it as you describe if the occasion permits.

You know, I agree with you absolutely on Feldman's "Swallows" [*The Swallows of Salangan* (1960)]. I heard it in Buffalo & wondered that such elaborate posturings & verbalized defenses, such strenuous efforts to support an edifice finally add up to so tiny a voice, so small an object to be underpinned. It is out of embarrassment only—even granted one does not know one feels shame or embarrassment but calls it by some other name—that such phenomena as Feldman can emerge. The general prettiness & triviality balanced by the obsessive concern with the greatest amount of public currency & "cover-story" prestige is part & parcel of the end of the 19th-century Romantic posture, the vertical man, who thinks he is unique enough to blot out the sun. I for one am utterly fed up with art & artists based on such unholy premises. Pity those who can't read the *Mene Tekel* [i.e., "Mene, Mene, Tekel, Ufarsim," Daniel 5:25] on the wall. On the other hand I don't assume a posture of superiority because I recognize their weakness. I am too long familiar with my own & the whole fabric of human frailty to permit myself even the slightest itch of self-satisfaction. *Vale* Feldman!

I am delighted things are working out in the dep[artmen]t & especially pleased that you are convinced by Suderburg's abilities.[2] Incidentally, another former student of mine, Stephen Albert,[3] is currently staying in Montreal & I've urged him in a letter just written to get in touch with you. Steve has won the American Acad[emy] in Rome Prize for 1965—& well-deserved too. He writes with great passion, exerts remarkable control over his means which are still basically traditional—has a fantastic sense of timbre. He will be a true artist, one of the few of his generation (Steve is about 26). […]

Will you be surprised if I tell you that from Feb. 20 to the end of March I wrote the fl.-cl.-vl.-pno. piece I talked about?[4] I put it that way only because I myself never anticipated it would come like that. It is being reproduced & I will send you a copy. There is still so much to say which only a long talking session could take care of. But only to add that you must know how much I too value our friendship and what it means. […]

George

18

4 MAY 1965

My dear Istvan,

Here I am sitting in the hotel room in Cincinnati, Ohio answering your two wonderful letters. I think I mentioned I would be here for the activities which comprise "An Exposition of Contemporary American Music"—not too good a title—but we shall see. Last night I gave the opening talk which seems to have been received very warmly & apparently as far as I can judge with understanding. Saturday night Max Rudolph conducts the *Zodiac* for the first time anywhere.[5] I am looking forward to that. This afternoon I'll attend rehearsal—it's not a difficult work—but full of changing configurations of color & gesture. But to get back to your letters (what a treat!) & the question before us: the McGill lecture. I don't have to tell you how absolutely delighted I was with your reaction to the *Contra*. If it is as good as you think it is—& I as well—then perhaps I've made something really worthwhile. You know this is the work where I tried for the first time to employ other composer's music, either to quote it (there are very few direct quotes) or to transform it & establish it in a context of my own invention.[6] Now I feel greatly encouraged to go on & am planning to follow this general plan of action in a large chamber ensemble work just commissioned by Fromm Foundation [*Music for the Magic Theater*] and my 3rd quartet (commissioned by myself!). Ideas are in the back of my head for both & as soon as school is over & my desk cleared of ephemera I shall fight the bull again. The *Contra* will be performed in Bowdoin College, Maine Aug. 18. Could you come to it? I would like very much to share my first hearing of it with you, my friend. Now down to real business. Your suggestion re a lecture entitled "Music of Today" followed by a subtitle falls in perfectly with what I did last night here. It would read "Music of Today: Aural Fact or Fiction?" My talk is about the problem of making the art work, composing itself in today's world with particular emphasis on the struggle with the abstract tendency which prevails in the art generally. I branch off in this talk—for the first time—I talk about literature, film, painting & draw analogies to show correspondences. At the same time I try to show exactly what we are dealing with today when we try to compose music. There is a great deal I don't say—there simply isn't enough time. As it is the lecture is 45 minutes long read at a normal pace with places to breathe. I'm worried only about one thing—I have not planned musical examples & wonder if you would prefer that I work them in. It can be done. I will be glad to follow your suggestion here & take any other suggestions you have. If you & your colleagues find my title suggestion & subject matter fits your plan then we have only to arrange the time. I shall want to hear from you about this.

Gene and I were very pleased too by your response to Paul's poem. It is frighteningly beautiful & I always find myself amazed at the beautiful lucid images he made. […]

George

19

25 MAY 1965

My dear Istvan,

Your letter with your talk at Univ[ersity] of B[ritish] C[olumbia] theory program came yesterday & I hasten to reply so you will have the papers back in time for your trip to Vancouver. Evidently it is the same in Canada as in the States: no one seems satisfied with the way theory goes; & indeed it is very difficult. I liked your approach very much (especially your polite & kindly expressed skepticism re the B.C. approach which I think is overdone, fussy & maybe even a time-waster ultimately). What you call Auditory Pattern Perception is "right on the nose" since all you need to do is to substitute "Conception" for "Perception" & you are talking about the composer's work, his problems, etc. Unfortunately I can't be of much help in any specific sense. I know nothing of the technical literature on auditory perception (just scraps here & there & I never remember who said what; some scholar!). But if the task of theory is to guide the student toward an aural grasp (meaning mental, of course, but not verbal; I'm afraid there are no verbal equivalents) of compositional structure, then it is clear he must be led to an understanding of Gestalt, context, field, etc. He has to hear the totality first, then analysis. I think one of the greatest difficulties with teaching music theory is that we always start from grammar & grammatical details & get lost on the way. Could we not deal with questions of continuity & discontinuity right away by stressing the fact that different historical languages (modality, tonality, etc.) all develop different emphases & degrees of expectation as to the actions of pitches & rhythms. I think if we taught music as an auditory pattern of parallelisms (counterpoint, harmony, polyphony) & serialisms (successive happenings) we'd be closer to the way the brain functions (see Von Neumann's *Computer & the Brain*).[7] Repetition in music is analogous to self-perpetuation of genes & chromosomes, cellular structure etc. (again Von Neumann). Why not teach repetition & reiteration as self perception? The whole question, seems to me, is to find a way to teach theory as the organic structure of musical thought; & since musical thought is only a special form of thought & the whole process of thinking, the closer we get to the way the brain & nervous system operates the closer we get to music. We must teach the principle of masking which affects aural depth (Ives was the master here) on the relationships of parts in a context (yet Schoenberg writes *haupstimme* & *nebenstimme* knowing which voice is to be heard prominently, or the way composers treat a number of voices in a given context). I find that fascinating to see how in a quartet or quintet all sorts of relations are established: one; two between any of the four; three between any of the four; etc. Look at a quintet & see how it is divided. The composer is always thinking in combinations. Listening then should arrive at the same.

Well, here I am blowing off a lot called steam but not giving you any help at all. But one final word: I have always felt that theory should be taught according to how the composer functions, not according to abstract schemata which are only about themselves (Schenker, for ex[ample]).[8] The composer's ears are like anyone else's; only his sensibilities are more intense. That's why he composes; he "catches fire" as J. Maritain says about the poet.[9] Well, that's only a metaphor for saying his brain is bursting hot with ideas because anyhow the brain is hot; it's an energy system. And music is its corona. […]

George

[…]

20

29 DECEMBER 1965

My dear Istvan,

[…] First, about your work. The news that you've completed about 9 minutes is good to hear—is there no chance you could finish it before Sept. 66? I feel it is so unique and remarkable a conception that I want to see it burst on the world as early as possible.[10] It had its own effect on my work—not in terms of similarities but in the sense of utter release & freedom from the past, the conventional rut & groove. Your work is for me a basic statement so new & vital in spirit that it will shake everybody & everything up. It will make the current "avant-gardists" appear like so many Czernys & Moscheles. It will make them obsolete! I have the distinct feeling that between the two of us music is reviving its drooping spirits; and, if the world—which is already mad—doesn't go completely off its rocker & blow us all up, music has a chance to become valid again. The mind will be freed & the energies of the heart released from the deep-freeze.

I don't know how to describe my new work. It is called *Music for the Magic Theater* (after *Steppenwolf* by Hermann Hesse). It is somewhere between 20 & 23 minutes long, three sections: 1) "collage" (assemblage); 2) transcription of Mozart Adagio from K. 287 which I remember telling you about; 3) "collage." Once it's copied I'll send you a score which will speak for itself—I hope. I can tell you that I feel it is the best thing I've ever done, the freest, the richest, the most deeply felt. It is strange how the external discrepancies of language fade away and Mozart lives comfortably side by side with sounds & structures completely opposite to his. I think above all I have been trying to say that only the paradox is viable, that only opposites belong together & in making them manifest we reassert the tension of existence itself which is a multi-structure composed of multi-combinations. A cross-section of life is a like a Dagwood sandwich—it's got everything in it. I want "every thing" in my music. The problem is to choose. Do you think that you could fly to Chicago for its performance?[11] I don't know when that will be yet—perhaps this spring—but I would be very happy if you & Bea could come. [...]

George

NOTES

1 A version of this, entitled "Aural Fact or Fiction: Or, Composing at the Seashore" (1965), appeared in Rochberg, *Aesthetics of Survival* (1984), 177–88; rev. and expanded ed. (2004), 187–98.

2 Robert Suderburg (b. 1936), student of Rochberg who, like his mentor, abandoned twelve-tone procedures in the late 1960s.

3 Stephen Albert (1941–92), a student of Rochberg in the fall of 1963; his symphony *RiverRun* won a Pulitzer Prize in 1985.

4 *Contra Mortem et Tempus* (1965).

5 *Zodiac* was premiered in Cincinnati on 8 May 1965 by the Cincinnati Symphony, conducted by Max Rudolph.

6 *Contra Mortem et Tempus* contains references to the music of Berg, Berio, Boulez, Ives, Varèse, and Webern.

7 John Von Neumann, *The Computer and the Brain* (New Haven: Yale University Press, 1958).

8 Heinrich Schenker (1868–1935), one of the most influential music theorists of the twentieth century.

9 Rochberg did not recall the precise location of this reference, not surprisingly since both Jacques and Raïssa Maritain use the imagery of "poetic fire" frequently throughout their voluminous writings. A few examples, chosen at random: In *The Situation of Poetry: Four Essays on the Relations between Poetry, Mysticism, Magic, and Knowledge*, trans. Marshall Suther (New York: Philosophical Library, 1955), Raïssa writes: "Is that not what Rimbaud said? 'The poet is really a stealer of fire'" (7). And Jacques Maritain: "It is in no sense a matter of diminishing the role of the intelligence, nor the importance of intelligibility, of human experience, of conscious metaphysics involved in the poetic work, especially when that work is a tragedy for example, or a drama or epic. I say only that the fire of creative intuition must be hot enough to consume these materials, and not to be extinguished by them" (62). And in *Creative Intuition in Art and Poetry* (New York: Pantheon Books, 1953), Jacques Maritain speaks of "external materials to be integrated in, and transformed by, the fire of creative virtues" (112), "the fire of spiritual communication" (145), and, further: "For reason and calculation in the poet are there only to handle fire, and if 'enthusiasm' means fire, there is no writer without enthusiasm (touched with reason-gloved hands). So much the better if in the handwriting the pen is controlled and diligent: the words will burn all the more. It is not, furthermore, with regard to inspiration and poetic intuition, it is with regard to pas-

sion, 'brute' passion, associated with them but spiritualized (made 'intentional') in the creative fire, that Novalis and Arnim demanded coolheadedness" (248).

10 Presumably Rochberg is referring to Anhalt's *Symphony of Modules*, which was completed in July 1967.

11 *Music for the Magic Theater* (1965) was premiered on 24 January 1967 by the University of Chicago Chamber Players, conducted by Ralph Shapey.

1966

21

4 JANUARY 1966

My dear Isty,

Imagine two wonderful things happening to you on the same day: I came home from Swarthmore College where I heard a beautiful performance of my *[La] Bocca [della Veritá]* for oboe & piano played by two young, incomparable musicians (from N[ew] Y[ork]), Ronald Roseman (oboe) & Gil Kalish (piano), sat down to dinner with my girls & read through the day's mail, saving your great letter for last (the dessert!). So your words which convey so much warmth & friendship & human-ness were the second of the two (but only in order of occurrence). Our deepest thanks for your good wishes and to all of you our hopes & wishes for a rich, fruitful '67 [*sic*] and for the great success of the first performance of your music. I think it's wonderful you should be asked to conduct your *Symphony [of Modules]*.[1] That will insure its best presentation providing of course you get the number of rehearsals you've asked for. The one time I conducted my own orchestral music in public was, for me, a very great experience—but I must confess it scared the hell out of me. I often get the urge to do it again but that can wait. I should tell you that your score & tape have been with me for some days now and I have listened & looked intently, trying to supply in my feeble imagination the live speakers. In many ways it is fascinating what you have generated out of the text (which, undeniably, is strong & beautiful—a projection of faith & hope in the still untapped resources of man & time)—the pulsations & waves of vocal sound, the densities accumulating & dissipating—but I need to hear the totality before I can say anything meaningful. This much I intuit: that it is a rich statement in grays & blacks of sound which converts the surface of this sector of contemporary music into an exterior skin beneath which pulses life & strength. I am happy to hear that there is already a demand for the work & hope it meets with success wherever it is done.[2] […]

I was very interested in what you said about Weiss's[3] play. I too read it—before I saw it. Here we have a remarkable instance where the script is literally only a blueprint for the living organism. We saw a production in Williamstown (near Tanglewood) this summer & were very impressed by the power & surge of the production with its combination of drama, rhetoric, music, ballet, tableaux, etc. As to the ideational control of the play: I think basically I have Weiss's condemnation of man's inability to rise above his limitations, in fact to rationalize those limitations as truth & liberty, to make murder so central to his fanaticism & self-righteousness. The whole subject requires hours of talk—which I miss having with you. I see in the Vietnam War, for example, a prelude & preparation for the ultimate conflict of this century. It is presented to us as a "just" war, etc., etc. But what the U.S. government is really doing is gradually, carefully building bases for planes, supply depots, harbors, roads, etc. to handle the logistics of a great land war in Asia. We will probably have 1/2 a million men in Vietnam alone before this year is out not to speak of the numbers of men in Cambodia & Thailand, etc. And every nuclear device the Chinese drop only brings us closer; for each one intensifies the fear & hysteria which I suspect really grips Washington. I hate to blow smoke in anyone's dreams but I can't see how all this will end except in a catastrophic war. Yet precisely because I feel the immanence of it all strongly, it forces in me the necessity to work even harder & I live even more intensely if that is possible. Perhaps I am all wet; and all I'm doing is scaring myself into hard work—a delicious irony & certainly back-assward. But some of us are screwed to the left & I always felt that that's how the lattice work of my neurology goes. […]

I'm off to N[ew] Y[ork] Jan. 16 to 21 for a series of Ford Foundation meetings (Contemporary Music Project) & when I return will go to Chicago for the first performance of the *Magic Theater Music*. Meanwhile I've read proofs of the *Contra* & the *Nach Bach* for harpsichord & will soon of my Trio [No. 1] for piano, violin & cello. It looks like CRI will record the *Contra* (& possibly the *Bocca* for violin & piano).[4] The old *Bagatelles* & *Duo Concertante* for violin & cello will be released this year on Advance Records label.[5] I also must put in order my *David, the Psalmist* for tenor & orchestra which we just did at the University. It's an early work—1954; but I found it very beautiful. So you see I have plenty to keep me busy. Fortunately there are still 6 months of my leave. I want very much to have a really big chunk of the *Passion* done before going back to *l'accademia*. […]

George

PS: Speaking of books of real interest, do you know *Labyrinths* of Jorge Luis Borges?[6] He's an Argentinean writer of power & poetry, concentrated, dense—quite remarkable on the whole. I find something of what I'm doing in his aesthetics which rests, on one level, on "ars combinatoria." Somewhat more esoteric & difficult to penetrate is the *Tibetan Book of the Dead* which is replete with wisdom & magic.[7] Without knowing it my *Contra* & also *Black Sounds*[8] belong to this realm somehow. The patterns of East & West merge in the face of ultimate things.

22

7 JANUARY 1966

My dear Istvan,

Reading Camus's *Notebooks 1942–1951*, I find this last entry [7 March 1951]: "Any fulfillment is a bondage. It obliges one to a higher fulfillment."[9]

I am in bondage again. The *Magic Theater* music is finished, copied in ink. Before I write again—this is a terrible problem; I am always "giving-up," but can't give up. I must let go, live as Camus puts it only "in the circle of flesh" with those I love & those I do not love but cannot avoid (so much of our lives is spent with the latter). While I was nearing the end of the copying (I will arrange to have a copy made for you & sent off next week), there began in me the stirrings of the "stage work," the non-opera with operatic scenes, oratorio tableaux, etc. that will have to wait till next fall when I will be on leave—free of "duties," "obligations," the gray dust-bin of the world. If I can, I want to finish the stage work by the time I'm 50—another 2½ yrs. After that—*qui lo sa*? It will be 1968. Will we be in Hell again? America has gone off its rocker. This Vietnam business is nothing but a form of national insanity. It's the end result of pursuing Christian ethics & morality interpreted through the image-making of American institutional life—education, business, government, advertising, communications. Will we even get to 1968?

The *Magic Theater*—the music has a color of gold for me. It extends the qualities of the *Contra* beyond my fondest hopes. Even the 6-minute transcription of the Mozart "Adagio" belongs, is intrinsic, feels right. In some unconscious way I think I absorbed something from your second Symphony [i.e., *Symphony of Modules*]. You will be able to judge that when you see the score. I still have an (almost) insatiable desire to see your work again, to live in it, to know it as thoroughly as one can. I can be relentless, unfortunately. So be forewarned that I won't let up pressure on you to finish until you do! It's as much pure selfishness on my part as friendship for you & love for what you're doing. *Sempre avanti, amigo*!! […]

George

23

23 JANUARY 1966

My dear George,

It has come to this state: if someone would show me [a] hundred scores, each by a different contemporary composer and you would be one of them, I would unhestitatingly point to yours, because your language [has] achieved a singular personality by now. Intense, of the temperature of white heat, an extremely flexible articulation, achieved by the most economical possible means, a memorable ear, a unique integrating personality steeped in a series of traditions which coexist in a hierarchy of relationships … and many more attributes, each of which contributes to a beautifully expressive whole.

All this I came to feel and think about as [a] result of the three "reading-throughs" of your *Magic Theater*. A wonderfully beautiful piece, George, what you have written. It speaks to one as if you have written it in the course of a single inhaling. The line, including all the protrusions of course, is etched with a remarkably steady hand. […] Your going into and out of various quotes is subtle, effective and telling. The big Mozart quote is a truly beautiful body of sound.[10] Next time I'll read it through in the "proper tempo." I now understand the reasons why you felt such elation in working on the piece, and having brought it to such a satisfactory conclusion. It is a free yet superbly controlled organism. It gave me (and continues to give me), also, a tremendous lift, inspiration! […]

Your good words about my piece [*Symphony of Modules*] mean a lot to me. You can be certain that I push it toward completion with all that I have, discounting that portion of one's juices which is claimed by other, seemingly unavoidable, commitments.

I have now 13 minutes ready, 258 measures. It now looks that the piece will have one or more tape-voices, probably optional, but I am not sure of this yet. The total length will be about 26 minutes. It will be ready, if health permits it, by the end of the summer, the latest. There is some interest in a first performance by a Canadian orchestra, but it is quite uncertain still, because of the unusual difficulties involved. Another matter of interest: a publisher expressed interest in a facsimile edition of the work; also nothing definite as yet. […]

We were very grateful to receive the *Chelsea* 17 issue with Paul's writing in it.[11] "The Silver Talons of Piero Kostrov" is truly amazing. Where did Paul get this insight, this serenity, this sensibility? And what is even more mysterious: an original voice, fully developed. There are other attributes: there is a purity of expression, utter lack of clutter, a dignity of the kind I remember having experienced in reading the parables of Kafka. In these writings Paul appears in full force as a man who can forgo any posturing, any blandishing of heavy words and/or issues: the distilled vocabulary and the soul behind it will do the magic, all alone. And all that comes through with a clear, round ring of a bell. […]

Istvan

[…]

24

30 APRIL 1966

Dear Isty,

It was very good to hear from you & especially the pending good news—commission, full professorship et al. Absolutely count on me to write a letter for you. It will be a pleasure to advance your cause. In any case however I hope these references are really only formalities & that your promotion doesn't depend on them. Whatever way it is, nothing will give me greater pleasure than to give my opinion of one Istvan Anhalt and his work & worth! […]

I'm delighted you've been asked to write some music for the [Canadian] Centennial & sure you will "whack" out something first class.[12]

You can't imagine how interested I am in your assessment of the N[ew] Y[ork] proceedings you attended. I don't know whether I told you I refused to join this group.[13] It would take too long to say why here but suffice it to mention only this: the identification of so-called composers with the present academic scene spells the end of the "artist" except for the hold-outs & other mavericks who see music as a something-beyond-human sociology. From the little you said I sensed you were not exactly jumping with joy over what was going on there. Re our

Penn Contemporary Players & Mel Strauss:[14] Mel has recovered miraculously from a very severe heart attack (he's only 35–36). He should be able to resume work next fall again after a long summer's rest. The Players are hired by the dept[artmen]t (except for those students who are of professional caliber; for ex[ample] one of the percussionists you heard was Joel Thome—a very gifted composer & conductor).[15] Mel's plan is to develop a nucleus of players in the Phila[delphia] area on whom he can draw for any kind of performance. So far he's been very successful. I could tell you more about all this next week which I hope will be in Tanglewood. We've just rented a large house (very elegant!) & plenty of room for friends to stay & visit. So do everything possible to come.

There have been a few performances of music in N[ew] Y[ork], another one (of *Contra*) coming up May 10. The biggest news item is that I got a Guggenheim [Fellowship] next year which will help support us while I'm on leave. […]

George

25

18 SEPTEMBER 1966

My dear Istvan,

[…] At best this is only an interim note to tell you it was good to get your last letter & to hear of the progress on the *Symphony [of Modules]* & your plans for the work you are dedicating to Paul [i.e., *Cento*]. If it is at all possible, Gene & I want to be present at the first performance—very much.

I have been working furiously since we returned home—no let-up. During the summer (Aug.) I was approached by Lincoln Center Repertory Theater to do the music for their opening production of Ben Jonson's *The Alchemist*. I read it & agreed. Since then it has been a kind of madness around here, working day & night. I wrote about 20 minutes of music in 10 days & have just finished copying the scores of the 22 numbers (some very short, some 2½ minutes). Tomorrow I go to N[ew] Y[ork] for 2–3 days to record the music. Previews are Oct. 1 to Oct. 11; gala opening Oct. 12; public opening Oct. 13. By the 15th I should be finished & can perhaps return to my own old pace & pick up where I left off. […]

George

26

4 OCTOBER 1966

My dear Isty,

I'm back from my alchemical experiments, a little worn at the edges to be sure but free now to resume a more "normal" existence. We recorded the music Sept. 19 & 21 & a week later despite a terrible cold which no doubt was the result of fatigue & exhaustion I went back to put together a 1/2 hour tape of the 22 sections as "audience" music (before the curtain). Recovered sufficiently, Gene & I went Sat. nite (Oct. 1) to the first preview. To be absolutely honest we were very disappointed with the production in general. It is not bold enough nor intuitive enough. The director lost his nerve somewhere along the line and stuck too close to cliché-conventions for me, worked too thinly for another. All of this of course relates too to his fear of really using the music. He insists the actors must be heard. I don't deny this. But there are places where their gestures & movements animated by the musical environment I tried to create would come across with more point and vigor than relying on <u>what</u> they say. The fact that the music is on tape means of course that by a mere turn of the dial you can negate the <u>presence</u> & therefore value, dramatically, of the music—or enhance the play by letting it rise to hard-edge audibility & give the whole scene color & life. If the truth be told I'm afraid I lost this battle (& I had started off with high hopes because I believed in the play—still do—& in the ideas the director & I had worked out together; furthermore, believed in the efficacy of turning to the theater as a viable, if occasional, way for a composer to function. Now I'm not so sure anymore). Anyway, the music remains intact—my first "comic" music, a kind of musical commentary on the essence of Jonson's characters & the music of the times. For now I shall let it rest; but I have in mind to make a work for chamber ensemble out of it one of these days.[16] [...]

Imagine now that we're into the fall school is underway for you again. I hope it's not too burdensome. Seems to me that the most important thing for you is to be able to complete your *Symphony [of Modules]* and the new work you describe so graphically [i.e., *Cento*]. I look forward to both more than I can say. I have this awful sensation now & again in varying degrees of intensity that our world is burying us in the debris of daily routine; & freshness & spontaneity & vigor & energy are all being drained away by the monolithic nature of our culture. That's why I feel so strongly for your work because I know it is unique in this blighted time of ours. I don't mean to sound black & depressed. Actually at the moment I'm not. But I maintain my anger at the impossibility of 20th-century life. Our only recourse I suppose is to fight harder for what we believe in & maybe most of all not to get side-tracked too much or too often. […]

George

27

30 OCTOBER 1966

Dear Isty,

[…] I intend to write a fuller letter during the next week but for now am seeking your advice: John Cage has just written asking for a page of mss. or a mss. for a collection to benefit the Foundation for Contemporary Performance.[17] I remember his asking you for a mss. too. What did you do about it? And do you think I should comply & if so, with what? I'll wait to hear from you before deciding. […]

George

28

16 NOVEMBER 1966

Dear Isty,

Your letter helped me to decide what to do re Cage's request: because it is short & I don't have any particular feelings about my pencil scores I'm sending him the score of my *Nach Bach*—the harpsichord piece I wrote at Tanglewood this summer for Igor Kipnis [1930–2002]. As soon as it is printed (it's in the works now) I'll send you a copy. I think you will enjoy it.

I'm in infinitely better shape now than I was the last month or so. Now that I have gotten into my big work for choruses, soloists & instruments (orchestra, chamber groups) [i.e., Symphony No. 3] I feel my energies returning, my spirits rising, my feet on the ground again. I won't describe my mood & condition before now except to remark that I felt like 90—not a Casals 90 or even Picasso 85 but spiritless, depressed. Thank God (only in a manner of speaking though) that passed & I can work again & feel like getting up in the morning. I'm engaged on a large section which is truly "ars combinatoria" based on as motley a crew of sources as even I could imagine: Schütz cantata "Saul, was verfolgst du mich," Bach chorale preludes on "Durch Adams Fall," fanfares from

Mahler symphonies (1 & 2), Beethoven's *Marche Funèbre* ("Eroica") fugue which combines with a "tonal" fugue [that] I plan on the words of the Schütz text which combines with the tune of "Durch Adams Fall" which permits me also to use a long passage from a Mozart piano sonata (same motif as Beethoven's & my fugue theme, i.e., a portion of it which happened "accidentally"), etc. I'm most excited by the prospect of composing the fugue ("real"). If all goes well I should finish the sketch by Xmas. Then I can proceed to another section, etc. I want by the end of the spring to have completed at least 5 sections of the work. So far it looks like there will be about 15 (long & short), some purely instrumental, some "songs" for solo voice & chamber, etc. My confidence in the approach is considerably helped by recent discovery of the Argentine writer Jorge Luis Borges whom I recommend to you.[18] It turns out he had discovered this "world," so new to us, many years ago & applied it to literature which in his hands turns out to be metaphysics & philosophy of cosmic proportions. He is 90 & blind & very, very great indeed. His use of "correspondences" is for me spine-tingling. I can't tell you how sorry I am the New York party is off. I was looking forward more than I can say to our getting together. *Patienza*. […]

George

PS: The latest issue of *Musical Quarterly* carries an article on your friend.[19] If you get a chance read it. My copy has not arrived yet! […]

NOTES

1 The composer was to have conducted the work with the University of Toronto Symphony Orchestra but withdrew ostensibly due to lack of sufficient rehearsal time; the *Symphony of Modules* still awaits its premiere.

2 The reference is to Anhalt's *Cento* (1967) for twelve-part mixed choir and tape.

3 Peter Weiss (1916–82), German dramatist, painter, and film director, whose family settled in Sweden in 1938; he became a Swedish citizen in 1946 and a member of the Swedish Communist Party in 1968; the play in question is *The Investigation: An Oratorio in Eleven Cantos* (1965), a drama based on the Auschwitz trials held in Frankfurt, 1963–65, which the playwright had attended.

4 *Contra Mortem et Tempus*, Aeolian Chamber Players, CRI 231 (1967); there are no recordings of the violin/piano transcription of *La Bocca della Veritá* which the composer made in 1965, but the oboe/piano original (1957) has been recorded twice: Ronald Roseman, oboe, Gilbert Kalish, piano, Ars Nova/Ars Antigua AN 1008 (ca. 1971); and James Ostryniec, oboe, Charles Wuorinen, piano, CRI 423 (1980).

5 *Twelve Bagatelles*, for piano solo (1952), David Burge, piano, Advance Records FGR-3 (1966); *Duo Concertante* for violin and cello (1955, revised 1959), Daniel Kobialka, violin, Jan Kobialka, cello, Advance Records FGR-6C (1969).

6 Jorge Luis Borges, *Labyrinths: Selected Stories and Other Writings*, ed. Donald A. Yates and James E. Irby (New York: New Directions, 1964).

7 *The Tibetan Book of the Dead; or, The Afterdeath Experiences on the Bardo Plane, According to Lama Kazi Dawa-Samdup's English Rendering* (New York: Oxford University Press, 1960).

8 *Black Sounds (Apocalyprica II) for Seventeen Winds* (1965).

9 Albert Camus, *Notebooks: 1935–1951*, trans. and annotated Justin O'Brien (New York: Alfred A. Knopf, 1963–65), 2: 270.

10 *Music for the Magic Theater* contains references to the music of Beethoven, Miles Davis, Mahler, Mozart, Stockhausen, Varèse, and Webern.

11 See "1964," note 3.

12 Anhalt's *Cento* was commissioned by the University of British Columbia Chamber Singers, Cortland Hultberg, conductor, for Canada's centennial in 1967.

13 The American Society of University Composers, whose first annual conference Anhalt attended in April 1966.

14 Melvin Strauss (b. 1929), conductor of student ensembles at the University of Pennsylvania; he led the University of Pennsylvania Orchestra in the premiere of *David, the Psalmist* on 8 December 1966. He is presently an Adjunct Professor of Music, Emeritus, at Wesleyan University in Middletown, Connecticut.

15 Joel Thome (b. 1948), American composer, conductor, and percussionist; he teaches composition at the Conservatory of Music, Purchase College, State University of New York.

16 A concert version of *Music for "The Alchemist"* was prepared between August 1966 and November 1968.

17 John Cage's book *Notations* (1969), designed to benefit the Foundation for Contemporary Performance Arts, contains pages from manuscript scores of over 250 composers; Anhalt is represented by a sketch from *Symphony of Modules* (1967), Rochberg by a sketch from *Nach Bach* (1966).

18 See note 6 above.

19 Alexander L. Ringer, "The Music of George Rochberg," *Musical Quarterly* 52/4 (October 1966): 409–30.

1967

29

13 FEBRUARY 1967

My dear Isty,

By now the premiere of *Cento* has taken place[1] & we are very eager to hear how it went. If you just say the word, we shall try to arrange to come to Montreal to hear it. Please understand that my initial response was basically only to one-half of the total sound world of the work. Hence my inability to say more. It is a rich idea & an imaginative production & I look forward to experiencing it fully and live. I look forward with anticipation to hearing you say: come; it's all what I wanted it to be. Come hear it. [...]

The *Magic Theater Music* was given in Chicago Jan. 24. Gene & I went to hear it. It was a good, not a perfect, performance. Ideally, I can imagine something better still. The response to it was what I expected. Lots of puzzlement, a few strong rejections, a few strong acceptances. It's the business of the quotes which puts people off, especially those who think in the old terms of being "personal," "original."[2] For me it all works in some crazy kind of way. It's very much like what one of the players said to me: "I have the feeling it's right—but it shouldn't be." On Thursday I go to N[ew] Y[ork] to record the *Contra* for CRI. I'm glad this will be available on records eventually.[3]

For the rest, I'm staving off as best I can devils from inside & outside, trying still to discover some tranquillity, some heart-ease. But to live in a mad world such as ours is never easy. I've even given up reading the Sunday *N[ew] Y[ork] Times*. It's easy to follow the general shape of external events via TV. I like it best when I can lose myself in a good book. Recently

I read Céline's *Journey to the End of Night*. A powerful, lyric verbal singing, all about the human heart & its travail.[4] Beautiful but terribly sad. Perhaps there is really nothing else. I look forward to hearing from you soon with a happy report of *Cento*. […]

George

30

28 FEBRUARY 1967

My dear Istvan,

I was intrigued by your vivid description of how you went about getting the *Cento* into shape for the Vancouver performance. But to have the courage to rewrite it—that takes guts of an extraordinary kind, especially these days when few people have the capacity to face the difficulties of art & the imperfections of their own efforts. I hope the new version comes very close to what you want and will wait for your word about March 10th. I'm very eager to hear it—for many reasons, but mostly for its own sake (more about this later). I'm sorry though to hear you're so caught in the mesh of so many "identities" as you put it. It becomes increasingly difficult to accomplish one's basic goals in a world so complex & so demanding of our energies. In this connection let me only quickly mention what I have recently arranged with my administration: after next year I shall no longer be chairman. I can hardly describe the pleasure I feel at this prospect of being released from a situation which weighed increasingly on me. I shall be free of all sorts of chores, pettiness, problems—in short, the works. You who know it all too well I'm sure so you can appreciate what I am trying to say. It is in fact the best birthday present I can imagine inasmuch as I give up the chairmanship June 30, 1968 & July 5 I shall be 50. From then on I shall teach a few courses & devote the rest of my time to my own work. I like to think that you can win a similar freedom for yourself in the next years so that you can produce the powerful & beautiful works which I know are in you. In the final analysis it is more important to the world that real art be produced than that institutions run smoothly—which they don't do anyhow since they are such breeding grounds for all sorts of human foibles. For myself, I can't be so sure (and this is not false modesty) that the change in the outer circumstances of my life will necessarily help me produce real art; but I want to spend the rest of my life making a good try at it. That's the very least. In any case I sense no lack of fertility in you despite the many demands of your life. Sometimes too—I'm often forced to admit this when in the midst of my own maelstrom—the very intensity of existence creates a special inward quality which enters into the music we produce, a quality which burns away excrescences & superfluities leaving only the nuclei of ideas.

Recently Luciano Berio was in Phila[delphia] to give a lecture on "Problems of Musical Theater." He is himself a very likable man, although I found his lecture very poor & his music merely stimulating but not convincing. Nevertheless, his way of dealing with words (musical theater forces composers more & more to the problems of the playwright) stirred me to various levels of reaction; & linked up with your *Cento*, though only superficially, in the creation of vocal densities. All of which gave me a sufficient sprint of energy to tackle the same or similar problem in one of the sections of my *Passions [According to the Twentieth Century]*. This particular one happened to be one of 5 I sketched in Buffalo, all of which I intend to make use of eventually, in one way or another. Yesterday I completed the section. Meanwhile, I was able to finally visualize the sequence of sections which will comprise Part I, roughly 60–70 minutes of music. I suppose the work itself is my own ultimate contribution to what is now called "musical theater" although when I started it in 1959 I always thought of it as a "non-opera" (with operatic tendencies in some places). Part I will be made up of:

1. First Lumia for orchestra, ca. 5 minutes of "spatialized" music in which I hope to convey some sense of the ineffable which surrounds us & out of which we came & to which we return. To be composed.

2. "Saul, was verfolgst du mich" for solo quartet, double quartet, 2 choruses, orchestra; also some actor-speakers who make their "appearance" in the instrumental-vocal climax of the section. This is a giant collage (Schütz, Beethoven, Mahler, Ives, etc.) about 30 minutes.

3. "Deus Cujus Hodierna" for 2 choruses, speakers, some percussion. About 9–10 minutes. This text is from the Catholic liturgy dealing with the slaughter of the innocents.

4. "Deus Cujus Hodierna" and "Ayl Molay Rachamim," the Hebrew litany—memorial service. Mostly solo voice (cantorial). About 10 minutes. To be finished.

5. "Was willst du hin, Gott, war ich sterbe?" by R.M. Rilke for solo quartet & instruments. About 10 minutes. To be composed.

6. First Black Piece for orchestra. About four minutes. This is already composed, as are the second & third Black Pieces. They will be the counterparts of the Lumias, also three in number.

This is my present plan. My hope is to complete the sketches of Part I by summer, then make the score. What remains to be done in subsequent parts will be enormous & I must have the patience & courage to see it all to the end ultimately. For the first time I have a rising sense of confidence that somehow I can do it. That it will occupy me the next few years goes without saying. But there is in me the feeling that I must do this thing even if it means nothing but “old works” of mine will be performed & nothing “new” will come out. There is much, much more to say but this is already too long. I look forward to seeing you March 10 & hearing the *Cento* if all works out all right. […]

George

[…]

31

22 MARCH 1967

My dear Isty,

It was wonderful to spend those few days with you & your family, surrounded by the sound of your *Cento* which is still vivid & strong in my memory and the sight of your evolving *Symphony [of Modules]*. (I'm very serious about coming to the first performance. I wouldn't miss it for anything.) […]

Hearing *Cento* three times engraved its essence & texture on my mind forever. It is a unique conception & a beautifully realized artistic statement. You cut right to the heart of not only the psychological problem brought on all of us by our present mode of existence but also the musical problem of stating or representing this dark condition. All superfluousness is burned away & only the carbon & the core of truth is left to hear, to experience, to contemplate. This “cannot be bought.” *Cento* inhabits the same region as Camus's *The Plague* [1947] or some of the stories of Borges—the deepest reaches of 20th-century consciousness which few dare to plumb. But you dared; and you succeeded. Since ours is such an intense “feedback” (as you say) relationship it shouldn't surprise you then if I tell you that you gave me the courage to tackle, head-on, my *Passions* first sketched in Buffalo in 1964 which in a curious way touch on the style & technique of *Cento* as you will see. I plowed ahead & have made the final draft of No. 1 & No. 2 (No. 2 needed much less reworking than No. 1); and now I am forging ahead on No. 3 which will take lots of labor to bring to a final draft. The forces generally are 2 choruses (large), sop. & alto soloists, 3 male speakers (baritone, bass, basso profundo), 6 men's voices (little chorus), 3 trumpets, 4 horns, 3 trbs, percussion, tape (chiefly for recorded "quotes" in No. 3). It is a theater work; & as such I have some ideas for lighting, TV cameras, slides, film. The essential technique is collage: sound (instrumental, vocal; speaking, whispering, etc.) & visual elements constantly shifting & changing. I want to do a 4th & 5th also; but whether my energy holds out to encompass 2 more after doing No. 3, I don't know. If not now, then I can add them later. The important thing is to drive through No. 3 right now. I found the title I was looking for: *Passions [According to the 20th Century]*. What do you think?

The more I've worked on them the more convinced I've become that this is the answer for me to the whole business of music & drama. It simply ignores the question of whether opera is or isn't valid any longer & starts off from different premises & mental sets. It is drama which counts. With music alone one can be dramatic in an abstract sense, i.e., not about anything concretely specific; the minute you apply this "natural" propensity of music for every shade & nuance of gesture (every kind) to the theater by relating the musical affects to human feelings rooted in personal/collective experience then you can move freely when & as you want. I've discovered that while everything to be used must be composed as though they were "musical elements," music itself must not overburden the situation. There must be plenty of open spaces for speech & visual. Then when music returns it is ten times more effective than if you were letting it go on endlessly, a steady stream which absorbs everything. Dramatically, I'm not dealing with plots or even situations. It's very difficult to describe what I am dealing with—except to say there is a quality of the epic largely created by the juxtaposition of old & new, Latin/English, Hebrew/English; paralleling ancient happenings & contemporary ones (the Biblical slaughter of innocents/the 6 million); Hecuba/every mother (who is also a queen & wife); Beethoven's dream of brotherhood/Hitler's madness; etc., etc. It's all mixed up in a crazy sort of way which works for me on paper so far. What happens if it ever goes into production? I shudder to think of all the things that could be wrong in a practical way as far as a theater goes.

[…]

George

[…]

32

4 AUGUST 1967

My dear friend,

[...] Gene & Chessie & I will take off for the [New Jersey] shore the last week of Aug. I think I can survive it if the weather is good, if I take along a few good books—especially if I take my 3rd Symph[ony] sketches along & continue working on the score which I began a day or two ago at long long last. I'm more sorry for my sake than for yours that the premiere of your *Symphony [of Modules]* has been put off to the spring of '68. I mean: I have an avid hunger & curiosity and sense of deep excitement to hear those fantastic pages you've dreamed into life. Ever since I first saw them they have been for me a stimulant & stimulus to greater and greater freedom, notationally & musically. We all feed on our experience & develop hungers & needs in certain directions. I have come to look to your work as a source of energizing my own internal processes. It is also very curious how your *Symphony [of Modules]* suddenly gave a new dimension & brought into the perimeter of my own range of possibilities Cage's ideas. What I mean is that you have given Cage's vision a concrete, realizable, musical dimension through your own unfettered imagination. In truth what I'm saying is that you are infinitely superior to Cage. What he offered as theory and abstract potential you have realized as concrete actuality linking freedom of gesture, design, notation, timbral combinations to control, shape, direction, power of utterance, human feeling. What you say about our being part of your family—and it works the other way around too you must know—links up with my sense that we are brothers in mind and spirit; though we have different ways of expressing ourselves in our work, behind the difference is a profound similarity, one based on a sense of human life and human art which reaches toward a larger vision of both, something cosmic—not mystic, cosmic in an ancient sense of the connection between man & the gods which is to say between man & the god within man. We are both striving always to free ourselves from the pull of matter by releasing the energy in matter which is consciousness (the paradox is intentional). [...]

I did nothing more than show Alan's work to George Crumb & Mel Strauss.[5] The work is on such a high level, especially from such a youth (chronologically), that it speaks for itself. I hope he will be able to attend the performance. We couldn't pay his fare but we can arrange to put him up if he decides to come. I have spent the summer knocking the pieces together, working especially hard at ensuring a good season of performance of music. I have also been spending a great deal of time with the scores I will conduct with the orchestra and chorus (Handel's *Israel in Egypt* & Verdi's *Four Sacred Pieces*). I must confess I feel a great excitement at the prospect of making music with such forces (my trepidations extend to whether we will have a good turnout for both since they are extra-curricular; & from year to year you never quite know what you will wind up with. Also to whether or not I can pull it off at all since this will be my first major effort on a regular consistent basis). It's also a way of staying in touch with & penetrating even more deeply into the mystery which is music. […]

George

33

5 NOVEMBER 1967

My dear Isty,

I had been wanting to tell you what a joy it is to have your *Symphony [of Modules]* with me at last. But everything has been happening at once and so far, beyond only brief glances lacking sustained continuity, I've had no real chance to enter its world, to savor its richness, to swim in its element. One of these days I will withdraw from the travail of my daily existence just to have the necessary peace & quiet to read your fabulous work. This past week & 1/2 has been especially difficult. Hugh H[artwell][6] left just before our first orchestra concert which went off very well indeed, in the case of the Mozart *Prague* quite extraordinarily but simultaneously a terrible tragedy was playing itself out. One of our best graduate students, Dennis Marshall, who was doing his dissertation on Ives with me, had already died in his apartment of a cerebral stroke & no one knew it until after the concert was over. You can imagine the aftermath, the shock, the unbelievability of the whole thing. When Hugh returned from his trip to Montreal Monday or Tuesday I saw him & he gave me your greetings. By then he had heard the sad news. In a small depart[ment] like ours the students are very close & their relation to the faculty is free & open. Everyone felt Dennis's loss sharply. Their loyalty to each other is wonderful. Dennis will have an article published in *Perspectives* [*of New Music*] dealing with Ives's structural use of quotation.[7]

By now I have come to know & like Hugh very much indeed. He is a very gifted boy musically & it is a delight to work with him. I hope I can help him discover himself & bring his work to first stages of maturity.

Now I must plunge into preparations of Handel's *Israel in Egypt* which we perform Dec. 7. The experience of conducting has been very salutary for me. Besides giving me badly needed exercise (sic!) it also gives me a chance to make music as I feel it, to pour myself out through Beethoven, Mahler, Mozart, etc. (they are wonderful composers from the inside.) But this plus other duties conspires to delay my completion of the 3rd [Symphony]. I feel full of new projects but can't get to them. Next year, I keep saying, next year—when I teach only 2 courses & a few private students & am no longer chairman. Oh glory! […]

George

34

3 DECEMBER 1967

My dear Isty,

The recital of your bad experience with your *Symphony [of Modules]* upset me no end. How can such things be? How can they continue to go on? But they do; and we must suffer it because we are the ones to whom such things happen. How I wish I could have been there—at least to give moral support and what little comfort one can under such circumstances. One question: would it help if you took over the conducting of your own work? I can imagine that this can only add more hours of work & mountains of difficulty to an already overburdened existence. But while no one yet understands how to project what you've written perhaps the only solution is to take the bull by the horns & say if you wish to perform my music I will conduct it & nobody else. Is that possible? Is the recording entirely out of the question now? Perhaps by offering yourself as conductor you can still save the situation for both the recording & the premiere of #2 [i.e., *Symphony of Modules*]. […]

I am 2/3 through the 3rd Symph[ony]. The last 1/3 will be devilish hard. If I'm lucky I can attack it during the Xmas holiday. I want desperately to finish it by spring. (You see what I mean: the "work syndrome" is virulent). Meanwhile I must get through this work with Dec. 7 the climax of preparations for *Israel in Egypt*. Then the following week Ormandy does 5 perf[ormances] of *Zodiac* (the orchestral version of *Bagatelles*), the last in N[ew] Y[ork]. Then I have some talks to give here & there (in Feb. Portland, Oregon). So it goes. I am patiently waiting for this school year to finally end, put off the harness of chairman, & be free! Since *Nach Bach* (which I'm delighted you like so much) I've had the urge to write a "book" of piano pieces, some "take-offs" on whatever interests me, some “free”;[8] other ideas too. Heaven knows if I will find the time & energy for everything. […]

George

NOTES

1 *Cento* was premiered on 9 February 1967 in Vancouver by the University of British Columbia Chamber Singers under the direction of Cortland Hultberg, with the composer present.

2 See “1966,” note 10.

3 See “1966,” note 4.

4 Louis-Ferdinand Céline, *Journey to the End of the Night*, trans. John H.P. Marks (New York: New Directions, 1960).

5 Alan Heard (see “1962,” note 4); Rochberg's colleague George Crumb (b. 1929) became a professor and composer-in-residence at the University of Pennsylvania in 1965; for Mel Strauss see “1966,” note 14.

6 Hugh Hartwell (b. 1945), composer and teacher, a student of Anhalt at McGill University (B.Mus. 1967) and of Rochberg and George Crumb at the University of Pennsylvania (B.Mus. 1971; Ph.D. 1975); in 1976 he joined the faculty of music at McMaster University.

7 See Dennis Marshall, “Charles Ives's Quotations: Manner or Substance,” *Perspectives of New Music* 6/2 (Spring–Summer 1968): 45–56, reprinted in Benjamin Boretz and Edward T. Cone, eds., *Perspectives on American Composers* (New York: W.W. Norton, 1971), 13–24.

8 This would appear to be an early reference to the suite for solo piano *Carnival Music* (1971).

1968

35

2 JANUARY 1968; and
happy New Year to all!

My dear Isty,

[…] These weeks since early Dec. have been exhausting but I am back on my feet especially now that I've pushed the Symphony [No. 3] very close to the end. I wish there were some way to send some of it to you; but it's too early. Everything is still in an "unfinished" state. Once I reach the end of the work I must go back to the beginning & go over everything very carefully. My main concern is to make the work "sound." For this I must use every bit of experience & knowledge I have—& even that will not suffice. It is too huge in places for me to be able to gauge accurately what will happen. I have wound up using a gargantuan orchestra. Who will want to take a chance on such a work? Such considerations do not deter me, however. I see only bringing it to a conclusion in the way I feel it & hear it. The rest will have to work itself out somehow. And once it is brought to life? What horrible things will "they" say? I have committed every sin in the book musically speaking. I have "robbed" right & left: quoted, borrowed, transformed, etc. I have resorted to every "style" since @ 1600 till now—or just about. Besides which there is that great fugue in D minor which I wrote myself which combines with Bach's "Durch Adams Fall" & Beethoven's "Eroica" fugue. It would be wonderful if I can show it to you once it is finished. Perhaps even you, my dear friend, will think I've gone crazy. Yet everything I've done or tried to is made to seem quite plausible, natural & even viable by Leonard Meyer in his new book *Music, the Arts & Ideas* (Un[iversity] of Chicago Press).[1] His approach is intellectual, cultural-historical. A little heavy-handed but well-thought out. I suppose the coincidence of such a work being written & published precisely at the time I am deeply engaged in this way of working is a form of corroboration of its validity as an attitude toward composition. […]

I marvel that you are able to take on so much administrative work. I know very well the sense of duty & responsibility which drives one; but precisely I must release myself from this morality & its pressures so I can do my own work. The *Israel in Egypt* went well. Because of it I feel more comfortable as a conductor. *Zodiac* was a trial for me what with Ormandy's having to learn the score as he went along & putting up with the peripheral social aspects. By the time he took it to N[ew] Y[ork] it was well-polished. The umbilical cord is cut now & I wish it a long life. Igor Kipnis came back from his European tour & reported good things about the reception of *Nach Bach*. He takes it on an American tour soon. I'm expecting the *Contra* to be issued on CRI & the *Duo Concertante* for violin & cello on Advance Records.[2] I know how you must feel having your early works surface in the public arena while the really new works—those that represent you now—must wait. In any event it is not a bad thing if one's early music still lives. I look forward very much to hearing Gould's recording of your piano work.[3]

About the turmoil in this country: I am more & more disheartened by events. I do not trust or believe in [Lyndon] Johnson & [Dean] Rusk. Their attitudes are muddied with national pride (translate: stupidity) & their words are becoming increasingly dangerous—even threatening. […] For reasons I cannot explain I feel 1968 will be a year of great crisis—have felt this for some time. And now it has arrived I feel a little numb inside—wondering & waiting. All the more reason why I want to finish my Symphony [No. 3] & live as intensely as I can. Mostly I fear the extension of the Asian war & the rising tide of "Americanism" with its edge of cruel irrationality. There are too many "kooks" in this country who loved Joe McCarthy who are waiting for another chance. Well, all I know is we must talk, see each other, spend time together. I'm glad you will conduct your Symphony. It is an astonishing work & I will not rest till I have heard it! […]

George

36

24 MARCH 1968

Dear Friend,

Afterthoughts: for some reason I had the impression you were looking for someone to teach "theory." […] Now that I know you are looking for a composer—that alters the picture considerably & beyond. You know my views. There are all too few real composers. Hiller[4] is not one of them; & from the little I know of Brant[5] I had to think not here too. I could throw out names—undoubtedly all of them familiar to you. With few exceptions, I would have to ask: are they (in the real sense) composers? As to what a composer is in the sense I mean we are already terribly limited. If you don't accept my narrow definition the field grows larger. Potentially then:

Robert Erickson, Un[iversity] of Calif[ornia] at San Diego. An experimentalist of sorts. Very bright & knowledgeable. Around 45.[6]

Donald Martino, pupil of Babbitt. Understand he's undergoing crisis presently. May mean he will emerge (if he does) from the box of serialism & take a different direction. At Yale; currently on Guggenheim. Around 38.[7]

Bülent Arel whom you know. Also at Yale. Instructor (sic!) Around early 40's I gather.[8]

Loren Rush, currently working in computer music project at Stanford Univ[ersity] in California. Late 30's.[9]

William Bolcom, close & dear friend;[10] school-mate & friend of Bruce Mather;[11] powerful musician. Real talent lies in theater. About 29. Will Bill emerge as real composer? Chances are good, very good.

Andy Rudin, former student of mine, now at Phila[delphia] Mus[ic] Academy. Heavily committed to Electronic/Visual (makes his own films) mix. Strong personality. Have no way of judging how he will develop. Early 30s.[12]

When you're here in April can tell you of a few more people. It is so difficult because we are no longer talking about simple things—"composition" having exploded into multi-faceted possibilities few of which in my warped view ultimately worthwhile, i.e., mostly blind alleys. Where will we find the gift of poetry & passion joined to taste & discrimination all unified by the mystery of the soul which seeks transcendence? Science, logic, systems, methodologies, applied math & computer technology—it is to my mind the certainty which "musicians" attribute to these in their search for means which is the delusion from which they suffer. Just as it may be that Science itself is the great human delusion of our day. I am a thorogoing Blakean by now. Do read Koestler's *Ghost in the Machine* which is a devastating critique of man's so-called powers of reason.[13] We are apparently caught in a neurological bind: the inability of the "new brain" to coordinate its ratiocinations with the old one (the seat of our subliminal instincts). […]

George

37

11 APRIL 1968

Dear Isty,

[…] Your letter came today and gave me much happiness. I enjoyed your visit here more than I can say. It meant a great deal to all of us that you could share our life for even only those few hours. Especially I was happy that your being here provided occasions for enlarging the circle of admirers of your work. That circle will grow, of that I'm certain. George Crumb[14] was much impressed with your music and liked you. We had a long talk yesterday and George expressed powerful interest in hearing the new Symphony. That will be a time to look forward to: when it first springs to life! Our talks about my "Dritte" keep circulating inside & have provided just the right stimulus for a thorough scrutiny. Already some ideas for changes have come to mind. Would you mind very much if I quoted a part of your "First" [Symphony]? If you will give it your blessing I think I have just the right place for Anhalt!![15] […]

Along with everything else I am beginning to work out some ideas for my seminar in late 19th-cent[ury] music for next year. The notes I gave you relate to them, although from them it is difficult to see how they can be applied to actual music as an aid to comprehension of "cosmic" tonal design. I want to develop something called "metatonality" though one could say for example that the tonal spans of Schubert's B♭ major piano sonata derive from the same realm as Beethoven's 9th, Mahler's 9th—where the great tonal nodes are enclosed within D-B♭-G♭ (F♯) in any order (it being symmetrical). I'd love to have a chance to talk this over which you. […]

George

38

13 MAY 1968

My dear Isty,

[…] These have been difficult weeks. Thank God, only 4 or 5 more till June 15. I'm eager to get back to the Symphony [No. 3] & work hard & steadily on it. Meanwhile I'm busy wrapping things up at the Univ[ersity] & preparing a course for next year on the music of the 19th century. Today I go to N[ew] Y[ork] for a recording session of *Nach Bach* which Kipnis is doing for Epic.[16]

George

39

1 SEPTEMBER 1968

My dear George,

[…] Well now—where to start my story about my and our summer? (I'll want to come to what you have written, in the second part of this letter.) I might as well try to arrange the main subject-peaks of this European stay in a few bundles. Here they are: (a) Enclosures, (b) *Sprachkomposition* (it is usually talked about by using the German name, why? I don't know), (c) The 'STATE OF ELECTRONIC MUSIC or in other words Has the Medium REALLY Become the Message? Furthermore Youth, Internationale, Anarchy and finally Theatre & Life & Now. That is more than enough for a first account. […]

You know, George, how I went from a series of general notations to the specific notation in my *Symphony of Modules*. This is my most recent finished compositional act and [I] am glad that I did what I did. What next? I don't know.

Sprachkomposition. As I mentioned on the phone I discovered that quite a few composers did work in this idiom quite extensively in the past few years. Berio, Eimert, Ligeti, Stockhausen, Nono, Kagel,[17] etc., the poets Helms, Dufrêne, Kriwet, & Boehmer and others.[18] I knew of some of these activities but the scope of the whole I was unaware of. I am in the midst of trying to get proper documentation in order to gain proper perspective in this regard. So far I did not learn of the way *Cento* uses speech in any other work. (By the way I here enclose a copy of my Florence paper, brochures, and two clippings reporting on the Congress where I read it.)[19] The live feedback to my paper and to the playing of the *Cento* tape was of modest intensity during the congress, but then music seemed to be of lesser interest there than technology. But more of this later. […] (Incidentally, *Cento* will be done again in Montreal in April 1969, possibly by a group of actors. There may even be a scenic dimension in this performance.) I am still very much interested in working with speech, and will spend time on this for quite another while still.

The Florence Congress for Experimental Centres of Electronic Music, organized by the 1968 Maggio Musicale brought together a fairly interesting group of people, though with a few notable absences, those of Babbitt,[20] Hiller,[21] etc. To my considerable surprise most of the papers dealt with technology, and the concern with musical works, per se, was at a minimum, at least as far as the papers were concerned. The following papers contained complete works (or at least complete movements): Winckel's, Küpper's, Randall's, Xenakis's,[22] Stockhausen's, and mine. The daily tape-demonstrations, of course, have shown many more pieces, and of course there were the four concerts, during which works by Maderna,[23] Nono, Berio, etc. were played.

By the time I arrived at the Congress I had visited quite a few studios in Europe. The total impression quite overwhelmingly conveys the idea to me that we are living in a period of synthetic music when emphasis is given to instrumentation over musical product. Furthermore, the pure electronic music produced lately does not show significant advance over pieces done in the 1954–64 decade. The thought occurs to oneself: a poverty in artistic product is masked by emphasis on technology (both hardware and software, as in computer programming). One may present it in a more positive way: just because of the relative stagnation of compositional products, the need for updating related technology is being recognized and executed. Where lies the truth? As far as I am concerned I am still in the business of using tape as a medium, but, for the present at least, only in conjunction with "live" sounds.

The quality of the technological papers was, incidentally, rather mediocre. No new insight, no new departure was disclosed. In technology, these three things seem to be of some interest: (1) total computer generation of sound, (2) "live" electronic music (either the Mumma variety or the Synket variety),[24] and (3) the computer controlled analog equipment (witness the Zinovieff display in London's Art and Technology show which we visited before returning to Montreal).[25] During your next visit with us I'll show you the papers read in Florence, if you are interested. All in all I am fully confident in *Cento*. It will make its way slowly, if through no other way by word of mouth. (Though I hope that the published score will be reviewed, and in this rather sudden bandwagon of distributing electronic music on long-playing records, it will also eventually be recorded. (Incidentally Canada still is to produce its first electronic music record!)[26]

I am slowly running out of steam (and paper) but just a few words about the other topics:

Youth, etc. I have followed, while in Europe, very closely student activism, and I have now a much better understanding of it, although it is still woefully superficial. The following information I offer here without comment, and with some reserve.

(1) There seems to exist a Student Internationale now. Savio in Berkeley, Cohen-Bendit in Nanterre and Fekete at McGill all seem to act and talk from the same background.[27]

(2) The objective of this cutting edge of the student reform movement goes way beyond the desire to reform the university.

(3) Several of the leading organs, and/or leaders, seem to be speaking from an anarchist position.

(4) In London alone there seem to be about 500 "underground" publishing houses which bring forth a tremendous quantity of literature (poetry, pamphlets, periodicals, weeklies, etc.).

(5) Several (many? most?) North American universities and their society (staff, administration, student body, alumnae organization, civic *Hintergrund*) are inadequately informed of the nature, scope, and objective of the student activists and are in for some tough times and surprises before things will get better by the process of (hopefully) controlled change. (Am I speaking from my bourgeois background?)

(6) Student activism seems to be a part of a larger reform move[ment] which is in ascendancy (the Czechoslovak crisis may be but a part of this larger move[ment]. So is a part of the Black Movement in your States.)

As I went through countries and cities from Amsterdam to Rome, from Bologna, to Venice and Cologne, I saw/heard/read evidence which seems to sustain the above observations.

One of the most interesting things I saw/heard in Europe was a piece by the Danish composer Nørgård, entitled *Babel*, with the genre-definition scenic oratorio.[28] It was a total spectacle in the vein of the Theatre of Mixed Means. About 30 people were involved in it and it seemed to be a product polished through many rehearsals. (It was not a happening, though some of its events may have originated in a happening.) It was a most exuberantly performed thing by the 30 young people who threw themselves into it with terrific gusto seemingly derived from easy identification. It was presented during the Dijon congress of ISME [International Society for Music Education], a rather deadly affair otherwise, nominally devoted to novel technology in music education but in reality dominated by traditionalists (the apostles of the Kodály, Orff and Dalcroze methods and their sales cohorts), and children's choirs from Russia, Hungary and Czechoslovakia, and elsewhere. (In retrospect: what a juxtaposition is the Czech tragedy and the kid's choir of Brno, of about 40 children tightly packed in a semicircle in 4–5 levels and singing by heart without a break for about 90 minutes insipid work after insipid work. And the same holds true for the Russian choir. The Hungarians sadly continue with the contemplation of their music-spiritual navel, that is Kodály: the Hungarian kids sang about 90 minutes of Kodály, which was about 50 minutes too much. In this context (and it would have been the same even in a wider context), the Nørgård piece stood out remarkably with its freshness, topicality, and inventiveness.

Having read, while on the way from place to place, about the performances of the Living Theatre in France and Peter Brook's experiments in the Roundhouse in London I was keen of getting to see them if possible.[29] Well, it wasn't. I missed both. But I now feel that theatre (that is, this kind of theatre) is an important element in our place/time, and I want to see more of it. Your *Passions* came often to my mind in this regard, my dear friend, and I thought how sensitive you were in conceiving this work, and how appropriate it is. You said you want to nurse this work some more before you let it be on its way. I respect this, of course. Here I am speaking of the essential rightness of your selection of the medium, format and subject matter and of its white-heat quality. I am so interested to know what a director will do with it whenever you decide the time has come to launch it.

This brings me back to your letters in which you gave the good news of completion of your Third Symphony, the Webern paper,[30] the theory on metatonality (and the plan for new composition which you mentioned on the phone). Your liberation from administrative chores thus coincides with a terrific creative outburst. I am so happy about this, as anything you are accomplishing makes me as happy as if someone in my closest family would have similar satisfaction. […]

Istvan

40

15 SEPTEMBER 1968

My dear friend,

Your omnibus letter astonishing for its range of topics, comments, insights! I enjoyed it thoroly but must reread it. In the meantime I had been thinking of you & what you have to say—always so direct & illuminating—& am convinced your trip was infinitely worthwhile in every sense. […] What you say about the congresses, "speech composition" et al. left me with a sense of a vitality & force at work which, regardless of ultimate worth, in terms of results, confirms my continuing sense that we live in remarkable times. In fact, we are living out a true "apocalypse" on all levels. More than once something (latest news of riot, Czech invasion, S[outh] V[ietnam] war, a movie, a conversation, etc.) happens to make one feel "the world is burning up!" Yet the more fiercely it burns the quieter I feel inside. It's not a sense of "peace." Far from it. No. It is rather a sense of the inevitability of it all. I have been expecting it—as have so many. And now it is here one must stay in balance, achieve a true calm if possible. All of which is preface to telling you I am (& had been since middle of August) furiously at work on what I shall call "Sound-Pictures" based on Paul's Story "The Silver Talons of Piero Kostrov." For years I have wanted to make music of Paul's work. And I have found a way at last. It is for soprano & 11 instruments [*sic*], with some speaking & singing by the players themselves.[31] Twelve short sections divided into III interconnecting main parts. Essentially I have drawn from the story its chief images & a few lines of text for the singer. There are 4 "night pieces" & assorted other kinds. Mostly it is quiet, transcendent. Occasionally oppressive; released; wild. The 11 [*sic*] players never play all at once. Rather I draw on them for small combinations as needed. I'm using the Baldwin Electric Harpsichord for the 1st time—a very strange, beautiful instrument. I have finally achieved the "Electric Age!" It's due to be performed in Seattle Oct. '69 as part of a concert of my works; also the live version of the *Alchemist* music.[32] […]

George

41

21 OCTOBER 1968

My dear Isty,

Just a few lines to say that you should be hearing soon from either Hugh Hartwell (or someone else) re your invitation to the Penn student composers. The boys are working out a program & if the depart[ment] can supply some funds for expenses it will come about. Richard Wernick[33] who joined the faculty this year plans to accompany the group that goes up to Montreal.

I have been in a fever of work & just yesterday finished copying the score of my new *Tableaux*, "Sound-Pictures" from "The Silver Talons of Piero Kostrov" by Paul for soprano & 11 [*sic*] players. This is one of the two new works I promised Bob Suderburg for the all-Rochberg concert he is planning next Oct. in Seattle. The other one is the "live performance" version of the Alchemist music I had written for the Ben Jonson play & which I must now copy out. After that I will settle down to the long labor of copying out the IIIrd Symph[ony]. So my year is apportioned; & while I can't complain, I regret that I won't be able to go on to some new things I have in mind—at least not until all the copying is accomplished. By then it will be summer again & that means the shore (how I miss the sea, the sand, the openness of the sky, the burning intensity of the sun) and maybe—at long last—a trip to Europe. […]

When I have the *Tableaux* reproduced I will send you a copy. I think it will surprise you in some ways. Well, we shall see. In any case I'm eager to have your reaction. What has happened to plans for your *Symph[ony] of Modules*? I've learned more from that work than I care to say! […]

Gene & George.

42

3 NOVEMBER 1968

My dear Isty,

You should be getting in the mail soon my new work for soprano & 11 [*sic*] players *Tableaux*, "Sound-Pictures" which I based on Paul's story "The Silver Talons of Piero Kostrov." I will be eager to know your reaction once you've had a chance to read it. You will see it is different from everything else I've been doing—but it is not really a "departure"—as soon as I had finished copying it I set to work on the Music for the Alchemist & made out of the old music for the stage production a "live" concert version for 11 players, 2 groups—one of 7, a second of 4, plus incidental soprano. I finished it yesterday—800 measures with lots of tunes, "bim-bam," tongue-in-cheek—my best & only "comic" music to date. Both works will be done next fall in Seattle on an all-Rochberg concert along with the *Contra* and the *Magic Theater*. There will be two performances in January of the *M[agic] Th[eater]*: one with the Buffalo Philharmonic & the chamber version at UCLA. I will go out to Los Angeles to give a lecture in connection with the performance. In my present mood which is very polemical I've decided to leave off describing what I'm doing & instead, talk about it as a counter to all the "separatist" aesthetics abroad, etc. I want to pull out all the stops and talk critically about what is going on. Well, we shall see what comes out. Meanwhile before I get to the business of preparing the talk, I will begin to copy the IIIrd [Symphony] on which I did some more work this summer but have reached the point with it where I can't do any more. So after a few days of puttering around, taking care of little things, etc. it's back to work again. As you can see I have been working furiously—for lots of reasons not the least of which is that my schedule which is very light (Tues. & Wed. p.m.) permits it. But the real reasons have to do with a fantastic sense of internal pressure, obsession, compulsion—a way of staving off the unraveling of the world around us, a counter to the chaos which is descending. I feel like the world is burning up and perhaps there is only a little time to say & do, to "hear our voices again." Even with my tendency to exaggerate, this time I know there is no exaggeration involved. The world is changing before our very eyes and it has nothing to do with "progress." I feel as though Man were acting out an ultimate Revulsion of Himself. Well, enough of these bad thoughts. "We have come to say nothing. Let us Hear our Voices again." And sing and play, laugh and cry, make our noises like the crickets in the night. […]

George

43

9 DECEMBER 1968

My dear Isty,

[…] I am trying to push ahead on the IIIrd [Symphony] but lack the energy this morning. I watch it grow before my eyes—each day another page or two—and always caught up in oscillations of certainty and doubt, doubt and certainty that it is what I want it to be; or thought it was.

So it is a form of sweet relief to break off and start this new letter to you. I read your letter with that mixture of feeling which matched its contents. What you say about *Tableaux* means a great deal to me. As always I value more than I can put in words your generous response to my work. The fact that you recognize so clearly & directly what I believe is the essence of the work is a great joy to me. How else to put it? There is so little in the world around me which matches our fantasy/dream world; and to have another human being, a friend, who can live & breathe in a similar world of fantasy & dream, is a rare thing. While I find it difficult to talk about, I can confess easily & openly to you that composing *Tableaux* was a totally different experience from anything else I've attempted because I felt intensely the need to create in music & sound Paul's special world of tenderness & terror, love & fear—to capture if I could his lucidity, his sweetness; also his terrible knowledge of the near-impossibility of life for us coupled maddeningly with its beauty. I can only hope I've succeeded and that when the work is finally brought to life that through it something of Paul will radiate out to purify the world for a brief moment.

The other parts of your letter left me in another state entirely—angry for you over the fate so far of *S[ymphony] of M[odules]*—angry at the world of opacity & blind ignorance, of expediency, of lack of courage. Still while it is a struggle for you & I regret it exceedingly that you have to go through such a time with such a magnificent work, I retain enough faith to believe it will be done, someone will have the guts to do it. Now that you have a chance to discuss it with [Lukas] Foss it may be just the opportunity you've been waiting for. Please let me know what comes of your meeting with him.[34]

The offer of the Slee Professorship is great—& just the thing to accept if you can arrange it.[35] You sound weary of the problems of the faculty & how well I know that particular kind of burden which rarely lifts because of the endless round of repetition of details & human pettiness. You should get away by all means. It may sound cynical but I am completely convinced after my own 8 years of slavery that the only one who does not benefit from a sense of "high" moral purpose & responsibility is oneself. At our age it really becomes a matter of great importance whether one is going to give his substance away bit by bit to an unending series of people & things (who come to expect it &, as I learned last year, resent your withdrawing your person from aiding & comforting them & their small, selfish natures & designs) or decide in favor of living out the rest of one's life producing one's own work whatever it may be for better or worse. Under the conditions I'm discussing one is faced with the question of survival. Suddenly, "self interest" is freed of the taint of ego-centrism.

I don't mean to undermine your resolve—but Isty, do think more of yourself, your work, your own needs. Take the Slee if at all possible. [...]

George

NOTES

1 Leonad B. Meyer, *Music, the Arts, and Ideas: Patterns and Predictions in Twentieth-Century Culture* (Chicago: University of Chicago Press, 1967).
2 See "1966," notes 4 and 5.
3 *Fantasia*, for piano (1954), Glenn Gould, piano, Columbia Masterworks 32–110046 (1967); reissued in compact disc format, Sony SMK 52 677 (1992).
4 Lejaren Hiller (1924–94), a pioneering composer of computer-assisted music.
5 Henry Brant (b. 1913), Canadian-born composer and conductor who settled in New York in the 1930s, after studies at the Institute of Musical Arts and the Juilliard Graduate School. His music is marked by unusual timbral combinations and, taking his cue from Ives, an interest in "spatial music."
6 Robert Erickson (1917–97), composer and teacher; he became professor of music at the University of California, San Diego, in 1967.
7 Donald Martino (1931–2005), composer and teacher who has taught at his alma mater, Princeton University (1957–59), at Yale University (1959–69), the New England Conservatory (1969–81), Brandeis University (1980–83), and, since 1983, Harvard University, where he was the Walter Bigelow Rosen Professor of Music, Emeritus.
8 See "1961," note 1.
9 Loren Rush (b. 1935), composer, student of Robert Erickson (1954–60), founding director of the San Francisco Conservatory Artists Ensemble (1966–69).
10 William Bolcom (b. 1938), composer and pianist, best known for his programs of early American popular music (with his wife, mezzo-soprano Joan Morris [b. 1943]) and for his stylistically hybrid compositions, which juxtapose popular and "serious" elements. He and his wife both teach at the University of Michigan. Bolcom shares with Rochberg a fascination with the transcendentalism of William Blake. Both composers have set Blake's poetry.
11 Bruce Mather (b. 1939), Canadian composer, pianist, and teacher, who joined the Faculty of Music at McGill University in 1966. Rochberg is referring to the fact that Mather and Bolcom studied composition with Leland Smith (b. 1925) at Stanford University during the same period in the early 1960s.
12 Andrew Rudin (b. 1939), student of Rochberg and founding director of the Electronic Music Center at the Philadelphia College of the Performing Arts.
13 Arthur Koestler, *The Ghost in the Machine* (London: Hutchinson, 1967).
14 See "1967," note 5.
15 See "1984," note 4.
16 *Nach Bach*, for Harpsichord or Piano (1966), Igor Kipnis, harpsichord, Grenadilla 1019 (1968).
17 Luciano Berio (1925–2003), Herbert Eimert (1897–1972), György Ligeti, (1923–2006), Karlheinz Stockhausen (b. 1928), Luigi Nono (1924–90), Mauricio

Kagel (b. 1931), leading members of the international avant-garde in the 1960s, all of whom, in greater or lesser degrees, were involved in electronic and electro-acoustic music in this period.

18 Hans G. Helms (b. 1932), German music journalist, poet, linguist, and composer, based for much of his career in Cologne; his musical compositions of the late 1950s and 1960s characteristically incorporated the electronic manipulation of polyglot speech-sounds; François Dufrêne (1930–82), French sound-poet and visual artist who, extending the *bruitist* ideas of Luigi Russolo and the Dadaists, explored electro-acoustic extended vocal techniques in the early 1950s and 1960s; Ferdinand Kriwet (b. 1942), German poet and artist who explores the intersections between poetry, painting, and acoustic art; Konrad Boehmer (b. 1941), German composer, musicologist, and music theorist; he was associated with the electronic music studios of West German Radio in Cologne (1961–63) and at the Institute of Sonology in Utrecht (1966–68); in 1972 he became professor of music history and theory at the Royal Conservatory in The Hague.

19 In 1968 Anhalt spent eleven weeks in Europe touring various electronic music studios; on 13 June he read a paper on the recently completed *Cento* (1967) in Florence, during the Maggio Musicale, at the International Congress of Experimental Centers for Electronic Music; see "The Making of *Cento*," *Canada Music Book* 1 (Spring/Summer 1970): 81–89.

20 See "1961," note 1.

21 See note 4 above.

22 Fritz Winckel (b. 1907), Austro-German acoustician and musicologist; his published writings explore the connection between linguistic and musical structures, as well as aspects of acoustics, voice techniques, and electronic music composition; Leo Küpper (b. 1935), a pioneer of electronic music in his native Belgium; James Kirtland Randall (b. 1929), American composer involved with computer sound synthesis in the 1960s and 1970s, and professor of music at Princeton University (1958–91); Iannis Xenakis (1922–2001), French composer of Greek descent, one of the leading modernist composers of his generation.

23 Bruno Maderna (1920–73), Italian conductor and composer, co-founder (with Luciano Berio) of the Studio di Fonologia in Milan in 1954.

24 Gordon Mumma (b. 1935), an American pioneer of electro-acoustic music; Synket is the name of a synthesizer designed in Rome in 1964 by sound engineer Paul Ketoff.

25 Peter Zinovieff (b. 1934), British composer and inventor who founded, in 1969, the British synthesizer and electronic instruments manufacturing firm Electronic Music Studios (EMS), initially based in Putney, London; he was a pioneer in the musical applications of mini-computers in the 1960s.

26 Anhalt is mistaken; in 1967 Folkways released a recording under the title *Electronic Music: University of Toronto Studio*, Folkways FM 3436/FMS 33436, which includes works by Robert Aitken, Hugh Le Caine, Myron Schaefer, and others.

27 Mario Savio (1942–96), student activist and spokesman for the Free Speech Movement at the University of California, Berkeley, in the mid-1960s; Daniel Cohen-Bendit (b. 1944), a leader of the 1968 student uprising and general strike in France known as "Mai 68"; John Fekete (b. 1947), McGill University student columnist who gained notoriety for reprinting (from the U.S. satirical magazine *The Realist*) a controversial article in a 3 November 1967 issue of the student newspaper *The McGill Daily*, an act that earned him and his editors a reprimand from the McGill

Senate for contravening "the standards of decency acceptable by and in this university."

28 Per Nørgård (b. 1932), one of the leading Danish composers of his generation; *Babel*, scored for soloists, chorus, instruments, dancers, and mime ad lib, dates from 1965 (revised as *Nye Babel* in 1968).

29 Peter Brook (b. 1925), innovative and controversial British theatre director.

30 "Webern: Master of Harmony" (1968) (unpublished).

31 *Tableaux* (Sound Pictures from "The Silver Talons of Piero Kostrov" by Paul Rochberg) for "Soprano, Two Actors' Voices, Small Men's Chorus and Twelve Players" (1968). The work is scored for twelve instruments (with some doubling in the flute, clarinet, and trumpet parts) in addition to a large percussion section (two players on fourteen instruments).

32 *Tableaux* was premiered on 31 October 1969 by Elizabeth Suderburg, soprano, and the University of Washington Contemporary Group, conducted by Robert Suderburg; on the same program the concert version of Rochberg's music for *The Alchemist* was premiered.

33 Richard Wernick (b. 1934), composer, joined the faculty at the University of Pennsylvania in 1968, where he became conductor of the Penn Contemporary Players.

34 A performance of the *Symphony of Modules* by the German-born American composer and conductor Lukas Foss (b. 1922) and the Buffalo Philharmonic never went beyond the discussion stage.

35 Anhalt was the visiting Slee Professor of Composition at the University of New York, Buffalo in the fall of 1969.

1969

44

14 JULY 1969

My dear Isty,

It seems like "forever" since I last wrote. Finally the summer has reached a point of stasis and I can begin to think again and think about writing again. But all the while you've been very much on my mind: wondering how your work goes for you, the state of the *S[ymphony] of M[odules]*, whether you have some time off this summer & can get away with the family for a rest and vacation. I think the fact that you will be at Buffalo at least for one term is wonderful.

[...]

In late June I did 3 weeks at Temple Institute/Festival of Music and finished putting together a collection of 35 songs—which reach back to 1937 & up to now—for voice & piano.[1] Somehow this was part of a larger urge, before going on again to new things, to rescue from oblivion things which I still liked, among them a set of piano variations from 1941.[2] Now I'm thinking seriously putting my 1st Symph[ony] back to what it was: a 5-move[ment] work.[3] The prospect is frightening—all that work. Also the nagging question: is it worth all the trouble? Since there is no "answer" to such a question I'll have to decide on other grounds. I'm waiting word from Juilliard to find out if they've set the parts extraction in motion yet. Why do I sometimes dread the performance of the IIIrd [Symphony]? I wish there were some way to detach oneself permanently from what one produces in order to be free of all the inner doubts, uncertainties, vainglorious hopes—the whole kit & kaboodle of ego ties which constantly put us through the ringer. *Magari* ["I wish; if only"]. These are hard days in which to try to maintain the inner strength & purpose of artistic work. So much pure baloney in the air, so much terror & fear in the world, so much human ineptitude & incapacity. Somehow I have to gather my energies together again and keep going in the face of Vietnam, Black Separatism, Nudity, Civil Strife & violence. What a country, what a culture, what a time!

Perhaps the oddest thing of all that is happening to me is a growing need to confirm & reaffirm my Jewishness—not in the ordinary sociological sense, i.e., joining a congregation, observing the religious side, et al., but in the spiritual sense. Digging into the psyche to discover the connections with God or what we call "God" and Life, to find that quality of mind which made it possible to survive and be a Jew in the middle of Hellenic-Roman times, to remain free of all the corruptions which have dragged one people after another down. In a strange way the urge is tied up with music. I mean that music is being corrupted today, is being lost in the vagaries of "false idols." It has become unclean. If I can find my way clearly to both of these primary conditions of my life (and of life itself) perhaps the next decade, if it's granted me, will be fruitful for me. I feel very much on a threshold & not sure if the door before me will open or stay shut. […]

George

45

5 AUGUST 1969

Dear George,

[…] Yes you are right! We have to meet soon. The topics you bring up in the letter are such that short of writing 100 pages I cannot respond the way I should. The remarks about Jewishness. It is really uncanny, how similarly, on occasions, our inner development takes certain turns. In the piece (in fact I better say through the piece) on which I am working [*Foci*] I am groping towards an understanding of some facets of the collective psyche of our group which until now were far removed from my concerns. I have become very interested in reading certain parts of the *Zohar*, for example.[4] (Among other things it so Borgesian and/or Nabokovian at places, that it is quite uncanny.) Hassidism, Kabbalah, etc. I came to through this new piece. Well I will resist telling about it in detail here because the lessening of tension (the release, which may be the result of the description) may be detrimental to the work schedule. What a schedule: seven day[s] per week, from 10 a.m. to 10–11 p.m. in the studio (for the present) working on the tape layer of the work. There will be a "live" instrumental and vocal layer too. And if I am lucky the scenic aspects will be also tackled in some of the performances. (I am writing the piece for the Buffalo Center, [Lukas] Foss, etc.) The text is a fantastic assemblage; some of it written by me, some of it culled from a hundred of sources. Total duration about 31'.

The nature? Well something that speaks to us as, in the age of 7090 IBM computer[s], in the Moon Walk, in the time of distress of cities, of questioning youth, etc. Well—no! That may be too much to tackle. In fact the piece will have something "guarded," classical (Apollonian) about it. Well, that's enough. I will not tell more.

I am so pleased that you are your usual self, full of projects and plans. I'd love to come to New York for the premiere of your 3rd S[ymphony]. So, please, keep me posted of the developments in this regard. My *S[ymphony] of M[odules]* will, most likely [be] premiered by [Lukas] Foss in the Spring of 1970. On the programme will also be a new work by [Lejaren] Hiller. (I hope Foss will have at least 25–30 hours of rehearsal time!)

I am so preoccupied with the new piece that I had only marginal thoughts about the public lectures I'll have to give in Buffalo. (Incidentally, could you tell me of the kind of audience you had there? I was told to expect a mixed, lay-ish group.) At least one of the talks will be about the "new" literature for the voice. (In fact my seminar at SUNYB [State University of New York at Buffalo] will be centred on this topic.) […]

Istvan

46

8 NOVEMBER 1969

My dear Isty,

Just a few words to ask how you are and to tell you the Seattle concert was a great success. While I would have preferred 10 more hours of rehearsal everything was realized at a high level of performance & understanding. Bob Suderburg did a superb job & his wife Elizabeth sang beautifully.[5] The *Tableaux* turned out to be the work which made the greatest impact. I hope now it will enjoy its own existence.

I hope you are feeling better and are taking better care of yourself. I was very glad to hear you had relinquished your administrative duties. Makes real sense to me. When is the performance of your new work in Buffalo, when in N[ew] Y[ork]? It's unlikely we can hear it until it's done in N[ew] Y[ork] so I'd like to plan to set the day aside and look forward to seeing you & Bea more than I can say.

I ran into Hugh Hartwell at a concert at school last night & he says there's a rumor that you're leaving McGill to go to SUNYB [State University of New York at Buffalo]! Any truth to it?!? […]

George

47

20 DECEMBER 1969

My dear Isty,

I wish we didn't have to rush off like that without the chance to talk to you about your work & say goodbye to all of you. We skipped out of the hall during the applause of your work so missed seeing Bea & Carol (and Marion[6] & her daughter) before we left. We just made the 11:00 train![7]

I have been thinking about your work [*Foci*] and realize I must hear it several more times before I can really grasp it. But for whatever it's worth now here is my initial—provisional—tentative response. It is not a work about which one can say I like it or don't like it. Its very level of projection & motivation precludes that kind of simple gut reaction. Coming as it did after those monstrosities in the first half, it came across as a real work with shape & direction, with energy & purpose. I probably missed a great deal of both vocal projections & music because periodically I would concentrate on one and then the other in order to get at details & qualities. Generally speaking, however, I think I got an overall sense of the march of events & the shape they produced. The two most effective sections for me were the soprano music to the end & the rapid-fire taped "scherzando." Were you being ironic in setting that particular text for soprano in such a lyric style? It came across to me as irony—as though you were saying one can't justify lyricism if for its own sake. Don't know if I would agree; but then this may not have been your intention. I thought the bass drum strokes very effective ways to punctuate beginnings & endings. The idea of ending with the elephant bell is lovely.[8] I guess the one difficulty I experienced with the work was the nature of the texts—as far as I could understand them—projected via the taped voices. Because they are essentially anti-dramatic, I occasionally got the feeling of "documentary"-like comment on the state of things. Yet I felt you were striving for some level of dramatic projection. I wonder if the mixture of live & taped voices—as in *Cento*—wouldn't bring you closer to that goal?

Frankly, I would have preferred some live voices to break the consistency of the "broadcasting" feeling. I'm still not sure how I feel about the way you parallel the instrumental sound with the taped voices. I felt occasionally that they were constricted and wanted to break free of the dominance of the tape. I don't think that on the face of it it would be fair to compare *Foci* with *Cento* even though there is a kind of relation between them. I think *Cento*'s passion & rage gives it a different quality from *Foci* & I must hear *Foci* again at least 2 more times before I could really say what I feel its essential quality is. I would be happy to hear you talk your own way about it when you're back from vacation. [...]

George

NOTES

1 *Book of Songs*, for voice and piano (1937–1969), a collection of thirty-five songs compiled in April–June 1969.

2 *Variations on an Original Theme*, for piano solo (1941; revised 1969).

3 The Symphony No. 1 (1948–49) was revised several times: 1957, 1971–72, and 1977. The final version restores the five-movement original, although with changes in orchestral details.

4 The *Zohar* (or the *Sefer Zohar*) [The Book of Splendour] is one of the central texts of the Kabbalistic tradition, probably of thirteenth-century Spanish origin.

5 See "1968," note 32.

6 Marion Glasserow Gladney (b. 1925), writer, co-author of two autobiographies of actress Helen Hayes, *Our Best Years* (1984) and *Loving Life* (1987); she is Beate Anhalt's first cousin.

7 Rochberg is referring to the premiere of Anhalt's *Foci* (1969), which took place at the Albright-Knox Art Gallery Auditorium in Buffalo, New York, under the composer's direction, on 13 December 1969.

8 Anhalt found an elephant bell, probably of Indian provenance, in an antique shop in London; intrigued by the rich and varied sounds of this bell, he incorporated it into the score of *Foci*; identified in the score as a "middle sized elephant bell," it is among the last sounds heard, from backstage, as it fades to *pppppp*.

1970

48

17 JANUARY 1970

Dear George,

[…] I was of course pleased that you came to be a witness to *Foci*. I read, and reread, your response to this performance, and am grateful for your sincere act of agreeing to give so much attention and thought to this work. I respect your response, and, of course, it interest[s] me greatly. But I won't comment on it, because I still don't know how to talk about this work in an objective fashion. (I am expecting to receive shortly a tape of the performance. Perhaps listening to it will give me the necessary psychic distance for this, and possibly also for making some minor changes in it.) I also wonder how the visual part complemented the sound. Everybody in the audience saw this, but not I. Frustrating. […]

How is work? Hugh [Hartwell] tells me that your songs are beautiful. Could I have a peek? (I have to have the score of *Foci* recopied by a professional man, but if you wish to have a copy of this rough script I'll be pleased to send you one.) […]

Istvan

49

21 JANUARY 1970

Dear Isty,

[…] Hugh [Hartwell] was referring to the songs I wrote to Paul's texts. Or was it *Tableaux*? I'll do them with Neva Pilgrim April 1 here in Phila[delphia].[1] Right now I have no extra copies but I will send you one as soon as I can. There are 12 [*sic*] in this group and later (next year?) I want to do another set & again later a 3rd set.[2] I am suddenly obsessed by the desire to "sing" again, to leave off speculation & "new" things & do what lies closest to my heart. Of course the head keeps up its steady demands too so once again I'm attacking my problem from a "new" angle—actually an extension of what started 5 years ago with *Contra* & *Magic Theater*. I've just written 49 "caprice-variations" for violin solo after Paganini's theme (the same one Brahms wrote 2 books of p[ia]no var[iations] on).[3] Everything is there including Baroque, Classical, Romantic harmony & gestures as well as, of course, a good sprinkling of "contemporary" music. I felt good writing it. Unselfconscious. Happy to be able to think harmonically & rhythmically as though it were the most natural thing in the world. I passed the stage of writing tonally from a sense of irony to simply writing it. I'm more than ever convinced of the necessity to speak many languages—dialects to be more precise—& to match the gesture with the appropriate expression. My recent listening experiences confirm that contemporary music (or what we call "contemporary music") is a limited palette of essentially neurotic, constricted gestures. All of it perfectly true—but only of certain kinds of experience—the worst ones (alienation, trauma, nihilistic-destructive withdrawal, etc.). Susan Sontag & others have tried to make the old sense of dignity & nobility into something "campy."[4] Yes, that is true when they are sentimentalized. But I hear nothing of the sort in Brahms or Beethoven or Bach or Chopin. They have their truths & we still live within their sphere even if that sphere has been extended almost to the breaking point. I'm trying to say that I think we are the provincials not Beethoven. The very size of the old gestures (was looking through Bach B minor Mass today!) is still to my mind unbelievable & cosmic in every way (& without, mind you, electricity!). Well, you see I'm at it again—but anyhow the important thing is to find a way out of the contemporary cul-de-sac & to feel like a musician again. […]

George

50

10 JUNE 1970

My dear Isty,

[…] I've started a large cycle of songs for voice & piano based on a beautiful English translation of Bengali songs: *In Praise of Krishna*.[5] It is the "story" of how Radha falls in love with Krishna (God? Man?) and gives herself utterly. All the stages of sensual love are represented in the poetry. I am letting myself go completely in order to produce a genuinely lyric romantic expression. Somehow I feel the inward psychology of the female & can make the necessary projection. So far I have been sketching "tunes" mostly. One song is about 1/2 done & will set the stage for the kind of pitch language, harmony, treatment of prosody, of piano in relation to voice (always a hard thing to make come off convincingly). I was encouraged with the success of the songs I wrote to Paul's poems. Hopefully when this new cycle is completed, I can think about the next group of Paul's poems. My plan is to produce 3 sets with approximately the same number of songs per set as in the first one: Eleven. Perhaps once I'm "sung out" I will get back to instrumental music. The work for Israel in Dec. is done & should be there by now. I call it *Sacred Song of Reconciliation (Mizmur l'Piyus)*; for bass-baritone & chamber orchestra, text in Hebrew (Genesis; Isaiah; Hosea).[6] Work staves off depression which I feel every time I hear the TV news & read the newspapers. Incredible what has happened to the U.S. We can only hope things will take a turn toward sanity and restore a sense of balance, proportion & return to civilized ways. […]

George

51

3 AUGUST 1970

My dear Isty,

[…] I must confess I do not feel eager about going back to teach this fall. How I long for complete freedom! I have worked like a demon this year. Starting in Jan. the 50 *Caprice-Variations* for solo violin (based on Paganini naturally). Then the *Sacred Song of Reconciliation* for bass-baritone & chamber orchestra (for Israel) set to Hebrew, in the spring. And since June a new cycle of songs for voice & piano: *Songs in Praise of Krishna*. I've completed 11 of the 17.[7] I must confess I'm tired. But somehow I must do the other six most of which are sketched already at least on one level: the vocal line; which is where I always start—from the voice. I would love for you to hear Paul's songs & the *Krishna Songs*. There is a way if it would not put too much of a burden on you. I'm referring to the fact that since performing Paul's songs with Neva Pilgrim (who is a wonderful young artist in command of a remarkable instrument & sensitive nature) I gradually came to feel that I must do more of this. So I'm trying to "arrange" a few invitations to give a recital of the

2 cycles at different places. We'll probably do the new cycle here at Penn in the winter & again at Univ[ersity] of Illinois in March.[8] If McGill would be interested & can meet the fee for Neva ($500.00) & me (variable if necessary), we could have the added pleasure of seeing each other. But I hasten to add that if my proposal would in any way place work on your shoulders please do nothing about it. And should it not work out for whatever reason you have no idea what elation we felt when Gene read that part of your letter where you suggest you may be in Israel when we're there. It looks like we'll leave Dec. 5. The Kol Israel orch[estra] concert where I will conduct my (*David the Psalmist*) cantata for tenor & orch[estra] & also *Night Music* is Dec. 22nd & the *Sacred Songs* is Dec. 30. It would be wonderful if you & Bea were also there!

Your reading program sounds fascinating. I feel like a simpleton just writing! But between us reading anything these days but something distracting or mildly entertaining seems too difficult for me. I can't sustain the interest. But I'd love to hear you talk about all that stuff!

[...]

George

52

30 SEPTEMBER 1970

Dear George,

I have delayed this letter until I can write something definite about the idea of you and Miss [Neva] Pilgrim performing your songs at McGill. Well, the news, unfortunately, is bad. We shall not be able to bring this about for financial reasons, which stem from the following two considerations: (1) McGill shall celebrate its 150th anniversary next year, and all concert-moneys of the Faculty will go into the presentation of either McGill performers, or works by composers who have, or had in the past, an affiliation with the Faculty; (2) The available money is pitifully small, so little in fact that we have to find outside (CBC perhaps) support for some of the concerts. (For example it is doubtful that *Foci* could receive its Canadian premiere here, unless I find about $1,500 somewhere.)

Needless to say that I regret greatly that I have to postpone hearing your songs for a while. I regret it doubly: because they are Paul's and yours, and because, at present, I am more interested in the voice than in any other medium. (I am very interested how you are singing now!)

In fact the summer was spent entirely on reading on this subject. I cannot substantiate a statement to the effect that the musicological literature alone is found wanting in this regard, because I made but an unsystematic probing, to date. However, what this produced promises little enlightenment as far as deep understanding is concerned. Understanding that blows up the text until its atomic detail (Bolinger's word)[9] emerges, or until sound and meaning coalesce into a flash of insight (as Highet did it in his analysis of some English sonnets),[10] etc. Not that the linguistic stuff, or the psychological papers (many rather dreary accounts of poorly designed behavioristic experiments) add up to an "explanation." Far from it. The insight of the few psycholinguists, psychiatrists, or psychoanalysts who have tuned into the voice as a diagnostic (and/or therapeutic) dimension, while being of great interest to me, leaves me with a magnificent sense of non-fulfillment, that is, with the urge to go ahead and do something (write a paper, prepare a seminar, or even better dream of a new work).

Having caught a glimpse of the phenomenal complexity of phonology, and its relationship to phylo- and ontogenesis, I find it a great stimulation for conceiving new plans for works. What is needed now is the frame, or (using a different metaphor) the nucleus of the idea for a work, which will unify all vocal (supported or not) events, as they are grouped together in *Cento* and *Foci*.

I am, at present, in no hurry in beginning a new piece. I am fully occupied with trying to apply my newly acquired understanding of the *langue-parole* couple to works, such as [Berg's] *Lulu*, Ligeti's *Requiem* (it is a gimmicky piece, not better than Penderecki), Berio's *Sequenza III* (this work needled me more than any other. I just lacked conceptual vocabulary to think-speak about it. I think I have found a key to it), and Ligeti's *Nouvelles Aventures* (an important work).

Surprise: I have even spent time with Britten's *Peter Grimes*. He (Britten) has an uncanny ear for the prosody of 'Received English.' If he distorts it (and how) he clearly indicates personalities, psychic states, etc. and social statuses. […]

Istvan

53

3 OCTOBER 1970

Dear Isty,

[…] Just a few lines to say how welcome your letter was—& especially to hear that you are in better health. How I wish we could drop in on you! […] But it's really impossible. What with school (2 days a week), my own work & the meetings & rehearsals for the IIIrd [Symphony] in N[ew] Y[ork] coming up—I'm just managing to keep up with everything.[11] Also I must begin very soon to start practicing the piano parts of Paul's songs & to learn to conduct my *Night Music* & tenor solo cantata *David the Psalmist*—all to be done in Israel in Dec. So please forgive your old friend for not being able to join you in your woodland paradise. I am wondering: you think you & Bea could come down to N[ew] Y[ork] for the IIIrd [Symphony]? It will be Nov. 24, Tuesday night. One major problem: tickets are tight & as of now, I can't promise them to you. However, even if it turned out you couldn't hear the performance, Tuesday morning at 9:00 a.m. will be open dress rehearsal; so if you got to N[ew] Y[ork] the night before you could sit with us at the rehearsal. Please think about this & try, if at all possible, to work it out so you can be there. I've heard not a note yet but will soon. I need not describe the elevator-like oscillations of feelings, the hopes, the anxieties. There will be 400 people on stage! That alone frightens me—but also, I confess, secretly delights me!

I'm sorry circumstances won't allow a perf[ormance] of Paul's songs this season at McGill. Far more important, it seems to me, is that they should do your *Foci*. Perhaps by the time something should open up for the songs we could also do the *14 Songs in Praise of Krishna* I've done this summer & am almost finished copying out. It is difficult to describe them. They are a different world from Paul's songs. The new ones turn out to be very emotional, erotic-sensual, dramatic, romantic (or words to that effect)—a projection on my part into the heart of a woman in love: completely, intensely, totally female in her joys, ecstasies, fears & sorrows. I can only hope I've succeeded.

I think I understand what you're after—but why can't the problem be approached from the heart & not the head? Vocal sounds derive from the deepest recesses of our psyche & are formed by need. If that's the case, then the radiating concentric circles of meaning of words is what we need to reveal through music. How can psychologists or linguists help us understand what, in fact, we already know on deeply intuitive levels? Frankly, I distrust the behaviorists; & my contact with linguistics through 2 colleagues at Penn has suggested they have little to offer an art which is primarily synthetic because their discipline is primarily analytic. Remember Monteverdi's "music is the handmaiden of the word?"[12] That's where we are again, I feel. I want to take verbal expressions of intense emotional states (implicit as well as explicit) & enlarge & reveal those states in music which is lyric, clearly discernible in its shape & tendency & I suppose, as simple as Simon. I think you were on a different track from mine in *Cento*. But *Cento* succeeds despite its analytic approach to the words because it is dramatic, hot, altogether concrete in its intensity of projection. I think one of the difficulties with *Foci* is its lack of real drama, its too-close attention to abstract formulations. For me intelligence must be hidden in the structure of the music & not made one of the evident, component levels of the work. The reason for that I believe is that human intelligence is a different order of reality from the one which contains the possibility of music. The two are like oil & water.

The enclosed "reflections" tend to amplify some of what I've tried to say here. I wrote them for a memorial volume for [a] colleague-friend at C[ity] C[ollege] N[ew] Y[ork], Otto Deri.[13] I'm still out of step. Why that should be so is still a mystery to me. I used to call this all-too-prominent trait of mine: non-adaptive. Whatever the case may be, I am even less charmed or titillated or attracted than ever before by the products of our more "daring" colleagues. Berio impresses me; but fails to draw me to him. Penderecki repels me. Ligeti is too obvious (like the painter Barnett Newman).[14] In the end, I've discovered I have to go my own stubborn, simplistic way. Just to show you how incomparably out of step I can be, yesterday I determined to study counterpoint & fugue all over again at the earliest opportunity! […]

George

NOTES

1 *Eleven Songs*, for mezzo-soprano and piano (1969), was premiered by Neva Pilgrim, soprano, and the composer, piano, at St. Mary's Church, Philadelphia on 1 April 1970.

2 Rochberg set his son's poetry in two later works: *Fantasies*, for voice and piano (1971), and String Quartet No. 7, with baritone (1979), each of which use four of Paul's poems.

3 *Caprice Variations*, for unaccompanied violin (1970); the published score contains 50 variations in addition to the Paganini theme, which appears at the end.

4 See particularly Susan Sontag, *Against Interpretation, and Other Essays* (New York: Farrar, Straus, 1966).

5 *Songs in Praise of Krishna*, for soprano and piano (1970), based on texts from *In Praise of Krishna: Songs from the Bengali*, trans. Edward C. Dimock, Jr., and Denise Levertov (Garden City, NY: Doubleday, 1967).

6 *Sacred Song of Reconciliation (Mizmur l'Piyus)* (1970) was commissioned for Testimonium in celebration of the city of Jerusalem and premiered in that city on 5 January 1971.

7 The published version of *Songs in Praise of Krishna* contains fourteen numbers.

8 *Songs in Praise of Krishna* was premiered by Neva Pilgrim, soprano, and the composer, piano, at the University of Illinois on 16 March 1971.

9 Dwight Le Merton Bolinger (1907–92), American linguist; see, in particular, *Aspects of Language* (New York: Harcourt, Brace and World, 1968).

10 See Gilbert Highet, "Scorn Not the Sonnet," in *The Powers of Poetry* (New York: Oxford University Press, 1960), 190–96.

11 The Symphony No. 3 was premiered by the Juilliard Orchestra, Juilliard Chorus, and the Collegiate Chorale, with Joyce Mathis, soprano, Joy Blackett, alto, John Russell, tenor, and Robert Shiesley, bass, conducted by Abraham Kaplan, at the Juilliard Theater, Lincoln Center, New York, on 24 November 1970.

12 This is a recurring theme in Western thought from Aristotle to Wagner by way of Augustine and Aquinas, Luther and Calvin, Schopenhauer and Nietzsche, and others. Rochberg is referring to Monteverdi's celebrated debate with the reactionary critic Giovanni Maria Artusi; in defence of "modern music" or his *seconda prattica*, Monteverdi supports a practice that "considers harmony not commanding, but commanded, and makes the words the mistress of the harmony." "Il quinto libro de' madrigali—*Foreword with the "Declaration" of His Brother G.C. Monteverdi*" (1607), in Oliver Strunk, *Source Readings in Music History: From Classical Antiquity through the Romantic Era* (New York: W.W. Norton, 1950), 409. See also Rochberg, *Aesthetics of Survival*, 121; rev. and expanded ed. (2004), 111.

13 Otto Deri (1911–69), composer and musicologist, author of *Exploring Twentieth-Century Music* (New York: Holt, Rinehart and Winston, 1968). The memorial volume for Deri did not materialize; however, Rochberg's contribution, "Reflections on the Renewal of Music" (1972), appeared in *Current Musicology* 13 (1972): 75–82; reprinted in Rochberg, *Aesthetics of Survival* (1984), 232–38.

14 Barnett Newman (1905–70), American abstract expressionist/minimalist painter, a close friend of Mark Rothko and Jackson Pollock.

1971

54

2 APRIL 1971

Dear Isty,

I hope by now the score & tape of the IIIrd [Symphony] have reached you. The problem with sending the score was that the U.S. Post Office has size limitations so I finally got around to the Railway Express. Also since I couldn't send my own copy of the tape which I needed I asked Steve Albert, my former student & now close friend (he's extremely gifted),[1] to send you his copy which he was willing to do. Unhappily the mistake (poor trombone entry) which occurred early in the Schütz passage during the performance is captured "forever" on this tape & always upsets me when I hear it again. But in other respects it's okay.

How are you? Feeling well I hope & working. I am finally back to a reasonable routine & beginning to work again. I spent much too much time after getting back from Israel writing 2 lectures I had to give & practicing the piano parts of the new *Krishna* cycle which Neva Pilgrim & I did at the Un[iversity] of Ill[inois] on March 16. Happily, it went very well & the response to it was very strong. Ed London[2] who is there now asked me at a party the night before "why piano & voice?" Said it was "very German." Apparently he has not heard of song cycles by Fauré, Debussy, Messiaen, Copland, etc.!! On March 18 Neva & I did a morning program of Paul's songs [*Fantasies*] & repeated about 1/2 the new cycle. If our plans materialize next year we intend to give recitals of both cycles plus some others of earlier & later vintage (there are 2 transcriptions of "pieces" from the *Tableaux*). All in all I've discovered I enjoy performing. And in any case Neva is a superb artist & a joy to work with. […]

George

55

12 APRIL, 1971

Dear George,

Where to start? Many thanks for lending the score and the tape of your IIIrd Symphony. I listened to it with the students in the seminar the other day. As it started half of the group literally jumped! And from that on there was no slackening of attention until the last sound. The students (and myself, again) were gripped by the power and conviction of the piece. It is bold, unique, incredibly powerful, and your special mix, no one else's. It has a terrific streak of stubbornness in it, and at times it appears to me as an evocation to muster the forces of some of our great ancestors, coupled to your special brand of exclamations … I would not have been surprised to see J.S. Bach, Beethoven, and Schütz emerging from the wings, joining hands with you in this powerful appeal for humanity, and understanding. Strangely, stylistic consideration, meaning the mix, recedes into the background on second contact and the gross rhythm and vitality of the monument takes over with a firm grip … No doubt, no one but you could have written this work, and be proud of it!! […]

On April 2nd took place the Canadian premiere of *Foci*, at McGill. It was a far better performance than the one you heard. First of all I made numerous minor changes in the work, chiefly in the orchestration, and in the vocal line of Section 9. (It has become much more ornate.) Phyllis Mailing, Murray Schafer's wife, sang the solo part, and gave it a tremendous depth. I was very pleased with the response it elicited. The day after the CBC recorded the work in a grueling 8 h[ou]rs recording session, which produced an excellent collage of the various takes. It now seems that the CBC will bring out a record with *Cento* and *Foci* on it.[3] (I don't know when.) A detail: there was an entirely new visual complement to the piece, much more subtle than the first one. On May 21st the work will be performed in the CBC Festival Series in Toronto. (You see I am too getting back into shape as a conductor.)

As soon as all this dust settles, I shall start thinking on a new multimedia piece commissioned by the CBC [*La Tourangelle*]. The topic is rather forbidding: man's search for God (I wrote good first …!) They want it in combined French and English. Poor me; we are expected to contribute to the bridge-building between Canada's two warring linguistic communities. I am looking forward to working on it, though.

Now a news. I have resigned from McGill, in order to be able to accept an offer to become the Head of the Department of Music at Queen's University at Kingston, Ontario, a smallish city about 3 h[ou]rs of train ride from Montreal.[4] You may imagine the soul searching Bea and I (and the kids) went through until we made this decision. There are many reasons for it, and the foremost of them is the labile political climate in Quebec, which gives us a sickening *déja-vue* feeling. For 1971–72 our plan is to keep the house in Montreal, with me commuting to Kingston. It is also likely that McGill would want to have me as a Visiting Prof[essor] during the coming session, to allow them sufficient time to find a successor. […]

Istvan

56

16 APRIL 1971

My Dear Isty,

It was good to year from you—needless to say your account of your (& your students') reaction to the IIIrd [Symphony] was heart-warming. You are aware I'm sure that the work evokes as much puzzlement (if not dismay) as it does understanding, maybe more. But coming from you I take special pleasure in your feelings about it. About the score: I would be happy to let you keep it were it not for the fact it contains minor changes, etc. & I ought to keep it handy just in case. So if it will not be too much trouble do please return it at your convenience (no special hurry right now). […]

I was happy to hear that *Foci* has been recorded by CBC & will come out with *Cento*. Please let me know when the record is released so I can get a copy and listen at my leisure. The fact that *Foci* is now launched to your satisfaction & will be repeated in May is great news. Long life to you both!

It took me a little while to absorb the news of your leaving McGill for Queen's Univ[ersity]. I understand very well why you feel it necessary to leave French Canada—you are undoubtedly right to do so—I hope that once you are settled in Kingston everything will go smoothly and the demands on you will not be too heavy. So our warmest congratulations & best wishes! I look forward to August so you can tell us more about the new life ahead. […]

Once back from Urbana, I began to work again. There's not much to say yet except that it is a work for piano[5]—far from a "major" work in proportions or attitude—but I couldn't do anything large now simply because I lack the concentration & energy. Perhaps when school is over I can feel free of distractions & interruptions. But beyond all the surface stuff (which is always there anyhow) is a deep-seated anxiety over all the old problems—style, language, aesthetic—I never have seemed to free myself from the worry over it—nor can I write two pieces in a row with the same attitude or feeling; hence the perpetual boiling undercurrent of dissatisfaction with everything. On top of all this is the nagging need to finally put my 1st Symphony to rights—which means a great deal of work. Somehow there's the sensation that before I attempt [Symphony] no. IV the first 3 have to be the way I want them. Oh for the free and easy life!! […]

George

57

10 JUNE 1971

Dear George,

[…] The Toronto performance of *Foci* went almost as well as the Montreal one. One critic killed me, the other wrote with great understanding.[6] At present I am starting to work on my new piece [*La Tourangelle*] for the CBC. It will use again tape, instruments, & voices. I am in the reading stage now spending a great deal of time in the library. I feel that I am getting to sense the character of the piece. It will be at places terrifically passionate, at places icily calm … […]

Istvan

58

26 JUNE 1971

Dear Isty,

[…] Hugh Hartwell & his wife were here for dinner about a week ago & I read that horrendous, acrimonious "review" of *Foci*—actually it was the furthest removed from a review or report of a work I've ever come across. The man seemed to have an animus against Istvan Anhalt. He's either insane or an utter fool. I was very upset & angry for you. Such things are inexcusable, absolutely so. Still the best way to respond is to ignore it—which I'm sure you did. You have too much to do to be concerned, except in passing, with such idiocy. I'm glad to hear that the new work is forming itself. *Sempre avanti*!

I have one more movement to finish work on a piano suite of 5 movements [*Carnival Music*]: "fanfares-march"; "blues"; "largo doloroso"; "sfumato"; "toccata-rag." The titles already tell you something about the nature of the music. I won't describe it as a "light" work but it leans that way. It's "tonal"—though not without excursions to the periphery. I'm presently obsessed with the need to write genuinely tonal music with all the attendant aspects of melody, accompaniment, etc. It's like breathing clean air again. This necessity made it possible for me to go back to my 1st Symphony & revise it completely, virtually putting it back into its original 1948/49 form of 5 movements, reinstating large cuts made later. I'll make the new score this fall/winter. Also I have some notational revisions to make in *Tableaux*, about 1/2 of it. And after hearing the *Krishna* songs I've come to the conclusion that some of them need more work. So there's no end of work to be done. Meanwhile, the 4th Symphony is taking shape in my head & I'll get to it when all the present things are copied, revised, etc. At the same time there's my plan to do a monodrama based on Robert Lowell's *Phaedra* which he's granted me permission to use.[7] I have to clear it with his publisher now. Last but not least Gene & I have cooked up an idea for an opera. If we can get the rights I will go ahead. But that may be years from now. I especially look forward to discussing the opera problem with you. To date I have studied, listened to, etc. *Don Giovanni*, *Boris Godounov*, *Elektra*, *Rake's Progress*. This gave me a "spread" of styles, traditions, languages, etc.; the first two, it goes without saying, are incredible both as music and as lyric theater. *Elektra* is already too neurasthenic, it's unbalanced in its relentless fanatic concentration on achieving one single goal, dramatically & musically. The *Rake* is too self-conscious, too arch. One of the basic problems as I see it is to be able to distinguish & define musically, therefore dramatically, levels of action & feeling. The leitmotif-ridden style of *Elektra* allows no distinctions in levels. That's why even the quasi-recitatives are like arias & the arias like quasi-recitatives. Frankly I prefer Mozart's way. I will have to do a lot more studying & thinking before it's clear to me what attitude I want to take. All this will also have a bearing on decisions affecting the language question. An "atonal" style is deadly to opera—maybe not for a monodrama (but even [Schoenberg's] *Erwartung* sounds tiresome now). It's too screwed up, too tight. Especially in an opera where there are light or comic moments, the language must allow sufficient leeway for these effects to come through. And so on & so on. You can see why I want to talk to you about all this.

I'm reading a fascinating book which I think you'd enjoy too—the correspondence between Romain Rolland & Richard Strauss.[8] Try to get hold of it. […]

George

59

22 JULY 1971

Dear Isty,

[…] Since my letter to you the following has developed: my publisher has arranged for a recording of *Tableaux* with Vox to be done by the Monadnock Festival people in Keene, N[ew] H[ampshire] (players from N[ew] Y[ork], Boston, etc.).[9] Recording & live performance Aug. 21 & 23. So now I must plan to be there at least for the 18th or 19th to be at rehearsals. So now I'm afraid we won't be able to get together—which I regret more than I can say. Let's keep in close touch anyhow & once you're settled in Kingston let us know how things are. Maybe we can work out a plan for a fall meeting or winter.

I'm looking forward very much to the recording of *Foci*. Please let me know when it's released. Incidentally, about the IIIrd [Symphony] tape. Steve Albert has left Calif[ornia] as of July 17th. But if you already mailed the tape undoubtedly it will be forwarded to him. […]

George

60

30 SEPTEMBER 1971

Dear Isty,

[…] I'm sending you enclosed a long-winded diatribe re science which I read to the Am[erican] Assoc[iation] of Physics Teachers last winter. What surprised me was the number of scientists who agreed with me. When the "Avant-garde & the Aesthetics of Survival" which incorporates some of the enclosed appears in the *New Literary History* published by Univ[ersity] of Virg[inia] I'll send you a reprint.[10] I don't expect you will agree with everything but would like your reactions. Last night Gene & I went to see *The Hellstrom Chronicle*.[11] It shook me up. All day I've been asking myself how human beings can resolve the dilemma of attaining individual consciousness & freedom without eventually destroying the race itself. The excesses of capitalism & profit plus the arrogance of refusing to accept limitations of resources plus the parallel excesses of individualism & its arrogant refusal to recognize any restraints or limitations—these are the rampaging forces which seem to threaten us. And who or what can stop it? But we must go on with our work & make the beautiful symbols & metaphors—that is our real talent. […]

George

NOTES

1 See "1965," note 3.

2 Edwin London (b. 1929), Philadelphia-born composer and conductor; he has taught at Smith College and the University of Illinois and in 1978 was appointed chair of the Music Department at Cleveland State University, where, in 1980, he founded the Cleveland Chamber Symphony.

3 *Foci* and *Cento*, Phyllis Mailing (mezzo-soprano) (1929–2004) and Ensemble instrumentale de Montréal (in *Foci*), and Tudor Singers of Montreal (in *Cento*), both conducted by the composer, Montreal: Radio Canada International, 357 (MS-9398–9) (ca. 1972). *Foci* and *Cento* were reissued in *Anthology of Canadian Music/Anthologie de la musique canadienne*, Montreal: Radio Canada International, ACM 22 (1985). *Foci* was recently reissued again on compact disc, Toronto: Canadian Music Centre, Centrediscs CMCCD 10204 (2004), along with the first commercial recording of *The Tents of Abraham* (2003) and an Anhalt documentary produced and presented by Eitan Cornfield.

4 Anhalt became Chair of the Music Department at Queen's University in 1971.

5 *Carnival Music*, Suite for Solo Piano (1971).

6 John Kraglund, "Anhalt a Composer? Results Raise Doubts," *The Globe and Mail*, 22 May 1971. Kraglund's mean-spirited *ad hominem* review of *Foci* clearly transgresses the boundaries of professionalism: "But all efforts to recall one of his compositions that could be called unquestionably musical have proved in vain." By way of contrast, Toronto's other major music critic of the time penned a thoughtful and favourable response to the work: "*Foci* … is much more than a piece of music. It is an exploration of man's internal and external perceptions, a search for meaning amid confusion and a recognition of the failure of final answers." William Littler, "*Foci*: A Vivid Multi-media Composition," *The Toronto Star*, 22 May 1971.

7 Robert Lowell (1917–77), American poet who won the Pulitzer Prize twice, for *Lord Weary's Castle* (1946) and for *The Dolphin* (1973); his verse translation of Jean Racine's *Phèdre* (*Phaedra*) was originally published in New York by Farrar, Straus and Cudahy in 1961.

8 *Richard Strauss and Romain Rolland: Correspondence*, together with fragments from the diary of Romain Rolland and other essays and an introduction by Gustave Samazeuilh, ed. and annotated with a preface by Rollo Myers (Berkeley: University of California Press, 1968).

9 *Tableaux* (Sound Pictures from "The Silver Talons of Piero Kostrov," by Paul Rochberg), Jan DeGaetani, mezzo-soprano, and the Penn Contemporary Players,

Richard Wernick, conductor, Turnabout TV-S 34492 (1973). The recording Rochberg mentions does not seem to have materialized, at least not commercially.

10 "The Avant-Garde and the Aesthetics of Survival," *New Literary History: A Journal of Theory and Interpretation* 3/1 (1971–72): 71–92; reprinted in Rochberg, *Aesthetics of Survival* (1984), 215–31; rev. and expanded ed. (2004), 225–41.

11 This 1971 quasi-documentary film, produced and directed by Walon Green, features impressive microphotography of insects of the world and is based on the premise that insects, because of extraordinary powers of adaptability, could one day endure on earth where humans would fail; the film won the Grand Prix de Technique at the 1971 Cannes Film Festival.

1972

61

5 FEBRUARY 1972

My Dear Isty,

[…] Yesterday I finished my 3rd String Quartet which I've written for the Concord Quartet (a new & very young group). They introduce it in N[ew] Y[ork] May 15.[1] Wish you could be there! […]

George

62

14 APRIL 1972

My Dear Isty,

I'm writing this now so that it will reach you if you already returned from your trip to Hungary and if not, will be there when you do return. It was more than good to hear from you & to know that all is well. I look forward very much to reading your lectures and hope you had great success with them. What a sensation that must be—returning to the place you grew up, the place which saturated your heart & blood with so much that was good & beautiful and also terrible. But to return in triumph—that's the victory. I look forward to hearing more about it when you can find the time.

I knew when I sent you the "Survival" paper[2] that it might not meet with your entire approval; but we are old & close friends, like brothers, and it is important we know which way we are thinking. Besides it is very important for me, despite the fact that I am usually completely convinced at the time I believe something to be true even if later I should change my mind (and how many times have I already done that!), & have the resistance of a mind as sharp & keen as yours in order to test my ideas & feelings. What I wrote in no way excludes your interest in vocal composition and any other methodology associated with it. What I tried to say was that we must find our way back to making human statements which have such clarity of vision, such identity of profile, such mastery of means & the craft to use those means that the end result as art goes directly into the channels of the C[entral] N[ervous] S[ystem] & re-forms itself there as an intensely convincing experience. When I use the word " tonal" I mean it in the broadest possible sense including everything that exists & could exist whose primary qualities & characteristics are such that they do not go against the CNS but open it up to maximum response. In this sense *Cento* is "tonal" for me. I would have to experience *Foci* again to discover its shape & design; but knowing the incredible clarity of your mind, I would expect *Foci* to turn out to be "tonal" in this sense I'm describing. But undoubtedly you understand that at the present time I'm obsessed with the narrower meaning of "tonal" in my own work. The new quartet which gets launched May 15 at [Alice] Tully Hall, N[ew] Y[ork] (how I wish you could fly down to hear it!) is the closest I've come so far to grasping the essence of tonality. Aside from the obvious places (the Variations in A major, the Serenades in the Finale which are in D, etc.) I've tried to organize the whole work on the basis of simple & direct gestures with melodies & accompaniments. Probably the fact that the work is ironic in spirit will escape most people. They will I expect hear the "romanticism" of it. The real excitement for me in writing it was to rediscover the energy of pulse. There are 2 marches and also a great deal of *allegro vivace* which plays with & around the beat.

I'm about to launch into the monodrama based on Lowell's *Phaedra* (which he based on Racine)[3] and want to go even further into recapturing the force & drive of energies organized around pulse & beat especially so that the singer can literally ride on the motion built into the ensemble. The sense of this is of course very close to the old ways of Mozart & Rossini & Verdi (but not Wagner; or Strauss except maybe in *Rosenkavalier*) but just as close to Hindi music & jazz or even rock where the propulsive force is taken care of by percussion & releases the solo instruments or singers from having to do all the pushing. It also requires an objectification of the music, something difficult for me after so many years of Expressionism. […]

George

63

7 AUGUST 1972

My dear George,

It is a long time since I have written. It is not a long time since I thought of you. In fact you are often in my mind, a non-changing pattern for the past twelve years. In fact you were in my mind when I was in Hungary especially when I made a rediscovery of a long-lost friend (more of this later). I thought: how fortunate I am, not only did I reestablish a dear friendship, but I was also able to make a "new" one (yours) rather late in life for such a development.

So why not to start with Hungary (or did I write about this to you already? I don't think so). It was an event-packed, on the whole pleasant, and without reservation an exciting descent into the pit of the past, as well as the discovery of some new things. First the place: Budapest is a beautiful, sophisticated old city. I roamed the well-remembered streets, glanced up to windows beyond which well-remembered things were, and events took place 26 and more years ago. I sampled well-remembered foods, listened to familiar sing-songs of speech, and watched, listened, in general felt soaked in the ambience. I was a bit reticent of going back. I was afraid that I shall find Nazi-minded people, thinly disguised, who would awake in me hate and fear, and disdain. I did seem to have glimpsed a few such faces, but they were in the minority, by far. The country did seem to have changed, and especially the younger people 30 and under are a most appealing attractive lot. I have met with children (having visited schools from kindergarten to the Academy of Music), and young adults, and I was pleased to observe an almost general friendliness, openness, hunger for intellectual stimulation and a readiness to listen to the other man's ideas. There was generosity: people, students, young musicians appeared in my hotel and brought presents, leaving them at the reception with a brief note of "thanks for your talks," or an inscription in a score, etc. I met two superbly talented young composers, A. Bozay and Z. Jeney, both around 30.[4] They have to struggle all right, but are receiving performances, can eke out a living by writing music, and one of them is on a publication contract to the state publisher, which gives him a reasonable monthly income. Both write uncompromisingly and inventively. They are very well informed about the state of the art, and travel occasionally.

The greatest thrill for me was the meeting of an old friend J.-G. Szilágyi[5] whom I did not see for 30(!) years, and had no correspondence with him either. We came to know each other at the age of 19 and were friends for a few years (about 4) until the war separated us. He was a student of classical philology, and soon after obtaining his Ph.D. was sucked into the hell of WW II, just as I was, at the end of 1942. In 1944 he fell into the hands of the Russians, who made no difference at the time between a captured German SS man and a Hungarian Jewish labour-camp inmate. After 3 harrowing years in Russia he was let free. Upon his return to Budapest he got a job (the only available and remotely suitable at the time) at the Museum of Fine Arts, Antiquities Section. There he became interested in Etruscan art, and during the past 25 or so years he became (so our friends say) one of the foremost experts in the field in the world. Has published over 250 papers, and 5 or more books on the subject and at present is the head of the museum's antiquities section. He is a superb mind, alive to an incredibly vast spectrum of ideas, and data. He is not only conversant with the newest of artistic developments in art (he is very knowledgeable about concept art), music, and literature, but is able to integrate a new development with an old one through his enormous knowledge and perceptivity. I know of no other person who resembles what I imagine Borges to be. (Strangely he read no Borges, but often speaks with a mock-scholarly language, a form of his humour which reminds me of certain passages, <u>not</u> humorous, of Borges.) He and I walked through half-nights on at least 4 occasions while I was there, and savoured that thrill of rediscovering each other. (He made me very happy by letting me know that our meetings meant a great deal to him also.) There were other friends to meet also. I could write about several at length as well. But none of them came as close as J.-G. Szilágyi whom I would very much like to bring over here on an extended visit. (Wouldn't it be great if all three of us could be together!) These friends, the remnants of our old circle of poets, essayists, etc., and others met a few times while I was there and the warmth and intimacy was really moving. There are many details that would be of interest to you but I save them for our next meeting to tell you about them. I am certain that they will remain fresh in my mind. The only thing which was not right in Hungary was Bea's absence. Next time she'll come with me.

[...]

I shall mail you under separate cover the record of *Cento* and *Foci* which came out a few weeks ago, as well as a copy of my old *Fantasia* for piano which just was released by Berandol Ltd. The same firm will release shortly the study score of *Foci* also.

As soon as I got in Montreal from Kingston (July 3rd) I began finally the composition of *La Tourangelle* (the life story of Marie de l'Incarnation, the 17th-c[entury] French-Canadian nun, founder of the first Ursuline Convent in Quebec in 1639). It is a pantomime oratorio for a mime,[6] 3 live female and 2 male voices, many other tape-recorded voices, and a chamber ensemble of about 10 instruments. A children's choir will also be used either live or recorded. The work will be in 2 parts[7] and I am working on the first one which will conclude with her arrival in Quebec. There will be 6 sections (movements) in it and about the same number in the second part. The first part will be about 35 minutes [it became 64 minutes] and the whole work about double [that]. The piece is a CBC commission, and is scheduled for premiere in 1974. It goes very well and I have sketched about the half of the 1st part in a "first draft." The style of the work is rather eclectic and it flows so strongly (after all I have lived with the idea of the piece through several versions of the libretto now for more than a year) that I am almost a follower of its "voice," rather than its initiator. The "field work" of this piece is also of great interest. Readings into Canadian and French history, visits to the oldest Ursuline convent in Quebec, contacts with the nuns, Jesuits, etc. (Don't you think I went crazy!?) The whole thing came about because CBC asked me to write a piece about "man's quest for order and meaning in life through religion." I wanted to combine it with a Canadian framework. As it is, due to the strength of its central figure, it has (that is the theme) great depth, topicality, as well as universality. […]

Istvan

PS: There is question of publication of the texts of my Hungarian lectures. One way or another you will get a copy of these before long.[8] […]

64

21 SEPTEMBER 1972

My Dear Isty,

Since your letter arrived (a truly remarkable letter which Gene & I read & reread, talked about at great lengths & which is still with me because its expressions & images are so keenly human & vivid) I have been trying to find a space of time in which I could have the amplitude to reply, to tell you of our doings. Finally & at last today is such a time. Actually when your letter came I was in the thick of a new chamber work (for the Aeolian Ch[amber] Players)[9] which needed to be done before school started (which it now has) so that parts could be prepared in time for an adequate rehearsal period before the Dec. perf[ormance] it's scheduled for. In addition there was much commotion with my publisher who is an out & out rotter, bad faith again (the machinery starts to break down but one manages), much coming & going of visitors, etc. It has been a very packed summer & really a good one, perhaps one of the best in years. Gene & I took off for the shore (Jersey; our favorite place) in late May, stayed through the month of June. We put together an outline of our projected opera on *Steppenwolf* of Hesse (& are currently working toward getting an option to proceed with the work),[10] a quasi-libretto for a monodrama based on Robert Lowell's version of *Phaedra*; I wrote an article on Schoenberg for the centenary issue(s) of *Perspectives of New Music*;[11] we ate lots of fish; we sunned ourselves; […] we walked "on the Strand" a great deal; we read enormous quantities of stuff (I got hooked on *Black Elk*; & *Bury My Heart at Wounded Knee*, the story of how we did in the American Indians, became a form of racial penance every day when I could get to it).[12] In July we went to Aspen to attend some performances of *Tableaux* & *Magic Theater* which were done creditably. Colorado was beautiful. By the time we got back it was already the end of July & I had to get moving on the new chamber piece. Gene & I have begun to feel that we could live the rest of our lives as we did this summer. There's enough to do simply & together to make every day a full one of work. Frankly, while I enjoy teaching at the moment I'm involved, I begin to feel more & more it is a useless appendage to my existence & of course I'm beginning to try to figure out how I can "retire" early & still maintain a viable economic existence (*Piano, piano! Va sano, va lontano*. ["Softly, softly, go healthy, go far away"]). […]

I've rambled on endlessly about our activities but really want to tell how deeply moved I was by your account of your trip to Budapest. The image of the students leaving presents for you, the scenes of reunion with old friends, the sense of a world recaptured after it had seemed to be gone forever—I felt all of it through your words. Life in this century has been so incredibly difficult for so many people—& I can only guess what you must have gone through in those days when you finally had to leave everything behind & begin all over again in Canada. It's nothing short of an act of redeeming the very possibility of existence for people like yourself who has given himself to art & people rather than power & money that you went back in absolute triumph. I can imagine the sensations of wonder that it not only happened to you but that it <u>could</u> happen to anyone. And to regain an old & dear friendship. That is one of the sweetest of all things in life. I was more than deeply touched that you should include your thoughts of me in all of this remarkable experience. You must know, of course, that I reciprocate all your feelings toward me and regret only that distance keeps us from seeing each other more often. There are all too few people with whom one feels such a strong tie & undercurrent of deep connection that only to them can one open one's heart. Life being what it is, one learns to be guarded & wary & not to open oneself at all or at least not too much—an act of pure self-defense—but with you I have always felt a deep bond, a sense of brotherliness & spiritual communion. That's why what you say & experience is of primary interest & concern to me. It would be marvellous to make a threesome with your old friend from Budapest. Perhaps it will be a reality one day.

I'm intrigued by your plan for your new work & will look forward to progress reports as you get into it. I'm especially delighted *Cento* & *Foci* are recorded. When you can, please send me a copy. Your old friend is going in retrograde while you plunge into deeper & deeper mysteries. The middle movement of the Third Quartet which was introduced last May & seems to have made more than a little ripple is <u>tonal</u>; so are large chunks of the <u>Finale</u>; also the new piece contains an adagio in F♯ major/minor. So it goes. But perhaps to balance this tendency off, I find myself more & more involved in purely metric/rhythmic matters, am always "turned on" by Hindu sub-divisions. So some of this has found its way into the new works. I remain, as ever, unsatisfied with what is, with what I do, constantly trying to find another way to crystallize my dream of music & life. […] I keep wrestling with the 20th century.

If you could possibly make one of your old-fashioned jaunts down to N[ew] Y[ork] for Dec. 19—we could see each other & listen to the new piece together. I hope this will be possible.

Next summer Gene & I will go to Japan. I have been invited to read a paper for the <u>Int[ernational] Society for the Study of Time</u>.[13] I wish I could say I were confident of my ability to deliver a paper up to the quality of the other members of this august group of brains. It's far from false modesty. I've been reading some of their stuff (Brandon & Eliade, Whitrow & John Cohen, etc.) & admire enormously their erudition & command.[14] I'll have to start wrestling with the paper sometime this winter. It's not ideas I'm lacking for; it's the sense of certainty as to the best way to proceed not to speak of a certain sense of uncertainty about the validity of my ideas on time in music. In the end, I'll just have to grab the bull by the horns & trust to my intuitive sense of what is right. In any case, the prospect of seeing Japan is very exciting for both of us.

[…]

George

65

11 DECEMBER 1972

My dear Isty,

[…] I feel I have entered into an entirely new & different phase of existence—but can hardly describe or depict it for you or myself—perhaps if we could talk I could find a way to express it—one thing is certain: it affects my whole outlook on life & music, has intensified my sense of the worthlessness of so much that human beings seem to value & pursue while at the same time it has brought me to the center of my obsession with music—holy music—yet I feel totally inadequate to find the way to formulate in pattern & design & structure what grips me—for now anyhow—perhaps in time it will emerge.

I thank you for your music—the piano piece is a beautiful, rich, feelingful soundscape of sonorities—it gives the piano a true voice.[15] Having the recording of *Foci* & *Cento* has made it possible to get closer to both. I have always liked *Cento* for its peculiar poetry, its intensity & drama—it comes across with great presence & no diminishment of the power of a live performance. Forgive me, but I suppose I will always remain outside of the aesthetic of *Foci*. There are beautiful parts (definition 2; prefacatory [*sic*], the last section with soprano); you see, I've chosen the more obviously "musical" parts revealing completely my conservative stance.[16] I think that it is the speech elements which I can't absorb, which remain "foreign" to my hearing. Intellectually, I find the organization of the work brilliant and always focused, centered—it has its strange way of compelling one's attention. You'll have to put me down as an old back-slider, I'm afraid, though because I want to hear the instruments & singer rather than the spoken elements. […]

George

NOTES

1 The String Quartet No. 3 was premiered by the Concord String Quartet at Alice Tully Hall, New York, on 15 May 1972.

2 See "1971," note 10.

3 *Phaedra*, a monodrama for mezzo-soprano and orchestra (1973–74), based on texts adapted freely by Gene Rochberg from Robert Lowell's play based on Racine's *Phèdre*.

4 Attila Bozay (1939–99), Hungarian composer, a graduate of the Liszt Academy of Music in Budapest, where he was appointed professor of orchestration and composition in 1979; Zoltán Jeney (b. 1943), Hungarian composer, a composition stu-

dent at the Liszt Academy of Music in Budapest and with Goffredo Petrassi in Rome; he was a leading figure in Hungarian avant-garde circles in the 1970s; he joined the faculty of the Liszt Academy of Music in 1986, becoming head of the composition department in 1995.

5 János-György Szilágyi (b. 1918), leading authority on Etruscan art. Curator Emeritus of the Greco-Roman Department, Museum of Fine Arts in Budapest.

6 The mime aspect was subsequently dropped.

7 The second part was never undertaken.

8 These lectures were not published in Hungarian but were incorporated later into Anhalt, *Alternative Voices* (1984).

9 *Electrikaleidoscope*, for amplified flute, clarinet, violin, cello, piano, and electric piano (1972), commissioned by the Aeolian Chamber Players and premiered by them at Town Hall, New York, 19 December 1972.

10 Because of the prohibitive fee demanded by Hesse's son for the rights, this work was abandoned. Previously, in 1965, Rochberg used *Steppenwolf* as the source for the title of *Music for the Magic Theater* and quotes a passage from the novel at the head of the score.

11 "Reflections on Schoenberg," *Perspectives of New Music* 11/2 (Spring-Summer 1973): 56–83; reprinted in Rochberg, *Aesthetics of Survival* (1984), 46–68; rev. and expanded ed. (2004), 36–58.

12 *Black Elk Speaks: Being the Life Story of a Holy Man of the Oglala Sioux*, as told through John G. Neihardt (Flaming Rainbow) (Lincoln: University of Nebraska Press, 1961); Dee Brown, *Bury My Heart at Wounded Knee: An Indian History of the American West* (New York: Holt, Rinehart & Winston, 1970).

13 "The Structure of Time in Music: Traditional and Contemporary Ramifications and Consequences," in *The Study of Time*, vol. 2, *Proceedings of the Second Conference of the International Society for the Study of Time, Lake Yamanaka—Japan*, ed. J.T. Fraser and N. Lawrence for the International Society for the Study of Time (Berlin, Heidelberg, New York: Springer-Verlag, 1975), 136–49; abbreviated and slightly revised version reprinted in Rochberg, *Aesthetics of Survival*, 137–47.

14 Samuel George Frederick Brandon (1907–71), Professor of Comparative Religion at the University of Manchester; see, in particular, *History, Time and Deity* (Manchester: Manchester University Press, 1965). Mircea Eliade (1907–86), Romanian-born philosopher of religion; from 1958 until his death he was affiliated with the University of Chicago; see, in particular, *Cosmos and History: The Myth of the Eternal Return*, trans. Willard R. Trask (New York: Harper, 1959). For Whitrow see "1963," note 1. Rochberg did not recall the reference to Cohen; the reference may be to the psychologist John Cohen (b. 1911), author of such books as *Human Robots in Myth and Science* (1966), *Psychological Time in Health and Disease* (1967), and *Homo Psychologus* (1970).

15 Presumably the *Fantasia* for piano (1954), which was published in 1972 (Toronto: Berandol Music) and recorded by Glenn Gould (see "1968," note 3).

16 *Foci* (Toronto: Berandol Music, 1972); Rochberg is referring to the following parts of the score: "Definition 2" (Section 4), 30–35; "Preparation" (Section 8), 70–88; and "Testimony" (Section 9), 89–120.

1973

66

23 DECEMBER 1973

My dear friend Isty,

So much time, so many events (private and public) have taken place, so much of what we call "life" has flowed past us since I last wrote. It was not negligence or forgetting that kept me from being in touch but a crazy combination of being taken up by much activity so that the surface constantly seemed in a constant boil and of being inwardly (& paradoxically) silent, withdrawn, at loose ends, disaffected by a world I no longer recognize even though somewhere I always dimly suspected its possibility. But let me drop this gloomy tone & before launching into a brief account of our lives this year wish you & Beate & your lovely girls the very best of everything & especially health for the coming year so that work & dreams may be realized to the extent being human allows. For Gene & me it would be an especially happy time to be able to see you all & spend time together in the old way—sitting around a table somewhere talking, exchanging views & stories, being alive together. But until that can happen I must, like the old shoemaker, stick to my last. Work has piled up and must be accomplished even while a large part of me longs to be free, to roam the world seeing old friends, doing nothing in particular. I'm sure you are thoroughly familiar with the syndrome.

To begin somewhere I was deeply involved with work & papers until we left for Japan late June to attend a conference of the Int[ernational] Soc[iety] for the Study of Time. I read a paper,[1] listened to mountains of other papers for a week at Mt. Fuji. From there we went to Kyoto & then after 6 days to Tokyo for a few days, then home—very reluctantly!

We loved the old Japan of temples & shrines, *Noh* & *Kabuki*; we were even intrigued by the new Japan but it is frightening in its intensity, technology, all-consuming passion. We heard some music, not nearly enough; met some lovely people, including musicians, walked about as best we could in the awful heat that lies on the Kyoto–Tokyo belt like a pall, drank in as much as we could from trains, buses, taxis, ate food that delighted us. In short we had a marvellous time. That was all before the energy crisis of course. I can't imagine what the effect of the crisis will be ultimately on a Japan which is bent on being as "modern" as possible. But even the glimpse we had, especially of the old culture, made an indelible impression. When we arrived home the culture shock was enormous. We had become thoroughly enchanted with the diminutive Japanese (though the young are elongating), their refinement, their physical attractiveness. Suddenly here were all these hulking, big, fat, bland Americans! It was weeks before I got over it! Maybe that was what caused my small intestine irritation which got the better of me in August–Sept. but finally simmered down & seems to have cleared up. Fortunately I began a sabbatical leave this fall so that I was totally on my own and once recovered could get down to work again.

The spirit of Japan entered so strongly that the new piece I've just finished for the Baltimore Symphony contains more than an indirect reference to *Gagaku* whose melodies I find both incredibly elegant & sad at the same time; & whether Mahler ever heard them or not some spiritual cross-cutting is there. The piece which I call *Imago Mundi* will be done in May.[2] It is different in so many ways from my IIIrd Quartet that I fully expect everyone who thought that now they knew what I was up to will be completely discomfited & wonder at my inconstancy & inconsistency. Incidentally, I'm sending you a copy of the IIIrd Quartet and hope you won't find it too regressive. Now that *Imago Mundi* is finished Gene & I hope to go south for a rest & vacation for 10 days or so. When we return I want to finish my *Phaedra* for soprano & chamber orchestra which I began in Feb. of this year. By spring I need to begin work on a violin concerto for Isaac Stern which the Pittsburgh Symphony has asked me to do.[3] That's as far ahead as I dare to think. I have an all-pervasive sense of our heading into very difficult & strange times. The stranger the feeling the more resistant I feel, not to the idea of change itself but to the kind of change. Still I have to add that somewhere in the dimly perceived future following these new conditions we're already in I sense an alleviation, a brightening, a new health & sanity, even a music which will be beautiful again (that may be pure wishful thinking!). But for now the immediate reality is on us and the old world into which we were born & grew up into & even helped make in part in small ways is being shed, leaving me feeling curiously empty, anxious, puzzled, constantly beset by the uncertainty of every human enterprise including (& sometimes especially) my own. I live mostly with the sense that everything is leaving us but our defiant will to live & the passions that flow from that. In a curious way it's like feeling that the 20th century which was a very bad nightmare in so many ways is over & done with & we're in a tunnel leading to the 21st, we're somewhere between & we no longer have what we thought we had (however much we may have resented or disliked it), nor do we have or know what lies ahead. In such situations (& I'm sure this is far from the first time) we are quite literally reduced to whatever nature blessed & cursed us with. I speak very generally of course & maybe very incorrectly. But in some crazy odd way it all sheds a new light & new necessity on music & making it. What kind of music? For what purpose? These days I feel only one answer which is as stripped down as can be: to comfort ourselves in the dark, to enliven our presence, our passage. Nothing more noble than that. […]

George

NOTES

1 See "1972," note 13.

2 *Imago Mundi (Image of the World)*, for large orchestra (1973), commissioned by the Baltimore Symphony Orchestra and premiered by them, Sergiu Commissiona, conductor, at the Lyric Theater, Baltimore, 8 May 1974; the work makes use of elements and gestures of traditional Japanese *Gagaku* music.

3 Concerto for Violin and Orchestra (1974), commissioned by the Pittsburgh Symphony Orchestra for Isaac Stern and premiered by them, Donald Johanes, conductor, at Heinz Hall, Pittsburgh, 4 April 1975.

1974

67

9 DECEMBER 1974

My dear Isty,

It was good to get your letter and the news that *La Tourangelle* was in the final, final stages of completion. You know my best wishes go to you for its successful production. If it comes at a time when we are free I'd love to make the trip to hear/see it.

Paul's memorial concert was a great success in every way. Gene & I were more than gratified by the way everything turned out—musically & humanly. There were two works on the concert: Schoenberg Suite Op. 29 (& an excellent performance of it) & the 1st performance of a large work for mezzo & chamber ensemble by Jay Reise,[1] who is a former student of Hugh Hartwell—both of whom in their day held Paul's scholarship. The fact of this kind of connection with genuinely gifted young men has given the creation of the scholarship itself a special kind of reality & meaningfulness.

The concert, itself a high point, came in the midst of what has been for me an incredibly busy & at times difficult period. Since Sept. I have been working at the score of my violin concerto (for Isaac Stern) & only just finished it this past Friday. I suppose if I didn't also have to teach parallel with the intensity of my crazy way of working things would have been easier. As it is I find myself welcoming the close of the term & look forward with special pleasure to our trip to Sarasota in Jan. for 10 days just to be in the sun & away from paper & work. But this will be all too brief since, on the returning, school starts again & I must turn to thinking of how to write some new works which are commissioned. It is not the writing of more music which I sometimes dread—quite the contrary—the appetite & need for that is as strong, perhaps stronger than ever. What I dread is the constant language problem. Since the *Magic Theater* & *Contra* of almost 10 years ago not two works have been the same at least in outward appearance; & I find it increasingly difficult to find still another way, another approach, no matter how subtle the shift of attitude. The violin concerto is a good case in point & I will have to hear it before I can honestly judge what I have done. Since the first performances are in April in Pittsburgh I'll know soon enough. If there's the slightest chance you can come to hear it in New York April 15 at Carnegie please let me know. I'll try to get tickets for you. It would be good to see you again & have one of our old talks which I miss so much. […]

George

NOTE

1 Jay Reise (b. 1950), American composer, student of George Crumb, Hugh Hartwell, and Richard Wernick; Robert Weiss Professor of Composition at the University of Pennsylvania. The work performed on this occasion was, presumably, *Movements of Imagination*, for soprano and large chamber orchestra (1974). See also his article, "Rochberg the Progressive," *Perspectives of New Music* 19/1 (Fall–Winter 1980) and 19/2 (Spring–Summer 1981): 395–407.

1975

68

16 JULY 1975

My dear Isty,

The time rushes by & suddenly it is the day before the birth of your *La Tourangelle*. I wish I could be there.[1] Nothing would make me happier than to hear your music with you and to have a long talk like we used to. You'll understand I know when I say that I am working again (a piano quintet which must be ready this fall) and can't break away—especially since I am only at the beginning.[2] But I wish the new work all success and a long life. […]

George

69

22 JULY 1975

My dear George,

[…] The premiere of *La Tourangelle* did take place on Thursday last week, and the work was very well received. (One of the critics said it was one of the shortest hours he has spent in recent years in a concert hall …).[3] It is a strange piece stylistically, and I am very eager to have your reaction to it. I shall not have a tape until sometime in the fall, after we have assembled a final tape of the several "takes" during the last rehearsal and that of the performance itself. […]

When will a tape of the Violin Concerto become available? Good work on the piano quintet!

Istvan

NOTES

1 *La Tourangelle* was premiered, in a concert performance, with Mary Morrison and Roxolana Roslak, sopranos, Phyllis Mailing, mezzo-soprano, Albert Greer, tenor, Gary Relyea, baritone, Marius Constant, conductor, at the MacMillan Theatre, Faculty of Music, University of Toronto on 17 July 1975.

2 Quintet for Piano and String Quartet (1975), written for Jerome Lowenthal and the Concord String Quartet and premiered by them at Alice Tully Hall, New York, 15 March 1976.

3 See John Kraglund, "Memorable Moments in Uneven *Tourangelle*," *The Globe and Mail*, 18 July 1975, and Louis Applebaum, "Premiere of a Major Anhalt Work," *The Whig Standard* (Kingston), 19 July 1975. Applebaum (1918–2000), an important Canadian composer in his own right, perhaps best remembered for his many scores for films, television, and radio, wrote in his review: "The oratorio, cantata or whatever conventional label one might wish to apply to this unconventional work, is written for five singers, a chamber orchestra of 16 players, two tape machines and sundry assistant conductors, page turners, tape starters and volume controllers. It is played without a break in just a bit more than an hour and it turned out to be one of the shortest hours I have spent in a concert hall in recent years."

1976

70

5 FEBRUARY 1976

My dear Isty,

I've just come up for air after another concentrated spate of work and decided it was time to be in touch with a friend whom I feel I've neglected—but you understand, not intentionally—it seems as though the last 2 years have gone solely into work & the more I work the more I withdraw from a world which I find less & less congenial even at the very moment it seems to have decided to do more than glance my way occasionally—my long-standing sense of the paradoxical nature of human existence responds to this corroboration of intuition & also decides to let it be—since there is nothing one could or should do about it but go one's chosen way. Tonite I am besieged by a desire to see you, talk to you—to find out what has happened for you in your life & your music—all the things that count. I have not quite reached the stage of an old army friend who became a music critic in Cincinnati, then moved to Chicago to edit a magazine. He used to say: "when I want an intelligent conversation I talk to myself." Very Shavian, but the time for Shaw seems past & I frankly confess I have very little need to "talk" these days—even though life throws plenty of people in one's path who feel their existence only in the words, & not very enlightening ones at that. Since the Violin Concerto which Stern continues to play I've written a piano quintet which will be launched March 15 in N[ew] Y[ork]. It is one of those compendiums (about 50 minutes) in which I've thrown just about everything meaningful to me. As you know by now, I'm obsessed with the juxtaposition of tonal & non-tonal ideas; & as I go further in the tonal direction things are simplifying on the surface, complexifying beneath. I've just finished a baker's dozen *Partita-Variations* for piano solo[1] which pushes the juxtaposition even further, i.e., the tonal sections involve double c[ounter]p[oin]t, fugue, imitation, the non-tonal stretched in one piece, a rhythmic canon on a row (sic!), to my old stomping grounds. So it runs from A to Zerialism. With all these forays comes the increasing need for absolute classicism, the Haydn-Mozart kind. I like what Mozart wrote to his father: to the effect that he wanted the surface of his music to be appealing, attractive & the implicit level to be "learned." I think sometimes of the, depending on my mood, appealing surface of the human form (preferably female) & the incredible complexity it unifies. That may be a poor metaphor for what I have in mind but it indicates the direction I'm being pulled in. […]

George

71

19 FEBRUARY 1976

My dear George,

[…] Our lives go as follows. The major musical, etc. events of the last year were: the premiere of *La Tourangelle* on July 17th, in Toronto, in the MacMillan Theatre of the U[niversity] of T[oronto]. Marius Constant came from Paris to conduct it (the CBC has footed the bill, since the work was commissioned). It went well, after 19 hrs. of rehearsal time, which was far from extravagant given the duration (1 hr. 5 min.) of the work. The story takes the life of the "heroine" (Marie de l'Incarnation, the first Ursuline Superior in New France) up to the day of her (and her companions) arrival in Quebec in 1639. This performance meant a great deal to me as I poured much of myself into this work, or to say it better, I grew with it into unexpected directions between 1971–75. (Sometimes I was surprised at myself having gotten involved with her life, altogether.) But here it is and you can read the outline of the story in the program notes, a copy of which I am sending here. I do have a tape of the performance which is reasonably good. It is a large reel and I could only play it to you if we have a suitable professional machine. The idiom of the work is one that I have difficulty in describing. The central thread is constituted by 3 sopranos who, together, comprise the voice and personality of Marie de l'I[ncarnation]. Two live male voices declaim, sing as figures contemporary to her. About 12 tape-recorded voices represent a historical and a contemporary backdrop, and this is completed with two tape-recorded (for economic reasons) boys' choirs, one in English and one in French. (Incidentally, the work is in these two languages.) The overall character may be guessed at by the genre name I employed in suggesting a pointer to the audience: musical tableau in seven parts. The language (musical that is) is one that helped me to relive in a fashion the early decades of the 17th century. There are juxtapositions and superpositions of styles, and these are made to "melt" in various ways. In one part for example I wrote a six-minute-long quasi-Couperin-ian rondeau for piano, that starts out "all right," but gradually anamorphoses into something else. It is one of five "layers" in the fourth movement ("Isaac"). Etc. etc. It is hopeless to try to describe the piece. You have to hear it. I am very eager to know what you will say about it.

From your letter I sense that you have stepped up the level of intensity and concentration of your work. This is what really matters, apart from one's family. (But the children slowly detach themselves from the home, as it should be.) But is there something else, too, for you? Comparing myself to you I appear to myself as being almost leisurely with the job of putting things down on paper. For example I am spending an inordinate amount of time on an article about Ligeti's *Nouvelles Aventures*. The pages just grow ... I guess it will be more than an analysis. Perhaps it is a model for how to perceive a certain type of work.[2]

We shall be on sabbatical leave in 1976–77. Only one thing is certain about it. Our base away from home will be Cambridge, England, where I shall be working together with some linguists, and shall have some contact with the University Music School. [...] An eventuality that would bring me back to Canada is the prospect of the premiere of my *Symphony of Modules* by the U[niversity] of Toronto Symphony Orchestra under my direction. I was to do it last fall, but had to beg off it due to other work here. The premiere may take place in March, 1977.[3] Incidentally, I have accepted to serve another five years as head of dep[artmen]t (of which the first is the sabbatical). You may think I am crazy to do this. Possibly. But possibly the main cause is that I am bad at accepting orders (direct or veiled) ... In any case I don't mind this. One has to work at Queen's long hours anyhow, and I am used to the job. This term I am also teaching two courses in analysis, one of them being about post-1950 music. [...]

Istvan

NOTES

1 *Partita Variations*, for solo piano (1975–76), was commissioned by Etsuko Tazaki and premiered by her at the Kennedy Center, Washington, DC, 4 December 1976.

2 This eventually appeared as chapter 3, "Ligeti's *Nouvelles Aventures*: A Small Group as a Model for Composition," in Anhalt, *Alternative Voices: Essays on Contemporary Vocal and Choral Composition* (Toronto: University of Toronto Press, 1984), 41–92.

3 See "1966," note 1.

PART THREE

THE AESTHETICS OF SURVIVAL AND ALTERNATIVE VOICES (1981–1985)

Our "differences" I see as differences of, call it, personal proclivities, tendencies of mind and nature; and as I see it we share in too many things for those differences to matter that much. *Au contraire*, they forge an even closer link between us because I see them as complementing each other; i.e., it's as though your more "rational" initiating tendency all the while you are completely sensitive to and reaching over to the more feeling side of things forms the complementary polarity to my more "non-rational" initiating tendency while I strive to make my intuitive understanding of things clear and lucid, more "rational."

—Rochberg (January 1985)

George and Gene Rochberg, Newtown Square, Pennsylvania, February 1999. Photograph by Graydon Wood. Philadelphia Museum of Art.

1981

72

18 MARCH 1981

Dear Isty,

It is a wonderful feeling to have re-established our old friendship and I know you & Bea will be here in a matter of weeks. This is not even an "interim" letter. I shall pull out all the stops! When we last talked I was literally on the verge of finishing the orchestration of the opera;[1] and now, as of Monday, I can say it is actually done! What terrorizes me at odd moments is the fear that it won't work; or it will work but with massive revisions, etc. These kinds of fears have haunted me all my life; & there have been those times when they were prophetic! I am still sane enough & balanced enough to know whether I have done something good or not. In the case of the opera, despite the occasional seizures of doubt & worry, there is a strong sense in me (and in Gene whose judgments I've always trusted) that it is a strong & rich work. The surface of it is comic and essentially light; but as the tragedy of our Hero, China Astor, gathers force everything darkens. The opera is drawn from Melville's *The Confidence Man* which was his last published novel (in his lifetime) & which was rejected on all sides. It's not hard to see why from the vantage point of more than 100 years. When he published the book in 1856–57, America was feeling its oats—opening the west, building the railroads, everything in ferment and a general sense of Providence looking after her special child, the U.S. of A. Melville saw darker things: the abuse of trust & confidence, the illusion of progress, the corruption of values, the treachery of what he called "the man-show." How Melville would have bristled if he had heard that fool Nixon saying: Don't tell us what's wrong with America! Tell us what's right with America! Gene took the book which is horrendously convoluted & intuitively woven (no criticism actually of the book as far as I'm concerned; its very convolutions make for a curious richness of texture which makes his point even more telling!) & "simplified" it for theatrical-musical purposes. Besides weaving into the stuff of it the Con[fidence] M[an] himself she managed somehow (and brilliantly) to juxtapose the naiveté of our hero & heroine (his wife) and the trickery & worldliness of those around them. She underlined the opposition between "The Sober View" & "The Bright View" (Melville's terms). At the same time she told the story of China Astor simply & clearly and showed how the illusion of "The Bright View" can destroy the romantic, the idealist, the naive who approach life without defenses. The best part of it all for me is that she kept it from ever becoming didactic or preachy. For my part, I wrote a kind of music which is totally different for me—though not in all respects. I solved the problem (with Mozart's, Verdi's, & Puccini's help) of the aria/or song, the arioso &, I hope, narration—narration being the hardest part of it because there's always the danger of the music collapsing into dullness. The work is replete with solos, duets, trios, quartets. One of the special joys was treating the chorus as a "character," that of the town of Crystal City on the Mississippi where it all happens. I always loved *Boris* for its choruses; & even admire Britten's *Peter Grimes* for the same reason, though I like little else of his. Well, my dear old friend, this gives you a bird's-eye view of the work. Perhaps when you're here I can show it to you. I'd be happy to have your reaction. Strange we should both turn into "opera composers!" I need to know more of what you yourself have done. […]

George

NOTE

1 *The Confidence Man* (1980–82), libretto by Gene Rochberg after the novel by Herman Melville, commissioned by the Santa Fe Opera and premiered in Santa Fe, New Mexico, William Harwood, conductor, on 31 July 1982.

1982

73

7 FEBRUARY 1982

Dear George,

It is a day to be happy and celebrate: I got back a friend. You! Or, to put it better we proved it to each other that we have never lost our mutual friendship, which just slumbered during all these years while we went on in our separate trajectories (let's be more modest, at least for myself, and say: paths ...). It will, of course be of no surprise for me to find out that we have moved in parallel directions, at least to some extent, and during some of the time ... the discovery of our respective operas might be a first instance for such "aha" experiences ...

I shall resist the urge to launch into a 100+ page thing describing in detail the topography of our ups and downs during the years while we did not communicate in any other way but through thoughts. A few highlights will do for the moment, awaiting the day when we'll pull up to your driveway, ring the bell and embrace you ... Then will come the cups of coffee, feet up on something and gabbing in any order we can only fancy ... [...]

I do not even know if you are up-to-date with our removal from Montreal to Kingston in 1971, chiefly on account of the political climate in Quebec, which you know well about. When the bombs started to explode and political murders committed, we started to get uneasy. For us it was more difficult to take (and was more effective as an agent of influence) that some of our French-Canadian friends found it quite in order that certain unfair practices against non-French-Canadian persons are being proposed, prepared, and put into effect. This has clinched it for us, and made the difficult decision to leave more bearable. When Queen's U[niversity] in Kingston offered the headship of the Mus[ic] Dept. to me early in 1971, Bea was rather desperate, and when we finally got here was unhappy for at least 2 years. Only when we moved into our own home here (very nice, across the street from the R.C. Cathedral), she started to find her equilibrium again. It was much easier for me as I came into a ready-made situation with things to do and contacts waiting to play ball with. The compositional work just continued here. It does not depend on *locus* as far as I am concerned. Queen's U[niversity] is a fine place to work in, a mature institution with lots of excellent minds around and a good atmosphere for human contact in a measure one wants to have. I shall tell you about the Department in April. In fact it was an ideal move (to come here) from my point of view. I found out I was able to listen better here to my inner voices, and the character of this historical city awoke in me interests that were slumbering for a while before.

When we came here I was at the very early stages of working on a dramatic musical tableau, centered on the "life & times" of Marie de l'Incarnation, the French Ursuline, who was an early 17th-c[entury] Canadian pioneer. Why this theme? Why she? Well, there was a CBC commission to write a piece on the theme of "search for order and meaning in life through the focus of religion—the search for God in other words." I just "wrapped" it around a person: she, who, as it turned out, was a very fascinating woman, living during a fascinating period. The work was premiered in 1975 and the score is about to appear as published by Berandol Ltd. I also hope I shall be able to bring a copy along for you in April next.[1]

Since that work (entitled *La Tourangelle*) I am busy with two projects: a book and another dramatic work (I am not certain that I want to call it an opera, for reasons better left to tell about for our *viva voce* exchanges).

First about the book: it is called *Alternative Voices* and it is a collection of analyses & essays on contemporary "innovative" music (vocal & choral) for the voice. In it I am trying to speak substantively about the techniques that are involved, as well about the interdisciplinary relationships. I am also trying to trace the major recurring surface or "deep" themes that one can identify in this repertoire. The book, to be published by the U[niversity] of Toronto Press is in the hands of the copy-editor, and can be expected to appear hopefully before the end of 1983. Here I have a request to make. The only work by you that I included in the bibliography of scores is the *Passions*. Is there another work (or works) by you I should include? Please send me information about this, telling me about titles, years of completion, whether the work is published, or not, etc. This is fairly urgent, although could possibly wait until April. I am quite happy with the book. It is not a pedant's job (I couldn't have done it that way), although there is much information in it, but an idea book, and a picture about the way I came to think about other people's music. (About my own it is still a mysterious affair, and I am quite content to leave it in that happy, twilighty mist …)

The other project is a big one, too. I just completed the "short-score" of it (ca. 2½ hours). It is about John Winthrop, the first resident governor of the Massachusetts Bay Company, a paradigm of puritanism in America.[2] Of all people, why he, you may ask. There are several reasons for this. Given the bilingual and binational reality of Canada's (that is white Canada's) coming into nationhood and the present very sharp struggle between the two groups—the one (the French) clearly identifiable, the other (the English, Scotch, Ulstermen, those fleeing from South Africa, etc.) more amorphous. The earlier piece, based on the French heroine, demanded (from me) a "balancing" work. Looking for a figure from an Anglophone background, on this continent, roughly from the same historical moment, I found none in what is present-day Canada. But, then, Winthrop was not an American but a New Englander, whose foreign-affairs concerns dealt with about as much with the area north of Boston than with the territory south of it. Moreover thousands of Yankees immigrated in the period 1750–1775 into Nova Scotia from Massachusetts, Connecticut & Rhode Island. Hence a founding father of early 17th-c[entury] New England must also be considered a founding father of a segment of English Canada also.

The second reason in choosing Winthrop is because he was a fascinating man, with big dreams, but with a great deal of political savvy also. His failure in building a "Citty upon a Hill" is a failure that occurs, and reoccurs time again: we all carry in our hearts a Citty begun but never quite completed, perhaps because it is impossible to bring it about. The remaining questions are then: what did he manage to build, at what cost, and what way these influence our lives today?

There are still more reasons. Winthrop was an emigrant/immigrant, so am I. Winthrop is the spiritual ancestor to many fine persons I worked with together at McGill & at Queen's. I know their way of thinking and functioning (as a tribal-ethical comportment), yet they remain exotic enough figures for me to write about them. Finally, the group represented by Winthrop is a kind of underdog today, not so much in lacking power and money but more as having lost in some way public esteem. The WASP is in a way in bad odor, he is accused with all sort of ills, both in the shape of historical analysis, but also as a matter of current responsibility. There is, of course, much truth in the adverse criticism, but the whole thing might be coloured also by extraneous components that make the process somewhat suspect. Having studied the history of English Puritanism, and also the early history of the New England variety, I have the view that the theme is very complex, and there is a need for much circumspection when one approaches the question. In working on *Winthrop* I developed quite a strong feeling for the man, and see him & his little community in & around Boston as if I would have shared some of their experiences myself. Sometimes this was quite uncanny ... I save the details for April.

What does this amount to as production for the past 10–11 years? About 3½ hrs. worth of music in all, in the mode of historical accounts (through the "lens" of 2 psychologically extremely powerful persons), and an "idea-book." I am at peace with this, because I grew enough with this material, and this suggests that the available time was perhaps as well spent as can be expected.

I can hardly wait to hear from you news. I will have much pleasurable activity ahead of me while I shall endeavor to get up-to-date with what you have done during the past decade. In this respect I want to tell you that in 1977 (or was it late 1976?) in London we heard your Violin Concerto in the Royal Festival Hall. I think Previn conducted, but I don't recall the name of the violinist.[3] I was much moved by that work and while listening to it I heard you sing ... my old friend ... It is a beautiful piece ... Why didn't I pick up the pen right then and there? It is difficult to answer a question such as this. Perhaps I wanted to remain silent just a little bit longer, for some reason or other ... But you were not silent. You spoke through the Concerto ... [...]

Istvan

[...]

74

28 JUNE 1982

My dear Isty,

Again the time has evaporated & suddenly it will be time to leave for Santa Fe and whatever fate is in store for *The Confidence Man*. We leave July 4, Sunday. Rehearsals begin the next day. I'm remembering when you & Bea were here that we were irritated with the business of the singer who was raising such a fuss about her part in the opera—the Angel of Bright Future. You'll be happy to know the problem has been resolved for the better. She was released from her contract by Santa Fe after we had a meeting with her in N[ew] Y[ork]. She proved to be really impossible; & she's been replaced by Deborah Cook who is a fine coloratura & is eager to do the part.

We remember your visit with deep feeling. We should never again let so much time elapse without seeing each other. I hope the trip to Williamsburg proved to be everything you both wanted, relaxing & restful. I can imagine you have been home since your return finishing the orchestration of your stage work & putting your book to rights. You can't imagine what a strong impression *Winthrop* made on us. Whatever modesty you may have where your text is concerned, it gave Gene & me the sense of a large frame, poetic & dramatic in character. We hope when it sees the light of day the work will be immensely successful.

Strangely coincidental that our inner drives have led us both to the stage. (I don't speak of the books—but that too makes the coincidence stranger.) Last week I spent 2 days in Ann Arbor with W[illia]m Bolcom who is editing my essays & will provide the introduction for them [*The Aesthetics of Survival*]. We hammered out a shape for the book, edited some of the essays. There's a great deal left to be done yet. But that will all have to wait till Bolcom finishes his part & we're back from Santa Fe. I'm hoping that the mss. can be "put to bed" before we leave for Israel in late Oct. What tragic events in the Middle East. I'm afraid there's no chance for peace until the Arabs are willing finally & at long last to concede Israel's right to exist. In the meantime the outlook is very bad & Israel has to contend with a largely unsympathetic world. I suspect whether or not we actually <u>will</u> go to Israel depends on what happens this summer vis-à-vis the PLO, the Syrians et al.

I don't know if you ever read Paul's story "The Silver Talons of Piero Kostrov." In 1965 [1968] I wrote the large chamber piece I call *Tableaux* based on images from the story. Now Gene & I are preparing to make it into a stage work, actually a "drama" with music rather than an "opera." We have worked out the complete script this weekend. Now the rest is up to me. I will draw on *Tableaux* music & some of the songs I set to Paul's poems & write some new music. It's so completely different from *The Confidence Man* that no parallels of any kind could be drawn between them. It is entirely "surreal," contained, intimate. There are 2 singers—a soprano and a female "pop" singer who will function on different levels. The actors only speak. Besides them there is a dancer, a chorus of 3 men (ten., bar., bass) & a mimed role. I see already writing this will be quite different & perhaps more difficult than doing another opera. I have to find ways of meshing the music into the action so that at times it is pure background, at other times it is foreground. As yet I don't know when I can get to work. Probably after we're back from S[anta] F[e].[4]

Once we're at S[anta] F[e] & rehearsals are on their way I'll drop you a card to let you know how things are going. Gene is suddenly full of anxiety. She says if it were only my work she'd look forward to it knowing it will all come off well; but since she's involved … of course I understand completely. It's her DEBUT! She has a right to be nervous & anxious. I'm not exactly calm myself—but I'm keeping the lid on! […]

George

75

[Santa Fe, New Mexico]
24 JULY 1982

My dear Isty,

Three w[ee]ks have gone by in the thick of daily hard work for all concerned; next w[ee]k we go into dress rehearsals and next Saturday we will find out whether or not we've made an opera that works. I go from feelings of near elation to near depression *cum* frustration. I'm much too impatient for results but have had to learn that things do begin to come together. The singers are generally good with one exceptional singer (Deborah Cook, our Angel of Br[ight] F[uture]) on one end & an excellent "character" singer but with a not-too-good voice (Joe Frank, our Barber) on the other. The stage direction [Richard Pearlman] and conductor [William Harwood] are excellent & very hard-working. Gene loves the set; I can't tell yet until I see it working, i.e., with lights, people moving etc. Yesterday was the best day so far—singers and orch[estra] and I began to hear what I wrote. But whether it all hangs together, for that will have to wait for the 1st orch[estral] dress [rehearsal] Thursday night. Meanwhile I'm trying to stay calm. Gene is a blessing in that regard. She has much steadier nerves than I! […]

George

PS: If the stage-hands reaction to the music is an augury, then perhaps all will be well! […]

76

16 SEPTEMBER 1982

Dear Gene and George,

[…] It said a great deal to us that you not only had us in mind before leaving for Santa Fe, but while there also, even to the extent of taking time to write in that exciting & busy period for the two of you. I sensed the pre-premiere excitement from George's words and then nerve-testing experience of seeing a new work take shape in stages … But this was a special event, given the magnitude, nature and complexity of *Confidence Man*. I shall try to find you *viva voce* during the next few days, but in any case write also about this experience which must have been quite something! We were with you in heart/mind on the day of the premiere, wishing that we were bodily, also, there, participating more fully … […]

You must sense how much it means to me that you like the concept and text of the Winthrop story as I assembled it for this "pageant." Today, having completed page 350 of the orchestral score, I reached what appears to be about the halfway point in the piece (counting pages). In terms of the form: Part One is done and I am well into the first section of Part Two. I am happy with what I have so far and am pushing ahead with it. It will not be complete by the end of this year, consequently I have to get used to the idea of completing (say) the final 15–20% of the score while back in a teaching job (although with a relatively light course-load) as of Jan. 1. Yet another job that will land on my desk is the typescript of my book with the copy editor's comments requiring God knows how much attention, time, etc.

This is a rather breathless and mono-chromatic note, somewhat impatient under the skin, feeling the pull of empty score pages … […]

Istvan

77

24 SEPTEMBER 1982

Dear Isty,

How terrific to get back from N[ew] Y[ork] where we were to see & hear *Der Rosenkavalier*—birthday present for Gene—and find your letter & those great pictures! When I read that you were pushing past the 350th page of your score and that you would have to continue toward completion despite teaching I had a rush of memory and an even greater rush of sympathetic understanding. But despite "small" obstacles you'll get it done I know—and it will be beautiful! […]

It would take too long to write about Santa Fe but I can at least indicate a few things about the whole experience which had powerful negatives—many of which I slowly comprehend. To come right to the point the production in terms of set, lighting, direction went <u>against</u> the opera; and were it not for the strength of the libretto & the music would have killed it entirely. We trusted the director—Richard Pearlman—thinking he understood what we wanted but instead he had developed an entirely different conception from ours and virtually presented us with a fait accompli once we got to Santa Fe. By then it was virtually impossible to undo what he had set in motion vis-à-vis set & lighting design. We were handed a completely filled stage from side to side and front to back which made movement, entries & exits difficult to execute easily or quickly. Everything became clumsy, awkward, ponderous; & the effect of all this was to slow down the pace of the opera. We fretted and fumed—mostly to ourselves because we literally did not know how to deal with the situation. We learned a bitter lesson which of course will stand us in good stead in the future. Despite everything the singers did their very best—and some were indeed excellent—and the conductor & orchestra played their hearts out. Audience responses were good and at least for the 3rd perf[ormance] very enthusiastic. The worst of it was the viciousness & harshness of the critics, most of whom thought the production excellent! (from all over the U.S.) who seemed to decide that 1) our approach to Melville was all wrong (& inevitably <u>theirs</u> far better; overnight they had become <u>literary</u> critics as well) 2) the music wasn't "contemporary" enough. Beyond all that many of them made a <u>political</u> issue of my embrace of tonality, referring to the New Right & other hogwash of a similar nature. This sheer quantity of the criticism turned the whole thing into a momentary nightmare. (I was especially enraged because Gene was involved—this was her first time to suffer directly the stupidity of critics—but she quickly recovered her balance I'm happy to say.) Inevitably this kind of treatment of a new opera is bound to scare off other opera houses and the present silence from their direction continues this. Nevertheless we're ready with a revised version (prepared since being back) when they are ready. We've tightened & pruned to achieve greater internal consistency and intensity.

All that's behind us now. I am gathering strength and ideas for 3 new works I have to write and simultaneously we're making preparations for our trip to Israel. Hopefully by the end of Oct. when we leave things will have settled down in the Middle East; but frankly I am not optimistic. Israel exists in a sea of local & world hatred—and how can we call that "existence" when she must be in constant state of physical defense just to survive?

I wish I could have written a better "story" but reality is what it is. […] Be well & *sempre avanti*!

George

78

20 NOVEMBER 1982

Dear George,

A delay again in responding to a letter from you (24/9/82) and what a letter! I've been waiting for it, because I knew that it will tell the story of Santa Fe. I am one with you in your feelings and thoughts. The experience with someone else imposing their Procrustean bed (visuals, movement, etc.) of ideas on one's own can be (and is often) a harrowing experience. I came to the view that a stream of visual information can detract from rather than add to, the musical experience, unless there is the most sensitive and calibrated interrelation between the two. Already as a 16–18-year-old I have found myself keeping my eyes closed during opera performances for the very same reason. And this is why I don't conceive *Winthrop* as an opera, but rather as a musical pageant, as if some nefast [i.e., wicked] influence would have to be kept at bay in the very use of the word opera, at least in some of its interpretations. When a music, such as that of *Confidence Man*, has so much drama in it it demands its own suitable, & commensurate, visual complement. The same with *Winthrop*, for which I either am envisioning an actionless (but costumed and possibly also light-programmed) presentation, which would be simple enough to mount (and cheap too), or, alternately, a visual side consisting of a series of *tableaux vivants* against a pitch-black background, one giving away to another, each representing a historical deictic (a moment of time/space) instance or alternately a frame of mind (which would bring it close to the concept of the aria itself). The number of these tableaux would have to be fairly large though hence this type of presentation would be difficult and expensive to mount (in 1977, in London, we saw a marvellous presentation of Gorky's *Summer Guests*[5] by a theater ensemble—Theater am Hallischen Ufer, I think it was, under Peter Schaufuss's direction I believe—which was in part done in such tableaux, which alternated or coincided with carefully controlled mobile scenes). Echoes of *Last Year in Marienbad*![6] Marvelous experience it was; it paralleled some kinds of experiential time experiences. But back to

Confidence Man. From your account I am happy to read that the music, both vocally and orchestrally "worked." The enthusiasm of the singers and players must have been the best evidence to support your own conviction in this. Let the critics jump in the lake. We have to write what is dictated from the inside and by now for us, in our 60s, the inside voice must count only. Now the revision: anyone who scrambled (like Mahler for ex[ample]) to polish a score between rehearsals or performances knows of the process. Regrettably, economics don't allow us to "try out" 15 times in Buffalo, Cleveland, etc. before getting to N[ew] Y[ork] C[ity] or say Santa Fe.

But, what's essential, you now have a tried, polished, and experienced work, ready for the 2nd, 3rd, 4th, series of performances that are bound to come, and let then the critics discover new angles to your and Gene's exciting recreating of a slice of Melville's world.

The best news I can give you is that there is nothing more to write about than *Winthrop*, on which I am working at high 7/7 pace from morning till late into the evening. I have just completed the review & orchestration of Section 7 ("Boston … a Citty") which turned out as the longest mvt. yet of the work: 102 pages of full score and ca. 19 minutes in duration. No wonder: what I am trying to tell about here is the fortunes of Boston's people from the moment of disembarkation from Winthrop's fleet in June of 1630 to about 7 years later. It is a story that begins with an almost motionless stupefaction resulting from finding oneself face to face with a jungle. From this state of bewilderment/fear the group lurches (or [is] goaded into) a feverish work activity. Judicial/political/economic structures appear soon, and behind this one hears the pulsing of a continent (its indigenous people, that is, who are heard, but not seen yet) … and so it goes. There are numerous other features that succeed in a quasi-cinematographic sequence … (Now this sounds very deliberate, even pedantic; I hope that in the piece this appears as red hot drama, compressed to the very limit of intelligibility …) In a day or so, I am ready to begin the movement that tells the story of the trial of Ann Hutchinson that also seals her death warrant, as well as the tragic fall of Winthrop from the pedestal as an idealistic, utopian politico-social innovator … Probably I mentioned to you while we were with you that there are no heroes or villains in *Winthrop*, only people who try with the best of their understanding, and who "succeed" to a point, and then "fail." What "succeed" and "fail" mean in this context I am trying to tell in the work.

Another full letter would be needed about matters related to present-day problems besetting the State of Israel. I won't even begin to write about this, beyond saying that I was very disturbed by the killings that went on in those 2 Palestinian camps in Beirut. I am very curious what impressions you will have gathered about Israel's political situation while there. Please let me know how you see this situation.

I still have ca. 200 score-pages to finish (I now have 506) from *Winthrop* which is by far the biggest work I ever wrote in any sense, probably. The book just came back from the copy-editor and I have to consider his suggestions for changed wordings (no structural changes, fortunately) before it could go to the printers. The illustrations also are a headache. […]

Istvan

NOTES

1 See "1975," note 1.
2 *Winthrop* (1984) was premiered in a concert performance by the Kitchener–Waterloo Symphony Orchestra, with the Elmer Iseler Singers and the Stratford Boychoir, Raffi Armenian, conductor, in the Centre in the Square, Kitchener, Ontario, on 6 September 1986.
3 The British premiere of Rochberg's Violin Concerto took place at the Royal Festival Hall on 17 March 1977 with Isaac Stern, violin, and the London Symphony Orchestra conducted by André Previn.
4 This work does not seem to have materialized.
5 Maxim Gorky (1868–1936), *Summer Guests* or *Summer Folk* (1903).
6 A 1961 film by Alain Resnais on a script by Alain Robbe-Grillet (b. 1922) after his novel *L'Année dernière à Marienbad* (1961).

1983

79

10 MARCH 1983

My dear George,

[…] *Winthrop* is complete as of this past Monday. (Did the sound-waves of my big sigh of relief tinged with joy reach your soul's ear in Newtown Square? It ought to have propagated itself that distance …) Its vital "statistics": about 2½ hours of playing time, 741 pages of full score (of which 12 are double left/right pages); 6 solo voices (3 Winthrop's, Margaret Winthrop his third and longest living wife, Ann Hutchinson, his great antagonist in early Boston, a "herauld" who assumes diverse roles while pronouncing this or that [but do <u>not</u> think of him as a narrator, which he is not]), a mixed chorus (S[oprano], Mezzo, A[lto] T[enor], Bar[itone], B[ass]) of at least 24 voices (they better be of solo quality), and a boys' choir of about 12 voices.

I wish I could describe the essence and spirit of the work, but I resist attempting it right now. It may suffice if I just say that it is a "full" yet often "stylized" statement. The objective evolved slowly into the strong wish to portray individuals in particular situations, and as far as Winthrop is concerned show him at a number of crucially important moments in his life, hoping that these will form a chain giving a sense of his personality from his youth to his day of death. All this is surrounded by the two choirs who sing, speak, declaim, shout, etc. across an appropriately diversified spectrum of expressions. The orchestra (of a minimum of 30 players, possibly more if the strings are multiplied) is made to support with strength/colour the vocal strata. If presented in concert the orchestra will have to be muted somewhat, if used in a pit, it should "speak" with enough body from the depth. […]

What next? Of course the selling job. The work was not commissioned (although it was supported by a generous foundation—The Floyd Chalmers Fund—award that secured extra time away from the University) which had the advantage of letting the thing go the way it wanted to, without the constraints of agreed-to-conditions imposed extraneously. But now comes the hassle. There is a group in Toronto that could do it, one which has (for some reason) the right of first refusal. I'll know soon enough what comes from that corner. If the answer is "no," I'll try whatever promises any hope. I feel very strongly about the piece. I want it to be heard. […]

Istvan

[…]

80

2 JULY 1983

Dear George,

[…] I think our last letters met somewhere above the Adirondacks. In mine, I wrote about the completion of *Winthrop*. Presently I am in the process of finding one, or more, organizations that would undertake the premiere. (Estimated cost of a scenic presentation: a cool $1/2 million, Canadian, I should add.) The role of a salesman/impresario is a novel one for me and I don't particularly like it, but will persist with the exercise. […]

I just finished writing to Joseph Tal[1] (I do hope that he is still around; I haven't been in contact with him for about 10 years), as part of preparing our first visit to Israel in the fall of 1984. (Before that time, I hope we shall have the chance to hear you and Gene tell us about your latest impressions and opinions regarding the country and its people.) […]

Istvan

[…]

PS: I am enclosing a text telling about *Winthrop*. I wrote it, principally, for the purpose of promoting the work, especially in Canada.[2]

81

19 JULY 1983 | 135

Dear Isty,

[…] It's been a packed spring & summer so far. The Oboe Concerto is finished & in the hands of the N[ew] Y[ork] Philharmonic though it probably won't be scheduled until '84–'85.[3] I'm now "emeritus" (somehow I can never really relate to these academic honorifics); but as far as "life" goes, far from retired. The *Aesthetics of Survival* ms. is now edited & should be set in type by the end of the summer (isn't it curious how we parallel each other with books etc.). Meanwhile I'm having my journals (dating back to early '50s) typed with the idea of approaching a commercial publisher to bring them out. I'll probably have to get an agent to handle this for me. So far haven't the vaguest idea how you go about it. Also planning two "theoretical" books which I'll work at over the years between pieces of music—one having to do with chromaticism, the other a kind of miscellany catch-all where I want to write about subjects that have always interested me, some getting long treatment, some short—like slow and fast against each other in music, Beethoven's phrase echoes etc. Immediately ahead is a piano quartet I've promised. Then a large orchestral work for the Chicago Symphony [Symphony No. 5] which I should deliver in the next 2–3 years.

I'm sure you & Bea will more than "enjoy" being in Israel. In many ways it's both wonderful and unnerving at the same time. It's precisely that kind of paradox, the coupling of opposite extremes & the spectrum which I find characteristic of Israel these days. I don't know where you plan to make your headquarters but if possible make it in Jerusalem. And if Josef Tal can help you spend your time or rather stay at Mishkenot Sha'ananim,[4] you & Bea will be comfortable there. It was set up by Teddy Kollek[5] for artists, composers, writers who visit Israel and overlooks the Old City (the Valley of Gehenna [Hinnom in Hebrew] between). For now all I'll say is that when I think of Israel I grow sad. There seems to be no way to extricate herself from embroilment with the Arabs. Simultaneously Israel is becoming "orientalized"—a development to be deplored. Nevertheless it remains an amazing place. And Jerusalem—it's the Golden City for me despite its modern pimples! […]

George

82

15 NOVEMBER 1983

Dear George,

I had to put off, time and again, conversing with you, dear friend, because the never ceasing surge of things demanding urgent attention around here. I wish I could write that all this activity relates to preparations for the *Winthrop* premiere. Alas! This isn't the case. Since mid-June when we returned from a beautiful trip to France I did move stones around (believe me they seemed heavy in some instances) hoping to find some evidence of practical interest in the opera. Well, the word is out at least in our corner of the woods, that the piece exists, and that it is a "big" one, and slowly the view gets noised around that it is a good piece, that will be difficult to ignore on the long run, at least. I wrote letters galore, spoke with frightened administrators, and even to a potential conductor of a choir here specializing in "newer" kind[s] of music, but apart [from] appreciative &/or positive responses I have nothing to show ... yet. I am far from being disheartened, in fact I was expecting this kind of reception, given the size & weight of the piece. (The early production-cost estimates range between a 1/2 and 3/4 million $, Canadian I should add.) Here I am then with my big project, with lots of umph left in me for further sales-fights to get its public-soul under the light of the day. More of this as things develop. [...]

Well that's almost all. There is hardly any time for anything else (brainwork that is) than a bit of reading. I have just finished A. Sachar's *A History of the Jews*,[6] that I found gripping, and almost everywhere convincing. (He writes a bit ambivalently about some Kabbalists, A[braham] Abulafia, for example, about whom I found Gershom Scholem's account more credible, to the point, and interesting.[7] Another problem spot relates to the contemporary scene in Israel. But, admittedly, this is a most knotty topic to write about for a Jewish author, who is determined to see an overwhelmingly spotless picture, where there are some warts on the body politic in the perception of some other observers. I couldn't do it better, probably, and am glad that I don't have to be face-to-face with the problem. The situation might/would be different if I would be engaged writing a piece on a Jewish theme, something that I am contemplating to do, if I feel strong enough for it, somewhere down the road.)

Apropos Israel: I have written to Joseph Tal quite a while ago, and had no answer. What do you know of him? Bea and I are thinking of a trip to Israel in the fall of 1984, and would like to take up contact with the

Music Dept. of the Hebrew University. Can you suggest a name, or two, whom I could write about this? […]

Keep well, and let me know about the premiere of the Oboe Concerto, as well as of other new projects. […]

Istvan

[…]

NOTES

1 Joseph Tal (né Gruenthal) (b. 1910), German-born Israeli composer, director of the Israel Academy of Music (1948–1952); in 1965 he joined the faculty of Hebrew University, eventually becoming the head of the musicology department. Tal was an early pioneer of electronic music in Israel and, like many of his generation, he worked his way through strict dodecaphony toward a less constrained musical language. His six symphonies, composed between 1953 and 1991 and recently recorded under the direction of Israel Yinon by the NDR Radiophilharmonie (CPO 999 921–3 [2003] and CPO 999–922–2 [2004]), provide an excellent overview of his musical journey.

2 "*Winthrop*: The Work, the Theme, the Story," *Canadian University Music Review* 4 (1983): 184–95; reprinted in *Istvan Anhalt: Pathways and Memory*, ed. Robin Elliott and Gordon E. Smith (Montreal and Kingston: McGill-Queen's University Press, 2001), 375–84.

3 Concerto for Oboe and Orchestra (1983), commissioned by the New York Philharmonic for the oboist Joseph Robinson, premiered by them, Zubin Mehta, conductor, at Avery Fisher Hall, New York, 13 December 1984.

4 A non-profit organization in Jerusalem which serves as an international cultural centre and guest house for visiting artists and scholars.

5 Theodor (Teddy) Kollek (1911–2007), Hungarian-born Israeli politician, mayor of Jerusalem (1965–93).

6 Abram Leon Sachar, *A History of the Jews* (New York: Alfred A. Knopf, 1965).

7 See Gershom Scholem, *On the Kabbalah and Its Symbolism* (London: Routledge and Kegan Paul, 1965), and *Kabbalah* (New York: Quadrangle/New York Times Book Co., 1974).

1984

83

20 MAY 1984

Dear Isty,

Our books must have crossed in the mail and when yours arrived I spent the rest of the day reading as much as I could—mind you, not every word—but in an effort to get a big design of it and dig into its essential core. Unfortunately I had to put off writing you right away (which was my first impulse) because things were pretty hectic here. Mostly the excitement had to do with Gene's getting ready for her trip to Russia where she's been since last Thursday. […] I stayed behind to work on my Fifth Symphony which I'm writing for Solti & the Chicago Symphony.[1] It's beginning to open up and with luck & hard work I hope to have the first mov[emen]t sketched by summer. After that (if that) I'll aim for its completion by the new year. I keep hearing Solti's voice saying: "Don't wait too long!" And just yesterday talking with David Raksin, a Hollywood composer (he "wrote" the scores for Charlie Chaplin's *Modern Times*, *City Lights*, *Laura*, *The Day After*, and others I don't know about);[2] he said when I told him about Solti's "caveat": "That's because he waited eleven years for Lutosławski to finish his Third Symphony!"

I was fascinated by your book [*Alternative Voices*] for a number of reasons, among them the immense reading and scholarship that went into your writing it, the absolutely clear sense of a "chronicle" of an aspect of 20th-century composition, the clarity & elegance of your prose (no easy accomplishment that. Which reminds me: Someone recently raised heated objection to the demand that art criticism needed to be clear, lucid. What they said was: "All this talk about clarity is very

Fascistic ... and I don't like it!!" Talk about politicizing a situation where the "normal" traditional standard for clear thinking and clean prose suddenly becomes suspect! Bloody nonsense). But more than all this something started to rise to the surface as I read—and especially after finishing the "Epilogue"—which came as a bit of a "shock"—though not really a surprise—that is to say, I began to realize something very paradoxical (and I who love paradox was even more drawn in by your book as a whole)—namely, that here we are, you & I, close, close friends for over 20 years which has developed a deep sense in me (and I feel in you) of brotherliness ... and we are at opposite ends of the aesthetic poles in re the whole question of values inherent in the works of, especially, the post–WW II period and more generally modernism itself. Frankly the image of two people like ourselves stretching hands across this aesthetic gulf is what produced the "shock." I don't think I'm exaggerating; and if I do exaggerate our positions it's not to separate us in any sense. This is a case where friendship bridges all gaps! But to get to the basic point: aside from the not unimportant fact that you know the vocal repertoire <u>thoroly</u> and I have an absolutely minimal acquaintance with it, we seem to divide on the question of whether the horrors of 20th-century "reality"—its societal & political evils and ills which continue unabated and may keep boiling until some unspeakable climax we all dread occurs—is fit subject matter for art generally, music particularly. My ultimate reasons for finally rejecting modernism have to do with my intense belief that whatever "realities" an artist or composer deals with they must be transformed such that the pain induced in the social being is raised to a level beyond the phenomenological in the artistic being. No one can doubt the "sincerity" of today's composers who wish to deal <u>directly</u> with the raw effects of political crimes et al. but "sincerity" is not an adequate substitute for the transformational process which goes into making art. Picasso's *Guernica* is a good case in point. Miraculously he turned his personal horror at the bombing of that helpless city & its people into an enormous statement whose meaning is inescapable even to the casual eye. At the same time he produced a painting which satisfies every demand one can make on painting per se. Where you place a high value on Berio and Stockhausen (among others) because you believe they have captured in text and sound the essence of their subject matter (the awful unpalatable nature of 20th-cent[ury] man's experience), I remain unsatisfied because I don't believe they have transformed their material into what I consider art to be—however skillful & ingenious they may be in carrying out their designs.

After reading the "Epilogue" which is surely a marvellous statement in itself I couldn't help but feel: here are two books which emerge almost simultaneously which promulgate opposite views ... and written by close & good friends. And I chortled! Life is wonderful, *n'est-ce pas*? Together we have laid out virtually the whole spectrum of 20th-century music—from end to end, from a celebration of modernism to a declaration of what a lot of people are calling the postmodern (a term I have no personal use for)! Remarkable coincidence! But then, Isty, I don't believe in coincidence. Somehow I think all existence is fated—though not determined in the absolute sense—and it was "fated" that we should be the authors setting forth the aesthetic differences which seem basic to this very time. Naturally, I'm eager (to say the least) to get your reaction to all this. [...]

George

[...]

84

27 MAY 1984

George, dear friend,

Your letter of May 20th arrived this past Friday, and your great book [*Aesthetics of Survival*] a few days earlier. Just as you, I feel I must write to you now even before I could say that I have absorbed well enough what is in your book. There is so much in it that to get to this point will take me some time. I am going to live with your book for a long time to come returning to it time and again when I want to listen to its special voice, yours, my friend and brother. Whether a coincidence or not (and I tend to agree that probably it is not) it will remain a part of our shared mythology that we became authors and composers of operas at about the same time.

As to substance: yes on the surface we would seem to represent differing viewpoints on some aspects of contemporary music and art, and these appear to be rather far from each other on an imaginary fan of aesthetic choices. But, I must say, that I have trouble with a metaphor such as this, because it does not begin to reflect the true depth of the issues involved, nor the complexity of the context one has to cope with. So let us allow that, yes, there are differences between our respective outlooks. But why should one find this to be surprising or troublesome? I not only can live at peace with this notion but feel very positive about it. Difference or no difference, I have a tremendous feel[ing] of closeness, of affinity, for your kind of commitment and an admiration for the sharpness of your apperception, the courage with which you are appealing to the sense of responsibility of the artist, for your eloquence, and for the clarity and poetry of your language. But there is something else besides. I hear in your prose a familiar cadence and intonation: that of a latter-day prophet who saw the monster and rose to do battle with it, whatever the consequences may be. Perhaps prophets have no choice. Perhaps you and I had no choice either but to go along our respective paths that, in retrospect, are shown by our footsteps. There might come along a third person one day who would declare us to be similar, despite certain obvious divergences between us. Perhaps one of the common elements so identified would be our Jewishness, which I have had much trouble to define since a long time. But, lo, here it echoes in certain sentences in these two books. Has this Jewishness something to do with the circumstance that we are the champion survivors among all nations? Or/and with a self-imposed obligation to periodically—occasionally ill-received—emit warning calls (prophecies) for all—Jew and Gentile alike—to hear and heed? Tell me, what do you think of this?

And even if there would be reasons in the minds of some for us to go on the mat to wrestle, with the overall difference between our two interpretations of contemporary art on our minds, I would refuse to do so. We are no narrow scientists, as distinct from the truly great ones, and there is no reason why we should reject the possibility for a still longer synthesis that would accommodate our thesis/antithesis duality if this is at hand. What I rejoice in is that you are as you are with your articulation of the world through your music and word. (As to the latter I derived enormous pleasure from articles such as "Humanism versus Science" and "The Fantastic and the Logical," among others. They are eloquent and beautiful.)[3]

I sense, that, as a composer and writer, you are in full motion, at or close to the peak of your powers. I feel pretty good about myself, also, from these points of view. If our artistic modes of expression, and our words about music, differ in some measure, then, so be it. I like this tension between our respective poles. Why try to attenuate it by mediation? It would reduce what I feel to be a positive & a creative force. Rather, let us keep on singing our respective songs; the clearer, the more individually telling, the better. One day you have "included" me in your music. To have heard my own reflection in the mirror and frame of your 3rd Symphony, was a marvellous and enriching experience. I felt that <u>you</u> gave me something by accepting a part of me.[4] You, of course, your musical thinking, has become a part of me since a long time ago, although it would take quite a few more words to explain (horrible word, this one) in what fashion this occurs. So let us remain ourselves, and mix whenever it seems fruitful … but we want no homogenization, please … Right?

Just one more word along these lines: I am greatly touched that you found merit in *Alternative Voices*. This is very important to me and helps me to go on. […]

Istvan

85

16 JULY 1984

My dear Isty,

[…] Up until @ July 1 I was working hard & shaping the opening sections of my symphony for Chicago. I really felt I was getting somewhere when the bug hit—but so swiftly & angrily. I'm still not up to the kind of effort it will take to get back to the extension of the 1st movement. But I hope I can before the week is out. I've been reading a great deal—all kinds of things—mostly what has taken my fancy is rereading Troyat's biography of that great mad genius demi-god Tolstoy.[5] What a spirit & nature. I keep wondering what he would have thought of the way the world has gone in this century. He died in 1910—so missed the 1st WW which I can imagine would have enraged & saddened him beyond everything. I saw an 1½ hr. documentary of WW I (films from Germany, France, England, Russia, et al.) which stunned me with the utter stupidity of what we so euphemistically always refer to as "mankind." Such pride, arrogance, wrong-headedness, lack of understanding, brutality; such unwillingness on all sides to let go of all the falsities that govern men's behavior when they are in positions of power & authority. Stick a uniform on someone, give him a high-sounding title, tell him the fate of the country, the church, the people, the something-or-other depends on him—and suddenly everything that is possible to imagine that is against humanity emerges. Which leads me to the U.S. election in Nov. I despise Reagan & everything he stands for but see no hope in Mondale (or any of the Democrats for that matter: so many small people, *luft menschen* I call 'em). I dread Reagan being re-elected but Americans are so trivialized by our culture by now that there's no doubt in my mind he'll be reelected. […]

George

86

31 OCTOBER 1984

Dearest Friend, George,

Difficult to face up to it: I made you wait for over 3 months with these lines, after receiving your letter (a *cri de coeur* it is!) of July 16, 1984. […]

On the 1st of Sept. I retired from Queen's. […] I am yet to find my bearings. September was busy with CBC work (a jury, ISCM [International Society for Contemporary Music] Festival in Toronto, the preparation of a box of recordings of mine that is scheduled to be released in the spring of '85, etc.).[6] The enclosed autobiographical sketch (also for a CBC album) I wrote in the summer. It will help to fill some "white spots" in your perception of the past of your old friend. In August I thought I came to the point of having generated enough interest in *Winthrop* for putting together a package (a "consortium" would be a better word) for its production. […]

I am very interested in your new symphony [No. 5] for Chicago. Give me a glimpse of it whenever you can. (I still recall the marvellous one-man performances of parts of your opera while we visited you and Gene!)

I seem to be in a word-phase now. I am reading Michel Foucault's *The Order of Things*, a little by Derrida (*Dissemination*) and Ricoeur's lucid *Interpretation Theory*.[7] I find these French thinkers writing in terms of a different (several different) metalanguages than those anchored in the English, North American, positivist, empiricist tradition. We dig (normally) Popper, Russell, and in a daring moment go even for Wittgenstein. But these Frenchmen (<u>all</u> spiritual heirs to Mallarmé, directly, or by the intermediary of a Barthes—if this is the correct genealogy) think/speak/write differently, using ellipsis, metaphor, and other artifices of poetical/rhetorical discourse much freer than those closer to our turf. Often it is frustrating to read Derrida, or Julia Kristeva,[8] but they lure one on … (Did you read a popularization of this bent in Umberto Eco's novel—a best seller by now—*The Name of the Rose*?[9] The semiotic subtext hangs out rather obviously, and the historical condition clashes with the editor's cutting scissors … "but Signor Eco this is too much <u>even</u> for the schooled N[orth] A[merican] reader … you just <u>have</u> to compress this into not more than 1,200 words <u>at the outside</u>!" I seemed to hear here & there in this work.)

But what about writing music, my friend, you say. And rightfully so. Am I starving myself out for another protracted stint with musical matters? Or am I working on what Foucault would call a new (in this case personal) *epistème* (knowledge field, or some such), just because I, too, am perplexed, dissatisfied, unhappy with much (but by no means all what I see surging around me. The new magical potion: computer literacy ...; the new frontier: space exploration; ... robotics (the new Golem) which is what Abraham Moles,[10] in a recent lecture at Queen's, called the most recent stage of the Adam-Pygmalion-Prometheus-Homunculus-Golem-Frankenstein-Robots (of Karel Čapek)[11]—factory without workers line (see also N. Wiener's dream: the human use of human beings, turning into mass unemployment). He calls such a line a "mythogramme."[12] But what position to take that would not be that of the Luddites? How to think about models that have meaning for a North American trade-unionist, a manufacturer, a politician, to a Chinese worker, as well as for the mother of a starving child in Abyssinia? What has this to do with music? Or can music do without asking this question? Things are so complex, and seem to be getting even more so. This past weekend I attended a 3-day colloquium on "Symbols in Life and Art." Do I now know better what the boundaries of the concept denoted by the word "symbol" are? Yes and no. Someone (Cantwell Smith the religious historian from Harvard) flung the challenge to his audience: "I should like to hear a discussion, for instance, on my notion that to call a cow a cow, for example, is a metaphor."[13] This, of course (or is this not naive to say so?) has little to do with the murder of Indira Gandhi. Little do we know the true destructive range (as distinct from potential) of words. Little do we know to what extent we are manipulated by gesture, tone, situation, innuendo, and the like. (A main theme of *Alternative Voices* ... But did I say this clearly enough ...? Some commentators think I only wrote about the avant-garde. Not true.)

Not surprisingly our concerns echo each other, although they are not identical. Some persons (friends) imply, or even say to me, that I should write smaller/shorter works. (Read: easier to perform, on account of forces and cost.) But one does what imposes itself. For me, this will be a song cycle next.[14] (Can one still write one for voice with piano?) But a little part of my world must be allowed to get into even this slighter work ... it has to say something! [...]

Istvan

87

7 DECEMBER 1984

My dear Isty,

When your letter & autobiographical sketch came I read them through immediately & with such a sweep of conflicting emotions, of joy for you and sorrow for you. I wanted to drop everything and respond right away but I was so deeply involved with the orchestration of my Symph[ony] #5 that I had to put off answering till now. The score is done, thank God, but it was followed by a heavy cold *cum* fatigue which, in the nature of things, are "cured" by lots of sleep & rest. I realize all too well now that at my (our) stage of life one should be more chary of one's energies & forces and not keep on tempting the Fates. It's a matter of changing pace, not throwing oneself totally & completely at what one is doing—which has been my lifelong habit. It'll be hard to do but if I want to "last" I'll have to find a way. […]

I was fascinated by your autobiographical sketch and marvel at the things you went through and survived. And the story of how you came to Canada was very moving. Yet, as hard as your young years were (and mine, but in a totally different way) I have the sense we were lucky when you think of the horrors that our parents' generation and ours went through in Europe. We are each here in our own way to tell our story through our music and words. Without spiritual fortitude it would be impossible to come through any sort of difficulties, whether physical or psychological.

Next week is the week I launch my Oboe Concerto and as you can imagine it will be "heavy" but I'll get through it somehow. Joe Robinson, who is the principal oboe of the N[ew] Y[ork] Philharmonic, is a superb artist and if [Zubin] Mehta takes things seriously things should go well. I think what will ensure his complete immersion in the work is the fact that it will be recorded commercially (New World Records) the day before the last live perf[ormance].[15] As you can see from the card Gene sent there are other perf[ormance]s coming up but they are far enough in the future so I don't have to think about them as yet. What I am thinking about because it is absolutely fresh in my mind & heart is [Symphony] #5. Part of the reason for pushing so hard to finish it is that Solti wanted to see the score at the end of this month in order to decide if he can schedule it for the '85–'86 Season. And that is what I hope will happen. It's about 23 minutes long, one continuous outpour from beginning to end. Of course there are distinct sections but eventually they all interlace in the

Finale. I "invented" what I think of as a circular form, the opening statement being the core out of which spiral in successive fashion episode 1, develop[men]t 1, epis[ode] 2, develop[men]t 2, episode 3 and *finalmente* the summation which gathers everything up. Since "5" is crucial in symphonic numerology, I put "everything" I could into it—but judiciously, not wanting to overload. In this day & age of a dying culture I felt impelled to reassert the old human values of charged feelings. Many will probably take it as "romantic." That's superficial. If anything it is against Nuclear Death and the Beast of the human spirit. […]

George

88

8 DECEMBER 1984

My dear Isty,

How could I neglect to send my warmest congratulations & bravos on your retirement? Which is why I'm writing this addendum to yesterday's letter. Although you indicate in your sketch an ongoing internal connection with the academic life—am I right in this?—separation from it formally can't do any harm. In fact, I myself am convinced—as you probably know—the so-called rational environment of the university is fundamentally antithetic to the pursuit of art. But be that as it may I can't imagine you're not happy after all the years to be free to wander as you will—mentally, musically, psychologically, spiritually. In my own case leaving the academy behind was like a new lease on life, a release from things that had grown onerous to bear. But why go into all that? It only amazes me I stuck it out so long—23 yrs.

I was very interested in your latest reading—Derrida, Ricoeur, et al. I've had little time to read in these directions—& frankly even less inclination. Deconstruction(ism) as I have gathered from other of my readings leaves the mind, the spirit & the universe even thinner than the old positivist notions. What is fascinating tho is how the human mind in this century insists in ever-increasing degrees of intensity in stripping every possible layer of "natural" meaning from human experience & taking "knowledge" (so-called) even farther & farther away from life as we experience it to some oxygen-free zone of abstraction. I find most intellectualist word-game playing these days more & more antithetic to the life I feel & see around me—chaotic, horrendous, unbearable though much of it is. I see a wild dance going on that most of humanity is partaking in (Dance of Death?); and I see the intellectuals distancing themselves as much as possible from this mad dancing. Even if the dance were gentler, more "civilized" (which it's not been for nearly all this century) the academics sit on the sidelines, like disdainful wall flowers. As music is part of the dance, and a very big part at that, I prefer to be there myself. Still I have my own needs (rational?) to comprehend as much of what's going on as possible. So I have been reading the great and remarkable Wm. James and find myself shouting inwardly hallelujah![16] In many curious ways he's probably more pertinent today than he was in his own time. And for spiritual insight I always find myself going back to Owen Barfield, the English writer now in his 80s. If you don't know him I would recommend *Poetic Diction* which he wrote when he was 26–27, *Worlds Apart* which is an astonishing book in many ways and especially *What Coleridge Thought*. He is a master of the English language, writes with consummate lucidity and has a power of "reason" unmatched these days. If you don't know Barfield yet please try him. I think you'll find him intensely rewarding even should you not agree with any of what he says (although I kind of doubt that!).[17] […]

George

NOTES

1 Symphony No. 5 (1984), commissioned by the Chicago Symphony Orchestra and premiered by them at Orchestral Hall, Chicago, Georg Solti, conductor, on 30 January 1986.

2 David Raksin (1912–2004), prolific composer of film scores. Raksin provided the now-classic score for *Laura* (1944), with its famous title song, as well as the score (with additional music from Virgil Thomson's *The River*) for *The Day After* (1983). Of the two Chaplin films, he worked only as an arranger of Chaplin's music for *Modern Times* and has no connection with *City Lights* (1931), whose musical score is by Charles Chaplin and José Padilla.

3 "Humanism versus Science" (1970), in Rochberg, *Aesthetics of Survival* (1984), 164–73; rev. and expanded ed. (2004), 135–44; "The Fantastic and the Logical: Reflections on Science, Politics, and Art" (1973), in ibid., 189–203; rev. and expanded ed. (2004), 199–213.

4 In a letter of 11 April 1968 Rochberg asks: "Would you mind very much if I quoted a part of your 'First' [Symphony]? If you will give it your blessing I think I have just the right place for Anhalt!!" Rochberg uses a brief gesture from Section VII of Anhalt's Symphony No. 1 (bars 290–93), which begins in the second half of bar 327 and ends in bar 343, after which the music returns to the D minor of J.S. Bach's chorale prelude on "Durch Adams Fall ist ganz verderbt" mixed with a fugue of Rochberg's invention. Joan DeVee Dixon, *George Rochberg: A Bio-Bibliographic Guide to His Life and Works* (Stuyvesant, NY: Pendragon Press, 1992), fails to note the Anhalt quotation in her list of borrowed material in the Third Symphony (192–93).

5 Henri Troyat, *Tolstoy*, trans. Nancy Amphoux (Garden City, NY: Doubleday, 1967).

6 *Anthology of Canadian Music*, Radio Canada International ACM 22 (1985), a five-LP collection of Anhalt's music, including an autobiographical sketch and program notes by the composer.

7 Michel Foucault, *The Order of Things: An Archeology of the Human Sciences* (New York: Pantheon Books, 1970); Jacques Derrida, *Dissemination*, trans. with an introduction by Barbara Johnson (Chicago: University of Chicago Press, 1981); Paul Ricoeur, *Interpretation Theory: Discourse and the Surplus of Meaning* (Fort Worth: Texas Christian University Press, 1976).

8 See, for example, Julia Kristeva, *Desire in Language: A Semiotic Approach to Literature and Art*, ed. Leon S. Roudiez, trans. Thomas Gora, Alice Jardine, and Leon S. Roudiez (New York: Columbia University Press, 1980).

9 Umberto Eco, *The Name of the Rose*, trans. William Weaver (San Diego: Harcourt Brace, Jovanovich, 1983).

10 Abraham Moles (1920–92), psychosociologist, pioneer in the field of cybernetics and information theory; see in particular *Information Theory and Esthetic Perception*, trans. Joel Cohen (Urbana: University of Illinois Press, 1966).

11 Karel Čapek (1890–1938), Czech writer; see in particular *R.U.R. (Rossum's Universal Robots)* (1921, trans. 1923).

12 Norbert Wiener (1894–1964), American mathematician, pioneer in the field of cybernetics, which term he coined from the Greek; see *Cybernetics: or, Control and Communication in the Animal and the Machine* (New York: MIT Press, 1961).

13 Wilfrid Cantwell Smith (1916–2000), Canadian philosopher of religion and theorist in the field of comparative religion.

14 Presumably *Six Songs from Na Conxy Pan* (Hat Dal Na Conxy Panból) (1947), for voice and piano, an English version of which was prepared by the composer in 1984.

15 Concerto for Oboe and Orchestra, Joseph Robinson, oboe, New York Philharmonic, Zubin Mehta, conductor, New World Records 335 (1984).

16 See William James, "Concerning Fechner," in *The Writings of William James*, ed. John J. McDermott (Chicago: University of Chicago Press, 1977), 529–45; see also Rochberg, "Fiddlers and Fribbles, or, Is Art a Separate Reality?" *New Literary History: A Journal of Theory and Interpretation* 18 (1987): 257–79; reprinted in Rochberg, *Aesthetics of Survival*, rev. and expanded ed. (2004), 145–64.

17 Owen Barfield (1898–1997), *Poetic Diction: A Study of Meaning* (Middletown, CT: Wesleyan University Press, 1984); *Worlds Apart: A Dialogue of the 1960s* (Middletown, CT: Wesleyan University Press, 1963); *What Coleridge Thought* (Middletown, CT: Wesleyan University Press, 1971).

1985

89

7 JANUARY 1985

Dear George,

Finally, the peaceful hour to respond to your marvellous letters from Dec. 7th and 8th ... Where to begin? Perhaps with the question: how did the performances of the Oboe Concerto go? And the recording session? Please tell me about these in some detail in the next letter. We, of course, got the card with the impressive list of performances. Which orchestra will do the Fourth Symphony? (Come to think of this: I don't think that you have written to me about that work yet. It might have been 'born' at the time when our correspondence was in a state of hibernation ... True? In any case, there is a lacuna in my mind about this that has to be filled. Is the work published? Recorded? I must catch up ...)[1] Is the Cello Quintet a fairly recent piece?[2] (Yet another blank spot!) And now of course your shiny new [Symphony] #5! I am so delighted that you have it. Triumph echoed from your lines ... the wrestling was over ... and the work stands ... to be seen and heard ... Your description of its form is fascinating: a beautiful, quasi-classical, conception. Of course, how can one begin to hope to mirror the information-rich tissue of a full score with linear sentences that tend to channel the mind of the receiver into modes of imagining that are doubly misleading: 1) with regard to the work, and 2) with regard to the composer and his working methods? I guess, the issue is that between a manageable description and the natural history (if not anatomy, or even better the biochemistry) of the creative process. I could make a good case for the usefulness of everyone of these descriptive levels, depending on the objective to be served by the account, the time available, etc. In a word: your description (composer to composer) was at the right level: it triggered a long chain of thought reaction that fed on what you wrote.

You are marvellously productive and I am looking at my own productivity, priorities, accepted obligations, etc. over the decades, not to speak about more basic layers. Then I say to myself: turn away from that moldy mirror, and look at your friend ... Yes! So, here I am rejoicing with you at yet another major achievement. I'd love to see the score, and of course hear the work played. Again: keep me posted about Solti's decision regarding the premiere.

I sense that you cannot be swayed from doing what you are doing by anyone's applying buzz words, such as "romantic" to your handiwork. What does a label, such as this, really mean? At the close (last page) of the enclosed lecture-text[3] I am asking the question: what is old? In fact this is the question that got me on to writing the lecture that I am to read in about 2 weeks' time in Calgary and Edmonton, and possibly also in Vancouver. (At U[niversity of] B[ritish] C[olumbia] they want me to read—as a "premiere"—'What Tack to Take.'[4] They might schedule a 2nd public lecture, while I am there.) Having completed *Alternative Voices* I became curious about the degree of applicability of its methodology to "old" musics. In fact this was not a new idea, basically, as I have been teaching a "basic" course (undergrad) in Analysis that followed, somewhat, the path taken in "Pst ... Pst ...".

I sense that there is an area where our respective ways [of] looking at things differ considerably, but I have some difficulty in finding the words that would locate it in our respective approaches. This has unmistakably appeared in the diverging (or so it seemed) paths our compositional orientation followed from the mid-'60s onward. It also shows in the kind of books we came to publish about the same time. I am pretty certain that what I shall say here can be (and ought to be) shot full of holes, by either one, or both, of us, as soon as the ink dries, but I try something anyway. It might have to do (that is our difference) with the way you sense life in which we all swim. Now, quite a bit has been written about fishes that are not supposed to be aware of the water in which they live. But we are the kind of fishes who feel it to be their business to sample, test, gobble-in, spit-out, etc. all over, all the time, cyclically ... the element in which (through which) we exist. Now what is this 'element'? Society, a political environment, a span of history, an epistemic cornucopia from which we pick and choose? (No, I do not know "your" Barfield,[5] but will check him out ... but you may 'postpone' checking out "my" Foucault.[6]) So, here it is: let's call it our own, individual, pictures of the world, both as the synchronic fiction goes, and also as the impossible-to-cope-with diachronic complexity. Whatever! We do have, as we (everybody!) must have, our working world view, every moment of our lives. Now your world view includes a great deal of wealth and depth of perception, fueled by a marvellous intensity that is your very own in its chemistry and of the rarest quality in power. This world view also includes exclusions: not only on account of not having the time to get to know closer something, but rather as, having understood the gist of that 'stuff,' you say: I don't want anything to do with this. (Now, we all have to do this. The question pertains on the mix: what is 'included' and what is being 'rejected.') When you were using in one of the letters the expression "natural" meaning, I think you have put your finger on that (or one) central organ. I said: here might be a key to our differences in outlook with regard to some things, that become even more important by radiating out their influence into more peripheral activities, for the 'outside' to see, hear. Perhaps I should say a word, how I see the notion of "natural meaning." Well I am skeptical about interpreting it in any way that would confine it into a specific episteme (epistemic 'space')—centered, politically, or socially biased or ethnocentric etc. notion. To me 'meaning' is not an independent entity, however it might be conditioned by some of our cerebral constants. To a very large extent we have an enormous scope to fashion our collection of recipes for meaning. We are not static when it comes to this, although there are likely to be more, or less, active periods in one's life with respect to developing one's notions concerning the 'meaning' of meaning. My entire involvement with the human voice derives from this: I wanted to envisage the most diverse, the richest, the most profound model I was capable of that would give me that "compost heap" from which I could grow my life as a man, father, teacher, composer, writer, friend, adversary, etc. ... all the roles one is assuming I needed for this help. In fact: to have come to the point when I knew that I need this (linguistics, for ex.) or that (x, y, z) was already a sign-post in the journey in what I regarded as being for me the right direction. The order of the day for years was expansion in the direction of 'humanistic' fields. (With a single, conscious, decision reached in the summer 1961, I rejected any further "experimental" work with new technologies of sound-production & composition. I have done this while driving north from Murray Hill, N.J. where I spent a week with M.V. Matthews, learning of the computer music project he conceived at the Bell Labs.)[7] This got me where I am now, my dear friend. I hope that you will see in the paper "Pst ... Pst ...", despite the discrepancy in size, a counterpart to, a complement of, *Alternative Voices*. Now, when it comes to my music you may see in the score of *La Tourangelle* the willingness to allow for the same range of diverse approaches to meaning, spanning & sampling the thousands of possible uses of language for the purpose of achieving meaning that is authentic, comprehensible, apposite, concise, and artificial in the way that I feel is the best expression. When you'll know the score of *Winthrop* you will recognize there an even greater diversity, spanning a range, including, among other types of utterances also, artificial representations of diverse rhetorical modes and the collective death rattle of a band of Indian men & women (the Pequots) who were murdered by a punitive expedition mounted by the Bostonians, in the mid-1630s (1636, I think).

But there is another aspect in which we may differ, although here I feel this might only appear as a divergence. You seem to profess a dark view of the prospects of the world. Yet, you go on creating with a magnificent sweep and energy, as if celebrating man's power to have yet another, possibly many other, chances for self-correction, renewal, and the like. Your life, as I know you (and cherish you dear friend), sometimes puts into question what you in a moment of outrage or despair, are saying in words about the world. Basically, despite the forebodings, the warnings, I feel that you are someone fuelled by a forever unquenchable hope, and even trust, in the human collectivity. You feel like some of our Biblical prophets, from time to time: warning, reminding, castigating, uplifting, speaking in a crystal clear, intelligible language, to enable the multitude to understand, since everyone must contribute to survival, if indeed that should be possible. Now, where you and I stand as brothers in this business is the fundament, the ground, namely the abhorrence of glossing over things. We are for telling as it is, but focused through abstraction and transcendence. I feel that I have moved quite a bit closer, musically, to where you are, with *La Tourangelle* and *Winthrop*. Precisely because the total range must include Palestrina, Bach, etc. However, what matters to me most, both humanly & musically speaking, is the potentiality of choice inherent in the total range over which I have a conceptual control, while envisaging personal & social action, as well as compositional language, process and structure. This field is, at any one moment, and at every moment, the picture of my mind. Its propensity for inclusiveness, catholicity, is, I feel, under control, and is not spiralling out into the blue yonder ... Enough of this tangent. I feel I had to say it, because you said certain things that indicated concern on your part that just might have a bearing on what I just finished writing.

With the lecture "Pst ... Pst ..." out of the way, we'll get on the road to Alberta & British Colombia with good cheer, hoping that it will also be some sort of vacation which we both need at this moment. With that trip over, and all the other smaller projects that I had to look after since "retirement" (a blessed state, I see it exactly as you do, after 35 years in academe ...) also behind me I can begin a new phase. I understand how you feel about the university not being a place that is conducive to artistic output. I see this as a 2-faced situation. Negatively, for the reason you've mentioned. Yet, I see in it something inevitable, given some cultural-political realities. But what matters to me most is that, by having made my living within a university, I have become a different composer, from what I, probably, would have become, should I have had to make ends meet in a Conservatory or on Tin Pan Alley or Hollywood. And this holds true for the entire Anglo-American-Canadian-Australian scene. One off-shoot of this, the rebirth of music theory, a mixed blessing some may say ... a fact to me. A fruit of the same old positivist tree ... but then there is in our corner of the woods other vegetation around & various birds (Cage-d, or not) that provide other alternatives ... In short: I have few regrets about my 35 years of bondage; however I am claiming now another 20, at least, for 'free' existence ... In other words: in a Conservatory I would never have come to the point of writing *Alternative Voices*; *Winthrop* also, if at all, would have been different. [...]

Istvan

90

15 JANUARY 1985

My dear friend Isty,

An envelope from you, large or small, is bound to contain all kinds of good and wonderful things and the one I just received especially so. Not having read Foucault I begin to see why you are drawn to him. The Heidegger quote[8] rings very strongly in me and suggests overtones of Barfield who also relates language to consciousness[9] as well as Walter Benjamin who writes in his *Reflections* that all things in the universe have "voice" and "speak" suggesting universal consciousness, all things having their form of "being" have their own language.[10] So in that sense the universe itself is a form of "speaking" and we are one of those forms "spoken" by the universe; and our speech not only reflects universal speech but reflects back on its source. That's why I've always believed that music, one of our primary forms of utterance, is a reflection of world consciousness just as world consciousness reflects itself in our music.

Our "differences" I see as differences of, call it, personal proclivities, tendencies of mind and nature; and as I see it we share in too many things for those differences to matter that much. *Au contraire*, they forge an even closer link between us because I see them as complementing each other; i.e., it's as though your more "rational" initiating tendency all the while you are completely sensitive to and reaching over to the more feeling side of things forms the complementary polarity to my more "non-rational" initiating tendency while I strive to make my intuitive understanding of things clear and lucid, more "rational." Taken all together we—or our different starting points—form an approach to a totality. Not unlike old musings of mine where I have tried to imagine what it would be like to combine <u>in one violinist</u> the qualities and capacities of a Heifetz and a Stern. Imagine the lofty purity of the one together with the gutsy, earthy passion of the other—both available when needed to the same performer. Or I remember after hearing Penderecki's Violin Concerto [No. 1 (1974–76)]—and while not liking it *in toto* admiring many things in it—wondering what kind of music would emerge from a composer who combined his <u>and</u> my best qualities? But somehow it appears nature has arranged it (by "nature," of course, I mean biology, genetics) so that each of us is <u>bent</u> in one primary direction and this predominant tendency diminishes the availability of elements of the opposite or complementary tendencies. Except—& this is the clue for me—where we <u>know</u> we are bent the way we are and because we need and value the other side of things, strive for them … and so on. You see the line of my thinking where we're concerned. So despite being different "compounds" of the same human stuff we nevertheless share many things & feelings in common including music <u>and</u> words. Lately my need for words, for saying, is stronger than ever. After completing [Symphony] #5 I re-worked an old essay and rebuilt it almost entirely. […] I call it "Fiddlers and Fribbles: or is Art a Separate Reality?"[11] Also I had 200 pages of entries from my journals from 1950 to '83 typed up and it's now in the hands of an agent. I'll probably meet with her in a couple of weeks to discuss possibility of publication. She seems to think she can place it with a N[ew] Y[ork] publisher. I'm not sure if all this verbal activity doesn't have something to do with advancing age, wanting to get a lifetime of experience and thought down in words before the final curtain. Even if the last act may still be a long one! And for many reasons, not the least of which is we are now both grandparents, may the last act be a long one for both of us—and for Bea and Gene. […]

The enclosed really should be seen in the context of the entire Dec. '84 issue of *Critical Inquiry*. I hope you can get hold of it at your univ[ersity] library perhaps. The issue contains a confused, sloppily-thought-out "reply" by a young avant-gardist which he calls "Can Modernism Survive G.R.?" In March will appear my response which I call "Kramer vs. Kramer."[12] The "controversy" was engineered by the editor of *Critical Inquiry*. I have no objection to that per se but the level of discussion to be worthwhile is not "high" enough, my respondent, one Jonathan Kramer, having seen fit to make his piece a personal attack on me. I've never really understood why academic "discussion" gets so acrimonious. (*Vide* the exchange between Krieger and Gombrick in the Dec. '84 issue of *Cr[itical] Inq[uiry]*.)[13]

Symph[ony] #4 goes back almost 20 years now. It's only now beginning to surface. The N[ew] Y[ork] perf[ormance] will be given by Alvaro Cassuto and the Nat[iona]l Orch[estra] Assoc[iation] of N[ew] Y[ork] (a young professional "training" orch[estra]). It belongs to the world of all those works I wrote in the '70s which are frankly "tonal" in the old sense. Except in this instance, the middle mov[emen]t is chromatic though not "atonal." (I have come to dislike all these distinctions—but how else to describe a mixture of dialects?) It's a 40-minute work with big romantic gestures, often dark & ruminative in cast—and as often serene in a sad way. Because I love it and believe in it as music I'm waiting for the day (if it ever comes) when orchestras will take it up. The quintet for 2 cellos is drawn from ideas I took from the opera [i.e., *The Confidence Man*]. It's a "divertissement" though not always light in spirit. There are probably other works I haven't told you about—not to keep anything from you but because I'm never quite sure whom I've told what! Also I must confess to a certain reticence always to be speaking about myself ... But I do want to tell you about the Oboe Concerto which I wrote for the principal oboist of the N[ew] Y[ork] Philh[armonic]. Right after my last letters to you we went to N[ew] Y[ork] for a week of rehearsals & perf[ormance]s including recording it for New World Records. It went better than I could have hoped. Joe Robinson, the oboist, is a first-class musician & understood the work, gave it everything he has (which is a lot) and Mehta took great care with it so that by the time we recorded it the work really came to life.[14] I was especially pleased that the players in the Philh[armonic] liked it & said so. Orch[estral] players as you know are a tough breed—and if you can convince them ... you know the rest!
[...]

George

91

13 APRIL 1985

George, dear friend,

From what follows you will see why this letter is so very late. First, then, I should give you an abbreviated account of what the situation was up here since Jan. 15, the date of your last note […], a call from the heart, in which you said things in a beautiful way. More of this later, as well as of your paper "On Modernism …" ["Can the Arts Survive Modernism"]. […]

Shortly before we left for the West there were signs of stronger interest in *Winthrop* (that is, producing its premiere) than before. For this reason I decided to put off everything (including answering your letter, my very dear, and understanding, buddy) and tackle translating 745 pages of full score into a workable piano-vocal/choral rehearsal score. (Actually: what I am coming up with is playable—in part—by a single pianist, who would leave out things, or, conversely, by 2 pianists [on 1 keyboard or 2].) […]

While I still don't have anything in writing, it now looks that the work will finally be premiered (but fingers will have to be kept crossed) in May, 1986.[15] The conductor is to be one of Canada's most experienced opera conductors (with an excellent *Wozzeck* to his credit). It will be a concert performance, unstaged that is, which pleases me greatly because I don't want any distraction resulting from half-digested, quarter-prepared scenic plans, and directorial egos for this 'first testing.' This means of course that I have to apply myself to the piano-vocal/choral score (to date only ca. 20% is completed) with renewed energy. There are other distractions in store, alas, but I am hopeful that I'll complete it in time for the rehearsals. You can imagine how much all this means to me. I feel very strongly about *Winthrop*: about its relevance to this noisy, fickle, dangerous, frivolous, fast world of ours. Will it be able to cut through the commercial din? Yes, I say, provided the organs of promotion (I hope some will be available) will do their job properly. I also feel strongly about its musical qualities, and how it is "new/old" or "old/new," not by design alone (your friend is less addicted to 'ratio' than you'd think, if indeed you do think along these lines), but on account of gut and feeling. Of course, there are pages of row-tables, set-tables stashed away in boxes (more stuff for the Library), but these are just lattices, jumping-off points, palette-surfaces, the raw stuff, as we well know. The work, in all, adds up to a musical ambience, that of Winthrop, his times and environment, as they were echoing in my head while I thought about them. Sometimes (with increasing frequency as the pages accumulated) the work almost dictated itself. I shall keep you posted about the developments.

Now, finally, I am coming to your wonderful letter [...] The way you wrote about 'speaking' will forever ring in my ears, especially this beautiful sentence: "The universe itself is a form of 'speaking' and we are one of those forms 'spoken' by the universe ..." The depth, the tone, the idea of all this reminds me of the milieu of the Kabbalah ... It sounds terribly old, sweet, and Jewish ... Or do I hear eastern echoes in it? Or perhaps theosophical ones? Perhaps it is an age-old wandering idea that suddenly found its moment of reincarnation as your pen touched the paper ...

We need not say much, anymore, about our 'surface' differences, which, on the evidence of your 5th S[ymphony] and my *Winthrop* might be found to be more insignificant than an 'outside' observer would think it to be at first blush. As to the 'inner stuff,' we are, as we have found ourselves to be ever since we first exchanged a word, marvellously, and comfortingly, close. Yet this 'closeness' does not threaten our respective identities, that are so securely grounded that they allow for the frank recognition that our vantage points are, indeed, not identical. And why on earth should they be (or even could be expected to be) more homogeneously in the same box? This brings me to your challenging article "On Modernism," a copy of which you've sent along with your letter.

First I want to say that it is a beautifully & lucidly constructed call for a broad-based change in cultural attitudes, supported by a wide-lensed analysis of what recently was, what is at hand, & what is likely to be in the next little while. On first reflection it reads to me as having emerged from a compositional-cultural-axiological stance that came about in your heart/mind/gut/brain in a spontaneous way. It evolved 'organically' (yet another biological metaphor), bringing you (a questionable metaphor positing 'outside and inside,' where there is only 'inside') to where you are, or, at the least, where you were during those hours/days while you crystallized the text of your paper: a frozen series of moments in time, during which the fluid process of thought/person turned into statement thus freezes itself, and exposes itself to response. (I am, of course, contrasting the ever-evolving process with the frozen, isolated, record/account, somewhat paralleling the sociocultural event of writing out a Bible from an aural tradition ...) While saying "you are here," or "I am there" I am again resorting to a metaphor, this time to a space-related one. And so it goes with language, as we so well know. What <u>does</u> matter, and what I want to underline is that this evolution in you was emotional, instinctive, in response to numerous inside and outside stimuli, and their interplay, & thus perfectly right, unassailable as an artistic choice. At least, this is how I see it. The rest is explanation, rationalization, finding apt parallels, witnesses, making use of this or that psychopompos, whom you are selecting (in the Sartre-ian sense) because you know they are leading you to where you already are in the first place. (Now, what about this as a space-related figure of speech?) You and I, are together, and in good and old company, when we think of the presence of memory in music, with its manifold ramifications. No problem here. However we do seem to have a problem with some other aspects of approach. I am getting to these now at the slight risk of generating a little heat, between the 2 of us. (Having spent more than enough time in the "kitchen" we can take the heat ...)

Why relegate the messenger of a difficult-to-accept ('bad') news to the dog-house? The grounds for the Dada, the neo-Dada, the positivist-oriented, etc. statements were apposite. They had to be made and were made. They introduced what I think is an interesting proposition: besides, or instead of, being "beautiful" (or arriving at "beauty," whatever that is) music can, and should at times, at least, aim at presenting the truth or some aspects of the truth, with its (that is music's) powerful means of selection, abstraction, framing, concentration, memory-play, suggestiveness, etc. etc. (But again: 'beauty' & 'truth,' in this sense, need not be mutually exclusive.) The many combinatorial matrixes, populated by an infinite semantic repertory, ordainable according [to] any one of the numerous imaginable syntaxes, allow us to reflect the world and thereby show us in the act of reflection, in that wonderful multiple mirroring act, that is also suggested by the picture 'Las Meninas' (I think by Velásquez), so well interpreted by M. Foucault in his *The Order of Things*. It is worth testing our memory capabilities whether or not they can cope with this or that formulation.

I have a little problem with the expression (on p. 320) [of "Can the Arts Survive Modernism"] "in the continuity of civilization and its enduring values." I am searching here for some qualification. 'Western' civilization only? Which periods of it? The music of which classes? I accept readily if someone says my garden is the garden whose shrubs, trees, etc. were planted by Bach, Haydn, etc. My own preference as to value systems are definable in such and such [a] way and they are related to such and such figures in the evolution of European/American thought. But then I am pulled in the direction of 'alternative' view points, that lure me out of the safe house that the line of Palestrina-Bartók built. I am (at times) lured out of the safe confines of the world defined by the number 12, out of the relatively safe world of a notational convention, and into the world which is beyond the notes. (I do know that your world also springs from the realm that is beyond the notes. But we seem to have gone from that shared compost heap in different ways, at times, to make our ornamental shrubbery grow.)

I also sense a subtle change in attitude toward 'modern' things in the paper as it evolves. At first you show a more-or-less negative attitude towards 'it' (although the 'it' is very difficult to pinpoint, and I am not sure that one has a good enough justification for beginning not earlier than with Marinetti and with *Erwartung*, both of whom/which define 1909 as an alluring *terminus ab quo* … What about, Mallarmé, Rimbaud, Baudelaire, etc?), but later on (p. 336) you are writing about synthesis. Now this is where we come together again. This I resonate to. This is my world, too. And I feel this is likely what will continue to evolve. And you have said it beautifully.

The sub-text of your paper is, I cannot help but feel it, suffused by an *Angst*. Even the word 'survive,' says it loudly. You seem to feel/think that we might just blow each other to bits. Granted. And it is something that should keep everyone with a bit of breath left in him/her to contribute to the thwarting of that ultimate menace & horror. I cannot begin to hope at the moment to be able to say anything else worth saying about this, so I stop. (This does not mean that I relegate the matter to a space under a carpet; far from it …) But you are transposing here something. It is not only the reality of the bomb that we should endeavor to survive, by such & such an act of resistance, etc., it is the reality of 'modernism.' (If I understand you well.) I would like to have here something else instead of a possible, hidden, equation: bomb ≅ modernism. (Please tell me if I misread this, and there is no such implication.) Yes, I am worried about the 'bomb,' about which I can do precious little, alas. But there are other things I am worried about that are a bit closer to my own customary field of action. I am referring to the vulgarization, commercialization, manipulation, etc. that shouts with ever greater force in the pages of the 'entertainment' (not art, mind you) sections of our newspapers, out of the frame of the 'tube,' etc. The din is enormous and the mass-magic is supported by an ever more heinous application of the democratic/elitist pseudo-dichotomy used as a poorly disguised curse. I need not say more, since we know what is at hand. Is music as we know it powerless in the face of this mass onslaught? Are concerts, opera, forms of communication & distribution of the past? If so, what are we composers whose heart/mind functions so much through the structuring of sound and making it into meaningful artifice? Dinosaurs? Are the young going to be able to muster the aural concentration necessary for the 'taking in' of a 50-min. symphony or a full-length opera?

I have not read Kramer's piece. […] And just as well, since you wanted to hear my response to <u>your</u> article, and much less so (if at all) my reaction to K's words. Nevertheless, I'll try to read the latter, too, and should I feel it useful I'll return to the topic. As a last word: your paper is an admirable & a tremendously courageous act, even if I cannot follow you at every turn. […]

Have you seen the TV double-feature *Wallenberg* ?[16] After a bad beginning it grew into good story-telling. Regrettably, there was <u>nothing</u> authentic to see from the Budapest of late 1944 & early 1945, but the spirit was not far from what I remember having been the case. Unfortunately it was a black & white distortion, showing lots of Jews as wonderful human beings, and, with the exception of a beautiful Hungarian countess, <u>not one</u> Hungarian who was anything but a bastard, or worse, a killer. Well, the reality was bad enough but there <u>were</u> decent Hungarians (I can thank my life to a few) who acted with humanity and much courage in trying to (and often succeeding in) saving Jews. (And we know, from recent experience, that Jews also have among them wild, cruel, psychotic men, killers too …) The telecast stirred me up, not a little, and compelled me to recall certain things. This suggested that I send to you here the text of a poem (I wrote <u>very</u> few in my life) which I wrote on a hot Sunday, in a dusty little Carpathian village named Elöpatak.[17] Sitting, as I recall it, in a courtyard, it just began to pour out of me. While I sensed that the really tough times still lay ahead (it was in 1943) I felt an overwhelming urge to imagine a future to be at least potentially so. I placed it in the environment of a 'garden-city' of medium size … (It is remarkable how close Kingston, with its many mature trees lining the streets in the older part of the town where we live and with the many gardens, waterfront, with its many friendly people in the university, among them several who stimulated me, and helped me to be who I am, in the shops … comes to that imaginary community whose mirage—the evocation of which—filled me with hope and strength that I felt I needed for the ordeal still ahead …)
[…]

Istvan

[…]

92

23 APRIL 1985

My dearest friend Isty,

Your great letter came in the midst of a swirl of things we're involved in (more of that later) but from what you wrote it's clear you're in your own "swirl." [...] I am more pleased than I can say to hear the news about *Winthrop*. If we can make it in May '86 we'll be there! [...] I think you're right to view an unstaged performance as positively as you do. That way you can concentrate on the music. Our *Confidence Man* came a cropper precisely because of wrong directions the whole physical production went in: cumbersome set, inappropriate costuming in crucial places, wrongheaded stage movement—and worst of all, directorial mindset. Oddly enuf, 3 years later we still occasionally hear of someone who "loved" it, presumably the music itself.

Before launching into answering some of your main points in re my piece on modernism—but not to neglect saying how glad I was that much of it struck you convincingly—a word or two about the enclosures. The "Fiddlers & Fribbles" paper is something I've been fiddling with for a couple of years & I was finally able to put it into what I hope is decent shape. As you can see I've helped myself rather liberally to "science"—but chiefly of course as metaphor rather than hard fact. My ambivalence where science is concerned won't escape your eagle eye I know. I tend to knock it on the one hand but when it suits my purpose I "use" it as I did when I talked about J. von Neumann in the book essay.[18] Perhaps you've gotten hold of Kramer's "reply"—which will make reading my response to him more meaningful—especially in "explaining" the tone I adopt toward him. In point of fact if I were a modernist loyalist myself he is the last person in the world I'd want defending what I believed in. In any case I hope you'll enjoy both pieces—although the only one I really care about is the "Fid[dlers] & Frib[bles]"—and look forward to what you'll say about them

You handed me a rather tough "assignment," old friend, with your probing points & questions in re my paper on modernism. Let me dispose of your concern about whether I attribute the bomb to modernism or equate the two. The answer for me has to be no to both, at least on the immediate surface of things. There's no way one could claim that modernism brought on the bomb even though both occurred in the era of the highest technological achievements & advances of the century. But there is a way I connect the emergence of both modernism and the bomb from a common Gestalt or ethos or world view (*Weltanschauung*) which has been on the march since the 17th century in the West, more specifically Europe and spilling over to & enfolding America in the 19th & 20th centuries. Of course you're right: "modernism" as an art movement and mind-set has clear roots into the 19th cent[ury], & perhaps its seeds could be traced as far back as the 18th cent[ury] with the *Sturm & Drang* mov[emen]t. All those writers & poets (Nerval, Novalis, Büchner, Baudelaire, Rimbaud et al.) who are already expressing disaffection, discontinuity, alienation where the combined aristocratic/bourgeois "values" of old Europe are concerned are proto-modernists in a way. Wm. Blake has a beautiful, apposite aphorism: "When the senses are released, the world will burn up."[19] (Incidentally, all the noise, the "din" as you call it, of our day that characterizes mass culture & entertainment is part of that picture of "senses … released," part of the basic revolt against self-containment or repression & inhibition, against civility toward our fellow man, against human "dignity"—which begins to sound rather stuffy in the context—and results in a world which begins to sound and look like a garbage dump in motion.) The political revolutions belong to this burning up of the world since they let loose internal (to the countries involved) & external hell & violence. Sounds suddenly like I'm against revolution vs. repression. I'm not—when it is a liberating force—but when it turns as it did in Russia to even worse repression than it presumably revolted against—then, yes, I am. Problem is, there's no balance, no stability of forces or opposing tendencies. There's, in part, the problem of modernism: by chucking traditional languages of art & substituting new ones—often purely arbitrary and with a half-life of 20 years or 6 months, it was no longer possible to produce works which pull opposites together or create interior richness out of diverse elements producing artistic fusion (think of the incredible symbolism in music of slow against fast and of contrary motion—both principles the very heart of old species counterpoint—apart from the rules of consonance & dissonance, themselves balancing opposite tendencies). The "symbolism" becomes very real in Berlioz's last mov[emen]t of the *Fantastique* or in Beethoven's Grand Fugue or *Hammerklavier* fugue, etc. Forces of opposite tendencies are pitted against each other & that's what, besides quality of mind, of ideas, of realization, makes these kinds of works powerful still. By destroying these balances, modernism took to the "single-idea" (but that too was in the air as I tried to show: the search for the single absolute dominant western region & culture generally—but not the East; the East has always understood the world is paradox & contradiction; traditional Japanese aesthetics built them into drama, *haiku*, music) and the single-idea itself either embraced chaos or uncertainty (aleatory) or potentiality (graphics); or sought to stave these off (serialism) by searching for absolute principles of structure & organization. But as we both know nothing stands, nothing holds & we're still "looking" for "the" or "a" way out. That still doesn't answer your powerful point about the "messenger of bad news"; that, I must confess is a hard one. Yes, I agree, we must know the truth of things, we must be, in that sense, realists & to learn to face what is. But does it follow from that that if a work of art symbolically or actually "represents" or tries to represent the terrors of the contemporary world, that it a) is telling the "truth"; b) is by virtue of that effort to tell the truth, a piece of art; c) is automatically protected from a justifiable critical view of what it is in itself as an attempt to make art? Perhaps this is where we don't see eye to eye—quite. I'm not sure yet & must hear from you on this very point. For me, while the chaotic horrors of our day are all too real, I'm not convinced they are "subject matter" for art unless their rawness is transfigured, transformed through the power of an intense artistic mind & nature. Here I suddenly think of Shostakovich's 14th Symphony—a kind of "negative" requiem, certainly his subjective "response" to Soviet brutality & death-dealing. Even if one grants this requisite "power" of artistic expression to "modernists" & I don't see why not, the other problems I've already alluded to come rushing in: the palette of means is too narrow, too limited & limiting, the tendency to use art to speak one's mind & heart directly to the issue becomes a little blatant & shorn of the transforming nature of art itself. It's damn complicated no matter which way you turn it—and it's not cut and dry by any means.

Anyhow, to go on & try to round off the picture I have of the problem: we've been to the moon and back & now we know there is another side to it—the dark side. That's my metaphor for our experience of the 20th century—we have discovered & lived in the dark side with a vengeance. As a result I take it as a given that man is at root not rational, though some of us try to be—and that his force & energy serve evil ends just as easily & often more readily than those we call "good." (Good for whom? is also a proper question. To a Marxist-Leninist, communism is good—or a good. But what if you're a Russian & don't agree & 'specially if you make your disagreement known publicly—by word & deed? We know what.) Aside from the epistemological questions/problems of what is truth & how do we know it, there are often "truths" beside the sad, heartbreaking ones of our pathology. I mean the sublimated, transfigured truths of Bach & Beethoven, Haydn & Mozart which still speak volumes to us. I don't know if Keats's "truth is beauty & beauty truth/that's all ye need to know"[20] fits our case because our case is so wildly exacerbated by terrible events. But to go on: "modernism" has become for me the symbol of an epoch ending (Blake again—"The world will burn up") & nothing can retard & halt what centuries before us set in motion. There is another ineluctable "truth": forces set in motion must play themselves out to the bitter end regardless of human consequences. But I also feel a new wave has been set in motion, one which you & I may not live to see & hear & feel but our grandchildren will—hopefully. The need for a new balance, a transformation, is felt & acknowledged on many sides; and it is not mindlessly Luddite in nature. It is supremely conscious I think of the need to set limits to science & technology but not to give up either. For us, it means to accept in purely personal terms what we value of the modernist legacy and find ways of adding it to a larger vocabulary which includes the pre-modern according to personal interest & need and out of both find our way to an art which speaks wholeness not partialness and speaks it in transformed fashion. I really can't say any more for now.

On the purely personal side these are busy days. Performances have taken me in & out of N[ew] Y[ork] a good deal this year. Just last week my 4th Symphony at Carnegie Hall with Alvaro Cassuto & the Nat[iona]l Orch[estra] Asso[ciation] of N[ew] Y[ork] (actually a young pros training orch[estra]) which came off very well. Thursday we go to Boston for the Brandeis Creator Award [Brandeis Creative Arts Award] ceremony where they're bedecking me with a gold medal (unfortunately I'm told it's not solid gold!) & then next week to N[ew] Y[ork] for their concluding ceremonies at the Guggenheim Museum. Early this month I went to my first meeting of the American Academy and Inst[itute] of Arts & Letters to which I've been recently elected. Their "ceremonial" as they call it is May 15. Then May 20th U[niversity] of P[ennsylvania] is conferring an honorary degree on me (they called to ask what kind of degree I wanted, anything they said. I settled for music. Something tells me I should have asked for "humane letters"). I feel a little odd, frankly, that all this should be descending on me in the "adolescence of old age" as they now call the middle 60s because I'm not always sure I've done what I set out to do. I remain "unfinished." I suppose that's the goad to continuing writing music. Right now I am working when all these distractions allow on a piano trio [No. 2] for the Beaux Arts and just finished the 1st mov[emen]t. […]

George

Forgive the Addendum—but the thought just struck me about subjectivity/individualism as seen through the "eyes" & words of Doris Lessing & Robert Bly. In her Canopian Chronicles (*Shikasta* is the 1st of 5 books & quite wonderful) she speaks of "The Degenerative Disease" which for her, i.e., the Canopians, is rampant ego, pure subjectivity & all its consequential ills as intrinsic to modernism.[21] Bly, a poet/philosopher, writes a book called *News of the Universe* in which he traces the course of subjectivity-objectivity in world poetry.[22] Fascinating essays (non-academic) separating sections of poetry illustrating his thread historically. Rich stuff & worth reading for itself regardless of how it sheds or doesn't shed light on the questions we're discussing.

I've just written Reagan urging him not to go to Bitberg. It is inconceivable that he doesn't understand.[23]

93

12 JUNE 1985

Dearest Friend,

[…] This cannot be a 'response' to your extraordinarily rich and very moving and touching words: in the free-flowing text of your letter, so spontaneous, so much—obviously—directly from the burning range of your heart/mind, so authentic … and then in the 2 papers. These pages cannot (and will not attempt to) touch upon every thought, invitation, challenge, appeal, etc. in your words … Should I be foolhardy enough (and unmindful enough of my great limitations …) to attempt this I would—to begin with—write to you dozens of pages … and when all done I would feel a dissatisfaction over not having done justice by you, by your depth of thought, by the weighty topics, and, finally, by my own amorphous, yet deeply felt emotions about these very themes that, once again, we share so much concern for. Well, then: I shall begin to say a few words of our present respective surface-realities, and after these I'll come back to the 'meat.'

I am so grateful that you told me about the Brandeis award, the U[niversity] of P[ennsylvania] doctorate (how generous and right that they asked you about the kind of degree you'd wish to have), and finally about the election to the American Academy. All these tell you something, and this is positive, sustaining, ways & means for saying (on behalf of individuals, groups, corporate bodies, segments of society, etc.) that your labours have been noticed as contributing to the *essor* ["expansion"] of good for many and saying 'thank you' for it. Who among us is so strong that can sustain his/her psyche (in the old sense, meaning life) without such good words of acknowledgement or the like once in a while? I am sure that you know how to 'read' gestures such as these and will absorb them in a fruitful way. Being your friend and a fellow seeker I am happy for and with you on account of these honours. [...]

A few days ago I completed the piano-vocal/choral score of Part One of *Winthrop*. 200 pages. The rest will bring it up close to 500 pages. I must be done with it by the end of October, the latest. The problem is that I have a commission for a song-cycle for Phyllis Mailing, which I have also promised for mid-October ... and I want to do something 'special' for her.[24] All this takes time and I feel a little bushed right now. [...]

The chief 'player' in the premiere [of *Winthrop*] will be the Kitchener-Waterloo Symphony Orch[estra] (with its 'core' of the Canadian Chamber Ensemble) under the direction of Raffi Armenian, Vienna-trained conductor-composer (the same stable from which Mehta is coming), one of the best opera-conductors of the country, with a fine *Wozzeck* to his credit (with the Canadian Opera Company). The other major partners are the CBC Radio Music Dep[artmen]t and Wilfred Laurier University whose fine chamber chorus, the Laurier Singers, complemented by a few professionals, will provide the vocal ensemble. The Canadian Council will be the 4th partner. For the six solo roles plans call for the best available Canadian singers, and I am delighted with the ones who are being contacted presently. The premiere will be the final event of a 3-week festival of new music. The conductor wants to perform, imagine this, *La Tourangelle* in the afternoon and *Winthrop* in the evening on the same day! We'll see ... There will be master-classes, lectures, etc. during the week preceding the performance(s): by the soloists, the conductor, and myself. It should be a busy week, indeed.

Let me get out of this swirl, from this recitation of action-to-come. I have to catch myself, pull on the brakes and stop looking 150 feet (or 10 months) ahead. We have to turn now to a different perspective. [...]

First that very complex train of thought that leads you to speak about 'modernism' the way you do. I can be, and am, at peace with what you say and with what is behind (at least I so think) what you say. What has happened, and what continues to happen as you exist, create, etc. is, so it seems to me, that you have reworked your personal ordering of your world, priorities, value systems, in order to be able to continue to exist better, fuller, and create, things for yourself, and for others. You have been, and are, creating your reality as a landscape painter who infuses a vista with mystery or with drama, or with whatever (à la Turner or

Cézanne), who paints an interior landscape for which the outside contours, topography are but jumping-off points. (I should also have mentioned that *nonpareil* artist of imaginary landscapes, Yves Tanguy, whose, ominously beautiful *Multiplication des Arcs* you may recall as having seen at the MOMA.)[25] You (or I) have the freedom to structure (and restructure from time to time) that epistemic base from which an artistic statement emerges, and then another, and so it goes in succession. To put it conversely: our 'gut' excretes the works and we—faced with our handiwork—begin to rationalize it, because we like to talk/write, or are expected to in a university environment. There we are, then, with our respective stories, words, opening ourselves up to attacks from left and right. As long as our art is good (I won't define this) we are justified in having created it, even if our words about it elicit misapprehension, malice, fed on someone's feelings being attacked, or by honest divergence in assigning values to different models for artistic restructuring of the world around the artist, so that he should be able to create with a greater peace of soul. Taken this way, from my seemingly (but not truly) perspectivist point of view, I am not only with you in your efforts to sustain your spiritual environment, and would defend your right & justness to do this, but can do so effortlessly as I am peering out from my own personal world ... These are far from being two solipsistic realms, as we are quite familiar with those parts of our worlds that do not overlap. What we note as being significant are integrity, authenticity of voice, and an ongoing 'wanting to do in the world' ... to show the world to itself, how it is, how it was, how it may have been, how it could be now, how it ought to be now, and how it should endeavor to avoid this or that morass that is a distinct possibility for some future if we do not watch out. Our orders are made up of bits and pieces of older, newer and imaginary orders as we might remember them, combine them, etc.

I cannot do better now—to illustrate one instance of this as far as I am concerned (if even at the risk of stretching your patience, dear friend)—than by trying to recall for you what went into the making of 'Isaac,' which is Section 4 of *La Tourangelle*. Here is the shell: the heroine, widowed at age 19, has retired—as a novice—to a convent against all existing rules (social) and regulations (ecclesiastical), leaving an 8-year-old son to the tender(?) mercies of the family (sister, brother-in-law), following what was an irresistible spiritual urge. Result: risking the 'sacrificing' of the little boy for some 'selfish' reason. Conflict between parental duty (eventually shirked) and 'higher' (God's) command followed. Spitting in the face of society, and its prevailing mores, ethics, order, etc. The episode was a real-life event for Marie de l'Incarnation. I sensed the potential for realizing this high-tension dramatic situation of so many conflicting forces & tendencies. But how? No single 'style,' no single polyphonic web of 'lines,' no single pulse could render this pulsing reality, this socio-psychic-mystical/inter-outer landscape that I so clearly saw/heard in my head. I felt the aggressiveness of her critics then and there in the town. I heard a voice speaking out of an ancient edict pronouncing anathema on persons who abandon their children, for whatever reason, and who as a result justly or unjustly torment themselves about their own parenting ... [...] And then the complex polyphonic mind of the heroine who is, at one and the same time, a child of her own time and place, yet different and sufferingly so. And then there are the children, the boy and his gang, acting as they do, responding to manipulation by some adults, as well as following a sense of mischief, not being aware of the torment they are thereby visiting on the parent of one of them, in their terrible and yet so appealing, innocence ... They launch, time and again, their taunting chants ... All this is underlined by the throbbing pulses (several) of a community *anno*, say, 1628.

What are the musical ingredients for this assembly? For Marie de l'Incarnation there are two layers: one is the piano piece—independently performable—entitled *La Fuite* (Flight), a Couperin-ian rondeau in a slightly 'modern' garb, a kind of semi-pastiche I wanted, but was unable, to write while I studied under Kodály at the Hungarian Academy during the late 1930s. It is a motoric, compulsive piece, with a returning *idée fixe*, yet one that is 'evolving.' This piece is, then, one of the propelling forces of the work. The other, outer, self is the layer of the 3 sopranos who vocalize with excitement, anguish, etc. and who finally utter that 'sigh of relief' that I have referred to in *Alternative Voices*. The 'townsfolk' is the *Sprechstimme* duo and some of the taped voices. The ecclesiastical decree of anathema (in 2 languages) is on one of the tapes, as well as are 2 boys' choirs (one in English, one in French—thus reflecting our present-day Canadian tensions that were only too palpable for us especially during 1966–1975). The chamber orchestra is yet another layer, throbbing, flowing, moving through that imaginary mindscape, and 'outer' drama. The polyphony resulting from these layers is harmonically controlled, but with an allowance for a certain amount of limited give and take as to synchronization ...

In toto, then, what this movement represents is a somewhat intricate intersection of my own past (and at the time of writing the work) present 'realities' and those of the work's heroine Marie de l' I[ncarnation].

The layers are, of course, stylized through limitations, various symmetries, redundancies, etc. The total result, then, is far from being a cheap bit (or at least so I hope) of *verismo*, but a kind of abstraction of a fairly involved mix. Now all this is explanation. When you will hear the piece (and the performance that I have is quite good, even if not the best, alas, that we had during one of the rehearsals) you will tell me if transcendence has been accomplished in your apperception, or not so.

So you see: I had to put this ('Isaac') onto paper because I sensed a rhyme & reason to all that seeming confusion. There was a superior order therein which also contained a hope, that existed for all these people, for those currents of thought, ideas & behaviors, that compelled/allowed them to unite in an interplay at a moment in time and in a place. This situation was for me not a frozen moment in time as that in a still life, but a swirl 'lifted out' from the river of time and shown again, compressed, abstracted, to suggest echo, resonance, empathy ... or whatever, that includes also victory over the danger of drowning in the whirlpools ... survival and the right to go on with one's own business, risk-taking, no risk-taking ... to do what has to be done.

I would be worse than foolish—naive—to offer this as a prescription for anyone, over the long run ... even myself. But at that time that had to be said. For the past little while it was Winthrop—John senior, that is—who surprisingly claimed that I search for myself as I was trying to bring him to life. (Of course our works write ourselves just as much as we write them. But the two are but two sides of the same reality.)

I hope no one, for a while at least, will try to pin me down for an answer (or two) about how much concern on my part goes into the composition business for such notions as beauty, harmony, truth-value, being apposite in a given context, or being clumsily out of place without wanting to be so for a super-ordered reality. For me the potential diversity & range is enormous, and I find that the designation of the territory to plow takes much time ... But slowly the bits & pieces do come together ... It's getting late now. I'll continue tomorrow by rereading first your paper on "Fiddlers & Fribbles" and following it in its path ...

13 JUNE

A fascinating paper: your 'F & F.' In more ways than one, for me to be sure and for many others also, I expect. I am with you in its conclusion and much of the time your trajectory towards it would run on closely parallel tracks with my own should I have undertaken this very trip to

Damascus ... It befits our age, time, person, to feel that we have to try to get more light about such 'final' things you write about with such white-hot passion. [...]

There is much persuasiveness in your argument and the lines of force that your assonances ("fiddlers and fribbles" 'slipping into solipsism') create add to this effectively at an almost (but probably not entirely so) subliminal level. I sense in the background of this beautiful paper the shadows of the seven archons, gnostic searches for ways and means that would connect man with cosmos, and which might help him to live what was in "*illo tempore*" (thanks Eliade) referred to by the word (I only recently stumbled on it) *heimarmene*, which, as far as I understand it, means both the cosmic order, as well as man's awe in face of it. And not only awe, but also not a little of terror in contemplating the vastness of the firmament and what is beyond it, as we are time and again reminded of it.[26] It is marvellous to read your conclusion about man being, and having been from the very inception, a part of the scheme of things. I, also, marvel at what we are (good, bad & all) and feel that the finest hour (on the scale of a cosmic clock, of course) for humanity may [be] yet to come. But I am not so certain of it. Even discounting the trendiness in pronouncements about ecology, there seem to be real causes of concern about this, as well as with the lunacy about "the bomb." Our shared faith in the fundamental "belonging-ness" of man is broadly based. We would be well advised to face up to what is destructive in us, as the followers of Zoroaster, Mani [founder of Manichaeism] and others did by recognizing the presence of Ahriman.[27] Koestler tells us that the enemy is within now, and that we 'turned sour' at one stage or other in the process of phylogenesis.[28] Possible, but probably unprovable. I totally share your seeing art as a very important part of reality. It is one of the pinnacles of existence in the creative mode. Yet the notion of the "creating spirit" might be seen today as a still broader category. It contains the sciences as they subdivide, split off, from each other, while only yesterday they formed what may have been regarded as unitary fields of inquiry ... It contains socio-political endeavor ... and in a clumsy and often revolting way it may also contain commerce, business, etc. (Many years ago a merchant spoke to me with some conviction, tinged with indignation, about his creativity that goes into his business—he was an importer of table-ware and similar goods.) I don't understand scientific creativity and even less so mathematical one. Our creativity, I feel, is of the first importance, and I tried to put it in words in the 'Epilogue' to *Alternative Voices*. In this sense I am totally with you in your assessment of man. If I prefer to think that at the moment of the 'big bang' man's potentiality (just as much as a cockroach's potentiality) was included but not necessarily the fact that he will have a pair of eyes & ears, and will, occasionally wear blue ties or nylon stockings, I may only be quibbling. But words are important to us, and I try to be more mindful as I am getting on in years, than I was earlier, of the many traps my own bumbling, semi-command of language hold for me. I am on guard to keep in check my own propensity for verbal magic, or to use it—whenever I allow it to sound—to good effect. […]

I do hope that you will like *Winthrop*. I feel that you will. In a parallel way I would like to hear one day your *Confidence Man*, very much! […]

Istvan

94

23 JUNE 1985

Dearest friend Isty,

As always your letter brings all kinds of news of life and work—and I continue to marvel at your sheer capacity for the latter. The news about *Winthrop* is terrific and it will come about I know. […] The prospect of seeing you & Bea is a joyful one. I hope Kingston is not so far away from Toronto that we won't be able to spend some time there together. Toronto is particularly fresh in my mind albeit in the abstract because I just finished reading Josef Skvorecky's *Engineer of Human Souls*.[29] Do you know Skvorecky or about him? He is a Czech novelist who chose to come to Canada after, I guess, being booted out in 1968 when the Russians "took charge" and teaches at the Univ[ersity] of Toronto. All the time I read his book I kept thinking of you because he writes about a writer who had to do forced labor under the Nazis as a youth. Though I find the book much too long & too repetitive (his countryman, Milan Kundera, is far more succinct & therefore more effective to my taste), it is a remarkable weave of story, self-reflection, political and literary musings going back & forth from the '40s to the '70s (when I suppose the book was written) and makes painfully clear the sickness of the Nazis and the Communists both before & after the Soviet take-over. He is obviously a man of deep & intense feelings for the concreteness of life and an equally deep & intense hatred for all abstractions which lead to political hell-on-earth. Again I kept thinking of your experience & what you must have gone through until you came to Canada. As an American I was as we say "spared" all this in the flesh, but must confess not in spirit. I share Skvorecky's very carefully veiled sense that "it can happen here" (remember Sinclair Lewis?),[30] that slowly, slowly America is losing its grip on its 18th-century foundations and that the right, the conservatives, the fanatics (both in religious fundamentalism and the political variety, "fundamentalism" always being lopsided—deaf, dumb & blind to everything but its own view) are gaining too much ground. It also has something to do with the incredible sentimentality that has swept through the American psyche, making it almost impossible any longer for political "leaders" & the common man to distinguish between truth & falsehood, between reality and its substitutes (like TV & movies). How else explain a phenomenon like Reagan—uttering sentimental crap every time he opens his mouth and SMILING. God, how that man smiles. All the time. And most Americans love it! Reagan sets the stage for Big Brother American Style. He too will smile; & people will be bamboozled into thinking "he's a wonderful man," "he loves America & us," "he will take us through the Valley of the Shadow of Death," etc. Skvorecky knows all this about Hitler & Stalin & their lesser lights. Unfortunately he doesn't know any more than I do how to fend off the next wave—but he senses its approach. Truth is, I feel ripped open by his novel and know the only way to keep from being sucked into depression and immobility is to get back to work myself.

I have to do a woodwind quintet for Australia[31] but I'm really thinking of 2 more symphonies.[32] It's in them I can work out my unhappily dark & oppressive sense of the madness of this world, present and future. Of all the insanities of the day Reagan is pushing Star Wars which will bleed us dry and all the while America can't defend itself against a flea, the current "flea" being of course the Shiite taking of hostages. The total bankruptcy of our state of being is revealed precisely to my mind in our so-called government's inability to understand and deal with anyone from the Third (<u>irrational</u>) world. It runs deeper than old-style politics. The big against the small, the greed of national economics and so on. It's become a struggle between a democracy irritated by its own loss of a grip on reality and totally irrational behavior on the part of rabid fanatics. Israel is in the middle—and that really hurts. The world is never tired of hounding the Jews, blaming them for everything—all the while nicely sidestepping their own culpability in how things happen & how they turn out. Sorry to "dump" all this on you—and I refuse to blame Skvorecky! […]

George

95

3 OCTOBER 1985

My dear Isty & Bea,

I can't tell you enough how wonderful it was to visit with you & to thank you for treating me as one of your family. The glow & residue of being with you is still there for me. I only hope I didn't upset your normal routines of life & work too much!

When I got home I polished my remarks on "inward seeing & iconic thinking" which I'll give at the Penn[sylvania] Conference Nov. 12.[33] It's being word-processed & when I get back I'll send you a copy. Later I will amplify it into a full-length article. There is still more material that needs to go into it before I can be satisfied. With that out of the way I'm back to the wind music & with luck hope to finish it soon. Gene & I were in N[ew] Y[ork] Tues. for the Prokofiev *Love for 3 Oranges*. Not very much music except for the "march" which is the only truly inimitable piece that threads its way through the opera. The production, though enjoyable for its sets, costumes & directorial schtick, is a perfect example of what has happened to opera these days. Directors treat the musical text as a 1) launching pad & 2) backdrop for their own fanciful conceptions against which they invent all kinds of quite arbitrary designs of movement & visual spectacle—and the audiences "seem" to love what they do. Although I can imagine how much more you would prefer a fully staged production of *Winthrop*, Isty, I think to be relieved of directors & sets & costume designers & all that paraphernalia will, in the end, serve your music better—at least initially. You know how I am with you in this whole thing & hope for its success as you do. *Thisness* will surely make its point. If tapes will be available of both works eventually, I'd love to hear them. […]

George

96

15 OCTOBER 1985

George, dearest friend,

[…] I was deeply touched by your Oboe Concerto, its intensity, dignity, serenity and passion, and the harmony that unites it all into a disciplined and most effective shape. While its Mozartean craftsmanship I could expect from you, it came across with such radiance & purity that it became a part of the essence instead of remaining 'just the vehicle'! This work shows up the vulnerability of 'class-terms,' genre-appellations and stylistic compartmentalizations (so many vestiges of the Aristotelian effort to see 'in categories,' that obviously was a great advance at the time & for a while after …). To me it just is, in its uniqueness, an instance of artistic truth/rightness, labeled G.R.'s Oboe Concerto, which in itself is but a mnemotechnic device for those who have heard the work. ('Heard' is, of course, another black box to open, eventually …) […]

Last Thursday a bomb-shell letter from the Kitchener-Waterloo Symph[ony] announced that for some (financial it seems) reasons they want to postpone the *Winthrop* premiere. During a subsequent telephone talk I became even more suspicious of this 'postponement.' In short I am, at present, in the dark as to what is going to happen. I've fired off several letters, of course, trying to pin down these slippery human beings. I've even consulted a colleague in the Law Faculty about what options I may have. A point to consider (and there are several others) is the ca. $20,000 expenditure to the 6 copyists whom I have contracted for the job, and my commitment to the donors of many thousands of dollars to me (Queens U[niversity], among others) for the purpose of preparing the parts, etc. <u>for this specific</u> performance. A messy situation, to say the least. I don't like the idea of a court action, neither do I like getting stuck with an expenditure of $20,000. Also, I am mad as hell, and this is <u>no</u> overstatement. I took some steps that make it possible for me to see a bit clearer about this by the end of this month. The present uncertainty will just have to be borne until then, in all likelihood. You see now why this is not the right moment to talk to [a] dear friend 'as usual.' I feel somewhat bitter and edgy, with an instinct to withdraw … But I just could not delay further writing to you. (Recalling our days together was a tonic, a breath of sanity in this crazy situation. Incidentally this was well expressed by J.M. Keynes somewhere: "We must pretend to ourselves and to everyone else that fair is foul and foul is fair; for foul is <u>useful</u> and fair is not."[34] I wish I knew where he said/wrote this.)

Sorry to end on a sour note, but you'll understand.

Istvan

[…]

97

15 OCTOBER 1985

My dear Isty,

As promised the short paper on "inward seeing" etc. and also the piece from *Physics Today* on "spooky action at a distance."[35] Now that the wind quintet (*To the Dark Wood*) I described to you in the Kingston airport is completed (except for some last-minute checking), I'm going to tackle the fuller version of "Inward Seeing." Almost too much material to fit together—and going to knock my head vs. such juicy topics as "experience and idea," "quantitative vs. qualitative"—small stuff like that. Must also read a new book by Howard Gardner on cognitive science called *The Mind's New Science*—heady, *n'est-ce pas?*[36] […]

George

98

11 NOVEMBER 1985

George, dear friend,

[…] Your paper 'Inward Seeing & Iconic Thinking' addresses itself to a very important topic, and you do this with penetration, commitment and eloquence. When you point to the central idea as a place where "totalities are born … projected outward … in some external … form" (what I left out is important, of course) I felt [like] saying: of course, that's it. How else could I account for seeing within a few seconds' time a whole section of *Winthrop*, for ex. Section 4, "Famous Brittany," which depicts the turbulent mid-1620s of pre-revolutionary Britain … Now this 'flash' was, I believe, the end result of reading background stuff, mulling things over, shifting, eliminating, deciding to include all 'operations' performed in a mixture of conscious & not-quite-conscious states of mind, until the mind (or a particular part of it) was ready to 'fire' the final integrative act, which consisted of a 'theme-complex,' a 'mood-assembly,' a pile of 'materials remembered,' another pile of 'seeing events that could have taken place,' and I cannot exhaust the list … The total bulk had almost a 'weight' in the total mass of *Winthrop*; it was to be one of the pillars of Act 1. At that point all was swimming in a soup of remembered text fragments. But it did have a formal-affective function in Act 1. All that was part of the 'flash,' but other stuff might have been there too. The months of work on that ca. 15–17-minutes-long section were spent deciphering the identities of potential subsections that tumbled out fast, and in an unpredictable succession from the head. […] The usual process of polishing through uncountable stages is still not over: as I am coming close to completing the piano-vocal/choral score I am still changing a detail here and there. But now the movement (and the whole work of which it is a part) stands I believe as an instant of a complex network of truths, shown. In all this I moved along as a quasi-somnambulist led by the hand—so to say—the insight of that 'flash,' a kind of gyroscope ...

178 | Now I only recently stumbled onto the info[rmation] that in Greek the word δεικνυειν (*deiknuein*, might be a close enough transliteration; I am uncertain, as I do not have Greek) means not only 'to show,' but also 'to prove.' Is it in this sense that Martin Heidegger uses the word 'showing' when he said "The essential being of language is Saying as Showing?"[37] Which I can (must) also apply to the section of *Winthrop* I just wrote about. If so (and I believe this to be the case) then by showing 'dramatically,' e.g., in a condensed, concentrated, intensified, abstracted (to a point) way a chunk of truth in much of its complexity, I might have also proven the truth being that. Even if it never happened exactly that way, even [if] no such 17 minutes of events-succession ever took place ca. *anno* 1626, it is truer than the unvarnished truthfulness of any real 17-minute-long sample that really has occurred. If so, art, by inventing from elements of a chain of truth, a fiction-abstraction, comes closer to the essence than much of the 'thing' as is, or was, could ever hope to achieve. You know all this, and more, but it came out as an echo to your beautiful sentence ... (I am very much looking forward to reading the 'big' paper.)

You see I am rather full of *Winthrop* these days. Worried about seeing the project coming unglued and apprehensive at contemplating some unpalatable alternative responses to such an eventuality. Presently all things seem to be in flux. The trouble is (one of them) that I do not know what I should believe to be true from what is being said. This is sad, but having an ear for the 'sub-text,' and some previous experience, I cannot but be wary of much that takes place (or does not take place) presently on the *W[inthrop]* front. I'll keep you posted. [...]

I must go now. Two things in parting. You might find relevant things to 'iconic thinking' in Michael Polányi's concept of 'tacit understanding';[38] also in T. Izutsu's *Language and Magic*.[39] [...]

Istvan

[...]

99

23 NOVEMBER 1985

My dear Isty,

[...] I have to tell you I was so taken with your description of your own iconic experience with *Winthrop* that I've incorporated most of it in my paper ["The Iconography of the Mind"]. If you object to my having done so, please don't hesitate to let me know—and I'll take it out. But frankly, it's so good & indeed perfect an example of precisely what I'm writing about I hope you'll allow me to keep it in. The paper is done in the rough; & even while it's being typed I'm already revising, deleting, changing it. Would you read it over once it's knocked into reasonable shape? I need & want tough criticism before it takes final form & I let it out of my hands, and I know you will be eminently fair in giving it your critical scrutiny. Please let me know. It will mean a great deal to me. In the overall sense I think it's more than ordinarily good because it goes to the heart of some very important & basic matters such as laying to rest old dualisms between reason & intuition, idea & experience, quantification & qualitative, objectivity & subjectivity. It also shows as clearly as I can show it <u>how</u> we "think" especially when making art is concerned although I don't neglect other "forms" of thinking. Somehow with this paper I have the feeling I've gotten closer than ever before to things which are basic & which keep cropping up in my mind—like an ostinato. […]

George

100

6 DECEMBER 1985

Dear George,

[…] I was tremendously touched by your decision to include something I spilled out about *Winthrop* in the new paper. Another bond between us? Sure! I have an odd feeling about us 'including' each other, in a reciprocal way, in several forms, the strongest of which are the silent ones, when one accepts as one's permanent 'baggage' a thought, an attitude, etc. of the dear and intimate friend, or soul-brother. It harks back, I sense, to an old old act between tribal brothers who may cut their skin to shed blood to be mixed immediately and then ingested by both. Just as much a symbolic act as the one we have and are (will be?) doing, to show something very dear, rare, and precious. […]

Sure you have heard my *cri de coeur* about *Winthrop*, the 'selling' of which costs me presently some heartache. What I am enmeshed in revealed itself as a complex situation characterized by a bevy of midwives, little money, some tender reputations, some (much) self interest, and so it goes … What else is new would someone near Carnegie Hall say. Of course … I see no villain/good guy oppositions either. So it boils down to fixing this or that. Last week my mood was deep purple about all this. Since, some hopeful signs have appeared. I'll know more in about 2 weeks' time. Keep your fingers crossed for me. […]

Istvan

[…]

NOTES

1 Symphony No. 4 (1976) was commissioned by the Seattle Youth Orchestra in celebration of the Bicentennial of the United States and premiered by them, Vilem Sokol, conductor, in Seattle, Washington, on 15 November 1976.

2 Quintet for String Quintet [double cello] (1981), commissioned by the Concord String Quartet and premiered by them (with Bonnie Thron, cello) at the Curtis Institute of Music, Philadelphia, on 6 January 1982.

3 "Pst … Pst … Are You Listening? Hearing Voices from Yesterday," *Queen's Quarterly* 93/1 (Spring 1986): 71–84; reprinted in John Paynter et al., eds., *Companion to Contemporary Musical Thought*, 2 vols. (London and New York: Routledge, 1992), 2: 977–92.

4 "What Tack to Take? An Autobiographical Sketch (Life in Progress …)," *Queen's Quarterly* 91/1 (Spring 1985): 96–107.

5 See "1984," note 17.

6 See "1984," note 7.

7 Max V. Matthews (b. 1926), electrical engineer who worked on acoustic research, from 1955 to 1987, at the Bell Telephone Laboratories in Murray Hill, New Jersey; he was the first to design programs for the computer generation of music (1957–58). From 1974 to 1980 he served as a scientific adviser to the Institute de Recherche et Coordination Acoustique/Musique (IRCAM) in Paris.

8 "Expanding on what Aristotle said twenty-three centuries before him, he [Heidegger] wrote: 'The letters show the sounds. The sounds show the passions in the soul, and the passions in the soul show the matters that arouse them.' To this he added, '*The essential being of language is saying as showing*'" (italics in original). ("Pst … Pst … Are You Listening?" 71; 977).

9 See "1984," note 17.

10 Walter Benjamin, *Reflections: Essays, Aphorisms, Autobiographical Writings*, trans. Edmund Jephcott, ed. with an introduction by Peter Demetz (New York: Harcourt Brace Jovanovich, 1978).

11 "Fiddlers and Fribbles, or, Is Art a Separate Reality?" *New Literary History: A Journal of Theory and Interpretation* 18 (1987): 257–79; reprinted in Rochberg, *Aesthetics of Survival*, rev. and expanded ed. (2004), 145–64.

12 Rochberg, "Can the Arts Survive Modernism? (A Discussion of the Characteristics, History and Legacy of Modernism)," *Critical Inquiry* 11/2 (December 1984): 317–40; Jonathan D. Kramer, "Can Modernism Survive George Rochberg?" *Critical Inquiry* 11/2 (December 1984): 341–54; Rochberg, "Critical Response: Kramer vs. Kramer," *Critical Inquiry* 11/3 (March 1985): 509–17.

13 Murray Krieger, "The Ambiguities of Representation and Illusion: An E.H. Gombrich Retrospective," *Critical Inquiry* 11/2 (December 1984): 181–94; E.H. Gom-

brich, "Representation and Misrepresentation," ibid.: 195–201; see also Murray Krieger, "Critical Response III: Optics and Aesthetic Perception: A Rebuttal," *Critical Inquiry* 11/3 (March 1985): 502–8.

14 See "1984," note 15.
15 See "1982," note 2.
16 *Wallenberg: A Hero's Story* (1985), directed by Lamont Johnson, starring Richard Chamberlain as Raoul Wallenberg.
17 Anhalt, "Mirage in Elöpatak," in *Istvan Anhalt: Pathways and Memory*, ed. Robin Elliott and Gordon E. Smith (Montreal and Kingston: McGill-Queen's University Press, 2001), 421–23.
18 That is, "The Avant-Garde and the Aesthetics of Survival" (1969) in Rochberg, *Aesthetics of Survival* (1984), 215–31; rev. and expanded ed. (2004), 225–41; for reference to Von Neumann, see "1965," note 7.
19 This is a rough paraphrase of the following lines from Plate 14 of *The Marriage of Heaven and Hell* (ca. 1790–93): "For the cherub with his flaming sword is hereby commanded to leave his guard at [the] tree of life; and when he does, the whole creation will be consumed and appear infinite and holy, whereas it now appears finite & corrupt. ... If the doors of perception were cleansed every thing would appear to man as it is, infinite. For man has closed himself up, till he sees all things thro' narrow chinks of his cavern." I am indebted to Professor Morris Eaves of the University of Rochester for suggesting this connection.
20 More precisely, "'Beauty is truth, truth beauty,—that is all/Ye know on earth, and all ye need to know.'" From *Ode on a Grecian Urn* (1820).
21 Doris Lessing, *Canopus in Argos: Archives*, vol. 1, *Shikasta: Re, Colonised Planet 5: Personal, Psychological, Historical Documents Relating to Visit by Johor (George Sherban) Emissary (Grade 9) 87th of the Period of the Last Days* (New York: Knopf, 1979).
22 Robert Bly, *News of the Universe: Poems of Twofold Consciousness* (San Francisco: Sierra Club Books, 1980).
23 In what many consider his greatest foreign policy blunder, President Ronald Reagan, arguing that German soldiers were also victims of Nazi terror, on 5 May 1985 placed a wreath at the German military cemetery in Bitberg where, among the 2000 or so graves, lie a small number of Hitler's elite guard, the Schutzstaffel (SS).
24 *Thisness*, duo-drama for mezzo-soprano and piano, text by the composer (1985), commissioned by the Vancouver New Music Society for Phyllis Mailing, premiered in 1986 in Vancouver by Mailing and pianist Richard Epp.
25 Yves Tanguy (1900–55), *Multiplication des arcs* (1954), oil on canvas (Museum of Modern Art, New York); colour reproduction in Karin von Maur, with essays by Susan Davidson et al., *Yves Tanguy and Surrealism* (Ostfildern-Ruit, Germany: Hatje Cantz Publishers, 2001), 127.
26 For a summary of gnostic cosmology and a definition of the word *heimarmene*, see Hans Jonas, *The Gnostic Religion: The Message of the Alien God and the Beginnings of Christianity*, 2nd ed. revised (Boston: Beacon Press, 1963), 42–43. Jonas translates *heimarmene* as "universal Fate," the "tyrannical world-rule" of the Archons, or rulers.
27 The name given to "the Lord of Darkness" by the Persians and Chaldeans.
28 See "1968," note 13.
29 Josef Skvorecky, *The Engineer of Human Souls*, trans. Paul Wilson (New York: A.A. Knopf, 1984).

30 Sinclair Lewis (1885–1951), Minnesota-born novelist, playwright, and social critic, who won the Nobel Prize for Literature in 1930, the first given to an American; his novel *It Can't Happen Here* (1935) is a portrayal of a fascist coup d'état in the United States, driven, in the words of the character Francis Tasbrough, by opposition to "the Jew Communists and Jew financiers plotting together to control the country." With reference to Lewis's title, Rochberg writes: "But unfortunately it is happening and now in High Gear!!" (letter to the editor, 6 May 2004).

31 *To the Dark Wood*, for woodwind quintet (1985), commissioned by the Earle Page Foundation of the University of New England, Armidale, Australia, on behalf of the Canberra Wind Soloists and premiered by them at University Hall, University of New England, 3 October 1986.

32 Symphony No. 6 was begun in the spring of 1986 and completed in January 1987. Only a few sketches survive of a seventh symphony (see "1989," note 8).

33 "The Iconography of the Mind: Inward Seeing and Iconic Thinking" (1985–86) (unpublished). There are three drafts of this paper in the Anhalt Fonds (MUS 164/F2,16): a first draft, simply titled "Inward Seeing and Iconic Thinking," dated October 1985; second and third drafts with the full title, dated 1985 and 1985–86, respectively, the final draft running to 116 pages.

34 John Maynard Keynes, "The Economic Possibilities for Our Grandchildren" (1930), quoted by Ernst Friedrich Schumacher in *Small Is Beautiful: A Study of Economics as if People Mattered* (London: Blond and Briggs, 1973). The quotation continues: "Avarice and usury and precaution must be our gods for a little longer still. For only they can lead us out of the tunnel of economic necessity into daylight."

35 N. David Mermin, "Is the Moon There When Nobody Looks? Reality and the Quantum Theory," *Physics Today* 38/4 (April 1985): 38–47.

36 Howard Gardner, *The Mind's New Science: A History of the Cognitive Revolution* (New York: Basic Books, 1985).

37 Martin Heidegger, *On the Way to Language*, trans. Peter D. Hertz (New York: Harper & Row, 1971), 123.

38 See Michael Polányi, *The Tacit Dimension* (Garden City, NY: Doubleday, 1966).

39 Toshihiko Izutsu, *Language and Magic* (Tokyo: Keio Institute of Philological Studies, 1956).

PART FOUR

POLITICS, RELIGION, AND SOCIETY (1986–2000)

The hirelings of the so-called "chattering" classes cooperate effectively, and with the help of promoters of a new class of linguistic mutations, our conceptual landscape was, and continues to be, subjected to a subtle yet brutal, near subliminal (for those who do not "deconstruct" these new linguistic horrors) brain washing.

— Anhalt (November 1996)

1986

101

3 APRIL 1986

My dear Isty,

I hope the cassette of [Symphony] #5 has reached you by now; and once you've had a chance to "assimilate" it, you'll let me know your reaction. I spent the 2 weeks following our return home recuperating. I was really exhausted, not so much from the musical side of the week in Chicago—that always has its tensions & pressures inevitably—as from the constant need to relate to the sideshow set in motion by the fact of the premiere[1] itself: interviews, a meeting with critics following the Wed. rehearsals (wouldn't have made it through that talk session without the help of a long bourbon), a reception at the office of Hizonor, the mayor of Chicago […] and various & sundry champagne receptions following both performances. After all these years, being "wined & dined" is really not my style at all—but the "musical life" of our times seems to insist on being more & more social. […]

Solti proved to be every inch the man & musician I have come to regard so highly. He was enormously sympathetic to the work, was quite generous with his praise privately & time professionally. The fact that I am not entirely satisfied with his performance takes nothing away from my feeling for him. We had about 3–4 hrs. of rehearsals including the dress run-through, no more—for the most simple of reasons: I had to prepare 2 programs that week, the concert with [Symphony] #5 Thurs. & Sat. and a Tchaikovsky concert Friday night!! How does one even get used to the maddeningly brief time available to prepare a new work? One doesn't—or I should say, I can't. When I express dissatisfaction with his way of doing

[Symphony] #5, I refer mainly to the tempo of the 5/8 section which is just under what it should be and consequently becomes too *pesante* & the fact that he doesn't allow the slow sections greater expansiveness and elasticity. Despite these flaws, it came off coherently and convincingly. The orchestra responded enthusiastically—always a pleasure when the people who play your music say out loud they like it—and the audience gave it a good reception. While "recuperating" I entered those corrections & changes I felt absolutely essential for greater presence & clarity where needed (in the tissues)—so now it is behind me. What I long for, since we're never really finished with a work until we hear it in its most ideal sense, is another performance—maybe next year—which will come as close as possible to the ideal. Meanwhile, now that I feel some energy again & the old noodle is beginning to perk a little, I'm circling around ideas for [Symphony] #6 which will be another *Geschichte* entirely. Someone expressed to me his feeling that the same spirit animates [Symphony] #5 that animates [Symphony] #2. Fine; & probably not a bad insight because both are compressed, hot, concentrated works. But [Symphony] #6 will be in 4 movements which already tells you something.[2] Wider range of gestures, a different orchestral palette, looser in a way. I hope work on & involving *Winthrop* goes well & not too taxing. As the man said, "I don't buy green bananas anymore." […]

George

102

20 APRIL 1986

Dear George,

What a powerful and gripping work your 5th [Symphony]! A tremendous opening, literally, like a wound torn open, or like a sustained wailing over the telling (no: showing) of something that has taken (or is taking) place … A work of enormous lines, sustained by whatever gave you the endurance to envisage it and put it on paper. Then the lyricism that told me of another inner song of yours, echoing what I retain of the Oboe Concerto, suggesting to me, my dear friend, that you are closer to Wittgenstein's Vienna then I ever was, though, at times, I have felt (and am still fancying) a close kinship to it. (How unbridgeably far that world was from the Budapest years of, say 1937–42 …) But back to your 5th … (yes it is a fifth, responding to whatever one would feel obliges one to say something about weighty matters … Are we thus retracing a mental/developmental tract blazed by that giant that still dares one, as if saying:

"… and you think you could open your mouth? What do you propose to say?" Well, you've taken him on alongside his awesome journey and held your own, on your terms because, as it turns out, you have your own trace, your own life, which had to be lived, must be lived, and shown as lived …) Do these make sense at all? As the words spill out there does seem to exist a thread … But this is not all: this beautiful (yet also terrifyingly so) work is a transcendent image, and as such art of a very high order. I could go on (even after a single listening that took place a few days ago), but is it necessary? You must have gotten that I love and admire the work a great deal and am happy that you've brought it off. A plateau in your output it is!

Things are gathering speed around *Winthrop*. […] Tomorrow I am off for Toronto where a meeting will take place about publicity related to the Sept. 6 premiere. Some drums will be beaten which is as it should be, given the size of the effort that goes into this production, and the increasingly defensive posture of serious music in this corner of the woods, at least. The symphony people will be there too and I should like to think that there will be some news about the engagement of the still not designated singers for 3 of the 6 solo roles. We'll see.

Enclosed is the tape of the March 6 Toronto performance of *Thisness*. It took place in a downtown church, one of the venues of the A[merican] S[ociety of] U[niversity] C[omposers] conference. […]

Istvan

103

27 APRIL 1986

My dear Isty,

The text of *Thisness* came a day before the cassette with your letter—all three found me wrestling again with a new orchestral work I'm writing for the Pittsburgh Symphony [Symphony No. 6] (more of that a little later) — — —

1 MAY

Something interrupted me—& I couldn't get back 'til today. What was it? *Chi lo sa*? Since the 27th I've listened to the tape of *Thisness* & read the text—and all the while I listened I kept seeing & hearing you go through it when I was in your studio & thinking how much more personal & sensitive your reading (however incomplete) … the atmosphere of the work hung on for a day or more. Searching, penetrating, probing the dark fringes. Still with me as I write. It's a true statement, a statement of "old age" as someone once said about those works which come from the heart of experience, of the sadness which becomes the inevitable accompanying *basso ostinato* of mature years. How could it be otherwise? That's what life is, despite those rays of light & love that come our way if we're lucky & open & receptive. We are there now, my old friend & that is our source for whatever we do 'til the end. I don't know whether it has anything to do with what used to be called "wisdom." That's too fixed & static a word for the huge waves which wash over me these days, too much the sense that we've lost our compass for wisdom because all around us something, indefinable & threatening, is loose in the world. In the face of terrorism, Soviet nuclear accidents which affect all of Europe how can one be sanguine & at ease inwardly? Hence your work, hence mine. No one has understood my 5th [Symphony] better than you & I shall cherish your thoughts & feelings as you expressed them. I said to Gene the other day: I have war on the brain. Whether I will eventually call [Symphony] #6 "In Tempore Bello" I don't know; but that is what dominates me as I struggle to give life & shape to what I feel & hear. I'm planning four movements (four beginnings & endings! that's why [Symphony] #5 had only one of each—the technical problem of how to start & how to end—one of the worst I know these last years) which will range far & wide. I have all the ideas, some clearer than others—can't really get off the ground unless I do—still not sure how I'm going to get my head around all the stuff that keeps rising to the surface—but I've made a beginning—and that's more than I could have said 3 weeks ago. What we do or try to do is the sanest madness I know—the rest? ...

[...]

George

104

1 AUGUST 1986

George, dear friend,

I just reread your wonderful letter from April 27th ... hearing you shouting through the turmoil and heat of the 'workshop' as you grope around with recalcitrant material and reluctant-to-yield form-ideas hammering out a beginning for your Sixth ... 'Pastorale' versus 'Opus in tempore bellorum' (actually the ultimate, that would call for "belli," is not upon us ... yet (?), but this plurality of intractable conflicts is much too much already, sounds not being in sync ... we cannot be in sync ...). It was generous that you, once again, shared with me these 'chemically' complex early moments in the coming into being of something new ...

As always I listened very carefully to the echoes my doings bounce off your mind ... This time it was *Thisness*. I see the rightness of your response, albeit in my perception the 'thing''s essence is not so much in being an 'old voice' (although, perhaps, this is true, also), but slightly to the southwest from it. Question: must an enactment of certain types of truths be, inevitably, and overwhelmingly somber? This crazy life goes on, people (at least in our little corner) live longer, eat better, etc. despite the increasing troubles all around ... What bothers me is the inexorable advance of vulgarization, and the inequity of life opportunity, depending where one was born. Is there some kind of contradiction between the 2? I don't know how to think anymore about the killing fields of Ulster, Punjab, the Near East, etc. Are we made in a way that induces us to kill? The ghost in the machine story ... are males worse in this than females? Or is this only cultural conditioning that is now in the process of change? How should I act when I hear about Nazi-type Jews on the loose in Israel? We soon need, I begin to feel, another 2–3 days to bounce off worries, ideas, on each other. (What a rare treat it was to have you here with us a few months ago ... !)

Yes, *Winthrop*. The cast is complete, and so is the checking over of the orchestra material (ca. 9 weeks of solid slavery). The premiere is set for Sept. 6th. [...] The principals and the choirs are already at work, though the adult choir (S.M.A.T.Bar.B., often divided up) will do most of its work towards the end of the month. Orchestra rehearsals will begin on Sept. 2. The public response is heartening. The leading papers in the country have run substantial 'advance' stories, with pictures (I have photos of several Winthrop portraits).[3] Quite an expectation is in the process of building up. (After all, the premiere of a full-length 'home-grown' work is not an everyday occurrence in 'cool Canada.') I hope that I shall be able 'to deliver' accordingly ... I am confident, as of now. [...]

Istvan

105

10 AUGUST 1986

Dear old friend Isty,

What I wouldn't give to be able to be present Sept. 6 to hear *Winthrop* come to life—but as it turns out we're leaving for a month's trip to Australia Sept. 25 (concerts, lectures & 1st perf[ormance], also 2nd, all of *To the Dark Wood*).[4] I think the pocketbook could manage two jaunts in the same period but not these old bones! So we will be there in spirit and I will call you before we leave for down-under to find out how it went—which Gene & I both hope will, as the parlance goes, "knock 'em dead." […]

The Marcia movement of the [Symphony] #6 is sketched. I'm currently debating whether to write two inside mov[ement]s (a scherzo & a slow one) to complete the work or settle only for the scherzo. I "reason" with myself: inasmuch as the 1st mov[emen]t (also sketched) is a large fantasia with much slow music surrounded by more dramatic & sometimes violent passages, do I really need an adagio & thereby push the work over 40 minutes? A real dilemma which I need to resolve soon. In any case with the outside mov[ement]s already in hand I'll tackle the scherzo next & see what my feelings are in re the adagio. […]

George

[…]

106

Southern Cross Hotel
Melbourne
11 OCTOBER 1986

My dear Isty,

It's morning in Melbourne. Gene's just gone off to see the town. I'm waiting for a young Australian composer, who wants to talk to me, to show up. Then I'll meet a group of them for lunch at some restaurant. We've been "on the road" for over 2 wks. & tho a little frayed around the edges from too many airports, planes, long & short hops, hotels, we're holding our own. Tomorrow we're off to Sydney for 3 days, then Canberra for the rest of the time here climaxed by an all-Rochberg concert at the Canberra Sch[ool] of Music Oct. 20. The Canberra wind soloists (excellent players in every way, esp[ecially] the hornist) will repeat *To the Dark Wood* which they launched in Armidale Oct. 3. I'll have a chance to work with them once again before the 2nd perf[ormance] so we can polish things. It's been a remarkably varied trip so far; first Tahiti, Gauguin country—soft tropical climate & people, the same colors you see in Gauguin's canvasses, then Armidale, high "tableland," sheep country, wide & broad undulating landscape, lovely people at the Univ[ersity] of New England who brought us here. They are in fact quite remarkable when you consider none of them are musicians yet the principals are all mad about music generally & contemporary music particularly. There are philosophers of language, of science, research scientists among them—warmest bunch of academics I've met in all my years of assoc[iation] with academia. We hated to leave there. Then on to Brisbane, a healthy bustling town on the move in a big way. Exemplary of what seems to be happening to Australia—they're intelligent & sensitive enuf to be building things like perf[ormance] arts complexes on the bank of the river which runs through the town. Gave a lecture at the Univ[ersity] of Queensland while in Brisbane. […]

The Australians seem to want "culture" desperately but don't seem to have developed their collective tastes sufficiently to protect them against mere entertainment. The art we've seen so far I would call "derivative-derivative" & the music—haven't heard enough yet to form any judgments. Heard a Requiem for solo cello by Peter Sculthorpe[5] who is acknowledged as one of the big 3 or 4 here which has the distinction of genuine feeling expressed clearly. The "idiom" leaves something to be desired. […]

Gene and George

107

20 OCTOBER 1986

Dear friend, George,

[…] I am delighted with the progress of your 6th. From what you've written you are 'half way home' already. What a series! What an achievement! To my mind (and experience) you are one of the true symphonists writing today who have the 'stuff' to sustain the weight of the scope/medium suggested by the word 'symphonic.' Let me know what your eventual decision is re the Adagio [of the Symphony No. 6].

Yes, one must feel in one single grasp the ebb and flow of the entire work. One of my questions (before the premiere) re *Winthrop* was about the tension/tempo curve of Act 1. The work starts 'slowly' with Section 1. Section 2 is 'tense,' but subsides at the end (it is the aria of John as a young man). Section 3 is a 'slow' love-duet. I was wondering if this 'slow-fast-slow' beginning—adding up to ca. 50% of Act 1—would work. Well, it does and did. What I was counting on (that the emotional 'temperature' and 'density' of Sections 1 to 3 will 'launch' the work powerfully) proved itself true.

The rehearsals were frugal as to time, to say the least, for, a work of ca. 140 minutes of playing time: 6 effective hours for the orch[estra] alone, 6 effective hours for orch[estra], soli and the 2 choirs plus the dress (with which—rather late—we moved into the concert hall that seats ca. 2000, with a fine acoustics of ca. 1.8 seconds reverb time). After the players got the hang of the harmonies, and the progressions, etc. (they had to, and did, learn fast) the orchestral stratum came to life 'by itself.' The problems pertained only to dynamic balance, which (some of which) kept on causing problems right into the performance. I was, and am, reluctant to change dynamics in the orch[estra] until I hear a performance in which the orch[estra] is in the pit, where I imagined them to be as I wrote.

When the voices joined in the excitement rose. Most (4) of the soloists were very good. The rest (2) adequate. The mixed choir (The Elmer Iseler Singers, Canada's best professional choir, augmented to 38 voices for the occasion) was splendid. They sang/recited/declaimed/shouted/whispered etc. up a real storm, or performed with exquisite subtlety their very difficult part. The boys' choir (ca. 25 strong) was so-so, but on the whole adequate, and without disaster. (I was worrying that the kids will feel lost when 'plugged' into the whole.)

The reception of the audience, that included lots of professionals, was and remains very gratifying. From the responses that came my way since Sept. 6 (and the broadcast of Sept. 14th) I might be allowed to conclude that the work speaks to people with different levels of sophistication in music: to professionals, including fellow composers, but also to amateurs of music, people whose expertise lies elsewhere. This pleases me greatly as I did want to reach people beyond the 'in crowd.' Correspondingly, and somewhat less importantly, the critics refrained from maiming, etc., but instead found it possible to be positive enough ... (There was only one critic from the U.S.: Robert Finn from the Cleveland *Plain Dealer* who wrote a long review in the Sept. 14th issue of the paper.)[6] The sub-text of the above is, of course, that I am relieved. The piece did not 'bomb,' just the contrary. Ca. 10 years of effort (including the past 2 years, most of which went into the preparations for this premiere) was not in vain.

Boston's WGBH (a member of the Public Radio Network) is desirous to re-broadcast the CBC September 14th broadcast, which comes to 3 hrs. together with introduction and intermission interviews. They are, presently, searching for the (rather modest) sum of money that will be needed.

A friend of Richard Wernick's,[7] who was at the premiere in Kitchener, spoke to him about the work. He expressed interest in seeing the score (in his capacity as dramaturge for the Phila[delphia] Symph[ony] Orch[estra]). Hence I sent him the score and the tapes.

Our vacation in England was restoring. The weather was perfect throughout. We walked and slept a lot and ate well. We had some reunions with people whom we like and did not see for a while. Also revisited some of the Winthrop-related places in Lincolnshire & Suffolk.

I am looking forward to reading your account about the Australian trip. […]

Istvan

108

10 NOVEMBER 1986

My dear friend Isty,

How time eats up our lives! I was no sooner back from Australia—an experience of a lifetime & not to be repeated in this one—wonderful in many ways, especially genuinely new lands & climates & peoples & languages—and half-recuperated from the trip back (there is nothing to make you sag like the depleting plagues of jet-lag) when I was off to Chicago to keep a promise I had made to the Beaux Arts Trio to attend their perf[ormance] there of the new (or recent) piano trio [No. 2]. It was worth it musically—for they played it with the same love, conviction & rightness of "style" they bring to Mozart or Brahms. […]

George

NOTES

1 See "1984," note 1.
2 The final version of Symphony No. 6 (1986–87) is in two parts: I. Fantasia: Allegro, and II. Marcia.
3 See John Kraglund, "CMC's Biggest Triumph May Be Opera Premiere," *The Globe and Mail*, 21 May 1986.
4 See "1985," note 31.
5 Peter Sculthorpe (b. 1929), *Requiem*, for cello alone (1982).
6 Robert Finn, "Canadian Pageant Unveils Elaborate U.S. Historical Work," *The Plain Dealer* (Cleveland), 14 September 1986. In a generally enthusiastic review, Finn singles out for special praise the closing pages of Part One, which he describes as "a kind of Protestant passion": "And the close of Part One is masterly—a choral-orchestral poem describing the departure of Winthrop and his followers for the new

world. The chorus softly intones a kind of farewell benediction ...; a slow, steady sea swell rises in the orchestra and the chorus chimes in with soft noises imitating the rise and fall of wind through halyards. It is a touch of genius." And in conclusion he writes: "At its best, where music and text unite successfully, 'Winthrop' is masterly. Even when they don't, it is still dramatically compelling in a theatrical way. Even when you're not quite sure what is going on, the ear is constantly surprised, delighted, challenged, confronted."

7 See "1968," note 33.

1987

109

8 JANUARY 1987

Dear George,

[…] Your letter from Australia was a treat. It must have been a strange experience. (The place seems to draw. Presently, 2 young former associates of mine—student copyists—are spending a year in Sydney, one of them studying with Sculthorpe whom she likes much, and are delighted with the Aussie way of doing things …) I admire your fortitude in exposing yourself to the rattling that such a displacement is likely to entail. I find myself becoming more and more a 'stay-put' one, and this seems to agree with me. (Mind you, I have not been tempted to go far afield. I don't know how I would respond. Only one trip abroad is in the works now. I am reading an 'invited' paper at the yearly conference of the Royal Musical Ass[ociatio]n to be held at London University in April. Their (our) theme is 'Words & Music.' I was asked to say my bit on 'new' music for the voice.[1] I am trying to see how I could get beyond where I left off with *Alternative Voices*. I have oodles of notes on scraps of paper, and a few dozen new scores, tapes, to consider for it. However it is unlikely that I shall be able to give more than—say—a week for pulling 'the thing' together for a ca. 45' long 'Spiel.') […]

Presently I am preoccupied with writing (on a 'rush' commission for an Oct. '87 premiere by one of the leading orchestras of the country, the National Arts Centre Orch[estra], a new orchestral work. It promises to be (as requested) about 20 min. long. I have (now) much pleasure in writing it (by the month's end—Jan.—I should have the 1st version of the short score done. It will be my first 'non-vocal' piece since the late '60s. (On that account I was a bit wondering what I would want to say purely orchestrally. But I need not have worried.) The provisional title of the work is *Simulacrum*. It has a hidden scenario, of a vague sort, and proves to be the framework vehicle for getting into territory where I wanted to go since quite a while by now. It will even be a kind of exploration (this is one aspect of it) of my own Jewishness, whatever this is.[2] Lately I've been reading about things Jewish and am much stimulated by the syncretistic richness of it all. I see now that what I thought (wholly in the 'gut' way) that there are many ways of 'being Jewish/etc.' has been felt by many before me. (Discovering the wheel, once again ...) Oh yes! But the nuances in my mix will matter.

Other stimuli included (this was before I was thrown into the *Simulacrum* whirlpool) reading *The Selfish Gene* and a book on the *Anthropic Cosmological Principle*[3] (the latter would interest you; the former is a frustrating, arrogant, yet interesting geneticist's vantage point view of existence). Another was a volume of a magnum opus by the philosopher Mario Bunge (the title escapes me momentarily) in which he takes a critical view of most contemporary fads (computers, A[rtificial] I[ntelligence], genetics, etc.).[4] An attempt of a polymath at sorting out things at our own level, where things 'are at,' presently. [...]

Istvan

110

18 JANUARY 1987

My dear Isty,

[...] Australia is now a kind of very pleasant memory, almost a dream of sorts. Humanly, very gratifying considering how many truly warm & intelligent people we befriended. "Professionally" (odd word, fully deserving quotes around it) everything went off like clockwork. [...] There were excellent performances, especially at the end in Canberra. Perhaps the most interesting residue of the trip are the 4 or 5 one & a half hour ABC broadcasts scheduled for March '87 & interviews I had in Sydney (6 hours in one day!) *cum* recordings & tapes of my music. The Aussies are in for a real dose. Along the way I was supposed to meet Sculthorpe but it never materialized. He's considered one of Australia's best composers but I don't know enough of his music or Australian music in general to comment on that judgment. I brought back an ABC recording of 4 orchestral works, one of them by Sculthorpe—but I much prefer a work called *Viridian* by Richard Meale to Sculthorpe's *Mangrove*.[5] It was with tremendous relief I settled back into my work again. I'd written out the score of the first part (mov[ement]) of my 6th Symphony before leaving for down under and once back at the desk pushed through to just @ 2 weeks ago & completed the second part. […]

I'm fascinated by your mention of Jewishness in connection with your new orchestral work. Perhaps you can tell me something about it. Curiously I've gotten involved with Jewishness (incidentally a letter came yesterday from a dear young woman, the wife of a former Israeli student who had to, for reasons of conscience so he claimed, return to Israel, even though if he'd stuck it out here in the States, he would eventually have landed on his feet. She remarked that the whole country is madly obsessed with the old question, "Who is a Jew?," largely because it's been forced on them by the orthodox. She says, in effect, there're tearing themselves apart. Sad, sad, sad). Because I have decided to rework the Iconography essay[6] into an expanded form, probably a book & in the process decided it was somehow crucial to discuss the 2nd commandment which prescribes the making of images. What a subtle complicated business comes out of it & I'll probably never get to the bottom of it. Along the way I came across a remarkable study (in 12 [*sic*] vols.) by Erwin Goodenough of *Jewish Symbols in the Greco-Roman Period*.[7] Talk about syncretism, especially in the Hellenistic period! […]

George

111

14 MARCH 1987

George, dear friend,

[…] *Simulacrum*, the new piece is done, copied, printed, ready for the conductor. Its size: ca. 21½ minutes, and it ranges over a considerable terrain of my personal landscape. (Are we not, forever, explorers of this inner map, getting to know the lay of the land better as we go on … or: we make the landscape as we wake up to get another beautifully rich day … Life is "nice," if at times terrifyingly so, but one lives, breathes and the grandchildren smile … and … oh … the hugs … enough.)

Now I'll go into the other 'mode' and shall string up words so as to allow the non-linearity of the landscape I stuttered about earlier not to be narrowed into falsity. Ostensibly, I'll be writing about music & words, but I am pulled by all sorts of hermeneutic sirens beyond a safe limit … I resist somewhat … but should I? … who cares … if 'they' think I am slightly … well … queer … (or do I underestimate my English interlocutors? They might be the real creatively crazy ones and I'll find myself as the square Canadian ...). So, you see, after all, I am deafened by the specter of a few echo-ghosts. Enough again ... The stuff I already have on scraps of paper promises an interesting possibility ... I might just be able to pull it off.

What you wrote about the second commandment is interesting. I am closing with a quote that is a 'motto' in the score of *Simulacrum*: " ... every word of the Torah has six hundred thousand 'faces,' that is, layers of meaning or entrances, one for each of the children of Israel who stood at the foot of Mount Sinai. Each face is turned toward only one of them; he alone can see it and decipher it." (G. Scholem in *On the Kabbalah and its Symbolism*, in reference to the *Kabbalah* according to Isaac Luria.) [...]

Istvan

[...]

112

3 MAY 1987

Dear old friend Isty,

I had visions of you & Bea happily roaming the English countryside in early spring last month. I hope it proved restful & restoring after all your recent labors. When will the new orchestra work be done? [Symphony] #6 for Pittsburgh w[ith] Maazel is set for Oct. 16/17/18.[8] Like all such "events" in my life this takes on the character of dream ... when I was young it was all so real ... now the only reality—and even there it has its dreamlike character much of the time—is the day-to-day life, especially now that I'm breaking new/old ground for a large-scale violin/piano work. I find myself literally between two worlds: Brahms/Beethoven sonatas which have taken on miraculous qualities, they are so right & inevitable in the way they are thought and realized as true chamber music dialogues; "provoking" myself with recent works by younger composers who design more than "think" their music though obviously thought goes into fashioning design. They are obsessed by "sound," color, texture; either the "harmony" is unidimensional as in some cases & lacks all progression in the old sense, or "layered" in other cases. I've been studying *Viridian* by Richard Meale, a 55± Australian. Very tasteful, tiny but well-shaped phrases passed through the orchestra with occasional "cadences" clearly tonal. And a young American, George Tsontakis[9] whom I recently met. A very talented, dark-spirited, serious mind. He builds everything virtually out of antecedents—there are no consequents. In certain moods I find it irksome because no line develops. Instead, it creates the impression of hovering around loci so that movement, even when he's rhythmic (& he is, more than most of his 35-to-40-y[ea]r-old contemporaries), occurs by accretion. Still I'm drawn to these things even though they lie outside my "natural" range of musical thinking. Where Brahms gives us unfolding thought expressed in often indelible ideas, they proceed atmospherically—cloud forms often—so that it's hard to remember anything specific.

My Octet [(1979–80), "A Grand Fantasia for Flute, Clarinet, Horn, Violin, Viola, Cello, Bass, and Piano"] was done in N[ew] Y[ork] early in April & on the program were works by 35–40-y[ea]r-olds. Astonishing how much talent per square inch they have. But no clear emotional signals came through their ingenious "designs." Do they feel? In their private lives I'm sure they do. Why not in their music? Are they afraid or inhibited or even perhaps embarrassed to speak with passion, to declare their personal pain or joy (if they're lucky enough to have joyous moments in life)? The one who impressed me most was a young Dane or Swede, Hans Abrahamsen.[10] Lots of energy, incredible color imagination. But added all up, I'm still not sure there is anything that is so powerfully said as to enter into the bloodstream of the (dwindling?) art culture of our day. Rereading *The Tragic Sense of Life* by Miguel de Unamuno, the Spaniard of the turn of the century.[11] What force, energy, power of life & spirit mixed with the dilemma of knowing that what awaits us all is death, oblivion, *nada*. But Unamuno says no: he opts for personal immortality against nothingness. He faces the contradiction head on. Takes your breath away. That's what I miss in these young ones, the dilemma, contradiction, painful paradox of life itself. Their sheer consciousness has diminished, no doubt the spiritual plague brought on by the 20th cent[ury] which has produced such a degree of fear & crushing anxiety—even to the race's chances of survival itself (Aids is the physical manifestation of spiritual loss of immunological capacity to rage against life and death) that artists generally can no longer come to grips with Fate or Destiny. Instead they escape into abstractions to protect themselves from too much pain. I was recuperating from a miserable strep throat some weeks back & reread T.S. Eliot. There you find the beginning of self-anaesthetizing, the self-distancing from painful awareness of life's dilemmas, mysteries. Eliot is English; Unamuno is Spanish. Perhaps there's the difference in how they go at it, Eliot reflecting at a distance, Unamuno on the Barricades raging at the injustice of possible oblivion, of the end of personal consciousness. I prefer Unamuno (and I'm not even Spanish!) though I feel Eliot's measured, sometimes almost stuttering inability to "say"—and sympathize greatly. Making pleasant conversation, being charming, delightful or even witty in art is fine but only as a momentary diversion, a pause to refresh, in the midst of the agon. The F♯-minor intermezzo/scherzo/caprice of Brahms's A major Sonata is such a moment. Thinking out loud so you can hear me Isty—that's what I'm doing. Art is for "warriors," not gentlemen.

I hacked out two chapters of the book between end of Jan. & end of March. Suddenly I lost all taste for words, for intellection, for dealing with ideas. Perhaps I'll get back to the book "later"—whenever "later" will be. In any case, they're being typed up & once they're proofread, revised, etc. I'll send you Xeroxes so you can read them & let me have your thoughts. After spending 2 months solely preoccupied with Judaism & Christianity in regard to images & words, I find myself more convinced than ever that the pagans for all their superstition were closer to the spiritual reality we face than either the Jews or Christians. Though the Christian message of love is certainly more appealing than the Jewish insistence on law. In time to come there will be new religions, whether better or more efficacious for man's purpose & needs, who can tell? I hope spring is touching Kingston with its warmth. The mystery of the Earth's self renewal always amazes me. So unlike ourselves—unless Unamuno is (somehow) right (somewhere).

[…]

George

113

5 DECEMBER 1987

My dear George,

On my cluttered desk lies your typescript of "The Second Commandment and Idolatry"[12] which I am about to read the second time over before entering into this note to you. Yes, I do have recollections of it. It 'spoke' to me, once again almost like a mirror, as it so happened on repeated occasions in our relationship over the past 25+ years. We do seem to travel on paths that for some reasons (and possibly these are the enigmas that interest me, if not the most, but in a 'peak' way) appear to be parallel to each other for longer stretches of the road than with any other person I cherish a lasting friendship. Whatever these 'causes' are (shared circumstances, shared totemic belonging in some way, and who knows, perhaps a genetic link also may lie deep in our chromosomes, attesting to a shared ancestry way back in time somewhere, perhaps in a German ghetto, or a village in the Pale, or who knows where) but there they are ... and once in a while they prompt me to regard, and call, you a soul-brother. [...]

News: I did complete the score of the new orchestra piece for Toronto's young Esprit Orchestra. Its title is *SparkskrapS*. It is one more piece in this latest series of directly inward voyages that started with *Thisness*. Its other source is Kabbalistic thinking: the sparks of the 10 Sephiroth, intermingled with the debris of the 'containers' that were to encapsulate their essence. Now this essence is the infinite 'light' of the Unnamable, the Unfathomable. No wonder, then, that such hypostases as Hokhmah (wisdom), Binah (understanding, etc.), Tiffereth (beauty or memory) etc. could not contain this essence. To say it in another language: our word-receptacles are inadequate means whereby to encapsulate the divine (read cosmic, read human, read scientific, read artistic ...) essence. They were made to try this but vainly; no wonder they burst, and all that remain are the debris of sparks and the scraps intermingled and the duty of all good men (women) is to sort them out (whatever this means for Tom, Dick or Sally). But a latter-date Kabbalist (I don't recall who he was) said that all that, sparks and the shards, express the physical, metaphysical, including the human universe, the 2 are but 2 sides of what is given. I found all these ideas (and of course they read/sound differently when expressed by a more 'qualified' interpreter) very moving and inspiring (*spiro*, spirit, etc.) and wrote a piece which has more contrasting junctures than most other of my things written to date. Having kept a time-log as I went along I clocked the piece at 22 min. 23 sec., almost the same duration as that of *Simulacrum*. (The premiere is scheduled for March 19, next.) [...]

Istvan

[...]

114

20 DECEMBER 1987

My dear old friend Isty,

What a beautiful & rich letter—what pleasure to share with you my thoughts/your thoughts & to be going down the same path virtually arm in arm. I am looking forward to hearing *Simulacrum* & when I can have a copy made of [Symphony] #6 will ship it off to you. Bravo on the new piece—you are on fire! And all success with it! I'm slowly approaching the end of the orchestral suite from *The Confidence Man*. Six sections which ascribe a kind of arc from the optimism (false) of the 1st section to the darker clanging of the last where the "truth" of things shows its nose, though perhaps not its whole face. I'll be glad to finish because I want (& need) to get on to new things (chamber music). The suite is a way of wrapping up the concerns & interests of the 70 yrs. I'm approaching in July which constitute the PAST. If the gods are with me & my strength holds out I want to plunge into new regions (though not novel or innovative in the sense "new" has come to mean in this benighted century).

The "Iconographic Mind" obsesses me. I keep making notes to myself. Reading G.S. Kirk on Heraclitus & his Fire which is the ever-living Kosmos in which we all share.[13] There I feel is the root source of all I'm trying to say & why it is impossible to separate word & image. You're absolutely right as far as my understanding goes about the word/image unity in Kabbalah. Except that you are far more knowledgeable where that is concerned. I may have to delve into it—don't know yet. The problem of course is that the "subject" ultimately goes in every conceivable direction & I must establish limits for myself in order to deal with what I feel is the central question: the transformation—evolution or devolution?—from a form of consciousness among the ancients which embraced the Kosmos & enfolded man into it and "modern" civilization of the West which separated itself off so sharply that metaphysics is "meaningless" to most intellectuals these days. I believe with Blake that man's sensory field shrank down to the analytic/rational/logical & ended up starving the soul & denying the spirit. While all this is going on in my head I keep asking myself: what are you doing? What have you undertaken? Well, like all important things in life, better to try & fail than chicken out & settle for comfortableness & ease of mind. Somehow I sense it's the hard things that will keep me alive!

Met Samuel Noah Kramer[14] last night at a friend's house at dinner. Amazing phenomenon of a man: 90+, looks 80, giving off fire & sparks, & works everyday writing papers on the field he helped to get underway in the States, Sumerology! Writing papers for festschrifts of former students & colleagues now approaching the youthful age of 70!! But people like him are lucky, at least in one regard: they have one thing to do; you & I have two!!! Words & Music. Strange that we should be so alike. Maybe you're right about the chromosomes! or common or related ancestry. […]

George

NOTES

1 "Text, Context, Music," *Canadian University Music Review* 9/2 (1989): 1–21. Reprinted in John Paynter et al., eds., *Companion to Contemporary Musical Thought* (London and New York: Routledge, 1992), 1: 272–89.

2 *Simulacrum* (1986–87); see Gillmor, "Echoes of Time and the River," in *Taking a Stand: Essays in Honour of John Beckwith*, ed. Timothy J. McGee (Toronto: University of Toronto Press, 1995), 15–44.

3 Richard Dawkins, *The Selfish Gene* (London: Granada Publishing, 1978); John D. Barrow, *The Anthropic Cosmological Principle* (Oxford: Clarendon Press, 1986).

4 Mario Augusto Bunge, *Treatise on Basic Philosophy*, 8 vols. (Dordrecht: D. Reidel, 1974–89). Presumably Anhalt is referring to vol. 7: *Epistemology & Methodology III: Philosophy of Science and Technology* (1985).

5 Richard Meale (b. 1932), *Viridian*, for orchestra (1979); Peter Sculthorpe (b. 1929), *Mangrove*, for orchestra (1979). Interestingly, in this context, *Viridian* is cited as the work that signalled Meale's break with modernism. See James Koehne, notes to *Richard Meale: Orchestral Works*, Adelaide Symphony Orchestra, David Porcelijn, conductor, ABC Classics ABC 8.770015 (1995).

6 See "1985," note 33.

7 Erwin Ramsdell Goodenough, *Jewish Symbols in the Greco-Roman Period*, 13 vols. (New York: Pantheon Books, 1953–68); abridged version, ed. with a foreword by Jacob Neusner (Princeton, NJ: Princeton University Press, 1988).

8 Symphony No. 6 (1986–87), commissioned by the Pittsburgh Symphony and the Pennsylvania Council of the Arts, was premiered by the Pittsburgh Symphony, Lorin Maazel, conductor, in Heinz Hall, Pittsburgh, on 16 October 1987.

9 George Tsontakis (b. 1951), American composer and conductor, student of Roger Sessions and Hugo Weisgall.

10 Hans Abrahamsen (b. 1952), Danish composer; he studied music history and theory at the Royal Academy of Music in Copenhagen, and composition, privately, with Per Nørgård and Pelle Gudmundsen-Holmgreen.

11 Miguel de Unamuno, *The Tragic Sense of Life* (London: Collins, 1962).

12 This unpublished paper, and its sequel, "Iconoclasm and Fear of the Image," are in the Anhalt Fonds MUS 164/F2,15.

13 Geoffrey Stephen Kirk, *The Cosmic Fragments* (Heraclitus of Ephesus) (Cambridge: Cambridge University Press, 1954).

14 Samuel Noah Kramer (1897–1990), Ukrainian-born American Assyriologist, author of numerous books on Sumerian history and culture; the Samuel Noah Kramer Institute of Assyriology and Ancient Near Eastern Studies was established at Bar-Ilan University in Israel in 1980.

1988

115

31 JANUARY 1988

My dear friend Isty,

[…] The Suite for orchestra from *The Confidence Man* which I had to let "hang-fire" through Dec.–Jan. is now completed. And before I gear up for some chamber music I must write, I want to settle a few details in the sketches for the 2nd Suite (from the same) for soloists, chorus & orch[estra], put them aside 'til I'm ready to sit down & write out another 200 pages of score. Neither of the suites is <u>for</u> anyone; so for the present there are no perf[ormance]s in sight, but when the spirit moves me, perhaps I will be able to interest someone in doing the orchestral one.

The second immediate project which Gene & I began […] is preparing a volume of <u>all</u> of Paul's poetry & his four stories. We're working with a young book designer on one end; on another, a young poet friend John Matthias[1] […] is trying to interest publishers of poetry in taking on the volume. If we can bring the two ends together, Paul's work will finally see the light of day. […] The last 4 days were spent in my writing a "Preface" for the volume in which I tried to weave together some biographical matters of import, comments on the design of the contents (four parts, the first three, the poetry, the last, Paul's stories), posthumous statements by writers, some of whom were friends of Paul's, and a final section where I try to "locate" Paul's work in the human/spiritual spectrum of things. Gene is typing it now & when we have Xeroxes made I'll send you a copy & would appreciate your reaction to the feel & tone of it (which I've tried to keep simple, direct, unselfconscious & unsentimental—yet loving). […]

It fascinates me that you are so deeply involved with the Kabbalah (I've read only Gershom Scholem [when] I was involved so heavily a year ago now with the possible meanings of the IInd commandment). In today's *N[ew] Y[ork] Times B[oo]k Rev[iew]* a piece by Harold Bloom on new anthologies of Yiddish poetry—& I suddenly feel a strong urge to read them.[2] Going back to my IInd com[man]d[men]t thoughts: were the early Hebrews (& subsequently the Jews of Europe & America) "alienated" or "self-alienated"? To me the question, probably unanswerable in the end, is of the greatest importance because Jews, as early Hebrews, are obviously fascinated by, drawn to, unable to resist ultimately pagan/Gentile culture. Yet they either refuse outright or are unable (for less consciously overt reasons) to merge with, be an unidentifiable part of non-Jewish culture. If we look at the present hell that has overtaken Israel, & add to that its internal discussions between secularism & fanatic orthodoxy, what in fact are we "looking" at? Merely nationalist or religious ideologies or something deeper? Something that wants, needs, demands to be separate from, different in kind & degree from everything & everyone else? I have felt this war in myself since I was 15–17. Once at a party I met a French-Jewish couple recently emigrated to the States. The wife looked at me with amazement as I dropped a Yiddish word to salt a phrase: "What, you're one of us??!" And I thought in my usual ironic/sardonic way about such things: you mean, lady, I don't "look" Jewish? Then comes the curious question: why do (most) Jews automatically assume they know instinctively what another Jew will "look like"? Or that out of any crowd of human faces they can pick out the "Jewish" ones? That can hardly be what being "Jewish" is or means. Then of course I read Hindu & Christian theology & end up thinking: and neither can I subscribe to your tenets even though here & there are gems of thought, experience, even wisdom. The quandary is hardly lessened when I remind myself of what Sartre said: a Jew is anyone others call a Jew. I've gone too far afield but I needed a little talk with you. Pity of it is, you're not here to enlarge the dimensions of it & add your thoughts & warmth to the heavy question. Whatever the human answer to "Muss es sein," historically, the "Es muss sein" can't be pushed away. […]

George

PS: A last thought: I have a young poet friend, Stephen Berg—well-published by now & very gifted, who lives & writes in an agony of self-doubt: About being "alive" here & now, about "who" he is, about the nothingness of the death that must follow life.[3] Nothing in his work suggests that any of his concerns are about being "Jewish." But yesterday, rereading some of his work, I began to wonder if what was plaguing him was not simply being "human" (hard enuf) but rather, buried under layers & layers of secularized living, a kind of "genetic" suffering that comes with being born a Jew. Then I start reacting badly to the whole question, i.e., reject it, because it insists on concerns with only partness and my deepest inclinations & thoughts when they are clear & palpable to feeling, sensation & even some form of cognition are toward & of wholeness, the oneness of man, of the universe, of what others call "God" but I think of as "world-consciousness." So back to the Pre-Socratic conundrum of the one & the many or what the Hindus call the "Measures of Fire" (not unlike your Kabbalistic sparks by the way!). Berg wants to be himself above all else. Yet how can he be "himself," a simple spark, which is only a sign of a vast unified essence? Es ist the problemma of modernische Menschen: to retain identity in a vast commune called "the universe." *Meshuggah*!! ["crazy"]

116

9 FEBRUARY 1988

George, dear friend,

[…] The way we are writing to each other, the directions of our current concerns indicate to me that, quite rightly, we are giving a thought to the 'rounding out' of our life's work. Is such a 'finale' possible? Can one ever hope to leave the scene without loose ends showing, without unfinished business, without some brew still bubbling on a back burner, or on another? I begin to think not. As one ties up one tissue's last thread, another's potential appears as an inescapable task to be tackled. Or, to put it in another way, the gears are still spinning and are demanding that one's will, one's urge to spin forth our tale, should begin to act putting ideas (musical or otherwise) into communicable shape as long as there is breath in us. Ideas like this spawned *Simulacrum* and *SparkskrapS* […]

The poem 'Afterthought'[4] just popped out at the year's end as I was working on 2 things: (1) reminiscences about a recently deceased close colleague at Queen's, the English scholar, poet, Coleridge-expert, George Whalley [1915–83],[5] to be used in a 'memorial' volume by his friends, colleagues, etc. and (2) a talk to be given on Jan. 5th at the Univ[ersity] of Toronto Faculty of Music about *Simulacrum* which had 3 performances coming by the Toronto Symph[ony] in that week.[6] (The talk connected my very old poem *Mirage* with the papers 'What Tack to Take' and 'Pst … Pst … Are You Listening? Hearing Voices from Yesterday,' *Thisness* and, finally, pointing to *SparkskrapS*.) The reason: I realized at about that time that for the past 3–4 years (since I completed *Winthrop* and *Alternative Voices*) all that I did (except the 2 wedding musics for Helen and Carol)[7] constituted either a continuation of my questioning things related to music for and by the voice (the minor concern) or attempted definitions of the 'self,' answers to the eternal questions: Who am I? Why am I here? What is my world? Etc. (the major concern). My interest in the Kabbalah was prompted by work on *Alternative Voices* which, as you know, carried me along into territories (such as magic, for example) which held absolutely no interest for me anteriorly. So it was an 'organic' development. I found in it (Kabbalah) a rich world which appeared to be as foreshadowing in a most interesting way psychology, linguistic analysis, phenomenology, at least as my very limited acquaintance with these fields indicated this to me. I suddenly found myself listening to some of these old Jewish mystics: Moses de Leon, Isaac ben Luria, Abraham Abul[af]ia,[8] and finding in them a kind of searching spirit, a kind of touching groping that seemed to me something I could feel close to. I did not know then that at least some of their insights & teaching had much in common with other Mediterranean traditions (one, or another kind of Gnostic ones, for example). I took them as <u>Jewish</u> thinkers and said to myself: lo, here are some of your origins. It felt good. Almost as if I would have become an auditor (I would <u>not</u> have qualified as a regular *Yeshiva bocher* ["scholar"]) in, say, the Safed Academy of Isaac ben Luria. A strong component in the joy of this exercise of matching the self with these avatars was the notion that in the 'finale' of my life, I ought to find a (for me) satisfactory answer to the questions: 'In what sense am I a Jew?' 'What is (are) the necessary component(s) in the notion of 'being' a Jew?" Of course these exercised that <u>other</u> assimilated old Jew, Sigmund Freud also. Shot through his writings (also reported by Ernest Jones in his biogr[aphy] of S[igmund] F[reud])[9] are remarks about this (if I remember: some speak of the capacity/propensity to stand alone in a hostile environment—in this case Vienna—during more than 3/4 [of a] century, 1860–1938—and stand up for one's ideas), culminating in his strange *Moses and Monotheism*.[10] For a long time (until ca. 1984) I thought that my credentials (including those that appear in a mirror) for being a Jew were forever vouched for by that impeccable authority on the matter: Adolf Hitler. Now I know better: this is not enough. I have to document myself, have to read, etc. But I do not know the language (hence I can only learn about the Kabbalah, etc. indirectly, in translation, that is not good enough), and other interests preclude a single-minded narrowing [of] one's involvement with this topic alone. Instead of wanting to learn to become a better articulated Jew, in his Jewishness, I want to do something else. I want [to] understand my very specific reality, which includes my Jewishness and being at peace with my entire past, even if that part includes a great disconcern for Jewishness. Much of my life consisted of interacting with non-Jews, and I like many of them, learned much from them; they were, are, and will remain parts of myself. (Witness the evidence of this in the 2 operas *La Tourangelle* and *Winthrop*.) One's being, that genetically-biologically determined organism, seems to exist in a finite series of interactions with other such organisms ... which process creates patterns, patterns of patterns, all expressible as 'records' (more or less ephemeral in nature). All is unavoidably and exhilaratingly complex, making one's brain and sensors jangle in the light, in contemplating the prospect of a little more interacting, a little more life, a little more catching, hearing, sounding, etc. I know one thing about Jewishness for certain: I shall never write a 'holocaust' piece. I cannot, and feel that [I] should not ever hope to want to attempt it.

The news from Israel (the killing & beating of young people in Gaza & the West Bank) is distressing for a Jew, like myself, who lived all his life as a member of a minority group. Is what is happening now in Israel the unavoidably natural consequence of the circumstance that the Jews in the State of Israel are a dominant majority? Do all majorities inescapably become intolerant, exploitative, insensitive, brutal, and, finally, morally corrupt? Or, is it a case of a dreadful scenario of fear feeding on fear, distrust on distrust, intransigence on inflexibility, etc. etc.? Political cowardice on the same from the 'other side?' (Please note that the Kabbalistic expression *sitra ahra*—the 'other side' is a synonym for evil.) We know only too well to be & to remain Jewish individuals with a full enough sense of self-determination, in more ways than one, in North America was, and remains, easy. How would we fare in present-day Israel? I cannot even imagine it. (We, once again, planned to visit Israel in 1988, but decided not to go for obvious reasons. This pains me from several points of view, but [I] am helpless to do anything about it.)

Yes, I sense there is a kind of solidarity among Jews that appears almost as a 'guaranteed limited credit,' as long as the other party does not disqualify himself for it. But very often the differences outweigh the surface of shared territory, and there seems to be little desire to stay with the contact. Could it be that we are related, through different kinds of shared 'interfaces,' to numerous different kinds of peoples? (Religion, profession, sex, contiguity, age, temperament, outlook, etc. are but a few notions that define these interfaces.) What make our, yours & mine, friendship truly unique in my experience, is the extent, diversity and manifoldness of our mutual interface. So much so, that we agree to pretend that a genetic parentity [*sic*] might not be an impossibility, a mere illusion (or a wishful thought).

Your introduction is beautifully written for the projected collected works of Paul. It brings me back to the days when I interacted with him in Newtown Square. It is a heartache thought and never will be anything else. I loved him then, and I love the memory of those hours. I am also grateful to you and Gene that you have allowed us to share in however a small way in Paul's being, and now, once again in his memory. (These words cannot begin to say what I feel about all this …)

The Toronto performances of *Simulacrum* were preceded by ca. 3 hrs. rehearsals that were worry-inspiring. But at the end things worked out well enough. There remained some rough spots (rhythmical, mainly) and there was a brief but painful premature violin entry in one of the 3 performances that mars the tape I have. On the other side of the coin, the timpanist and the woodwind principals were superb and the acoustics of the hall excellent. The National Arts Centre Orch[estra] completed its western tour last week during which they performed the piece 9(!) times. So, to date, there were 14 live performances and 4 national broadcasts of the work. A record for me.

SparkskrapS is moving towards its March 19th premiere. I am in the middle of checking the orchestral parts. […] In the same time I am working on a new paper for the *Contemporary Music Review* on text, context, music, once again. I feel I can add a few more things to what I said earlier on this topic.[11]

Last week we saw in Toronto Shostakovich's opera *Lady Macbeth of Mtsensk*. Very powerful stuff. Its drive, power, and inventiveness kept us in a spell during most of its 3 hours duration. It is also orchestrally right for that sordid tale, which he splendidly manages to universalize. And to think that it is the work of a 24–26 year old! Staggering. This sent me to the library for his alleged autobiography, *Testimony*, edited by (or, according to others, written by) Solomon Volkov.[12] What a tale! What an environment! What a persona! I cannot begin to describe it. If you have not read it, it would be worth your while to look into it. (Perhaps, to read the first half, or the first 2/3rd of it might suffice. There is quite a bit of redundancy at the end.)

[…]
Istvan
[…]

117

17 FEBRUARY 1988

My dear friend Isty,

[…] I'm inching along on the Second Suite [from *The Confidence Man*] & don't feel any particular pressure to finish in a hurry. By the spring though, I will increase my tempo of output because I know I will want to begin the new pieces I want to write. Oddly enuf, two works for violin & piano, one for the Int[ernationa]l Violin Competition at Indianapolis which will take place in '90, the other for a wonderfully gifted young violinist, Maria Bachmann.[13] She plays the Bartók Solo Violin Sonata like one possessed. At this stage I have no idea what will come out. And as always I approach new work with clutching feelings in my gut—trepidation, fear, anxiety, what have you. The only way I overcome it is simply to work. Then if I'm lucky comes the moment when the initial feeling dissipates & is replaced by excitement of discovery & a sense of having come into the clear. An old, old story and very un-Mozartean!

A letter the other day from dear friends in Israel, Yinam Leef[14] who studied w[ith] me at Penn. & his wife Tanya. Nami (as he's called) felt he had to return to Israel, a moral obligation. Tanya did not want to go (she's not Israeli-born). There's a real sense of impending tragedy in her lines. How can one understand the position the Israelis are in? Or understand the intransigence of 122 million Arabs who would be happy to see every Israeli dead? The fury of the young soldiers is understandable once you realize that if they are Sephardic Jews whose fathers, mothers, grandparents etc. lived among Arabs in Iraq, Morocco, Syria, wherever, there is a terrible hatred in their hearts for Arabs, quite unlike the Ashkenazi Jews who came from Europe. They are western in outlook & feeling, liberal to a fault whereas the Sephards are Oriental—& very like the Arabs themselves in certain ways except they are Jewish. 3½ million Jews trying to stay afloat in a sea of 122 million Arabs. A frightening picture. I hardly know the answer myself but feel the desperateness of the people who escaped from one hell or another only to end up in still a new form of hell. When Gene & I were in Israel last, in 1982, we found it terribly depressing. It was the fall following after the invasion of Lebanon by Sharon and Begin. The fact that Gene was feeling poorly those 3 months (from Oct. to end of Dec.) only darkened the sense of things for us both. I have no wish to return. I don't think I could bear it—now especially. And what is one to say about a country like the U.S. where Christian fundamentalists are entering the political picture in large numbers? What does that portend for Jews? A quandary everywhere you turn. And all this playing out of the cosmic drama on the surface of major events still says nothing about the questions you raise, the personal sense of Jewishness while living among non-Jews, many of whom are dear friends, often loved ones.

Have I ever mentioned my abhorrence of the religion of Judaism, its narrow-chested, nationalistic legalisms, rituals, tribal echoes—none of which I can identify with in the least? Of course, this is only part of my general distaste for all orthodox religions of whatever stripe. Yet I am religious, my life is dominated by a sense of the awesomeness of whatever powers fashioned this incredible universe & maintains it. I think more than anything I relate very directly & strongly to the American poet Robinson Jeffers's view: that "God" is unconcerned with man, & that man is only a small part of what is—though in his fevered mind sees himself as the major part & as God's favorite "son."[15] Jeffers loved mountains, the sea, plants, animals, the stars—the whole creation but kept his distance from man. The paradox is that in his private life he was a loving husband & father and friend. If you've not read him yet (this is his 100th year of birth; he died in 1962 at 75), I think you have a real experience ahead. Reading him during the days of my recuperation gave me solace & strength and beauty. He's that kind of artist—very rare these days. An avowed anti-Modernist (declared as early as 1919), he spreads before the heart & mind an incredible panorama of human passion & fury unrestrained, yet great inner peace, especially when he writes of the natural world & his relation to it. He was "trained" in medicine & science and ended up saying our "science" is all wrong! I have lived with the same sense. The new develop[men]ts in neuro-science however lend some hope. If we can discover what it is in our neurological makeup that determines our sleeping & waking hours, our passion for the arts of music, painting, poetry, our ability—so natural—to love (and hate; the obverse of the coin), our power to sustain this weak reed that we are against forces stronger than we are, and not least how & even why we "think" as we do we shall eventually learn much that old sciences and humanities have been either unable to talk about or even show any serious interest in. Just to start thinking about the autonomic forces that guide & maintain us is already to give one the curious sense that we are not our own "masters" (a lovely old fiction!), that we ride powerful waves & undercurrents which in fact are in themselves the very manifestations of (what we call) "life" itself. As a doctor friend told me recently if we had to manage all the subtle interrelationships of our personal autonomic systems there wouldn't be enough time! […]

George

[…]

118

24 MARCH 1988

George, dear friend,

I just reread your wonderfully alive letter (Feb. 17) full-of-ideas, spread out in a quasi-free flow 'from friend to friend,' 'from mind to mind,' and, yes, 'from heart to heart.' […]

The situation in Israel distresses me greatly. I am afraid that that small country, to which—through its people mainly—I have an attachment, is likely to have to undergo a process of brutalization. Its leader-politicians, not daring to take the risks of compromise/peace, will opt for what they consider to be, militarily, the lesser risk, and will hang onto land and handle Palestinian outrage, opposition, hate, etc. with the iron fist and the finger on the trigger. Niceties, ethical considerations, first, will have lip-service paid to them; later the brutality will be rationalized and it may end with the unapologetic & uninhibited use of raw power. Witnessing all this (and I do hope & wish that I should prove to be wrong in my dark expectations) from the safety of North America will cause anguish, splitting of conscience and who knows what else. In Israel, the price will be, of course, much greater. Now, this should not be read as an indictment of the Jews in Israel, alone. There are multiple power-games in progress in the Near East presently, as we know, and each participant trumpets its own apperception of things, events, ideas, in its own language, the result being a fantastic heteroglossia, that may reduplicate that of the Tower of Babel. Or, was the Tower of Babel like the mess we are witnessing right now? What would be needed is a super-synthesis that would offer the framework for a resolution of this crazy tangle of theses & antitheses. Someone (the U.S.?, the U.N.?) should offer dozens of billions of dollars to the peoples of that region with which to build that synthesis. The money could come out from funds saved as the result of partial disarmament of the great powers. I am thinking about a big Marshall Plan for the Near East. Pipe-dream, probably. But, this seems to be the only hope for getting out of this deadly spin, in which the 2 groups are caught up while they are shouting at each other in a mutually unintelligible language.

The fundamentalists menace is, of course, an even greater one. I attribute it to a number of factors: (1) every human being needs an epistemic-ethic-etc. framework/foundation upon which to build an existence. Even a severely schizophrenic individual tries to find 'the patterns' according to which life supposedly takes place. (2) People have varying need to have control over themselves, over their own destiny. For a certain period, probably provisionally, they may vest this control in 'another' (king, dictator, teacher, physician, judge, parent, etc.). (Now, wherever that authority figure fails, this creates havoc.) (3) People with little intelligence/education/experience opt for simple models and for the peddlers who sell these models. The model and its 'controller/dispenser' is a source of mental solace/security for the individual who agreed to submit him/herself to both. (4) Each creed imposes insidiously a 'private' linguistic universe on its adherents, and this, often badly loaded, tongue plugs the ears/minds, preventing other messages to penetrate it. An old and sorrily obvious story … […]

I share your inability of identifying with the legalistic and ritual aspects of Judaism. Yet I was attracted to it (Judaism) without knowing what I would find in it. Maimonides's *The Guide for the Perplexed*[16] I put down after ca. 40 pages. But will return to it later, possibly. But what did catch my imagination was Jewish mysticism, as described in the books of Gershom Sholem, especially the *Kabbalah*.[17] One result of this the new orchestral piece *SparkskrapS* which was premiered this past Saturday in Toronto by The Esprit Orchestra, a group of young/'younger' professionals that specializes in recently (say, post-1970) composed music. The performance, while not 100% in detail, went well and I am very pleased with it and with the reception the piece got. It will be broadcast by the CBC on April 10th. (The producer tells me that the duration of the work turned out to be 25 min. 14 secs. Almost exactly the duration of my first Symphony.) Another detail: on Feb. 6 *Winthrop* was broadcast in its entirety by WGBH (Boston). This broadcast almost coincided with the 400th anniversary of John Winthrop's birth. […]

My next musical project is in a foggy limbo. I know what kind of thing I would like to do, but I do not have the 'framework' for it, as yet. It might take me quite awhile to get going with it. […]

Istvan

119

20 AUGUST 1988

Dear old friend Isty,

[…] Whether I ran true to form or not I don't know & can't say but during all the weeks of high temperatures and high humidity I managed two things: to walk every morning (as early as possible, sometimes 6:30 a.m.) for 20–30 minutes which did me much good and wrote 3 mov[ement]s of a 5-mov[emen]t violin/piano sonata, in fact the inside mov[ement]s II, III, & IV.[18] Now I'm "relaxing" with a new prose piece which I'll send you in time (looking forward to yours!) before I get back to the sonata to do I & V, the outside mov[ement]s. Impossible to tell you anything specific about the new music except to say I feel I cut a few new or at best different grooves. II is a "Sarabande," slow, noble (I hope) in spirit, classical in temperament (something I've been after for a long time), tonal in essence but not necessarily in surface execution. III is a Scherzo Capriccioso based on an old sketch from the war years which I ran across one day while looking for something else. It came as a complete surprise & suggests that once past a certain p[oin]t in one's devel[o]p[men]t a good idea remains a good idea regardless of what may have transpired in the interim. So it's full of *spass* and maybe *schtick* at times which still crop up in me from time to time (I'm the kid who when he got bored in class made gargoyles to vent some energy that schools tend to bottle up!) All I can say about IV is that the categorizers who are always with us will undoubtedly, if they care enough, label it romantic or neoromantic esp[ecially] if they read the heading over the 1st system, *Ardentemente*. As though living & feeling & writing at the end of this crazy century to be ardent about anything is anachronistic, a throwback to … what, the 19th century? Man remains what he's always been: a passionate creature. But perhaps that would come as a surprise to some. The "News" paper is being publ[ished] by *Annals*, the Journal of the Am[erican] Ac[ademy] of Political & Social Sciences which sits here in Phila[delphia] & where I read it during the spring at a conference.[19] […]

This fall is full of things that demand my attention and/or presence, some tho not all are performances. Also by hook or crook I must finish the sonata. Gene & I are also very involved, she more than I, in seeing Paolo's poetry & stories through to publication by an English (sic!) publisher (Aquila).[20] The hope is (the book) will be released Nov./Dec. […]

Life for us humans has a way of accumulating "events." I understand your "floating," wonderful sensation when it comes, a little weightless, a curious sense of unhampered peacefulness ... But rare ... Sometimes it comes when I'm writing music, as when I wrote the "Sarabande." Too often we feel the force of gravity, the heaviness of being. Kundera has wonderful things to say about all that (lightness vs. heaviness of being) in his novel *The Unbearable Lightness of Being*.[21] Do you know it? Really worth your while if you haven't read it. He also has a great passage on *Muss Es Sein?/Es Muss Sein!* In the same novel. He is one of the "characters" in the piece I'm writing now called "A Three-Way Mirror."[22] The other two are the American poet Robinson Jeffers & the Indian philosopher Ananda K. Coomaraswamy. An unlikely trio if there ever was one yet strangely compatible through the "distortions" of my lens. [...]

George

120

27 OCTOBER 1988

My dear old friend Isty,

Yesterday I delivered the mss. of "A Three-Way Mirror" to my typist. A relief beyond all relief to unburden myself of it for a time, i.e. 'til I must proofread the typescript. Eventually I will send you a copy & will be eager for your reaction. I've delved into neurology. Probably a rash act, but the only way I could get at what I was (am) after. Whether it "succeeds" or not is not the point for me. Rather that it was the only way to go in trying to get to the bottom of what we are. Below levels of consciousness, culture, language, ego, our tendency toward self-exaltation (even when we achieve uncertainty, ambiguity, ambivalence, doubt, despair, the focus is always <u>ourselves</u>, a focus that blinds us to whatever it is that "ourselves" derive from & rest on). All this in an effort to <u>understand</u> something I've observed working in myself <u>and</u> others I'm close enuf to to guess at. Whatever it is it is a <u>strange</u> sense carrying elements, aspects, overtones of something other than what we "normally"—even abnormally—think is going on, i.e., at the root of things including ourselves. [...]

On the personal side, these have been busy full months. The violin/piano sonata is being copied. Next year its first performance. There have been some gestures—all lovely in their way—saluting my 70th. A collection of piano pieces by former students over the many years at Penn. & young colleagues. Lincoln Center Perf[orming] Art Library in New York will mount an exhibition of stuff (mss, memorabilia, etc.) next Oct. through Jan. 1990 (sic!). A bibliography will come out next spring—

being prepared by a young lady who is truly a femme forte.[23] Last week a concert at Haverford College was "dedicated" to me on the occasion of the first perf[ormance] of a splendid work for solo piano & beautifully played by Curt Caccioppo [*sic*], its composer, based on solmization of my name (he got a C major triad plus a B6 & D out of it!).[24] I was in Pittsburgh last Monday night for a perf[ormance] of the old *Magic Theater Music*. At the reception which followed a birthday cake! All very surprising to me (I who have lived most of my life without expectation) & beautiful in its demonstration of feelings I'll not name. […] Meanwhile I have to occupy myself with rehearsals of Symph[ony] #6 which the Curtis Orch[estra] is preparing along with 3 other "finalists" for the run-off at the Friedheim Award Competition in Washington at Kennedy Center this Sunday.[25] But I must be in Syracuse because of a prior commitment.

Surrounding all this "private life" activity is the tension of the election in less than two weeks. Last night Mark Russell,[26] political satirist supreme said: "I understand if Bush is elected 1000 people are moving to Canada. And if Dukakis is, 10,000." Then he added: "That's sad for Canada." True enuf: we survived 8 years of that smiling idiot con-man, Reagan, & if need be will survive Bush. But what is really frightening is that America can no longer distinguish between reality & fantasy, between the genuine article & the ersatz. Kitsch has taken over the media, the culture (by & large) & the people. Bush "smiles"—& people say "he's a nice man"—so they think they can trust him. But he's an empty shell, a zero human being who wants power so fanatically he'll do & say anything to get it. Most people don't realize (or remember; Americans have no sense of history at all any longer) that the same crowd that engineered Reagan's two terms are engineering Bush's campaign. If he's elected, I can only predict dire consequences. The problem with Dukakis is he's a decent man, un-electrifying; doesn't know how to "smile" & put on a show (Americans can no longer distinguish between TV "shows" & political "shows." It's all run together). I'm not holding my breath exactly. But I am deeply concerned. We'll know soon enough what our fate is. As I see it, the major problem for the world is that America still affects it powerfully & profoundly. A president who can't resolve the many dilemmas facing the U.S.A. will not comprehend its relation to the rest of the world & could have a powerful negative effect. […]

George

[…]

121

1 NOVEMBER 1988

Dear George, dear Friend,

[…] We both seem to be writing a lot these days, and in a speculative vein. Our pathways may seem, and are, different, but the end point, trying to understand a little bit more of what makes a human human, is probably the same. I do it by relating music to the world and the world to music, in an infinite regress of interacting mirror-images. You do it your own way, trying to understand the very structure of your nervous system. The more I am looking at, and run along, the swirls of spirals the less inhibited I become about harnessing intuition in the hope that it will lift me off the 'ground' and whisk me through the air … But I feel 'written-out,' written 'dry,' after having squeezed out a number of papers during the past year. I felt that these are, sort of, 'afterthoughts' to *Alternative Voices*, the 'beat' that was mine for so many years. Now, I am ready and eager to get back to music (once again paralleling your involvement with your Sonata for violin and pianoforte). I am presently intrigued by another subject for a musico-dramatic work and have spent much of the past 2 months reading up on it. Yes, I am being unclear, concealing, etc., but I cannot help it. I must conserve the last amount of the 'inside' pressure, that would dissipate if I would 'open up' more … Also, I need escape hatches. The resolve to do the piece is still very 'iffy,' the 'pieces' are not together as yet. I hope to have a better feel of the whole business in another month or two. […]

Istvan

[…]

122

22 NOVEMBER 1988

George, dear friend,

Isn't it wonderful: with age and the increasing focusing inward that age brought along for both of us, respectively, we still can, and enjoy, listening to each other. Wrapped in our respective soliloquies, into which we suck in fragments from the world around, we still open up, from time to time, to each other and bear witness to each other's doings and sentiments. […]

Your Pf.-Vl. Sonata … when & where will it be premiered?[27] Please let me know. And I hope I shall hear the work soon after that. (My only Pf.-Vl. Sonata I dedicated to my father. It dates from 1953 [1954], I think.

But much of my recent *Simulacrum* (1987) for orchestra relates to my father and my paternal grandfather ... You see I am still conversing with their memory-images ...).

Final word: our respective political wastelands. You have Bush & Quayle and we have that windbag salesman Mulroney. What was so depressing in our election was the new 'low' in language and miserably partisan & self-serving campaign in some, most, of our newspapers. Slander, innuendo, etc. filled the air. Yes, there were questions asked about priorities, culture, etc., but at the end the bottom-line boys (and girls) carried the day. For another 4 years, or so, we shall be governed by a crowd that takes its keys from business, for whom art means box office receipts, for whom Art means Entertainment, and vice-versa, for whom an 'event' is a 'gala' reported in the society columns, preceded by the appearance of some 'stars' performing safe, old, chestnuts ... Of real art, new creation, they shy away, with mistrust, and probably, let us admit, in a number of instances, with some justification, since that kind of art sometimes (though not always) can be upsetting, even subversive of 'received' views, and 'safe' assumptions ... It is likely to demand concentration over a longer period ... But enough of Jeremiads. I am quite content that I am living at peace, get my pension, can write what I want when I want it and lo and behold can hear it played with the help of 'public' money after investing some time (sometimes) in salesmanship, as was the case with *Winthrop*, which involved an outlay of ca. $130,000 Canadian. A bargain, wouldn't you say? (So the picture isn't all bleak.) [...]

Istvan

[...]

123

7 DECEMBER 1988

Dear Friend,

A gripping, moving and deep-reaching paper: your 'A Three-Way Mirror.' It obviously is a labor of love, and profoundly personal. It is obvious also that you must have thought about these ideas for a long time and with great care. And these ideas, which you express in a compelling, flowing, language, are, of course, among the most vital we can only think of. What are we? How did we become what we are? What is the relationship of the species to the individual? How to rate what divides men from each other, in comparison to what is identical in every individual of the species? Some of your theses made me think of those ideas that have been recently presented as the various 'degrees' (or modalities) of the anthropic principle. And, of course, your concluding idea of us having 'gotten off on the wrong track' (please forgive the crude paraphrase) at a point, or other, in our 'progress,' is far from 'easy' to face up to. [...]

What else is happening, you ask. 'Something' is happening. I am, since the beginning of Sept., edging, ever so gingerly, closer and closer, to a theme, a topic, a group of historical personages, with a strong central figure, with the notion that perhaps, PERHAPS!?!?!???!!!, yes perhaps, I may compose something about (with) them. Of course I am hedging, and profess a hardly concealed mixed feeling of excitement/terror and delight. By now the 'investment' in reading (I don't dare to count the pages, books, etc.) is considerable, yet the escape hatch is still open. My hero is a very difficult, almost an enigmatic character, and I am still at quite a distance from him, hence I don't 'hear' his voice well enough yet. He is very complex, and I am afraid, to an extent at least, I might have to reinvent him, with generous disclaimers, apologies, etc. But I am close to being hooked and if so, I am going to spend with the work quite a bit of time, I would expect.

Now, am I being a little bit naughty, by not stopping talking in riddles, etc.? Well, I am convinced that no word is necessary in such a defense, before you, dear friend. You know it all too well, yourself. So, let us agree that from time to time I just might let some bits of news get out from here ... not more and not less than something to keep you posted that something is brewing ... your friend has not as yet hung up his skates ... Presently, of course, the essential task is the extent of the information that I feel I must, and can, have. Soon, a plan, a rough scenario, may appear, and, following this, I will start writing the first very rough version of a libretto. This is a very exciting process. I feel I have been invited to join a society, a cabal, a fraternity: I can listen in, can enter any and all room(s) I wish, and ask any question (however intimate) from all persons involved. Of course you know exactly what I am babbling about.

My little concern (just lurking in the back of the head) is that I might not last the duration ... So what. It would remain a torso, a dream, an interrupted sentence, or the like. As it is ... I am filling pages with notes and the more I am scribbling the more the 'thing' takes shape. The eventual composition of the 'notes' will be but the last act. The 'notes' are in the process of formation/assembly (my own little/big jigsaw puzzle, for which I am inventing the model and make up the 'pieces') already ... [...]

Istvan

[...]

NOTES

1 John Matthias (b. 1941), Ohio-born poet, Professor of English at Notre Dame University, where he teaches modern literature and creative writing.

2 Harold Bloom, "Still Haunted by Covenant," *The New York Times*, 31 January 1988. The anthologies in question are: *The Penguin Book of Modern Yiddish Verse*, ed. Irving Howe, Ruth R. Wisse, and Khone Shmeruk (New York: Viking, 1987); *American Yiddish Poetry: A Bilingual Anthology*, ed. Benjamin and Barbara Harshav (Berkeley: University of California Press, 1986); and *Selected Poems of Yankev Glatshteyn*, ed. and trans. Richard J. Fein (Philadelphia: Jewish Publication Society, 1987).

3 Stephen Berg (b. 1934), American poet, founder and coeditor of *The American Poetry Review* (1972). Since 1963 he has taught at Temple University as well as the Philadelphia College of Art.

4 Anhalt, "Afterthought," in *Istvan Anhalt: Pathways and Memory*, ed. Robin Elliott and Gordon E. Smith (Montreal and Kingston: McGill-Queen's University Press, 2001), 424.

5 Anhalt, "Remembrance," in *George Whalley: Remembrances*, ed. Michael D. Moore (Kingston: Quarry Press, 1989), 142–47.

6 Anhalt, "From 'Mirage' to *Simulacrum* and 'Afterthought,'" in Elliott and Smith, eds., *Pathways and Memory* (2001), 412–25; originally presented as a lecture to the Faculty of Music, University of Toronto, 5 January 1988.

7 *A Little Wedding Music,* for soprano and piano or organ, text by Gerard Manley Hopkins (1983), composed for his daughter Helen's wedding to Axel Jordan on 1 May 1983; *A Wedding Carol* (1985), for soprano and piano or organ, text by the composer, written for the wedding of Anhalt's younger daughter Carol to Branch Greaves, 17 November 1985.

8 Moses de Leon (d. 1305), thirteenth-century Spanish Kabbalist, author of *Sepher Hazzohar* (*The Book of Brightness*), a version of the *Zohar*, one of the two classics of Kabbalism; Isaac ben Solomon Luria (1534–72), Kabbalist and student of Jewish mysticism who originated the concept of *zimzum*, the belief that God "shrunk himself" so as to leave a void in which to create the world; Abraham ben Samuel Abulafia (1240–ca. 1291), Sicilian-born Spanish Kabbalist and Talmudic scholar.

9 Ernest Jones, *The Life and Work of Sigmund Freud*, 3 vols. (New York: Basic Books, 1953–57).

10 Sigmund Freud, *Moses and Monotheism*, trans. Katherine Jones (London: Hogarth Press and Institute of Psycho-analysis, 1939).

11 Anhalt, "Music: Context, Text, Counter-text," *Contemporary Music Review* 5 (1989): 101–35.

12 *Testimony: The Memoirs of Dmitri Shostakovich*, as related to and edited by Solomon Volkov, trans. Antonina W. Bouis (New York: Harper & Row, 1979).

13 Sonata for Violin and Piano (1988), commissioned by the McKim Fund in the Music Division of the Library of Congress and Concert Artists Guild for Maria Bachmann; *Rhapsody and Prayer*, for violin and piano (1989), commissioned by the 1990 International Violin Competition of Indianapolis.

14 Yinam Leef (b. 1953), Israeli composer, a student of Richard Wernick, George Crumb, and Rochberg at the University of Pennsylvania, where he earned his doctorate. He is an Associate Professor at the Jerusalem Rubin Academy of Music and Dance.

15 Robinson Jeffers (1887–1962), Pennsylvania-born poet who, in 1914, settled in Carmel, California, a geographical area that informs many of his poems. See *The Collected Poetry of Robinson Jeffers*, ed. Tim Hunt, 5 vols. (Stanford: Stanford University Press, 1988–2000).
16 Leon Roth, *Guide for the Perplexed* (Moses Maimonides) (London: Hutchinson's University Library, 1948).
17 Gershom Scholem, *Kabbalah* (New York: Quadrangle, 1974).
18 The published score of the Sonata for Violin and Piano (1988) has four movements: I. Sarabande, II. Scherzo: Capriccioso, III. Ardentemente, IV. Finale.
19 Rochberg, "News of the Culture or News of the Universe?" *Annals, AAPSS* (American Academy of Political and Social Science) 500 (November 1988): 116–26.
20 These publication plans fell through, but see "1964," note 6.
21 Milan Kundera, *The Unbearable Lightness of Being*, trans. Michael Henry Heim (New York: Harper, 1984).
22 "A Three-Way Mirror" (1988), unpublished ms., Anhalt Fonds MUS 164/F2,17.
23 Joan DeVee Dixon, *George Rochberg: A Bio-Bibliographic Guide to His Life and Works* (Stuyvesant, NY: Pendragon Press, 1992).
24 Curt Cacioppo (b. 1951), American composer, pianist, and musicologist; Ruth Marshall Magill Professor of Music at Haverford College; PhD Harvard University (1980), where he studied composition with Leon Kirchner, Earl Kim, and Ivan Tcherepnin. The work in question, dedicated to Rochberg, is a cycle of eleven pieces for solo piano entitled *Ciclo metamorfico sul nome d' un Maestro* (1988); previously, on 12 January 1985, Cacioppo, on a program which included three of his own pieces and Schoenberg's *Six Little Piano Pieces*, Op. 19, gave the American premiere of Rochberg's *Four Short Sonatas* (1984) (which is dedicated to him) at Merkin Concert Hall, New York. Critic Tim Page noted that Cacioppo "played with such genuine love for this music—with such an awareness of its quirks, shards, angles and shadows—that he succeeded in guiding the listeners through the most tangled musical terrain" (*New York Times*, 20 January 1985). The world premiere of *Four Short Sonatas* was given by pianist Michael Caldwell on 7 June 1984 in Palermo, Italy.
25 Rochberg's Symphony No. 6 received second prize in the Kennedy Center Friedheim Awards (1988).
26 Mark Russell (b. 1932), American comedian and political satirist.
27 Rochberg's Sonata for Violin and Piano was premiered by Maria Bachmann, violin, and John Klibinoff, piano, at the Ambassador Auditorium, Los Angeles, on 10 April 1989.

1989

124

11 JANUARY 1989

Dear George,

[…] I am quite a bit closer to thinking about undertaking writing a new opera now than when I wrote to you some cryptic words about it the last time. Yet my escape gear is kept in a good working order, just in case … But I will tell you here a bit, with the understanding that: (a) you won't hold me to this undertaking, should I decide, at a later date, <u>not</u> to go ahead with it and (b) since matters are as uncertain, still, you agree not to breathe word to anyone apart [from] Gene about it. Well, then, here it is. I now have the outline of an 'opera fantasy' on the life of Julius Robert Oppenheimer of Los Alamos fame.[1] Do I need to say more? You will immediately sense the awesomeness of an undertaking of this sort and size. I should not (for my sake) get into the details, beyond saying that for the past 4 months I have been immersed in reading about him, his circles, time, environments, discipline, and related concerns. This has proven to be a corpus of very considerable size, and I have just begun touching upon archival materials and conducting interviews with a few select persons who were close to him. I now have the outline (Draft One) of a libretto: 3 acts, each containing 12 shorter, or longer, scenes. I could go on, but shall stop right here, because suddenly (that was 3 weeks ago) work on *Oppenheimer* (this is a working title) had to stop as a result of a 'phone call 'out of the blue.'

A few days before Christmas I was informed 'officially' that the Music Director Elect of the Toronto Symphony[2] wishes to commission me to write a piece for him & the orchestra, a work that would begin the

1989–90 season's first concert. Dates: Sept. 13, 14, 16. Despite the very closeness of the deadline, I felt I cannot, should not, turn this invitation down. You can easily see that other projects had to move to the back-burner, which they did, as I undertook, almost immediately work on the new piece. Actually, the 'nature' of the program of these concerts, which, first, struck me like a minor lightning bolt, gave me an idea about the new work's character. I explain: my piece, an 'appetizer,' if I cannot do 'something' with it, comes before that icon, that giant of an icon, the 9th Symphony of B[eethoven]'s. Imagine, the predicament! Once again, I cannot, should not, get into a verbal description of the tack I am taking right now. Words would get in the way of the music I am trying to 'hear,' from the 'inside,' so to say … Eventually, there will be a story, and you will be, most likely, the first person, after Bea, of course, to whom I shall have the pleasure of telling what got transacted … So, for the time being, be patient, dear friend.

So, you see, from this slightly light-headed text & script (as if I would be slightly drunk, and in a state which some ancient Greeks would have called a poetic mania, one of the kinds of madness they recognized) that I am having an exciting, if quite a bit worrisome, time … (Will I be able to pull it off, in kind, and on time … ??) […]

You wrote about frustration resulting from trying to mesh brain with scientists. I know the feeling … Yet one is drawn to those 'other kinds' of minds because [of] the secrets they are wrestling with. With this thought, which also is a part of the Oppenheimer story, I take leave, from you, dear friend. Do write … of yourself. […]

Istvan

125

3 MARCH 1989

Dear old friend Isty,

It was a wonderful surprise the other night to hear your voice and esp[ecially] good to have a chance to talk. I sensed you are in the throes of your present work. Actually you caught me in a released state for I had just finished the *Rhapsody & Prayer* & had sent it off to my copyist the day before.[3] It is rare indeed for me to feel "at ease" with myself & the world, and if & when it comes, it's usually just after having given birth. So where there were no works for violin & piano before (except for much earlier things long rejected) now there are two: the 29' 4-mov[emen]t Sonata of last year and the 8½ minute *Rhapsody & Prayer*. Happily I was able to keep them apart, i.e., make them different from each other. I must have mentioned in the past at some point the horror I have of repeating myself consciously? Those unconscious gestural, phrasal, structural characteristics—those we can no more help than the way we walk or talk. I'm referring to the kind of self-replication that takes place because artists fear leaving off that by which they are already known or recognized, what most people call "style," etc. The ability to be the same yet always different was the great thing about a Mozart, a Beethoven, a Brahms. The same yet different: an unchanging core at the root of all change. Rather similar in spirit yet disparate enough to the idea of order in chaos, chaos in order. Have you read James Glieck's [*sic*] book *Chaos* yet, the story of a new science (since the last 20–25 years)?[4] Quite astonishing, destroys the grid-lock of the old everything-must-be-predictable science probably forever. Introduces into science the qualitative without abandoning the quantitative; and for someone with the right kind of mental energy (translate: young!) and interested in art and how it "works" a potential bonanza of analogous findings. Astonishing to me how things keep opening up, laying bare "secrets" of nature that had been ignored or bypassed because they didn't seem important. About the science: chaos, two things that are central to it would seem equally central to music, self-sameness (what I call "self-replication" in the motivic/molecular sense), i.e., the tendency of patterns to repeat themselves and scaling, i.e., proportionate sizes, the tendency for a small pattern to reflect itself in the much larger pattern or vice versa. I find such notions quite beautiful to contemplate and very satisfying to both mind and spirit. And for those like myself who are "religious" but intolerant of orthodoxies, doctrines & dogmas such notions have even a spiritual aura, esp[ecially] if you believe as I do in world-consciousness, i.e., a suprahuman intelligence (but not a personal God) at work in all of nature. Which explains that crazy tack I took in "The 3-way Mirror." Mind you, I'm not complaining, but I have a very strong feeling that no one understood what I was getting at in that piece. Most people are offended if you assault man, species: *homo sapiens* (misnamed) head on. Why? Because they feel personally attacked. Also of course they're mighty uncomfortable with the idea that they are not really in charge—which is what I was saying when I gave so much attention, emphasis to the autonomic nervous system. All of which suggests that we still need to grow up, to mature enough to begin to admit error, mistakes—in short to learn true modesty in the face of forces and powers far greater than our own. Ironic in the extreme to point to Gorbachev & the Russians as exemplars of what I've just said. No American (Canadian?)

would ever be caught dead admitting in public that America has made serious mistakes. It was attempted briefly in the late '60s/early '70s & then died a quick death. […]

George

126

13 APRIL 1989

Dear George, my special friend,

[…] Congratulations for the completion of your 2 pf. & vl. pieces. Interesting coincidence that you were called upon to write the two so close in time to each other. As to stylistic relationships: it is fascinating to read what you convey. On my part, I have to say, the whole thing is instinctual, I come to hear the stuff and write it down with numerous adjustments later. If people say that they recognize my 'voice' from one piece to the next, it sounds nice, but I am not conscious on account of what feature they are induced to making this observation. I guess my 'language'—musical, that is—is rather eclectic since *La Tourangelle* (1971–75). Anything goes, in any 'form,' that sounds 'right.' But things are apt to fall into some recurring patterns. E.g. the 2 recent orchestral pieces, *Simulacrum* and *SparkskrapS* are both single-mo[vemen]t works, the earlier one ca. 22½ min. long & the other ca. 24½. And now the newest piece (more in a minute about this) is also a single-mo[vemen]t work and its estimated duration is ca. 23 min. All three are 'idea' pieces (or what I called 'idea' works) since in each there are a few ideas that worked in me while composing them as not-so-secret notions. Do they 'surface' in the works, for others to hear? Perhaps yes for some and not so for others, I care little about this. All 3 works do 'work,' I think, as pieces of 'abstract' music, but for me they are this & something else added.

Now allow me to tell you about the newest member of this 'TRIO.' The name of the new work (which I completed yesterday in full score in a near breathless rush of less than 6 weeks) is *Sonance•Resonance (Welche Töne?)*.[5] Now you know that it is to be premiered in a concert in which it is to precede in time the 9th Symph[ony] of B[eethoven]. You told me on the 'phone some wise words about the non-relevance (in your opinion) of such conjunctions in a concert setting. I do go along with this for most occasions. But this occasion struck me differently, perhaps in spite of myself. I felt the weight of the occasion. The 'triumphal entry' into Toronto of the new Music Director Designate of the Toronto Symphony,

Günther Herbig, with this super-icon in our musical hagiography: the 9th. And myself as a preceding 'fanfare,' perhaps ... But, of course, this is nonsense, and as I found out later this is not what Herbig was hoping for ... (In fact I am not sure about this, and, it is not very relevant, either.) Enough for me that he knew my music, picked me out 'of the blue,' and gave me pretty much a *carte blanche* as to the piece's duration, etc. I knew next to nothing of him, and still know but little but what I do know is good, appealing & comforting as well as, well, inspiring. The idea that came to mind leaped out of B[eethoven]'s introductory sentence in the brief recitative to the 4th mov[ement]: "O Freunde, nicht diese Töne!" etc. In the sketchbooks one finds: "Nein diese ... erinnern an unsre Verzweifl." What despair did he try to repress? The echo of that resistance almost instantly 'generalized' itself in my mind, and penetrated this whole situation, commission & all. I kept hearing the very opening of the 4th mo[vemen]t: that 'terror-fanfare' (Wagner's term: *Schreckensfanfare*) ... What does that convey? That near *nonpareil* gesture in his output, or, for that matter, in the literature as I (limitedly) know it. I know that he wrestled with the 'technical' aspect of transition (never only 'technical': it required a sort of psychic bridge, a brief justification). But did this occur? Were things left unsaid? Which tones (*Welche Töne*) were left unsung? If at all, no one will ever know. And I am not privy to the secret, either. But what might be possible, I could guess at out of my own head, perhaps, perhaps, so I told myself ca. 3 days after I have accepted to write a piece for this coming Sept. 13 (to be repeated twice on the 14 and the 16). But at this moment I thought this is a madness. Why should I get entangled in such a situation? I resisted it for weeks and tried other tacks. But to no avail. The idea kept on coming back with more and more justification why I must try to go that way. Finally, and with a sense of uncertainty (fear is too strong a word for it, and it was not that), I gave in and threw myself into the idea and it carried me along to completion in less than 4 months of work, from the first sketches to the finished score. [...]

Istvan

127

21 APRIL 1989

Dear old friend Isty,

[...] So now we sit on the mountain top together and survey life and comment to each other on what we see (and hear) what we think meaningful (still) or not (usually my story; though yesterday I heard an old

Heifetz-Reiner-Chicago S[ymphony] O[rchestra] recording of Brahms's Violin Concerto which took my breath away and last night we watched Charlie Chaplin in *The Great Dictator*). But before I get too distracted and wander off from the main point which is the enclosed double canon which came about thusly: we'd been out to lunch, Gene & I, came home @ 2:00, read the mail which for me was mainly your good letter of 4/13; then I decided I would take a rest, before I got drowsy, but meanwhile was thinking of you & your turning 70 and suddenly began to hear a tune with the idea of turning it into a canon, lay there listening to it and thinking, felt refreshed and decided to go to my study to work it out.[6] Canons can be beastly things at times. After one false start, a double canon suggested itself and by 5:00 it was sketched ... But with one problem: Canon A is 9 bars long, B 11; I noticed that at each repetition they were 2 bars off, i.e., the pattern relationship kept shifting by 2. Question: how many repetitions or how many bars before the two canons return to their starting position? Since I'm mathematically all thumbs I called Chessie who's had to learn math to work on Babylonian astronomical problems. When I described the problem to her her response was: this is a Babylonian astronomy problem! I.e. having to do with pattern relations between cyclical periodicities which are asymmetrical (like sun & moon). After much discussion she decided perhaps it wasn't quite what she thought initially but, taking a suggestion I offered, had to do with finding a number into which 9 and 11 were divisible which, of course, is 99. She worked out a schemata which she's sending me which shows the 2-bar advance at each repetition. But the main point is that the initial pattern reoccurs in the 99th bar! Which oddly (and wonderfully) enough confirms the text: may you live to be a hundred! Still not sure absolutely this is the explanation but Chessie is going to track [it] down with her math pals. Mostly I'm struck (again) by the power of intuition. There's still much to write but I'll leave it for my next letter. [...]

George

128

26 APRIL 1989

George, dear friend,

Your wonderful gift arrived with yesterday's mail. What a surprise, and it touched me in a way, deeply, captivating a kind of happiness I have never felt before. The words that I shall put on the page will, I'm certain, remain inadequate for telling you 'how' and why.

Just your spontaneity, generosity and genuine feeling for a friend and wanting to express this on the spot, in the hour, it is something so precious for me that the only thing to do is to accept it, rejoicing in the fact that I have you as a friend, and our ongoing and still deepening relationship is such that a reserve-less acceptance is possible. I am sure you know what I mean ... So imagine that I give you a strong bear hug and with a broad smile tell you: thank you buddy, how nice of you, sending this splendid, affectionate musical toast-*cum*-exclamation (better: 'acclamation' for an intimate friend, perhaps). There is such an exuberance, *élan* and beauty and vigour in this double canon, and I particularly love its 'allegiance' to a Beethovenian gesture ... with its truly remarkable inner message of the 99 turns of the wheel ... wonderful. But its relevance extends to the new piece *Sonance•Resonance (Welche Töne?)* which you could not have known. It is my deep bow to our great master Ludwig van B. Today I counted in this score not less than 12 different (in part also 'in kind') references to the 9th S[ymphony] & to his language in general, my first venture in this direction to an extent, in which your preoccupations, and example, since the early 70s played a role. When you see this score you'll see right away what I mean. Dear friend, you made me so happy with your lovely manuscript! [...]

Istvan

129

4 MAY 1989

Isty, old friend,

So glad you enjoyed the canon. [...] I am casting about for ideas for 3 works, not exactly simultaneously but almost. I'm writing a flute/guitar duo for Elliot Fisk, a truly fantastic guitarist, but more a wonderful musician.[7] At same time I want to store up ideas for a cello sonata (w/pno) to complete the ones for violin & viola. *Finalemente*: to complete the triptych of Symph[onies] Nos. 5 & 6 with No. 7.[8] There are days I ask myself: why? Why do you have to drive yourself to distraction struggling up the hill again and again, Sisyphus-like? No answer of course fits just right except perhaps that there is no other way to be human, to keep searching, struggling to clarify by making something. Or so I tell myself. Some days it works better than others, this "telling" myself. However these works turn out eventually I'm so much in admiration of your recent outpourings. Truly wonderful. Bravo, my dear friend. May your muse continue to bless you! As I hope mine will bless me. [...]

George

130

230 | 22 JUNE 1989

Dear Friend,

[…] A little while ago I have written to you about my desire to write another opera of 'full' dimensions. I felt I wanted to complete a triptych with it, a work on a theme which would have a Jewish dimension to it, after the 'catholic' *La Tourangelle* and the 'protestant' *Winthrop*. I looked at several themes ('heroes' to wrap the 'thing' around) and thought finally that I had found one (a very problematic choice that) I was looking for. The usual work (reading, speculating, daydreaming, etc.) followed and things progressed well enough with interesting solutions and roadblocks (which often turn out to be sources for valuable details) emerging. At some point I felt that I should try to avoid all (some at least) the heartaches and uncertainties that I remembered re: *Winthrop*. In short, I began to look for a sponsor, or a group of sponsors, who would guarantee a production upon completion, who might even throw at me some commission money, and who might (if I found this necessary) fund a librettist or a co-librettist (with me) and a director who would start making some nonaggressive (hopefully so) input early enough. I did put quite an effort in all this: letters, telephones, trips, here and there; in the meanwhile I wrote out the first draft of a 3-act (12 + 12 + 12-scene) libretto and worked myself up into quite a lather about the whole business. During the past week or so things started to move towards a possibility about which I was skeptical, yet it (the glimmer) was there, it was difficult to ignore altogether. And, would you believe it, today came a 'phone call which indicated that this avenue (the only one so far) is not open. So that's that.

I am telling you all this, because it feels good to do so, and because it ties in with my earlier topic: self-realization through composing, and about the inevitability(?) of the whole darn process. If there is no way to stop, then my whole effort to secure backing, and its failure (to date) is of secondary import. A voice (there are others speaking also) says: you have no choice, but go on doing. Doing the opera? 3 acts? 4–5 years of work with a huge series of ??? at the end of the road? Or is one to have the option to choose among other projects? Of course, there is (we do have) some freedom, sometime … Even *Sonance•Resonance (Welche Töne?)* came about because I put aside fussing about the opera and started thinking about B[eethoven]'s 9th and what it means to my life in this world of ours. So here I am, playing out these variations on your wonderfully concise theme: why one goes on writing … I am sure you could pick up these, and weave your own variations growing out of my own glosses? tropes? marginalia? altered borrowing? We are both, with others, in this business ... *Basta*! [...]

Istvan

131

25 JULY 1989

Dear old Friend Isty,

[...] Yesterday or the day before I was listening to early symphonies of Haydn—Nos. 57, 58—and delighted in them utterly. Today I listened to 59 & 60 & suddenly felt real irritation at his jollity, his what-seem-to-be-perpetual good spirits. Why? I ask myself. No real answer—except my own wild vacillations of mood? Possibly though the fact that I've also been reading Ingmar Bergman's autobiography called *Magic Lantern*.[9] He was born one week later than I: 14 July 1918. I've always considered him a remarkable artist, not just in film, but in power of insight and understanding, one of the great men of our generation whose films capture the painful awareness of life in this crazy century. I don't know if you have a taste for such reading. I almost never do; but I've read his book twice now, the second time better than the first. What I like so much about Bergman is his passion, his skepticism, his ferocity of anger at injustices of life—yet tenderness & love & yearning break through unsentimentally. That's the secret of the man: he's unsentimental but full of wild feelings which life as we must live it cannot satisfy. I feel very close to such a man. I feel a kinship with him & understand his states of being. Evidently he made a conscious choice to give up making films after he wrote (faux pas!) after he made (better!) *Fanny & Alexander* [1983]. If you've not seen that you are missing something vital, something quite magical, "out of this world" as we used to say. I think he was wiser than I, for here I am still dreaming, agonizing, stressing over writing/making new works. Which means I'm accepting commissions (only those that interest me) which I fret over because finding new ideas or new ways of dealing with old ideas does not come all that easily or readily. The conflict arrives between a powerful desire to still be able to work & a profound need for tranquility, for cessation of pushing myself, pressing out the juices into some form or other of meaningful music, i.e., whatever juices are still there to be pressed. Sometimes the ambivalence, my inability to decide totally for one or the other, is positively maddening. Then it is I think: Rochberg, you have no character! So if something gets written, it's under a kind of duress.

It's Friday the 28th ... I had to break off but I'm back ... I just reread your June 22nd letter and am full of empathetic feelings in re the collapse of what looked like an opening direction for support of your opera. But as you yourself seem to indicate if you must write it anyway you will undoubtedly do it. Surely with your standing & reputation someone or other will come to the fore with the necessary wherewithal for a production, probably when you least expect it. But isn't it curious & more than interesting: we are exchanging thoughts & feelings about the same subject essentially.

Getting back to where I broke off, the duress I refer to is not necessarily personal or conditioned by private circumstances—though they can surely exist & be contributing factors—but more in the nature of the confabulated times we grew up in & live in now as what Gene & I call "the young old." (A generation ago people 60 & over were generally "finished" whereas that state doesn't occur now until somewhere between 75–80 & even there, there are exceptions.) The severe tensions under which, for ex[ample], the Soviet Union is falling apart economically, theologically & ethically; China is behaving ferociously and retrogressively; the U.S. is growing more & more openly corrupt (like the old Rome of the Emperors) and maybe on its way through the inner collapse of its schools, its morality, etc. to becoming a "third world" nation because it can't pay its debts & it can't run a hi-tech society efficiently anymore; while Europe is looking to 1992, the very best news in the entire century as far as I'm concerned—how could it be anything but what it is to try to continue to make art under the ferocious pressures of such a world? Which in an odd way is why I both love & get irritated with Haydn! Was it a dream, the 18th century, or was life really "like" what we hear in Haydn & Mozart? Or was it Beethoven who first opened his art to the reality of the tensions which saturate all human societies? Of course, there was for him the "small" difference of having a French Revol[ution] and Napoleon in the forefront of his day. I must confess I often go back in my own mind to the title of the 1st work I wrote after our Paul died: *Contra Mortem et Tempus*. And often feel, still, the intensity of struggling against this century of death and the cannibalism of time which eats at me daily. But then I marvel that I've not only written at all under these conditions but as much as I have. So it is paradox & contradiction piled on paradox & contradiction. Nothing is simple, or clear or direct except love—& love is the most complicated, overwhelming feeling we are capable of. So we have no choice you or I (and the thousands I sense out there just getting underway or already on the way) but to keep trying. I suppose "singing our song" is all that matters really, especially if we sing well, well enough so "others" will want to listen rather than turn away. I often wonder why any of us still needs "to listen." Mostly because—so says the small voice within—we are insufficient in ourselves & we need the corroboration of our lives & existences through what we feel of others & what they do & how it all affects us.

The strangest of all, for me, needs for "the other" is the need for God, a god or gods. More & more I'm convinced the old Hebrews invented Jehovah & monotheism as an outward expression of their own stern, austere, hammered out-in-the-fires-of-life psyche (collective?). Man has always (& still I believe) felt insufficient, incomplete in himself. He filled the metaphysical gap by creating a God or gods & also filled the cosmic silence which frightened him (still does I think) by talking out loud to such creations in prayer, song, ritual. The fact that these creations never "talk back"—no answer is given; just like all the radio signals going out to extraterrestrials but no answer yet (or ever?)—doesn't seem to matter. God (in this or that guise or form) "speaks" to man in codes, signals, mysterious ways; so long as men are content to believe in these hidden forms of possible communications between themselves & their deity, they go on believing because men must believe in something other than themselves. There I come to—utterly: God & gods, they leave me cold. I can't tolerate the simplicity & naiveté of belief in a personal god (still strong among Jews, Christians, Moslems). But that there is something suprahuman in power & in what we call "intelligence" which made the universe (of which we are only a small & possibly not too significant a part), that I can believe in wholeheartedly. The old cultural forms of Judaism, Christianity, Islam—they need to be put in mothballs & retired to the attic or the basement. They are all part of the old thought-forms which still bother us and produce bad tensions (*vide* Israel & the Arabs). What is beautiful to me, for ex[ample], are the slow movements of Mozart: they sound more & more like he was praying, to whom or what is less important than just the fact that he was steeped in the mystery of life & could pray. So old friend, our art is no mere entertainment for the delectation of "the others." Fine if it gives them surface delights & pleasures; but for those who need to be brought into the very essence of experiencing existence through music, we seem to have to undergo the "transcendences" you refer to, to suffer the tensions, also occasionally as "simple" (or "simply") humans, to enjoy our families, to relax with them, to laugh, perhaps when necessary even to cry. So I have babbled on forever it seems. I got carried away. I hope not too much. I'm still somewhat under the spell of reading Shelley & about him. I find to my delight his convictions (expressed far more felicitously & beautifully than I could ever do) very close to mine. [...]

George

132

21 SEPTEMBER 1989

George dear friend:

Time again has slipped by ... your most recent (July 25) wonderfully wide-ranging and 'out-of-the-heart' letter is almost 2 months 'old' (yet forever 'young'), and my response to it has been delayed until this moment. You have guessed the reasons: the premiere and the 'repeats' (2 'live' and 2 broadcasts to date) of *Sonance•Resonance (Welche Töne?)*. We just came back from Toronto, where we spent 12 days, working on and off on this production with the Toronto Symphony people and those from the CBC. The essence first: the piece 'works' just as I thought it would. I was delighted with what I heard (no surprises) and the receptions, where they 'count,' were very heartwarming. The conductor (Günther Herbig) and the members of the orchestra were very understanding and cooperative. They really gave in all of the 3 performances (on the 13th, 14th & 16th). Additional performances of the work are already lined up with the Calgary Philharmonic (in '90–'91) and with L'Orchestre Symphonique de Montréal (in '90–'91 or '91–'92). The critics (3 to date) were also positive.[10] To give you a flavor of the idea behind the piece I am here sending you the texts of 3 pre-concert interviews, which capture fairly adequately the dialogues upon which they are based.[11] It appears that it caught some people's interest that I stuck out my neck by acknowledging a chronotopic juxtaposition with Beethoven's 9th. Some may have wondered to what extent would I bloody my nose in the process. (The thought occurred to me, also, while working on the score, from time to time, especially in the early stages. But by the time I was half way through writing it I had no more worry along these lines.) As you can imagine (recalling your own positive experiences of this nature) I am relieved, relaxed and really floating on a cloud of happiness. [...]

Istvan

133

28 SEPTEMBER 1989

Dear friend Isty,

A hasty but heartfelt note of congratulations on the success of *Welche Töne*. I would love to hear it one of these days but "these days" will have to be postponed some: Gene & I are off to Leningrad, Moscow & Warsaw with Lorin Maazel & the Pittsburgh Symphony Oct. 4 & we'll be back @ Oct. 21 but then I'm off to Nashville for rehearsals & first perf[ormance] of *The Confidence Man* Suite (No. 1).[12] In Russia & Poland the Pittsb[urgh] is doing my #6 Symph[ony] which they introduced. So I'm a bit harried at this point because there are a lot of big & little loose ends that need to be tied up. […]

George

NOTES

1 Among Anhalt's unpublished papers is the libretto for *Oppenheimer: An Opera-Fantasy in Three Acts* (1990); there are also some musical sketches, but the project was abandoned. "What I had at the end (and to this day)," Anhalt writes, "is a three-act play, entitled *Oppenheimer*, unperformed." "An Operatic Triptych in Multiple Texts," in *Istvan Anhalt: Pathways and Memory*, ed. Robin Elliott and Gordon E. Smith (Montreal and Kingston: McGill-Queen's University Press, 2001), 369. See also Anhalt Fonds MUS 164/D1,65–97.

2 Günther Herbig (b. 1931) was appointed music director of the Toronto Symphony Orchestra in 1989 and served in that capacity until 1994.

3 See "1988," note 13.

4 James Gleick, *Chaos: Making a New Science* (New York: Viking, 1987).

5 *Sonance•Resonance (Welche Töne?)* (1989) was jointly commissioned by the Toronto Symphony Orchestra, the Montreal Symphony Orchestra, and the Calgary Philharmonic and was premiered by the Toronto Symphony Orchestra, Günther Herbig, conductor, on 13 September 1989.

6 "Double Canon, for Isty on his 70th," Anhalt Fonds MUS 164/B2,134. The text reads: canon 1—"Salutations on your birthday, May you live to be a hundred!" etc.; canon 2—"Istvan Anhalt, Istvan Anhalt, dear old friend, dear old friend," etc., signed "with much love, George 4/20/89."

7 *Ora Pro Nobis*, for flute and guitar (1989–90), written for Eliot Fisk and flutist Paula Robison.

8 A seventh symphony did not materialize. In a letter to the editor (6 May 2004) Rochberg wrote: "Remains a series of disconnected sketches—and now it's not likely they will ever 'connect up.' I can deal with words, but music is not possible: too exhausting."

9 Ingmar Bergman, *The Magic Lantern: An Autobiography*, trans. Joan Tate (New York: Viking, 1988).

10 Robert Everett-Green, "An Intriguing New Work from an Important Canadian Composer," *The Globe and Mail*, 14 September 1989; William Littler, "TS Goes Forward to the Past," *The Toronto Star*, 14 September 1989; David Barber, "Composer's New Work Wholly Original Creation," *The Whig-Standard* (Kingston), 14 September 1989.

11 "A Short Conversation with a Composer," *Toronto Symphony Times* 2/1 (September 1989), [p. 1]; David Barber, "Terrors of the Ninth," *The Whig-Standard Magazine* (Kingston), 2 September 1989, 1, 16; William Littler, "Daring to Second-Guess Beethoven's 9th," *The Toronto Star*, 9 September 1989.

12 The Suite No. 1, for large orchestra, from *The Confidence Man* (1987–88) was premiered by the Nashville Symphony Orchestra, Kenneth Schermerhorn, conductor, on 27 October 1989.

1990

134

27 JANUARY 1990

George, dear friend,

[...] I am faced with the decision-to-be-made of embarking on writing a new 3-act opera. But let me backtrack a little. I don't know if I told you of the theme of this opera. In any case I would prefer not to get into this since I need to build up an inner pressure in this respect. But I can and wish to tell you about some side aspects. I feel that I have a very interesting theme. After having written dramatic works about a Catholic woman (*La Tourangelle*), a Protestant/Puritan male (*Winthrop*) I was looking for a Jewish protagonist with whom I could identify. He (it turned out to be a 'he') had to have a kind of secular Jewishness which I know about from the inside (that is, my inside). This man also is a scientist, who made a great impact on society through his professional accomplishments. He is also a tragic figure, having been tossed down from some heights under unsavory circumstances which were characteristic of the terror of that time of history. The man has a strong mythical quality about him, which I should bring out in an eventual work.[1] Now where am I with all this? First as to substance. During a total of ca. 6 month-long on-again, off-again work on it, involving a modest amount of 'primary' research of sources (archival, personal acquaintances, relatives still around) and a sizeable amount of secondary material (books, articles, papers, etc.) I was at a point ca. the middle of November to face the question: what's next with the libretto? No new data was on the horizon. Am I to start writing the libretto with whatever I had? While knowing that what I had, then, did not allow me to get really close to the protagonist. What I felt was a kind of hesitation brought about by a double barrier: (1) I must be historically accurate, (2) I am reluctant to invent the missing material. This added up to quite a bind. I felt inwardly near immobile. So much so that one day in a burst of will I cut the Gordian Knot and started putting words on paper in two manner[s]: (1) synthesizing situations with the historical documentary stuff I had then, and by (2) writing fantasy texts: isolated words, word-pairs, lines, rhymes, etc. that came to mind as I pretended to hear my protagonists uttering. Within ca. 3–5 weeks I had a long text (based on the plan of an earlier outline of the plot) which was much too long, wordy, so much so that I called it a pre-libretto. I persuaded myself that this pre-libretto contains the libretto itself. I only have to pare it down, polish it, etc. Well, it didn't quite go this way. I did manage to reduce it and arrive at something which I called libretto (version 1). After having typed it out, the thing talked back to me as a surfeit of dialogues, interspersed by much too few introspective (aria, arioso) passages. Not good yet, although 'on the way,' I thought. At that point I felt I must demolish, consciously, my two barriers. I had to get away from the illusion of historical accuracy, and develop, instead, dramatically tight dialogues that will not do insult/injury to the essence of a truth, but would present this very truth in a garb which befits the medium. (After all, I wasn't writing a treatise!) The other barrier (shying away from generating intimately, candidly, introspective texts) was more difficult to kick out of the way completely. But after a few tries, one day the gates were swept away by a stream of poetry, the kind of which I never wrote; a kind (or rather kinds) which sounded authentic/plausible/believable coming from the mouths of complex characters. In short order, my inhibitions were lifted and soon enough I had over a dozen aria texts and ca. 10–12 arioso texts and some for lyrical duets. All this together came as Version 2. Versions 3 & 4 are the results of polishing/balancing work & making the dialogues colloquial instead of pedantically correct. Presently, a person is putting all this into a word-processor for subsequent stages of polishing. But I now feel I have an exciting and self-stimulating text, that says exactly what I set out to find in the first place. I am no longer bothered by the notions of authenticity. Instead, I acknowledge to myself that I have here a group of fictional characters who share quite a bit with historical figures of the same name and same station of life, and same (in great outlines) of life history. But the available record stopped at the bedroom doors, at the door of bathrooms. No records were kept of dreams, daydreams. Concealments (for whatever reason), many if not all, remained that: concealments. These had to be uncovered through fantasy. All this, or rather enough of it, I had to invent, which I did in a fashion. The result: a kind of amalgam that sits on an edge, the left of which is 'reality'(??) and on the right fantasy/conjecture. This not only fails to bother me. *Au contraire*: working at such borderline, in such limbo, situations is what really interests me: to work with such hybrids of documentary wedded to fantasy.

Now the second face of the coin, and back to risks, at least to 'tradeoffs.' What's next? I am in touch with an opera company which is interested in the project. We corresponded about it. They know me as a composer. They and I will sit down, once again, in the spring (by that time the libretto, in Version 'n,' should be quite 'mature') to talk more about it. One of the problems (theirs) that they are tying together a major commission for 1994–95 with the building of a new opera house which might, or might not, materialize. If yes, there will be a commission. If no, there won't be one. As simple as that. And as to the selection of the composer for the commission? The implication is that they might have, by now, a 'short list' of those they are considering. And I might be one of them. (My conjecture.) Well, that's this part.

Now where does this leave me with a project, of a kind which I was trying to describe here? I am, to put it bluntly, quite keyed up about it, yet I have some red lights flashing wildly in the background. What are you getting yourself into? Do you want to submerge yourself in this for the next ca. 4–5 years, with or without an assurance that the 'thing' will be produced? What would such a decision (especially without the commission) entail in terms of other projects not undertaken, wife, grandchildren put on hold. (For periods in our lives that cannot be substituted for, replaced later, etc.?) I enjoy enormously the interaction with the grandchildren. They challenge one's imagination. They are so eager to learn and are tremendous in absorbing and giving love. I don't want to shunt this aside in the interest of a new opera. Yet, Yet ... The 'thing' ticks in me. I feel a very close kinship to my 'hero' whose story, I feel, must be retold in the light I fashioned for him, and for whoever wants to listen to the piece. [...]

Istvan

135

19 SEPTEMBER 1990

Dear friend Isty,

[...] What I wanted to tell you is about the genuinely felt, warm & moving responses to date to Paul's book. I speak chiefly of writers—

poets, novelists, scholars whom we know. One novelist in London said: "Paul is the real thing." Coming from her (Eva Figes, apparently widely read in England, Canada, the U.S.) that is very heart-warming.[2] Because it says so simply and directly the most important thing any of us can say about anything: that it's authentic. An old poet friend said: "These are very very amazing poems—it is hard to say anything about them that is adequate." You can imagine how heartwarming it is to receive such responses. Of course, we brought out Paul's words as a tribute and a memorial as you said ... but, and I don't know quite how to put this, really far beyond that which of course is the intensely personal side, the father and mother side to a lost son which in and of itself is right and good ... but beyond that because the work as work demanded to see the light, demanded to be read by any and all who might take pleasure or delight or gain insight—by a host of possible reactions to writing that is imaginative and strong in its own way. And so we dreamed and talked and planned & hesitated & came back again for years. How does one bring out, physically realize in a suitably readable edition, at the same time beautiful in design—all of this. That we finally managed it is a minor miracle. And now that it is here and people are beginning to respond—and with hard work & luck perhaps we might even scare up a serious review in a poetry journal here and there—at least now we know, Gene & I feel that whatever could be done for Paul's work we have done and when the coda approaches its double bar at least we will feel that which we could do, we did. [...]

George

136

8 OCTOBER 1990

My dear old friend Isty,

It was a great pleasure to talk with you last nite and to have the sense that all is well. I'm sending you Paul's *Poems and Stories* which we published only a few weeks ago.[3] As you can imagine, it was in the works for a long time. There were often problems, sometimes what appeared to be insurmountable difficulties; but we persisted; and it exists now, all that Paul was able to write in one volume. What drove us was the realization that Paul's work had to be in the world in physically available form for anyone and everyone to read who was interested for one reason or another before we ourselves were too old to deal with it or had made our unsought-for departure to that "undiscovered country" from which no one returns. I hope you, and Bea too, may find things in the book which will move and even delight you. […]

Today I felt like I literally worked with pick and shovel. Why should a piano trio be so hard? Is it my age and the slowing down that I feel more and more, like it or not? Or is it that every direction one turns in, every possibility of language that you feel valid or still viable (and I'm sure that varies from composer, poet, novelist, painter, sculpture to etc. etc.) has already taken on either the dignified patina of great and worthy past use or is simply hoary with age or is already old hat, overused, rehashed? So that even Mahler's 8th which we were listening to when you called (a re-broadcast from Cleveland Orchestra) sounds unfresh, tattered and torn, grizzled around the edges … How to crack the husks of the seeds, even <u>old</u> ones. There are some seeds, pine/conifer cones which will open up and bear fruit <u>only</u> under the tremendous heat of fires, i.e., <u>forest</u> fires. With what does one stoke one's own fires? Old longings, new distresses like Iraq-Kuwait, old/new terrors and fears of the loss of friends, of one's own physical discomforts and illnesses? Freud wrote somewhere he could not work unless he were uncomfortable, perhaps even felt intense personal forms of distress. Is art the transformation of experienced pain—even Mozart? […]

George

137

14 OCTOBER 1990

My dear Isty,

I thought you and Bea might enjoy hearing the enclosed which was recently released. The Violin Sonata has come to mean a great deal to me because—and here I'm groping—it contains ideas and characters which I was after for a long time.[4] In a spiritual (not psycho-psychic) way, i.e., those things that have to do with what I call the "Not-I," it comes closest of all my recent works to states & aspects I keep finding in myself, in others, in nature. That it contains my "I" I have no doubt but only insofar as any "I" embraces and is embraced by the larger Not-I which is neither concerned with nor deals with individual biographies. I hope I don't make something which has become very "natural" to my inner state sound strange or detached, i.e., abstract or abstracted away from all that's concrete and real. […]

George

138

5 NOVEMBER 1990

George, dear friend,

[…] You wrote heartrendingly beautifully about Paul's remarkable book … a true monument to a rare and great talent … I am awaiting the right moment to show it to someone up in these parts who is able (would be able) to do something (a journal review, or the like) about making it known up here too … It ought to be known how Paul sang … The book is on my desk to keep the idea fresh, but there's no way knowing what might come along the next little while. I'll keep you informed, of course. […]

The [Violin] Sonata is a *cri de coeur*, passionate, lyrical, full of soul and sings throughout a flexible tale that freely cuts across 'slow' and 'fast' movements … it is a fantasia (fantasy) and a rhapsody that speaks here … the flow of free association of someone who has mastered the art of listening to one's own most intimate voices. It must be a pleasure to play and the performance is good. I think you are well served by your interpreters … Do you agree? The piece should receive many performances and, I think, will be received warmly by your audiences.

I alluded to work earlier. Actually, I am in no position to tell you anything precise yet. I can tell this much: a rather big project is brewing. We are very close to a decision. It all hinges on one of our governments. If this body approves a budgetary item (a big 'if' in these recessionary times) there is likely to be a commission for an opera. (A full-length affair.) I could have the answer before the end of this month, but, again, the doubtful period might just stretch out until the end of the year. The theme of the work is very exciting (I have been thinking of it for over 2 years by now), and if the thing is a 'go,' I shall have my work cut out for me for the next ca. 4 years, if not 5. I might be an optimist willing to undertake this at my age, but … what else is there to do with one's life … or, what else is better … ? […]

Istvan

139

11 NOVEMBER 1990

My dear Isty,

It was good to hear from you. I sense deep inner excitement but kept under wraps vis-à-vis the opera possibility. I recall your saying you had written one on the subject of a Canadian heroine, on an American hero (or antihero?), and finally you wanted to do something on a Jewish subject. This must be it. And if I know you at all you will do it, hell or high water. Speaking of a Jewish subject, have you come across any references to David Rosenberg's new transl[ation] of the *Book of J* with extensive commentary by the Yale savant Harold Bloom?[5] If not, hunt it down or up. May be of interest (central or peripheral, I can't say) to you. The one piece of fancy which seems to have American reviewers slightly tipsy is Rosenberg/Bloom's contention that "J" was a woman, sophisticated lady of the Solomonic court in the time of his son Rehoboam's reign, to whom Yaweh was still not an unapproachable, hidden god. Marvelous what the human mind continues to invent & spin into endlessly varied weaves of ideas, words, beliefs, opinions. I'm convinced we know very little that is incontrovertibly true. Like "man is an event in the life of Earth, as Earth is an event in the life of the universe." But to say "man proposes, God disposes" or "man thinks, God laughs" is to play at "wisdom" & "profundity." What kind of god did the Jews invent that he survived the crematoriums of Auschwitz? I recently read Primo Levi's book *If This Is a Man* about his experience in Auschwitz.[6] It is told simply, without flourishes of any kind: intellectual, psychological, verbal. Absolutely no posturing. The end result, i.e., the effect (on me the reader) is sheer devastation: that human beings called Germans could carry out in so literal, cold-blooded, mechanically robotic way a monstrous program of extermination and forced labor against anyone they considered racial inferiors. Levi tells no stories of "bravery"; only of death for most and seemingly accidental survival for a few. This attitude toward the Jewish God is mine: total rejection. He says at one point of an orthodox Jew who started praying in hopes of staving off being "selected": "If I were God, I would spit at _____'s prayers." If you haven't read P. Levi, consider it very seriously. But I recommend you approach it with care. At most I found I could only read one or two chapters a day—and it is not a long affair. Literally stripped to the bone, whereas *The Book of J* is nothing but flourishes, fanfares, lots of verbal fancy footwork. In the end a bit (or a lot, depending on your individual tastes, p[oin]t of view, etc.) repellent. […]

I'm on "holiday" for a week or so. This past week I finished a big chunk of a new piano trio. I'd say about 2/3's. I hope I can get back into it and complete it @ the new year. It has connections with the violin sonata you've already heard (glad you had a good response to it). Details of the Sonata dug deep into me, wouldn't let go & so rooted themselves in the trio and spread in new and unexpected growths & ways. The new trio is for the Beaux Arts Trio who are as you know superior performers.[7] I'm looking forward to my helping them prepare it. […]

George

NOTES

1 Anhalt is referring to Robert Oppenheimer (1904–67); see "1989," note 1.
2 Eva Figes (née Unger) (b. 1932), German-born British novelist, feminist, and social critic.
3 See "1964," note 6.
4 Sonata for Violin and Piano (1988), Maria Bachmann, violin, John Klibonoff, piano, Connoisseur Society CD 4178 (1990).
5 *The Book of J*, trans. from the Hebrew by David Rosenberg, with introduction and commentary by Harold Bloom (New York: Grove Weidenfeld, 1990).
6 Primo Levi, *If This Is a Man* and *The Truce*, trans. Stuart Woolf, with an introduction by Paul Bailey (Harmondsworth: Penguin, 1979).
7 Piano Trio No. 3 ("Summer, 1990") (1990), commissioned by the Philadelphia Chamber Music Society and the Pew Charitable Trust for the Beaux Arts Trio and premiered by them in Philadelphia on 16 December 1991.

1991

140

5 JANUARY 1991

George, dear friend,

Once again I'm late with this, a response (inadequate, I feel, it will be) to your Nov. 11 letter. Things are, still, in flux, unsettled as to 'the project,' and I find myself not quite 'in harness,' driving on to a goal/deadline, but I am not 'free,' 'in-between projects,' either, as this one continues to firm up in stages. 2 years ago, or slightly longer, I started a diary about this venture. This has grown, since, into a small book and there is much further to go (I hope) still. Since we spoke on the 'phone (so good of you to call, always a treat) I have in writing a formal 'statement of intent' to commission this opera from me, to be written on a libretto supplied (in the near future) by a very fine American/Canadian playwright. (My libretto, on which I've worked for almost 2 years was not acceptable to the company. Too 'literary,' they said.)[1] This amounts to progress for both of us (librettist & composer). What's missing? Money for commissioning fees. Some of it is to come from granting agencies, the rest from private sources, we were told. The timetable calls for a conclusion (agreement, hopefully) by the spring, the latest. In the meantime, I'm awaiting the slow birth of the libretto. Have you read Hans Busch's masterful compilations about the geneses of *Aïda* and *Otello*?[2] Other exciting tales, re collaboration between composer and librettist, are, of course, the correspondences of, respectively, R. Strauss, H. v. Hofmannsthal and R. S[trauss]-Stefan Zweig.[3] Do you know that Strauss's only daughter-in-law was Jewish, and he had to exert himself mightily in the 1936–1945 period to save her, and her two 'Mischlinge' [half-breed] children from the Nazi bloodhounds … There was a price to pay and he has paid it, with interest. I didn't know it until recently. As will turn out, the Jewish angle in the opera will not be overt, but something that will 'shine' (sweat?) through the personality of the central figure. He was a 'secular' Jew, as I see myself being; there are, and have existed many of the kind over the ages. Presently, I am reading the 5th volume of H. Graetz's *History of the Jews*.[4] Anything but up-to-date (publ[ished] in 1895), but chock full of information and very readable. It paints fascinating portraits … What a story! What a people! Virtuosos in survival, near all!

Just witness the present exodus of Russian Jews into Israel. I don't fault them for leaving the USSR, the contrary, after what we saw in Central Europe this past May. Nevertheless, what a choice! Getting into that whirlwind of the Israeli–Arab contest. But isn't this familiar? The choice, most frequently, for us, for our ancestors, was not between a hot spot and a peaceful asylum, but between an intolerably/dangerously inimical host/place/population, and a somewhat less inimical one.

There is, perhaps, no good reason for holding back info[rmation] about the central topic of the opera. Yet … while banana-peels are still around, I don't feel comfortable getting into substance, not as yet. Please, bear with me, dear friend. (I know you'll understand my nervousness, perhaps even superstition.…) I haven't, as yet, looked up the D[avid] Rosenberg book.[5] I did read P. Levi's *The Periodic Table*, but not his *If This Is a Man*.[6] (Do I want to read it after having 'visited'—an obscene word in this context—Auschwitz?) Levi's suicide/death occurred while we were in Italy a few years ago. For a full week the newspapers were full with the story, from many angles: reports, historical accounts, literary evaluation, his philosophy, etc. The whole nation (all across the political spectrum, so it seemed) was mourning a native son … No one came up with a firmly held hypothesis as to why he has committed the deed. Numerous commentators advanced the conjecture that it was the Auschwitz experience that killed him, after all those years, as if a delayed-fuse bomb … Who knows? Or will ever know.

My attention span for 'academic' prose has shrunk lately, as yours, also, seemed to do so … Lots of fancy sentences, lurking, still-unasked metaphors, ornaments of diverse sorts … too rich for the digestion … Good music is so much more concise, to the point, expressive … A recent case/illustration: Michael Tippett's 1970 opera *The Knot Garden*. I heard it only recently. Quite a piece. I didn't know how close we (he & I) can get at times. (Our respective circuitous routes were, of course, quite different.) Now, here is an energetic, still-creating 85-year-old! You & I, mere youngsters in comparison.

Glad to hear the news of your [Piano] Trio [No. 3]. I'm certain that it will join its intimate-eloquent-passionate brethren in your chamber-music works family. (I had the intention of writing some chamber works after *Sonance•Resonance (Welche Töne?)*, but the opera-to-be preempted this option/intent.) […]

Istvan

[…]

141

14 MAY 1991

My dear Isty,

[…] There's so much to say I'm not sure where to start. To begin, enclosed is the paper I gave at the Boston conference.[7] I found the Chinese who were there—mostly from Taiwan, although some of the young composers (@ 10 or so) hailed from Hong Kong, in one case from Beijing—to be extremely intelligent and warm people. In one particular instance I was deeply moved by what amounted to a heartfelt, deeply personal statement of existing mentally/spiritually/psychologically "between-two-worlds" state of being. The search for Chineseness (which the latest issue of *Daedalus* coincidentally devotes itself to)[8] is not unlike the old & present search for Jewishness. Although intensified by the Chinese being of different racial stock from the Caucasians whose culture (Western) they enter into & so admire and want to make their own; while Jews often can hardly be distinguished physically from other so-called white people. I confess I felt very drawn to these people on two counts: for what they are in themselves by virtue of intelligence & sensitivity, genes and old culture and for their striving to extend themselves toward the West. There are several authors in *Daedalus* who even speak of a Chinese Diaspora. Remarkable, isn't it? If you have the time & of course the necessary inclination I'm sure you'll find *Daedalus* worth probing into. […]

Preparing myself for the Boston paper I steeped myself in Chuang-Tzu,[9] Confucius, a marvellous *Book of Tea* by Kazuko Okakura written in English in 1907 or 1908 by this remarkable Japanese scholar/aesthetician who ended up acting as consultant & guide to Mrs. Gardener and her museum in Boston.[10] On the periphery of all this plus hardcore empirical stuff on current doings in China & Asia politically, economically &

culturally a friend gave me *Japanese Death Poems* an amazing compilation of poems (starting actually with the Chinese & then picked up as a Zen tradition by Japanese poets, monks, Zen Masters) written close to the time of departing.[11] What amazing people: stoic, quizzical, whimsical, stern, detached, tranquil, serene, puzzled, but almost never expressions of fear. Hardly a note for me to end on. So I'll just tell you a bit about the work I'm in the middle of now. You know for the last two years I've been involved in trying to understand & grasp so I could write for it the 6-string monster called the guitar. I went through something similar long years ago with the harp. But that noble instrument so beautiful to the eye and wonderful to the ear if treated right is child's play compared to the cliffs & abysses, gorges, ravines, rapids, traps & dangers of the "gittar." Somehow I managed two works for flute & guitar, the first a total reworking of the slow mov[emen]t of Bach's *Italian Concerto* which I call *Ora Pro Nobis* [1989] (and we surely need it, agreed?) followed by *Muse of Fire* [1989–90], a long fantasia-like probing of rarely visited corners of my soul. Because I like the guitarist who egged me on in the first place, Eliot Fisk, a brilliant performer, first-rate mind & human being, I'm writing a work for solo guitar based largely on old American pop tunes (things I played as a boy that have stayed with me) treating them as small treasures to be opened, revealed, examined, cherished, oohed & aahed over.[12] So I have delved into other & older regions of this old soul. […]

George

142

5 JUNE 1991

Dear George,

[…] I like your 'bells and drums' paper. (You have tempted me to read Confucius … perhaps one day.) I agreed with the core of your argument. But to remind ourselves: both Mozart & Beethoven were attracted to the exotic (<u>Turkish</u> musics, e.g.), perhaps in an attempt to go beyond comfortable Vienna … The exotic is akin to the fantastic which, in turn, is a twin of the dreamworld where 'things' may appear which otherwise would be denied access at the city-gates … But lately, I am beginning to perceive the traces/potential of/for the fantastic in the 'familiar,' the stuff close to home.

I made a double-take when I read your references to David Easton [b. 1917] in this paper. Obviously, you don't know, couldn't have known, that David is a <u>very</u> close friend of ours. He is Toronto-born and I met him while he held the 'Peacock' Chair in Political Studies at Queen's while also being a 'distinguished prof[essor]' at the U[niversity] of Chicago. This was in the 70s and early 80s. Upon reaching 63–64 he resigned from Queen's and eventually retired from Chicago. This was concurrent with his acceptance of a chair at the U[niversity] of California in Irvine where he now lives. As fortune would have it, he visited us here yesterday (he came in the framework of the Canadian Learned Societies biannual meeting, held here) and during dinner (our evenings <u>always</u> stretch out on the wings of stimulating talk) we talked about your paper (I made a Xerox copy of it for him) and related matters. He was very interested in learning about you & your paper. He asked me to tell you that the text of his you referred to has been enlarged for the book (I have it before me as I write this).[13] […]

'Things' have progressed in our negotiations with the opera company in question. Actually, they made a written offer of a commission to us and we are to meet within 2 weeks (so I was told) to hammer out details & to conclude a contract. Exciting … If all goes well, I can, finally lift the lid & tell you about the nature of the projected work. So, just a little bit of more patience …

The enclosed papers are connected. Please read them in the order suggested. I believe they will remain the last papers I write for a long time, if not forever.[14] I [would] rather write notes, in these days …

The news of your guitar piece is exciting. I know: it is a difficult medium & I have shied away from it until now. Shall be looking forward to more info[rmation] from you in this regard.

(In which way did you learn the necessary tricks?) […]

Istvan

[…]

143

12 JUNE 1991

My dear Isty,

[…] The radicalization of the American academic has reached a screeching/screaming climax—*moltissimo* noisy—& if you would like to "refresh" yourself, i.e., take a break from the hard labor of trying to make art, read Roger Kimball's *Tenured Radicals*.[15] Could be you have the breed blooming in Canadian groves of academe too, yes?!? Anyhow it's astonishing, isn't it, you & Easton should be old friends. Don't know when I'll have time to read his book but will certainly tuck it away in my head for future reference. (He's certainly one of the more balanced and humane voices in the grand circus of multiculturalism—and I might add intelligent. Passion, uncontrolled & unmitigated by willingness to face reality, short-circuits brains for sure. There are a lot of blasted noggins out there in American universities.) My thanks for your papers which I think you sent me while still in mss. The feeling of having read them before came over me as I perused them. Would be great if your opera contract came through. I've got my fingers crossed!! The guitar, that 6-string devil: whatever I "know" (that's still very little) I learned from exciting but exhausting sessions with Eliot Fisk the young guitarist for whom I wrote the pieces. Elliot is a brilliant musician & person. There have been times when I've felt from a passing word here and there that he suffers considerable frustration because his instrument (which he passionately loves) is not one of the major concertizing voices; & its audience is smallish compared to what it would be if he were a premiere pianist, cellist, etc. Anyhow, I have completed *American Bouquet*, 7 "versions" of popular music. In the fall Eliot & I will get together & what I've written will undergo revision for sure in order to make it more idiomatic, to release the guitar's voice, etc. I look forward to it but at the same time really dread it. I have come to hate making changes, having to revise, all that. Don't you sometimes get the feeling the world is unraveling right before our very eyes? Imagine, today Russians are electing ("electing"?) a "President" of the Russian Republic, and also voting on whether to change the name "Leningrad" back to "St. Petersburg" (Solzhenitsyn wants it changed to Petrograd). Leninism-Marxism's days are numbered. But will the Com[munis]t Party let go without a bitter battle? Can't imagine that! Faust has served his purpose for better or worster; time for Buddha. […]

George

144

11 AUGUST 1991

Dear George,

A humid day, this … just put some notes on paper … on the surface angry, gruff, but beneath an insecure restlessness, tossing and turning as if pushed by the reoccurrence of a bad dream, 'that' bad dream, an old visitor … Not me, put your mind at rest, dear friend, but a character from the opera that is still unsure of its birth, 4–5 years hence, though no longer of its conception. Riddles, and teasing … Yes and no. I am being teased, for the past 2 years or so, by uncertain (or overcautious or scared) opera administrators. But now, finally I believe, we (my librettist, I & our agent-lady in N[ew] Y[ork] C[ity]) have pinned them down: they must make a decision by the end of next month, the very latest; otherwise we shall cease talking with them. As you are guessing: 'things' happened on this front. Ca. 4 weeks ago I was convinced the project is dead as far as that outfit is concerned. But, since, the whole thing came back to life ... Now, I better swear you to the greatest secrecy, because, I feel, I cannot hold you in the dark about my 'theme' any longer ... Yes: for the past 2½ years I am thinking about an opera centered on the figure of J. Robert Oppenheimer of Los Alamos fame/shame ... whatever. (I succumbed to the rhyme ... the stuff of his life is much, much more complex than this simple pair of words ... The man is exceedingly difficult to 'pin down,' characterize; all ambivalence, movement, changes, and a few, difficult-to-fathom 'constants.' [...]

Now, you, also, know why we visited New Mexico this past February: Los Alamos, the site of the Trinity test (on July 16, '45), where we certainly picked up some extra radiation (though were careful while there) ... We saw quite a few 'old timers,' members of J.R.O.'s original team, including E[dward] Teller, who, as luck would have it, was there for a 3-day symposium while we visited L[os] A[lamos]. I spent quite a bit of time with Peter, J.R.O.'s son and only surviving descendant (now 50). My librettist [John Murrell] is one of the finest playwrights in Canada today. He, also, is 'bitten' by our theme and awaits the *dénouement* next month with the same intensity as myself. Please: don't breathe a word of this to anyone, apart from Gene, of course. And I'll assume that she, also, will keep it secret. (Eventually, the project, if a 'go,' will cease to be a 'secret.')

A different topic: Alan Gillmor, a fine musicologist at Carleton University in Ottawa, wanted to study our correspondence. (He already told me years ago that it would make an interesting book ...) The librarian of the Music Division at the National Library of Canada (where all my papers are, up to 1989) phoned me about this. I advised him that my correspondence is closed until I & my respondents are dead. And in 'special circumstances' (to be defined sometime in the future when I'll have time for it) this 'deadline' would be extended further. Now a question: what is your opinion about this matter, especially as it pertains to our correspondence? It would be useful to have this fairly soon. I, then, shall pass on the info[rmation] to the librarian. Another question: would you be able to tell me where the letters I sent you are kept? (Some might no longer be available, perhaps ...) If you could indicate their location it would help a researcher (Gillmor?) in the future. I think I might have a 'complete' bulk of your letters, some filed away separately (up to '85), the rest together with other yet-to-be-sorted-out correspondence. I think Gillmor might be a good editor, eventually. [...]

Istvan

145

25 AUGUST 1991

Dear old friend Isty,

In re this business of our correspondence: my feelings & thoughts are quite strong and definite <u>against</u> anyone—no matter their qualifications—bringing it out in a book while I'm alive. Isn't that your view too? That's what I got from your last letter where you bring up Allan [*sic*] Gillmor (unknown to me) and the call you got from the librarian of the Nat[iona]l Libr[ary] of Can[ada] Music Div[ision]. I don't know about you, Isty, but I'm not even "flattered" by such "interest." Either people are running out of ideas—on that score I think that already happened long ago!—or levels of "curiosity" have risen lately so that knowledge or what used to pass for knowledge is now being replaced by high-class gossiping <u>by</u> intellectuals <u>about</u> intellectuals (and artists, composers, poets, et al.) for intellectualism in whatever "form" seems appropriate. I've actually located a whole batch of <u>your</u> letters to me from recent times & more remote times, but there's no way I can possibly resurrect all you ever wrote & sent me because I'm not orderly that way and have tended to treat correspondence with even my closest friends as simply the pleasurable part of the business of living the quotidian. Would you like to have them for any particular reason? If so, just let me know and I'll send you a package of them.

These days are layered indeed—personal, very personal, world, history, local events (USA), on & on. To wit: a week ago Gene & I were celebrating our 50th year together in the state of what some have called "wedded bliss," we call "love and war." [...] Of course we now couple Aug. 18 [the Rochbergs' anniversary] w[ith] Aug. 19, the beginning of the failed coup in the USSR, also the end of the Communist Party as it turns out. Real reason to marvel at the unpredictable nature of the politics of man. But especially joy in my heart at the failure of one of the most monstrous-ever attempts to manipulate and engineer socially, economically, artistically, politically a vast conglomerate of human beings in an equally vast geographic area. My joy is linked also to the wide & growing acknowledgement that there can be no single answer to any life question or situation, certainly no monolithic, life-controlling/thought-controlling ideology which presses the human heart/mind/soul to stone and simultaneously demands allegiance, loyalty and praises to those who have raised such monstrosities over the lives of human beings. It also will take its toll—& rightly so—of further defenses of academic idiocies such as "political correctness" (I believe it was William Saffire writing in the *N[ew Y[ork] Times* not too long ago who said "p.c." means "political control," not what the p.c.'ers call it). So for the rest of our days Aug. 18 & 19 are linked indelibly; & to make it stick we are saving today's *News of the Week in Review* section of the *N[ew] Y[ork] Times* as a confirming "document." I still remember vividly Oct. 4 to 11, '89 in Leningrad & Moscow and the grim somber tragic faces of the people. I carried back (& away) with me the sense of a tragic fate ... if only I could have seen ahead to Aug. 19, 1991 I could have said to all those I saw in Red Square & other places ... soon, soon, you will be freed of your oppressors, you will begin to learn to live in freedom ... though it will be very hard ... for freedom means personal responsibility for one's acts, decisions, words as well as the near & far consequences of all of them ... You must decide from now on, no one can decide for you ... And so on/*Und so weiter.*

For your sake I hope your opera project takes hold w[ith] those externally involved, whoever they are. I can see how wrapped-up in it you are so can only wish you *buona fortuna*. I know the outlines of Oppenheimer's story, have even read a quasi-philosophical essay of his (something about "The Open Mind")[16] but oddly I don't share your excitement for what he represents. But it's your excitement & conviction that he's the right subject for your labors that count, you're the one who's writing it. Frankly, old friend, after this savaging we took nation-wide for *The Confidence Man* I lost all taste & interest in opera as such. Which is why I have since '82 concentrated so heavily on chamber & orchestra music. Only very lately have I felt the slightest tickle in my throat to "sing" again, i.e., to write any vocal music. But I've not done it yet—and I don't know if or when I will. I did finish the 3rd work for guitar—this one a solo work—in the spring, something I call *American Bouquet* based on some of my favorite old popular songs from my youth. They are neither "arrangements" nor "transcriptions" but some kind of essays in presenting the melodic & harmonic substance of these songs quite straight (no fudging, no dolling-up) in the framework of enlarged compositions. Don't know how else to describe them. Like the first two works, this is also for my good friend & guitarist *extraordinaire* Eliot Fisk. So I have made my "contribution" to one of the most difficult-to-compose-for instruments I know & will leave it at that, hoping that one or another of

the three will take hold & give pleasure if not insight.

Seems we're both involved in packing things up & shipping them off. Day after the children left I cleared out a whole closet full of scores, deposited them in 4 canvas bags which the music librarian & her male assistant schlepped out to their car to take to the Curtis Inst[itute]. In the two days following (Fri[day] & Sat[urday]) I put together a number of cartons of stuff to be hauled to the Lincoln Center Perf[orming] Arts library in N[ew] Y[ork], probably in Oct[ober]. Frankly, it is disorienting & discombobulating to have to deal with all this stuff which shrieks "The Past, The Past." But I am getting irritable enough as a result to know soon I will turn to the Present and try to write some "new" music. In the *Book Review* of today's *Times*, a most illuminating article on the business of Ezra Pound, noxious anti-Semite, self-avowed Fascist, and self-declared know-it-all poet whom some people still take seriously.[17] His amorality is enough to put me off permanently. I know we humans are sometimes poisonous combinations of good and evil. But I, as always, fail to see why such in poets, for ex[ample], needs to be excused. Man will always have art, good or bad; but he's never had enough good, i.e., moral sense (I say that despite the religions which claim morality). […]

George

146

1 SEPTEMBER 1991

Dear George,

[…] Gillmor/correspondence, etc.: We completely see eye to eye about this. No poking around in this as long as we are alive. What happens after is not my concern. I preserved your letters, because of you and because of my funny habit of squirreling away all papers that say something, that have some bearing on my life or the lives of those about whom I care. Who knows? Perhaps the circumstance that for ca. 20 years in my life (from 10 to 30) I often lived like a snail made me hang on to papers that defined a kind of interior '*locus*' for me … (Perhaps similarly to the relationship which the devout Jew had with the Torah, the Mishnah and the Talmud in the Diaspora … Who knows?) Now, what you may do, or not do, with the letters I sent to you is entirely your business. If you don't want to clutter up the house with them and if you don't choose to send them to one 'repository' or another, I'm certain the Music Division of the National Library of Canada would be glad to have them, near to your letters to me. […]

There is no need to add to the info[rmation] I told you about the possibility of the opera on J.R. Oppenheimer. This is my business and the whole thing is still 'touch & go.' I'll know more about it in a few weeks' time. Just one word before I leave this topic: it is difficult to know why one writes this, or that, kind of work. Probably the story of every piece is different. The same holds for me in this case. There is a very long tale about why I was, & am, attracted to this man's story. But this is not the right moment for getting into this. (His academic prose, incidentally, is stiflingly elegant and eloquent. J.R. Oppenheimer became a master concealer of his real face in public … One has to dig hard to get closer to the man's innards … much has to be imagined, or even 're-invented' …)

Strange, that you wrote about Ezra Pound. About a month ago I took out a volume with his *Cantos*, and 2 others about the man. I only sampled this stuff … The poetry, with its leaps & allusions has some appeal and he even induced me to look up some elementary explications of Chinese script, which fascinated him (and me too). As to his life, he was a pathetic figure, chasing, so it seems, a few crackpot notions, generalizations, which included some stupid notions about finance, Jews, etc. I was quite taken by his trial lawyer's private statement to the effect that E.P. was incapable of sticking to a topic beyond a sentence. The lawyer found him a pathetic, pitiable figure. I am a bit uneasy about the notion that 'it' is okay for poetry, but is to be regarded as 'pitiable' failing for life. But *Tristan* is a wonderful work and R[ichard] W[agner] was, at least sometimes (often?), a despicable character. Perhaps things are so tricky that one has to allow for the cohabitation of artistic genius and scoundrel-like thinking in one & the same mind. […]

Istvan

147

10 SEPTEMBER 1991

My dear Isty,

What a marvellous gift, your canon for our 50th![18] As far as I can make out you've conjured into existence a lovely little piece which has built into it "50"—but I'm not sure I've grasped it yet—other than 4 + 1 phrases in each voice which gives us 8 + 2 between the two voices expressing what appears to be a row—50 is locked in but I'm afraid I haven't quite got it yet. Anyhow Gene & I love it and thank you and Beate with all our hearts. I'm placing the embroidered original in the Lincoln Center holdings as one of our treasures. […]

George

148

23 SEPTEMBER 1991

Dear Gene and George,

[…] Now the numerology … This is really funny. Whenever, whatever, I count, 50 or 100 is likely to be the sum … and then the other references … Before I go into this little pedantic, silly, exercise (re: the numbers) you must promise to believe me that I <u>never once</u> gave a conscious thought to such attributes while composing this little (yet 'infinite') piece … Well, okay, here we go then . . .

Before the canon begins its <u>complete</u> (as distinct from <u>partial</u>) recurrence a whole step (2) 'up,' 4 × 13 beats occurred (the canonic 'sub-unit' of 13 beats 4 times; twice 'up,' twice 'down,' like a wave, yet with the 'net' result of 'ascent'). 4 × 13 = 52. Now these 52 beats feature the 12-tone row of the 13-beat 'unit' 4 times, for 48 tones. Hence: 52 + 48 = 100 in <u>each</u> part. Hence: the 2 × 50 occurs in each part, <u>doubly</u> celebrating the 100 years (50 for Gene & 50 for George) spent together.

Now the 'theme' of the canon, that occupies/fills the 13 beats. It 'tells' me this: it is a 12-tone row, which meant so much for George (and for me) during much of our professional lives, and perhaps it still does so. But this is a highly 'tonal' row, containing the 4 'tonal' triad types (major, minor, augmented and diminished) <u>and</u> the diminished 7th chord, each and every one of them with its (their) 'affective' load of 'happy,' 'sad,' 'irrational,' 'euphoric,' 'ecstatic,' 'pained' … articulating the emotional gamut we all lived through in our wonderfully and experientially full lives. These 'cells' line up (in a simplified form) like this (like a 'triptych'):

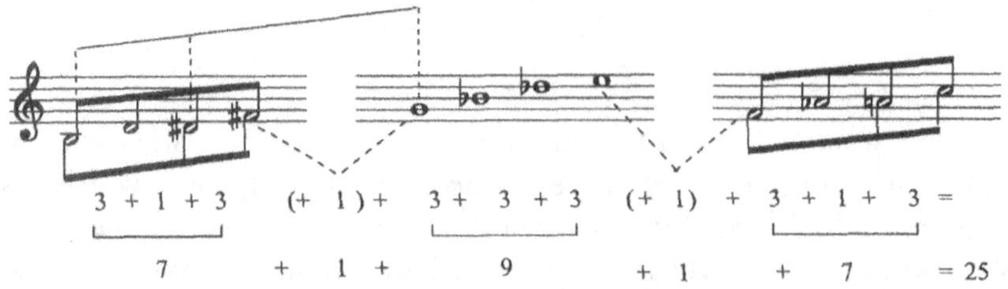

[This is also a palindrome …]

The 25 semitones in 'her' and in 'his' parts add up, once again, to 50. At this point I stop this exercise of omphaloskepsis [i.e., "navel gazing"] (a fancy word I stumbled on in my Webster, which gave me a chuckle a few months ago).

Well, here is the riddle, unmasked in its ... whatever the right noun to follow might be ... In all this remains the basic notions of love, infinite expansion, and holding a dear image of one's dear friends ... [...]

Istvan

NOTES

1 Anhalt is referring to *Oppenheimer* (see "1989," note 1). Upon the rejection of his libretto by the Canadian Opera Company, he entered into a collaboration with John Murrell (b. 1945), a Texas-born playwright who settled in Canada in 1968. Since 1999 he has been serving as Artistic Director and Executive Producer of Theatre at the Banff Centre for the Arts. See also *Istvan Anhalt: Pathways and Memory*, ed. Robin Elliott and Gordon E. Smith (Montreal and Kingston: McGill-Queen's University Press, 2001), 90n.34.

2 *Verdi's Aida: The History of an Opera in Letters and Documents*, collected and trans. by Hans Busch (Minneapolis: University of Minnesota Press, 1978).

3 *The Correspondence between Richard Strauss and Hugo von Hofmannsthal*, trans. Hanns Hammelmann and Ewald Osers (London: Collins, 1961); *A Confidential Matter: The Letters of Richard Strauss and Stefan Zweig, 1931–1935*, trans. Max Knight (Berkeley: University of California Press, 1977).

4 Heinrich Graetz, *History of the Jews*, 6 vols., ed. and in part trans. by Bela Lowy (Philadelphia: Jewish Publishing Society of America, 1891–98).

5 See "1990," note 5.

6 Primo Levi, *The Periodic Table*, trans. Raymond Rosenthal (New York: Schocken, 1984). See also "1990," note 6.

7 Rochberg, "The Bells and Drums of Confucius: Exploring Cross-Cultural Ways" (1991), unpublished ms., Anhalt Fonds MUS 164/B2,135.

8 "The Living Tree: The Changing Meaning of Being Chinese Today," *Daedalus: Journal of the American Academy of Arts and Sciences* 120/2 (Spring 1991).

9 *The Complete Works of Chuang-Tzu*, trans. Burton Watson (New York: Columbia University Press, 1968).

10 Kakuzo Okakura, *The Book of Tea*, ed. and introduced by Everett F. Bleiler (New York: Dover Publications, 1964). The mansion of philanthropist and art collector Isabella Stewart Gardener (1840–1924), modelled after a fifteenth-century Venetian palace, has been, since 1903, the Isabella Stewart Gardener Museum in Boston, Massachusetts.

11 *Japanese Death Poems: Written by Zen Monks and Haiku Poets on the Verge of Death*, compiled with an introduction by Yoel Hoffmann (Rutland, VT: Charles E. Tuttle, 1986).

12 *American Bouquet*, versions of popular music for solo guitar (1991), written for Eliot Fisk.

13 David Easton, *Divided Knowledge: Across Disciplines, Across Cultures*, ed. David and Corinne S. Schelling (Newbury Park, CA: Sage Publications, 1991).
14 See "1987," note 1, and "1988," note 11.
15 Roger Kimball, *Tenured Radicals: How Politics Has Corrupted Our Higher Education* (New York: Harper & Row, 1990).
16 J. Robert Oppenheimer, *The Open Mind* (New York: Simon and Schuster, 1955).
17 Richard Gillman, "Standing Up to Ezra Pound," *The New York Times Book Review*, 25 August 1991.
18 "Canon, For Gene and George on their 50th together … With love, and friendship, Istvan and Bea, August, 1991, Kingston," Anhalt Fonds MUS 164/D5,35. The text to this canon is as follows: "Dear friends, Gene and George Rochberg, fifty years together in trust, harmony, friendship and mutual love … on and on, deep into the twenty-first century with Chessie, Geno, Jacob and little Gemma … Dear friends, Gene and George …," etc.

1992

149

4 JANUARY 1992

My dear Isty,

[…] I'm truly sorry to hear you're still ensnared by that mountain of paper & the reasons it grew to such proportions. At this point I really have no words of comfort. Except: knowing you, you will not let it go to waste—it will issue in many things including the *Quartetsatz* for the Glenn Gould Memorial.[1] I just finished (as pure diversion) *The Lyre of Orpheus* [1988] by Robertson Davies & as I read it I kept thinking of you & the opera—because the entire plot of this (I think) fairly slight effort of his hangs on making an opera—should you read it I know you will smile at the naiveté of the author. I was delighted to see the piece on you in the *Queen's Quarterly*.[2] Not many of us attain to the distinction of making a difference in our own land & culture. I think it's terrific that you're finally going to make it to Israel. I only worry that you will see a land & a people with too many (unsolvable?) problems. The trajectory of my 3 times in Israel started at a great high (in 1963), leveled off (in 1969–70; or 1970–71, I'm not sure anymore) but still gave one the sense of vitality & capacity to deal with problems to finally a sense of weariness, exhaustion (in 1982, fall; following on the invasion of Lebanon by Sharon) which you could read on the faces of people wherever you were. Nevertheless, it is still a country & a people & a civilization despite all it must contend with. […]

George

150

14 JANUARY 1992

George, dear friend,

You are, as always, prompt with the pen, and effective with good advice. It was good of you to spring into action to facilitate some aspects of our upcoming trip to Israel. [...] I have on my desk a few books and historical map-sequences pertaining to the Holy Land. I am turning from one to another, in the hope that a sort of outline and geographical glossary *cum* a rough chronology will stick with me to lend a sort of framework to the sites and stories we are expecting to experience there. [...]

Yes the *Quartetsatz* is coming. Someone at the CBC is suggesting a title—something about Glenn G[ould]'s intellect or such. I increasingly am resistant to it. Something will eventually appear on the 'screen' when the piece will be done.

I am pretty starved for hearing live performances of my music, so it promises to be a treat to hear the Montreal Symphony (reputedly the best orchestra in the land) playing *Sonance•Resonance (Welche Töne?)* on Febr. 11–12 next. They gave the job to a Hungarian-born(!) guest conductor by the name Iván Fischer whom I never heard, or saw before.[3]

Istvan

151

17 MARCH 1992

My dear George,

Back from Israel ... a visit to which your advice, etc., contributed very strongly. [...] Before leaving for Israel we spent 5 days in Montreal in relation to the performance of *Sonance•Resonance (Welche Töne?)* by the Montreal Symphony Orch[estra], a splendid group, especially the strings, under Ivan Fischer, a youngish very gifted conductor, Budapest-born, as I am. We had ca. 3½ hrs. rehearsals and it was wonderful to experience how things came together. There were 2 performances and the reception was from positive to even better. (I listened, as always with eyes closed, and felt great ...) We got back on the 9th (after 14 hrs. on the plane) and on the 10th and 11th I had (in Toronto) rehearsals with the young Esprit Orchestra, which was to record (for a CD) *SparkskrapS* on the 12th.[4] Too little time, but again during the 3 hrs.-long grueling recording session (my first such experience) things came together and I think there are enough good 'takes' for assembling a true enough performance of the piece. So you see dear friend I had nothing to complain about hearing my music live these days. Also, before leaving for Israel I finished in draft the *Quartetsatz* (I call it *Doors ... shadows*) for the Glenn Gould memorial concert in September next. [...]

Istvan

152

17 JULY 1992

My old friend Isty,

[...] Gene & I are getting ready in more ways than one to leave for Grasmere, England where we'll listen to what I hope will be good (even if academic) talks @ Wordsworth, Coleridge, & Shelley; where we can walk in and around the lake country. [...] Going to Grasmere where Wordsworth lived & worked has driven me to read in a very serious way the works of the great Romantic poets as well as about them, biography and critical commentary. This has been extraordinarily efficacious because of 2 reasons primarily. <u>First</u>, I'm constantly being asked about (or "accused" of) my having been instrumental in bringing about "a" or "the" neoromantic movement here in the States; and suddenly one day I decided no one knew what they were talking about. That is to say, in order to talk about "neoromanticism" first you must know what "romanticism" is as an impulse and certainly how it manifested itself historically, esp[ecially] in the late 18th & early 19th cent[urie]s. Not surprisingly people who talk & write @ music rarely go deep & therefore tend toward the utterly superficial and/or the present variety of journalistic sophisticates. In either case they get everything usually wrong. Second, because the real impulses behind Wordsworth, Coleridge, & <u>esp[ecially]</u> Shelley are <u>nothing less</u> than the stages toward the transformation of man through both individual development & societal development both rooted in bringing about & maintaining political & social justice. (And if pol[itical] & soc[ial] justice come, can economic justice be far behind?)

The present state of the world and the absolutely immediate political situation in the States is in dire need of precisely what Shelley was so taken up with both in his poetry & his prose (which explains in a way what he meant by "the poet is the unacknowledged legislator of the world").[5] All week I have been watching the Democratic convention to the parallel internal thought of what these great minds & spirits were addressing themselves to & simultaneously thinking that perhaps it is no accident that our trip comes at this point. Though I recognize full well the danger of interpreting "world" events in purely personal, fated terms. Still, taken together these reasons connect to each other in astonishing ways in me, lift me out of more ancient ways of deploring the killing effects of the 20th cent[ury] in all directions, human, ecological, artistic, etc. and ending up as I frequently have depressed out of my mind. Now I feel that the root premises of what we call romanticism are precisely what is needed in this crazy world to heal hatreds, divisions; to replace mistrust and cynicism with trust and idealism. But a trust and idealism which are the opposite of naive, simplistic or sentimental hope/desire.

Without spelling all this out which would be to recap[itulate] the history & failures in that history of our species, it's possible to suggest a kind of renewed trust & idealism flowing from what Bill Clinton called in his acceptance speech last night "the new covenant" which, if passed through the story of <u>our</u> people, the Jews, would mean a tougher kind of morality & the responsibility which goes with it. So romanticism is not just "daffodils" or "music, when soft voices die" ... It is actually a directed spiritual storm which those amazing British poets released, a later infusion of what the old Hebrews released into the world. And now the need is once again for a great & major new infusion. To overturn a whole century, virtually, of horrors which were new forms of old plagues, each one whether aesthetic in form or social engineering with concomitant political perversions flowing from them or even scientific/technological "advances" (self-advertised as such by morally blind enthusiasts); and ultimately to return to deeper, humbler understandings of what the limitations inherent in being "human" are or may be, and therefore the revealed new grasp of man in relation to the physical world of which he is another variety or compound, the spiritual world which manifests in this physical form, both universe and man. But simultaneously I recognize the pitfalls, the pratfalls, the dangers of unbalanced expressions in political/social/scientific/philosophic/artistic enthusiasms rising to single-focus "belief systems."

So you see, my dear Isty, how at one and the same time I am launched on a new wave of larger, impersonal-yet-very-personal energy but haunted by the failures of the past and those that inevitably must still lie in our path because the world & man are not fixed entities & both are subject to contingency—yet there is still the "moveless wave" (Shelley),[6] "the still point at the turning of the world" (T.S. Eliot),[7] and "eternity in love with the productions of time" (Blake).[8] [...]

George

153

3 OCTOBER 1992

George, dear Friend,

Before starting to write this I reread your July 17th letter … I was able to devote more peaceful attention to it than at the first reading … So full it is with intensity, feeling, indignation, wanting to contribute to the righting [of] this crazily lurching ship, our human world (was it ever better … or are we getting ever more virtuosic in getting the gory news faster around, or trumpeting trivia with an ever greater decibel rate[?] … Oh, wonderful technology, to sell … what … detergent and warmed up, stale, 10th-hand *Kultur* …) […]

Words, words … I wrote quite a bit of these this year, and now I feel as being 'written out.' It started after I completed my first piece for String Quartet[9] in April (of this more later on, here …). I wrote a revised version of a brief text "The Bridge"[10] which is a sort of *cri de coeur* over our present nonsense here over the constitution, which is the result of only the most recent phase of the machinations of powerful elements among the political elites of a restive Quebec. Your elections and our constitutional referendum! Both within a fortnight. Both momentous, and potentially ominous watersheds in these terribly difficult times. So many people are hurting economically up here … people are put out onto pasture with no more than the flimsy repeat of some talk about the 'global economy,' 'restructuring,' … A post-Darwinian concept of the human species in the so-called 'developed' societies. (Yes, technologically, and perhaps also scientifically, 'developed,' but, as you so well say it are we so also, humanely, humanistically? We seem to be doing terribly. We haven't learned from the wars and slaughters with which this terrible century is filled …)

So what else did I write[?] … I thought, finally, I should write a few words of my dear maternal grandparents in whose home I lived from ca. age 14 until I was sucked into the Hungarian Army's forced labour camp system in Dec. 1942, at age 23. And I wanted to write about an old friend, László Gyopár,[11] a fellow student-composer in the class of Kodály, who was murdered in the same outfit I 'served' (was a prisoner in). One thing led to another, and then to another … etc. etc. and when the pen stopped I looked with disbelief at a pile of over 500 closely written pages of outpourings, about this and that and still something else … I decided to call this mountain "A Weave of Life Lines."[12] I had no courage to reread it. Put it away for a time when I shall be no longer around … Then I wrote a strange text to which I gave the title *Tikkun* which, as you might know, means (in

Hebrew) redemption, reintegration ... For me this (Kabbalistic notion) means an attempt at ascertaining if some bits and pieces of experience, thought, feeling could be made to coalesce into some sort of (however tenuous & temporary) unity ... Is this possible in this world of ours of raging multiplicity, pluralism, relativism of values, loss of faith in ... what? (What is that 'what'?) Presently, I am 'testing' this text whether or not it could provide the scaffolding of a piece for orchestra and a baritone solo.

Now back to the string quartet piece which the CBC commissioned me (1 out of 3 composers here) to write 'in honour' of Glenn Gould whose tragic, early, death occurred 10 years ago, when he was just 50(!) years young/old.[13] Several outfits up here joined hands with the CBC and organized a week-long 'international' Glenn Gould Conference, which also featured the first concerts in the brand new CBC Building in Toronto, with its fine Glenn Gould Studio (a little gem of a concert hall, seating 350, with excellent acoustics) and the début of the newly formed Glenn Gould String Quartet, composed of Malcolm Loew (Boston S[ymphony] Orch[estra]'s concertmaster, who was ill & had to be replaced), Steve Dann the principal viola in the Toronto Symph[ony], Mayumi Seiler, a wonderful Japanese-German fiddler, based in Britain & Salzburg, and New York's own Fred Sherry of the Lincoln Center, a wonderful chamber musician & cellist. The premiere took place on Sept. 24th and I have a long story about it which I am resisting to write down here. The result is an air check tape I have now of this single-movement work (playing time 12' 50") which I entitled *Doors ... shadows (Glenn Gould in memory)*. I loved writing it and after the concert it remained intact, but for small details which I consider fine-tuning. [...] It is a piece unlike any other piece I wrote. (No, I did not quote from the *Goldberg Var[iations]*, or for that matter, from any other J.S.B. stuff, either. In fact there are no quotes in it at all. It was not Gould's external discourse I was thinking about when searching for the notes ...) I'd love to play you this piece one day ... and if I don't get an even better performance than the present ca. 85% one I have now, I'll send you this one, eventually. [...]

Istvan

154

3 NOVEMBER 1992

My dear friend, George,

[...] Spurred on by your interest, here I'm enclosing a cassette with *Doors ... shadows (Glenn Gould in memory)*. The CBC asked me to write a piece for a series of memorial celebrations around Gould. (He would have been 60 this fall, but a stroke took him away 10 years ago.) I knew him. We spoke *viva voce*, on the 'phone, he even 'interviewed' me for some radio documentaries (and he played & conducted my music). Besides being a stupendous pianist, I came to know him as an enigmatic, even a little bit tragic, figure, with a tinge of the irrational mixed in within a very sharp and fast mind. So here is the piece, a kind of reflection on him. Behind it is the question: how does one 'decode' a complex person like G.G.? Of course, one doesn't. How does one 'know' anyone else? Difficult ... we show to the outside 'faces,' or only 'doors with shadows peeking out from behind.' How does one know oneself? A package of difficulties, this one too ...

The performance is quite good, even eloquent at places. I had but 15(!) minutes of rehearsal (in all) before this performance. I would like fewer glides, fewer long 'breaks' between 'events' [...]

Istvan

155

23 NOVEMBER 1992

George, dear friend,

[...] Your words about *Doors ... shadows* show so much: understanding (in a musical sense and in a sense pertaining to the 'human plane,' independent from this, or that, modality ... which tells me why we get so much stimulation/inspiration from a great book, a great painting, etc. But music is special! This is <u>our</u> field and I am increasingly grateful that I have <u>some</u> keys to <u>some</u> of its depths ... Our 'language' is like no other ... It can say so much simultaneously ... It is awesome ...) Yes ... a while ago I wrote of your 'understanding' before I got carried away ... To this I want to add generosity, empathy ... I am grateful ... Your words mean a great deal to me! I guess we are mutual witnesses to each other['s] doings and we 'resonate' in a sympathetic way to each other. Yet another thing to celebrate ...

As I suggested on the 'phone, the 'working' title you gave to your Wordsworth paper is poetry ... I'm so much looking forward to reading it, so please send it as soon as it is available.[14] [...]

About the enclosures ... Yet another small (or not <u>so</u> small) window to your friend's past. It needs a few words of Intro[duction]. This <u>memorandum</u> and one of the 'enclosures' to it, is a part of my most recent letter to Yad Vashem about Pater János Antal, the Salesian priest who saved my life in Dec. 1944.[15] After having found out earlier this year that Yad Vashem has what's called a Dept. of the Righteous (Who Saved Jewish Lives at the Risk of their own Life), I put Antal's name (and the names of the de Kerpelys who continued with the rescue ... in '44–'45) forward for a citation/honour by Yad Vashem. I am very anxious to get this posthumous award for that extraordinarily brave priest and for Mrs. Theresa de Kerpely and her late husband, too, who will be, within a week, 94(!).[16] She is living in Boise, Id[aho] and is still a dear friend, with whom I talk frequently on the 'phone. (She is near blind & cannot write/read anymore.) She is a gifted author of 7 published books of which the last is *Of Love and Wars* which is a voluminous autobiography that includes the war (WW II) years and thus our shared experiences also. She is a great lady. [...]

Istvan

156

24 DECEMBER 1992

Dear Friend Isty,

[...] I'm neither Christian, nor Jew, nor Muslim—all the God-oriented & determined religions are empty of meaning to me & make behavior based on any & all of these religions seem ridiculous or stupid or sometimes downright nasty—all this by way of separating myself from the local car dealer who has a big letter across his windows reading "Keep Christ in Christmas"—which translated of course means "buy more cars from me, your good friendly Christian neighbor"—good ol' American *capitalimus mit christus*. You will see from my Wordsworth effort I am declaring for Taoism (despite the fact I don't look Chinese). [...]

George

157

25 DECEMBER 1992

George, dear friend,

[...] I am escaping into my room for this communion, once again, with your splendid and illuminating paper 'Wordsworth's Mind and the Mind of Man.' What'll follow will suffer from the handicap that I couldn't bring myself to read *The Prelude*,[17] as yet, though I have it at home from the library. The reason? I am deep into a new venture (words/music, both by me) and the world of W[ordsworth] is too much of a powerful distraction, and would (could) even result in a 'derailment' which would take me weeks to 'right.' Your paper is different: it's a filter and a filtered string of ideas, expressed in a metalanguage that I can 'take' now, and enjoy, as I do cherish every word coming from you. The germinating idea, located/recognized by you is important and timelessly topical, even though [it] has come to assume a special resonance in our 'now,' presently. I agree with you: it is the old Adamic hubris, declaring (unilaterally), ignoring the signals unmistakable from flora & fauna that God gave the Earth to Adam to 'cultivate' (a 'soft' word this), enjoy, and exploit. (Wasn't this the pretext/pretense that was evoked by the early 17th-c[entury] colonists in North America, from La Nouvelle France to New England?) The buildup of your text is as striking as it is fascinating. [...] In the notion of the *Tikkun* (integration, redemption, 'putting together' ...) I sense a similar possibility for groping towards the ultimate cause and final unity of 'all that is.' (Perhaps in about 6 months' time I might be able to spin forth this for another little stretch ...)

I wouldn't worry about what the experts could be saying. You are not weighted down with the usual scholarly apparatus; are not aiming for 'tenure' or 'promotion' or whatever such mundane goal, but visiting Wordsworth's garden from your own neighbouring garden. What fascinates me is your affinity with W[ordsworth] & his chronotope. [...]

Istvan

NOTES

1 *Doors ... shadows (Glenn Gould in memory)* (1992), commissioned by the Canadian Broadcasting Corporation for the tenth anniversary of Gould's death and premiered by an ad hoc group calling themselves the Glenn Gould String Quartet on 24 September 1992 in the Glenn Gould Studio, Toronto.

2 Gordon E. Smith, "'Deep themes, not so hidden' in the Music of István Anhalt," *Queen's Quarterly* 98/1 (Spring 1991): 99–119.

3 Iván Fischer (b. 1951), Hungarian conductor, founding musical director (1983) of the Budapest Festival Orchestra.

4 *SparkskrapS* (1987), Esprit Orchestra, Alex Pauk, conductor, CBC Records SMCD 5132 (1993).

5 From *Defense of Poetry: Part First* (1821).

6 "One mind, the type of all, the moveless wave / Whose calm reflects all moving things that are, / Necessity, and love, and life, the grave, / And sympathy, fountains of hope and fear, / Justice, and truth, and time, and the world's natural sphere." From *The Revolt of Islam*, Canto 7, verse 31 (1817).

7 "At the still point of the turning of the world. Neither flesh nor fleshless; / Neither from nor towards; at the still point, there the dance is, / But neither arrest nor movement." From *Four Quartets*, No. 1, "Burnt Norton" (1935).

8 "Eternity is in love with the productions of time." From *The Marriage of Heaven and Hell* (ca. 1790–93), Plate 7, "Proverbs of Hell."

9 Anhalt seems to have forgotten an early String Quartet (1947) written in Paris for his teacher Nadia Boulanger.

10 "The Bridge: A Parable" (1991), unpublished ms., Anhalt Fonds MUS 164/F1,76.

11 László Gyopár (ca. 1918–44); see Gillmor, "Echoes of Time and the River," in *Taking a Stand: Essays in Honour of John Beckwith*, ed. Timothy J. McGee (Toronto: University of Toronto Press, 1995), 15–44.

12 "A Weave of Life Lines" (1992), unpublished ms., Anhalt Fonds MUS 164/F1,77–79.

13 The other two composers were Jacques Hétu (b. 1938) and Oskar Morawetz (b. 1917).

14 "Wordsworth's Mind and the Mind of Man," unpublished ms.

15 Enclosed with this letter is a nine-page typewritten "Memorandum Re: Pater János Antal," addressed to Yad Vashem, Israel, as well as a two-page photocopy of excerpts from an article by Sándor Dénes, "Szervezett segitség az üldözöttekért" [Organized Help for the Persecuted], in *A Magyar Katolikus Egyház és az Emberi Jogok Védelme* [The Hungarian Catholic Church and the Defence of Human Rights], ed. Antal Meszlényi (Budapest: A Szent István-Társulat, 1947), with handwritten commentary and translation in the margins by Anhalt. The Yad Vashem Museum in Israel was founded in 1953 to honour both Holocaust victims and non-Jews—"the Righteous among the Nations"—who "risked their lives to save the lives of Jews." Pater János Antal (1892–1967), a Salesian priest, provided refuge for Anhalt at this time, disguising him in the cassock of a priest and providing him with papers describing him as a seminarian; the composer's *La Tourangelle* (1975) was dedicated, in memoriam, to Pater Antal; see Gillmor, "Echoes of Time and the River," 15–44, and *Istvan Anhalt: Pathways and Memory*, ed. Robin Elliott and Gordon E. Smith (Montreal and Kingston: McGill-Queen's University Press, 2001), 15–16.

16 Theresa de Kerpely (1898–1993), Anglo-American writer whose second husband was the cellist Jenö de Kerpely. In 1944, Anhalt was sheltered in the de Kerpely home in Budapest after his escape from a forced labour battalion. The key documents are Theresa de Kerpely's first published novel, *A Crown for Ashes* (Milwaukee: Bruce Publishing, 1952), written under the pseudonym Teresa Kay, in which the leading character, Andrew Marton, is a kind of fictional composite of Anhalt and László Gyopár, his fellow student in Kodály's classes at the Liszt Academy of Music in Budapest, and de Kerpely's autobiography, *Of Love and Wars* (New York: Stein and Day, 1984). See also Gillmor, "Echoes of Times and the River," 15–44, and Elliott and Smith, eds., *Pathways and Memory*, 15–16.

17 William Wordsworth, *The Prelude, 1798–1799*, ed. Stephen Parrish (Ithaca, NY: Cornell University Press, 1977).

1993

158

21 JANUARY 1993

Dear George,

[...] I was, lately, helped by, finally, understanding the psychological relevance of the old Kabbalistic idea of *Zim-zum* (or *tzim-tzum*) which puzzled me for years. In case you are rusty about this here is what I think it (originally) meant, as a theistic notion. If God is everywhere in the universe how could he create anything else for which there would be no room!? A knotty little problem for some of our rabbis of old ... Well, they came up with the ingenious idea that the omnipotent, infinite, all-encompassing, etc. (the *Ein-Sof*) in his/her/its etc. wisdom (or 'generosity') imposed shrinkage on itself in order to provide the necessary *Lebensraum* for creation. Isn't this neat as a cosmological-theological notion? Until now it had no attraction-meaning for me. Then, suddenly, years after having encountered the idea, this came to mind: the *Zim-zum*, as many (most? all?) other Kabbalistic notions, concepts, has also a psychological dimension. In this case, the withdrawal (voluntary) of the 'creator,' to allow something else to be born, and expand, can also mean the voluntary 'withdrawal' of a parent, a teacher, another figure of 'authority' from the emotional, etc., space of a dependent (real, imagined, or potential) in order that the latter could realize the self. Now, you might smile at my primitive psychology here. [...] But this interpretation of the *Zim-zum* (1) helped to reinforce my instinct and (2) made me appreciative of some of these rabbis (Isaac Luria of Safed, foremostly) of old.

This brings me to your "declaring for Taoism" ... This intrigues me greatly, and I am disadvantaged by near total ignorance of the Tao belief-systems, mysticism, philosophy, religion, etc. The tiny bit I recall appeals to me, although I shall probably never achieve the "slowing down," the "distancing," the "calming of passions" and the "indifference to memory," etc. it contains, or at least I think it contains. But I share your distancing from "religion" if the word means dogma, observance, liturgy, prayer, etc. For me reading about the Kabbalah shows this kind of viewing of the world as a syncretic accumulation of Far-Eastern (some Taoist ones also) Zoroastrian, gnostic, Jewish ideas held together, as if in a sponge. I am interested in comparative religion which I view as an important part of the history of ideas. But this sounds false: it suggests some kind of knowledge which I don't have. From time to time I dabble in this or that; probe into this or that, trying to connect up these bits & pieces into my own little vehicle that carries me along from day to day. [...]

I found myself last summer so full of feeling about some people's woes in our world that I wrote a text-title: *Tikkun*, also a Kabbalistic notion, ca. 1,500 words. [...] The text-story is, I believe, very colorful and cries out for a musical "setting." After the premiere of *Doors ... shadows* on Sept. 24th, I set to work on *Tikkun* and wrote out the first draft of a piece (I call it a 'pluri-drama') for lyric baritone and orchestra in the following 3½ months. It is quite an extensive work, not less than 35 minutes. It will be quite a taxing vehicle for the singer-reciter who will have to convey a sing-song, etc. of half-dozen+ different personae in the piece. But the great problem might be that in the text I could be regarded as stepping on the tender toes of some establishment ideas ... Yes, there is an implied ethical—and perhaps unavoidably also political—dimension to some of the things in this text. Some members of the "Culture of Contentment" (John Galbraith) or of the "Manufacturing Consent" (Noam Chomsky)[1] set might take strong exception to some parts of this text. If so, I would have difficulty in finding a venue for the performance(s) of *Tikkun* given the circumstance that most (all?) of our orchestras increasingly depend on corporate donations to keep afloat. And it would not be the corporate executive who would say "nay" to *Tikkun*, it would be the orchestra (i.e., the artistic "decider(s)") who would bar it from inclusion on a program. But I might be overly pessimistic about this. So far, I have received plenty of signs of appreciation for what I was writing. I was (am) sustained by it and am grateful for it. Perhaps *Tikkun* will, also, find acceptance ... I don't have a commission for it, but I'll write it anyway, if I'll have enough strength for it. [...]

Istvan

159

9 FEBRUARY 1993

My dear Isty,

It's been an incredible period since @ Xmas—in the midst of work & plans for travelling for rehearsals & perf[ormance]s came the horrible shocking news of the death of our old & dear friend Steve Albert, one of America's truly gifted composers and only 51.[2] […] I can't tell you how hard it is still to take this in. Steve was a student of mine very briefly (for 1 term, fall 1962) & from there on joined the family you might say. A very intense, serious, searching mind, a large-hearted person of deep, sometimes overwhelming feelings which frequently threatened his own equilibrium & that of those close to him. […] For years Steve struggled for his inner balance which included his musical balance as well. Probably not 'til his forties did he achieve both in some measure. And certainly the music began to come. Not prolific but by the time fate cut his thread a good substantial body of works to his credit. This month Yo-Yo Ma was (is) repeating the Cello Concerto he wrote for him & recording it.[3] Some very touching & beautiful passages in the concerto. When Gene & I went to North Carolina for a holiday on the New Year I was ferociously depressed. The minute we returned on the phone mailbox a message from the *Guardian* in London asking me to write an "appreciation." It appeared Feb. 1 in edited, abbreviated form (as I knew it would; I had been forewarned).[4] I can't remember ever having had so much difficulty writing before. All the while I felt as though I were dreaming a nightmare & it wasn't true, I could go to the phone & call Steve up & there he'd be, cantankerous as ever. Isty, my old & dear understanding friend, I don't need to say it—but do: that life burdens us all too heavily; it is wayward & arbitrary; and if there is a "God" somewhere—be he Jewish, Christian, Muslim—he has no *Verstand* because he/she/it is simply not human & therefore can't enter into what is human—with all its pain, uncertainty, unreasonableness (only academics still prate about reason & reasonableness) layers-deep horrors. Oddly, it is not death which I fear: it is life itself. No Tender, Merciful, Loving "God" could have made such a world as now affects this time—but in truth why is this time <u>different</u> and/or worse from others? only in details, dimension, etc. Please forgive my bitter outcry. I'm very tired, from all the emotional *Sturm & Drang* […] which never seems to leave; & then on top of all that to Houston for 3 soul-exhausting days launching the new cello sonata w[ith] piano [*Sonata-Aria* (1992)] (Norman & Jeanne Fischer outdid themselves) followed almost immediately by a day in Newark w[ith] the N[ew] J[ersey] Symphony's 1st rehearsal of my 6th Symph[ony]. Flat on my back for 3 days after that. Then to N[ew] Y[ork] this Feb. 2 for dress reh[earsal] at Avery Fisher Hall, perf[ormance] Feb. 3; Lawrence (Larry) Leighton Smith (conductor Louisville Symphony) did a splendid job, finally home to recuperate & pick up the pieces of daily life & work again. How beautiful are the quiet, routined days, how almost soothing. […] I am finding stress unhinges my nerves, unhinged nerves weaken my legs, etc. Some of the joys of old age in America, land that I love.

I'm not surprised you're drawn back into Kabbalah. Each of us has a need for an esoteric tradition. Yours seems to be Kabbalah, mine first the *Bhagavad Gita*, now the Tao. Years back I read G. Scholem very slowly & carefully; then went back to it. For reasons hard to explain, it didn't take; Jewish mysticism—like the Christian variety, though differently & for different reasons—remains outside of me. It was a German-Jewish art historian friend refugee of 1933 who was studying counterpoint w[ith] me at the New School of Music in Phila[delphia] in 1946 who would introduce me to the *Bhag[avad Gita]*. I survived my 30s & 40s on that book alone. But knowing how you penetrate your material, I know you will make a fine new work, your *Tikkun*. No music for me now. I am now finally getting into putting together my book on *Chromaticism* (I'll send you the introduction shortly); and won't rest until it is completed.[5] After that I.I.L (as Tolstoy said: "If I Live") who knows what will follow. […]

George

160

23 MARCH 1993

George, dear friend,

[…] Steve Albert … a tragedy … I recall meeting him & his wife at your house during one of our visits. I recall him well: intense, <u>very</u> intelligent, sensitive, open and eager to reach out … Strange—but the circumstances of his death appear to pair up in my mind with the recent (few months ago) death, via car accident, of Christopher Lewis, a former student of mine at McGill, who taught at the U[niversity] of Alberta and lived since years in Edmonton.[6] […] Chris wanted, at the outset, to be a composer, but wisely switched to 'theory' at Eastman, for his Ph.D. according to Al Fisher[7] (formerly of the U[niversity] of A[lberta], now the new director of <u>our</u> School of Music). Chris grew into a terrific teacher

& a well-regarded (or better) theorist. […] One more life that ended in 'mid-phrase' … no 'closure' here … let alone a 'coda' …

You raise the question about life's 'sense' (this is my word, though), about "God" … wondering what drew me to the Kabbalah (thanks to reading about it in Scholem's words). My interest (only) in this is in its (the Kabbalah's) psychology *cum* attempt at concocting a thought-structure that its practitioners could accept (they talked themselves into accepting it) as a replica, or model, of the way we feel, think, are alone or are in mutual relationships, and in relationship to the cosmos and to the 'Maker of All.' It bespeaks of an epistemic plateau 'state,' or what-have-you. It is the evidence of an inner urge to understand 'deep' things, such as 'Maker,' cosmos, life, thinking, good vs. evil, and the like. No light stuff, this. And the hypostases in terms of which (for ex[ample]) I[saac] Luria expressed himself (via H[ayyim ben Joseph] Vital)[8] were recognizable concepts, like 'wisdom,' 'goodness,' 'power,' etc. On the other hand: the ecstatic Kabbalah (of A[braham] Abulafia, for ex[ample]) is more abstract and emotional … at least this is how I see it. (Moshe Idel, a youngish Hebrew Univ[ersity] scholar published copiously on it during the '80s.)[9] Actually, my slowly growing *Tikkun* is not a stranger to some of these things. (But I combine it with 'other' things, besides …) […]

Istvan

161

14 JULY 1993

George,

[…] *Tikkun* waits upstairs in my workroom for another push … Yes, the work does come along. In a week's time (hopefully) I'll be through this draft, which saw the drastic condensation of the text which I sent you. My rough guess is that I shrunk this text by about 35%, by cutting out, without caring for 'bloodletting,' much of those words that amounted to what I came to regard more as 'literature' as distinct from 'libretto.' It is now close to being a lean scaffolding which I have provided with music. My guess is that the piece will clock in at about 35 minutes performance time. It is a very dramatic piece; yet another of the 'interior' operas which gain by not being encumbered with sets, costumes … etc. It will take an enormously versatile insightful etc. etc. vocal artist, who will span the emotional/technical range of what the piece encompasses. It's ca. 10 characters (it is not about a multiple personality, though, but of someone, complex, to be sure, who witnesses, observes, interacts with, etc. with a host of others, and who internalizes some of these others and thereby becomes 'richer' himself …). I've done something similar—in idea—in *Thisness*, but here it will be realized differently … For one thing, the piece is through-composed and one situation/event/state of mind flows—modulates—more or less seamlessly into the next, with recalls, doubling-backs, self-referencing and the like … The "usual stuff" of music you would say, my dear, sensitive, experienced and 'knowing' friend … You see: I'm full of 'it' (*Tikkun*) and have the feeling that, yes, there might be (if all goes well) a birth of a new score in about 10–12 months' time … Wish me strength with the rest … […]

Istvan

[…]

NOTES

1 John Kenneth Galbraith, *The Culture of Contentment* (Boston: Houghton Mifflin, 1992); Edward S. Herman and Noam Chomsky, *Manufacturing Consent: The Political Economy of the Mass Media* (New York: Pantheon Books, 1988).

2 See "1965," note 3.

3 Stephen Albert, Concerto for Cello and Orchestra (1989–90), Yo-Yo Ma, cello, Baltimore Symphony Orchestra, David Zinman, conductor, Sony Classical SK 57961 (1994).

4 Rochberg, "Appreciation: Stephen Albert," *The Guardian* (London), 1 February 1993. Rochberg's appreciation of his former student includes a number of sentiments that reflect his own aesthetic journey: "Unlike those composers of his generation who joined the serialist camp or flirted with it briefly, Albert firmly rejected serialism as pernicious in favour of more open, tonally orientated possibilities which can be heard internally. To be able to hear what he wrote, and to write only what he could hear, led him to ways of melodic thinking and harmonic construction which eventually made the sound of his music distinctly his own." In his obituary of Albert, William Bolcom writes in a similar vein: "Both Steve and I studied with the American composer George Rochberg at different times and found George's example an encouraging way out of the then-all-too-apparent cul-de-sac of official modernism; although our three directions could not have been more different, our music has in common an opening toward the past in musical language in order to reach for a higher synthesis and breadth." *The Guardian* (London), 5 January 1993.

5 Rochberg, "Chromaticism: Symmetry in Atonal and Tonal Music" (1993–94), unpublished ms., Anhalt Fonds MUS 164/F2,18.

6 Christopher Lewis (1947–92), Montreal-born composer and theorist, a student of Anhalt at McGill University (BMus, 1968, MMA, 1971). Lewis's research focused on late-nineteenth- and early-twentieth-century music, particularly the music of Mahler; his doctoral dissertation, "Tonality and Structure in the Ninth Symphony of Gustav Mahler" (Eastman School of Music of the University of Rochester), was completed in 1983. According to his widow, Brenda Dalen, "Christopher spoke often

and fondly of his studies in composition with Professor Anhalt and greatly admired his music" (communication to the editor, 4 November 2004).

7 Alfred Fisher (b. 1942), American-born Canadian composer, pianist, and teacher; Director of the School of Music at Queen's University (1992–97).

8 Hayyim ben Joseph Vital (1543–1620), a disciple of Isaac Luria and a major source on Lurianic mysticism, a detailed exposition of which appeared in his major work *Etz hayyim* (*Tree of Life*).

9 Moshe Idel (b. 1947), Professor of Jewish Thought at the Hebrew University of Jerusalem; his publications include *Kabbalah: New Perspectives* (New Haven: Yale University Press, 1988), *Studies in Ecstatic Kabbalah* (Albany: State University of New York Press, 1988), and, most recently, *Absorbing Perfections: Kabbalah and Interpretation*, with a foreword by Harold Bloom (New Haven: Yale University Press, 2002).

1994

162

20 JANUARY 1994

George, dear friend,

This is the promised sign of 'life in progress' I envisaged when we talked on the 'blower' about a week ago. My head and 'emotion-tank' is so full, so beware (I should beware) as I am going to try to contain the danger of overflowing, spilling out, messing up the carpet, imposing your wonderfully patient and willing mind to listen to my 'other' in relation to yourself.

Now this 'other,' all the 'others' in relation to each 'other' (I'm just starting to glean the vastness of this literature, encompassing Buber, Bakhtin, Heidegger—the scoundrel/genius, yet another—Sartre, Husserl, etc. etc.) was on the top of my conscious mind during the past 4–5 months, as I was probing *Tikkun* (now called *Traces (Tikkun)*) towards the last double-bar (which it reached as no. 654, if I recall it correctly, a few days ago) ... In fact: the whole piece's one (there are several) core theme is the dialogical relationship between people, as distinct from, &/or complementary to, the monological one. Our adversarial political & economic philosophies, now so much in ascendancy, bespeak our loss of control over these dialogical relationships. The 'other' might be an adversary in a global 'Cold War' (winner takes all ...), or in a giant take-over battle among giant car manufacturers, none of whom questions the consequences of the isolation of social atoms, each sitting in his/her living room extension, in a make-believe privacy, as they hurtle at 60–70 m/per hr. on a highway towards the office, etc. until a traffic jam stops them all. [...]

I feel, and this pushed 'up' the idea of *Traces* together with other ideas, that technology is conducive to isolation, of separating people from other people. We find more and more electronic gadgets interposed between pairs of humans. Speed, the absence of the need to have to deal with (enjoy, endure, cope with, challenged by, surprised by, learning from etc.) 'others' is avoided in an increasing measure. And we are also removed, increasingly, from direct contact with nature ... [...] Produce is in heaps in the supermarkets, the seasons count only as variables in the prices, not in availability, etc. etc. I am no slouch in enjoying the amenities of technology (*vide* our jet trips abroad, fax messages, etc.) and have come to take them for granted. But there is a 'price' to pay. Authenticity suffers: CD is here, and concerts recede, is but one example for this gain/loss situation. And who are the sanctioners, the ones who tell/decide what appears in my TV window during the news, who write the manipulative editorials, the strong ones 'up there,' who demand and get millions per annum as salary & bonuses ... Question: why does one need millions of $ income per annum? I must say, I would not want my life to be different: we are relatively independent, can travel a little, pamper the little ones a bit, etc. etc.... It's remarkable how far a pension + a little savings can be stretched ... After all: it costs no money at all to gorge oneself in the treasures of the university library ... We live a charmed life, so it seems, & I should be & yes I am immensely grateful to whomever or to whatever I am able to partake, share in ... It is a good life and the least one could do is to think & write, which I'm trying to do. [...]

The reading which I needed (as usual) in the breaks while working [on *Traces (Tikkun)*], included the discovery of bridge literature joining Plotinus (+ followers) and several Kabbalist authors indebted to them. (It is another question how much Plotinus was indebted to Philo, and other early Jewish 'spirituals.') I just touched on Philo; and he and his place/times are fascinating, but of course his Greek/Jewish outlook, and metaphorical biblical reading is of great interest to me ... I also read some moral philosophy, Bernard Williams, the semi-philosopher, justice expert, John Rawls (*A Theory of Justice*) and that down-to-earth Scotsman John MacMurray[1] ... [...]

Istvan

163

14 FEBRUARY 1994

My dear Isty,

[…] Strange how our preoccupations always coincide: I have been reading Kathleen Raine's first-rate 2 vol. study of Blake's sources[2] & because of it plan to try to make my way through Thomas Taylor's (called "The English Pagan" because of his neo-Platonism) translation of Proclus's *Timaeus* commentaries.[3] And Raine's occasional references to Wm. B. Yeats's *A Vision* [1937] finally led me to the bookstore to buy it. A strange tale in which life is seen as perpetual conflict within self which is an even stranger compound of unmatched and unmatching (except under the rarest conditions) "faculties" and "principles" stretching back as well as ahead through many lives. I must confess today I am heavily weighted down with just this one I am living. […] So my dearest friend—almost everything is at a standstill in me. I don't hear anything. It is difficult to think. […] Somehow we'll get through this difficult time […]

George

[…]

164

7 MARCH 1994

My dear George,

[…] We are weighted down by that terrible massacre in Hebron by that Goldstein fellow.[4] […] The damage a single person is able to make, offsetting the yearning for peace by millions! We are also apprehensive about international ramifications … We were planning a (for Bea) nostalgic trip to Berlin (at the invitation of the Berlin city council) … But if things remain 'hot' we are wondering about the advisability of this …

Next Monday (March 14) in Budapest, in the Matthias 'Coronation' Church, will take place a world premiere which is of considerable importance to me: it is the premiere of the great orchestral *Mass* (*Missa*) by my late friend László Gyopár, who died a tragic death, at the age of 26, in the summer of 1944 (50 years ago!) near Stanislau, at the German–Russian front where we both were working in a Hungarian unit of Jewish forced-labourers. His death was awful and it lived in my mind ever since. I obtained (in 1950) a copy of his *Missa* which survived the war. This is now the only extant version; the autograph was lost with the death of

Gyopár's father in the late '50s. With the help of a former fellow student of ours, the noted & fine Hungarian composer and musicologist András Szöllösy,[5] the March 14 premiere will take place in the framework of the 1994 Budapest Spring Music Festival ... This means a great deal to me. ... Yet, I am afraid to go to Budapest for it ... It might be too much ...

Dear friend, my previous letter came to you as if from a 'peak' ... this one comes to you as if from a 'hollow,' if not 'depression' ... Perhaps I am tired after rushing through *Traces* to the last double bar ... Who knows? But I do know how close I feel to you my dearest friend in music and thought. [...]

Istvan

[...]

165

31 MARCH 1994

My dear Isty,

[...] What always interests me is how much more of a scholar you are than I. For all my delving I remember only what feeds my immediate and/or perennial needs/interests. I think that's how Yeats went at it. Nor am I surprised that scholars who value his poetry might turn a blind eye to his *A Vision*—or glaze over when it's mentioned. It's a very strange, if not downright weird, piece of work. Yet just as theosophy & spiritualism fed Kandinsky with no visible loss to his real work, ideas of reincarnation, karma, personality-formations based on conflicting tendencies seemed to sharpen Yeats's view (vision) of existence, people, events with no loss that I can see to his work. He's the poet who reaching I would guess roughly our present age & stage said: "Grant me an old man's frenzy, / Myself must I remake / Till I am Timon and Lear / Or that William Blake / Who beat upon the wall / Till Truth obeyed his call; / A mind Michael Angelo knew / That can pierce the clouds, / Or inspired by frenzy / Shake the dead in their shrouds; / Forgotten else by mankind, / An old man's eagle mind."[6] Great, isn't it? But not easy to reach for: An old man's eagle mind. [...]

George

[...]

166

11 APRIL 1994

Dear Friend,

[…] Your words, as always, so full of spirit, with soaring thought (yes "the eagle's mind" … what a beautiful transposition of figures: flight—flight of the imagination—mind! A beautiful conceit in this! I did not know it before … I'm grateful for the quotation, George, dear friend …) […]

Istvan

167

28 DECEMBER 1994

Dear old friend Isty,

Here is my "paper"—still a bit rough—which I will have transposed onto computer & will send you (for Robin Elliott) a good copy.[7] I hope you won't feel I've taken liberties or exceeded any limits of taste. Some of what came out surprised even me. Also I'm sending a copy of a drawing sketch (very large) a young friend Helen Mirkil made in preparation for doing a "portrait" on canvas.[8] She's a talented young woman and has a real "eye." When you first read my paper—I'm still searching for a title—read it as though it were one of my long letters, in this case longer than usual—and that the intended "reader" is of course yourself but also others—in other words an enlarged or extended "reader." The Clarinet Concerto sketch is done.[9] Now I must work up a Xerox copy for my copyist from which to extract a "piano reduction." Finally, the orchestration which I shall relax into. I've always enjoyed that stage. […]

George

NOTES

1 Bernard Arthur Owen Williams (1929–2003), Oxford-educated moral philosopher; see, in particular, *Morality: An Introduction to Ethics* (1972), *Problems of the Self: Philosophical Papers, 1956–1972* (1973), and *Ethics and the Limits of Philosophy* (1985); John Rawls, *A Theory of Justice* (Cambridge, MA: Belknap Press of Harvard University Press, 1971); John MacMurray (1891–1976), Scottish philosopher, Professor of Moral Philosophy at the University of Edinburgh from 1944 to 1957.

2 Kathleen Raine, *Blake and Tradition*, 2 vols. (Princeton, NJ: Princeton University Press, 1968).

3 *The Commentaries of Proclus on the Timaeus of Plato, in Five Books; Containing a Treasury of Pythagoric and Platonic Physiology*, trans. from the Greek by Thomas Taylor (London: The Author, 1820); see also *Thomas Taylor the Platonist: Selected Writings*, ed. with introductions by Kathleen Raine and George Mills Harper (London: Routledge and Kegan Paul, 1969).

4 On Friday 26 February 1994 Baruch Goldstein, an Israeli physician, entered the Tomb of the Patriarchs in the West Bank community of Hebron and murdered more than forty Palestinians gathered for early-morning prayer before being overpowered and killed by some of the worshippers.

5 András Szöllösy (b. 1921), Hungarian composer and musicologist, professor of music history and theory at the Budapest Academy of Music (from 1950); he has edited writings of Bartók.

6 The last two stanzas of "An Acre of Grass," *Last Poems* (1936–39).

7 The Canadian musicologist Robin Elliott (b. 1956), since 2002 Director of the Institute of Canadian Music at the University of Toronto, solicited a short prose piece about Anhalt from Rochberg for *Istvan Anhalt: Pathways and Memory*, ed. Robin Elliott and Gordon E. Smith (Montreal and Kingston: McGill-Queen's University Press, 2001), which appeared as "Reflections on a Colleague and Friend," 355–63.

8 Helen Mirkil (b. 1952), BFA (University of Pennsylvania and the Pennsylvania Academy of Fine Arts), MFA (Pennsylvania Academy of the Fine Arts). Her pencil drawing of Rochberg (1994) appears as the booklet cover art for a recent recording of Rochberg's Symphony No. 5 (with *Black Sounds* and the *Transcendental Variations*), Saarbrücken Radio Symphony Orchestra, Christopher Lyndon-Gee, conductor, Naxos 8.559115 (2003), and in the more recent recordings of the Symphony No. 2 (with *Imago Mundi*), Naxos 8.559182 (2005), and the Violin Concerto, with violinist Peter Sheppard Skærved, Naxos 8.559129 (2004), both with the same forces. An oil portrait by Mirkil, simply titled "Rochberg" (1995–96/2002), is reproduced, in colour, in *"Conversations": Paintings by Helen Mirkil* (Collegeville, PA: Philip and Muriel Berman Museum of Arts at Ursinus College, 2002), 6.

9 Concerto for Clarinet and Orchestra (1996), commissioned by the Philadelphia Orchestra and Wolfgang Sawallisch, premiered by them with Anthony Gigliotti, clarinet, on 22 February 1996.

1995

168

4 JANUARY 1995

George dear friend,

Your letter of Dec. 28 with "THE TEXT" written, as always, in your spontaneously, sinuously, flowing script, a beautiful script which—even to look at—gives me always a 'high' pleasure, arrived this morning ... another 'red letter' day, for this.[1] [...] I opened your letter, realized with astonishment that you have filled 54(!) pages with "THE TEXT" ... Wow! [...] Well, I read it in one enormous intake of ... what ... ? No noun comes to mind that could possibly complete, without stunting sense & feeling, the preceding sentence. I have to try then to describe, layer-by-layer, what thoughts & feelings your words gave rise to. First of all: your approach is about the best possible imaginable in the present context! But what a near-impossible task youngish Elliott invited you to undertake! Impossible as genre 'X'; ditto as genre 'Y'; and so on ... Instead of these you took an entirely original and organic tack, with a stroke of inspiration and by dipping into the well of our shared friendship. [...] The 'genre' you composed it in appears to me as a complex of multiple 'mirrors.' Although you are likely to know what I mean by this, already here ... I'll try to spell it out for 'the others' ... Mirror (1) You portray me (most warmly and generously) in words; Mirror (2) You portray yourself, often in paralleling our two personae, thus giving evidence of the great richness, depth, passions, etc., etc. in and of your own soul; as such you have shown the other mirror surface which constitutes the 'reflecting' surfaces of our exchanges and the sources from which these exchanges emerge; Mirror (3) You gave evidence and examples of the kind of dialogue we are engaged in (yes: your letters to me grew to such a depth and substance in the course of these past 34, or so, years); […] Mirror (4) You portray warmly and authentically a friendship (ours) which, in its kind, is extraordinarily important for me, as it grew, ever so organically, between, and by, the two of us.

In short: your TEXT is a mine of insight into an 'I,' into a 'Thou' and into the growth of this natural bridge that 'grew' between the two of us … Now that I am able to read what and how you have written for Elliott's volume, I don't feel any longer that you had to cope with an unwelcome chore, an imposition, but turned the invitation into something that is creative and 'telling' in multiple ways, including your way, also. I think your text is something that you had to write (unless you have done it, this way, already on an earlier occasion which, somehow, I doubt …). A final word is a 'thank you' for having taken the time to write this, especially when you had notes (the Clarinet Concerto) to think about!

Apropos the 'Jewishness' topic … I don't recall ever having sent you a copy of my brief text 'Indictment (An Old Story).'[2] I'm enclosing here a copy of it. […] I am also enclosing the initial pages of the full score of *Traces (Tikkun)*, with the final version of its text as is used in the score (for your eyes only, for the time being). My hopes about hearing this work came back from the dead … Two powerful institutions, the CBC and the Canadian Opera Co. appear to be in agreement about the intent of premiering the work. Presently, there is a budgetary phase where agreement is necessary before I'll know that it is a 'go,' or yet another futile, fruitless, try … I should know this within the next 6–8 weeks … […]

Have a wonderful 1995. And many thanks [for] that striking drawing of you by the gifted Helen Mirkil. She saw you as if belonging in a portal niche of Chartres Cathedral … a Jewish gothic saint … my dearest friend, George … with love … in reciprocity,

Istvan

169

13 FEBRUARY 1995

My dear Isty,

[…] In the interstices of feelings, major/minor artistic distractions I've been thinking @ your "Indictment," also text of *Tikkun*. Of late, as Hamlet said, I've lost all my mirth—so I find it difficult to respond to merging w[ith] the godhead, whatever that may mean. In my present indeterminate state I don't even know what such terms mean—or I've "forgotten." But "Indictment" started a whole train of various thoughts & ideas going off in every direction at once. Perhaps when I can organize myself I can write more coherently @ the Jews living, battling, surviving in a welter of every other "minority"—ethnic, racial, theological—also trying to live, battle & survive simultaneously. Suddenly it's all homogenized to my mind & all human beings face the emptiness of physical & spiritual space not knowing how to act in the face of finalities. The only thing I'm able to grant our insane species is the remarkable capacity to invent stories @ itself. To have—as we don't fortunately—immortality would be to suffer the most terrible ennui, because already at only 76 I find the endless repetitions—my own, others', [our] species cast in art forms & intellectual forms, not to speak of near & far news & gossip that filters through the dark scrim around me—unbelievably childish, infantile, tiresome, wearisome. […]

George

170

3 MARCH 1995

My dear George,

[…] I am intrigued by your reaction to my 'An Indictment,' and I shall be awaiting your eventual (if at all coming) further comments on it, or deriving from its theme. The end of the poem was a kind of surprise for me too … It just 'happened' if I recall it correctly. The one who was the 'indictor' appears to have experienced a sort of interior slippage there (not quite a Damascus insight, though). His words could be understood as revealing that while he <u>spoke</u>, a kind of debate was in progress in his mind/heart. While he was (I must guard against being too affirmative here) speaking <u>one way</u>, his subtext branched out in different directions! He began to <u>understand</u>, and at that point this understanding became strong enough to break onto the surface … giving the impression of revelation, contradiction, <u>sudden</u> insight, <u>incorrectly</u>, I should add. What might have happened is that the audible/readable text was, from a moment on, a less and less sustainable concealment of a slowly evolving thought-process … of an interior argument between the self and the self … The fact that I allowed 'God' to speak …? Perhaps I shouldn't have done this … All that this stands for is facing up to the cosmic mystery, the unanswerable question related to, or, rather deriving from, the existence of <u>all</u>, physical, spiritual, or whatever … And *Traces (Tikkun)* takes up the same point at <u>its</u> end. And I think it does it a bit more according to my present frame of mind ... It avoids totally the anthropomorphic crutch, and, instead, posits an end to a 'momentary' (say lifetime's length) convergence of atoms into a human being, with an 'identity,' 'name,' 'belonghood' (forgive this ugly construct) and expresses the desire to accept death not as an annihilation of 'identity,' 'name,' etc., but as a 'natural' process, i.e., a surrendering of the stuff one is made of, this near-infinitely improbable cosmic event, which a human being amounts to, to the common primaeval inventory of matter of the universe. I admit, this is a type of thinking that is influenced by the notion of the three anthropic principles ... True: one spends a lifetime acting, and leaving 'traces,' leaving the question open: do all these comings & goings & doings 'add up' (another metaphor, this) to a 'pattern' (can't avoid speaking in metaphors?), i.e., is a *tikkun* (my personal 'tikkun') possible? This is the theme of the new piece ... [...]

Istvan

171

29 MARCH 1995

Dear friend Isty,

I can't tell you how pleased and happy I am with your fulsome response. I hesitate to call it "praise." Somehow it strikes me as "unseemly" to use such a word in relation to an expression of loving friendship. You'll be glad to know, too, your colleague R. Elliott seemed quite taken with it. There is a world of things on my mind & in my heart but I don't think I can write an "autobiography" in one sitting. At most I can touch on a couple of things & leave others for another time. First, I carried in me your "indictment" for a long time. Actually it's still there. In the meantime I read Vol. II of Art Spiegelman's "Cartoon" (drawn in comic strip fashion) history of his father's survival of the Nazis, Auschwitz, the Holocaust which he calls "Maus."[3] Do you know it? If you do, then you'll understand. If you don't, then I strongly urge you to get it and read it. It is—as all such tellings must be—completely direct, unsentimental, unselfserving, unembarrassed in its attitude to life and death.

I don't know if it is not living, i.e., facing, the most fundamental questions of life & death at every turn that allows human beings to play the self-serving illusionary games they play, to take up the actor's profession of performing before the world ("show-and-tell time" as practiced so constantly now in American life), to practice hopeless "hope," to remain locked within the powerful frame of their loves & hates (never seeing them as though from outside themselves). This is I begin to think that which distinguishes Jews & being Jewish from virtually all other peoples—whether defined racially, ethnically, culturally. […] This in the year of the 50th anniversary of the Holocaust. Which tells me: those who hate Jews—and where is a short list of those who don't?—care not one whit for "history," its so-called "meanings," and so on. This sounds like, the way I'm putting it, <u>us vs. them</u>. Aha! But when you examine, however briefly, "them," it breaks down into endless combinations & fragments of other us'es and them'ses. But aside from making this "small" point of *homo chaoticus*' penchant for xenophobia, paranoia, fear of life in general, what I wanted to say was that the "world" somehow has <u>always</u> sensed & esp[ecially] now <u>after</u> the Holocaust that Jewish survival against <u>all</u> odds (Ashurbanipal, Sennacherib, Roman Empire, Catholic Church, Crusades, Auto-da-Fé, forced conversion/Marrano style, Russian Czars' pogroms, the Holocaust/Nazi-style) is strange, mysterious, unexplainable by any "normal" folk/mythic/or rational thinking. Therefore it partakes either of what "they" call "God" or "the Devil." And given the fearsome superstitiousness of the race, more likely the devil. This <u>evil</u>, therefore, must be stamped out. These Jews are an affront to our understanding of self, of what life is all about; a secret attack on our beliefs & convictions; a denial of all we hold secret—"we" being all the marvellous varieties of Christians <u>who hate each other</u> as well as the varieties of Moslems <u>who also hate each other</u>. Yet having recently read *Everyman's Talmud* by an English Jew of the 1930s[4] which tries to organize the subject matter of the centuries-long-in-its-unfolding Talmud, I can't find the "demonism" (though there is—surprisingly?—a section on *Angelology*. Those tough old Hebrews <u>believed</u> in Angels, arch- & ordinary ones, cherubim & seraphim) can't find the "secret"; in fact much of it strikes me as topical, purely so, therefore no longer applicable since conditions which gave rise to certain views, etc. no longer exist; or foolish; or fanatic. So I wonder at it all & think to myself: And yet you <u>are</u> a Jew after all. Why? The why? followed by ringing silence.

The Clarinet Concerto I'm happy to report is orchestrated. I'm still riding the wave of its completion combined with the sense it's a good work. Knowing myself as well as I do, that won't last & will be supplanted by the usual negatives of anxiety & concern about its intrinsic qualities, how it will be received, etc. Philosophically, of course, I'm way beyond all that. Which is to say: I am "beyond Good & Evil," I follow the Tao, I am as Arjuna learned from Krishna "unattached," not tied hand & foot to "the fruits of action." […]

George

172

22 APRIL 1995

Dear friend Isty,

I've been wanting to write you but what with finishing the concerto score, reading panel reduction proofs & sundry other things the time has passed until finally, this moment, I feel unburdened, "free at last," and what's more communicative. Is that surprising to you? These two days, yesterday & today, I feel as though heavy, oppressive burdens have lifted and—despite my powerful augers in re the Okl[ahoma] City bombing and all the fanatically stupid zealots in America & the rest of the world—singularly light-hearted. A rare moment which I know will fade and pass in another day or so & my old heavy nature will take over again. […]

We are contemplating a trip to Europe; perhaps will see Budapest for the first time. I will not see it, however, without imagining that I've just seen you turn the corner of some street in a priest's cassock! Fanciful though this may seem, not half as fantastic as this novel titled *Scandal* by the Japanese writer S. Endo.[5] If you can find the time, I urge you & Bea to read it. It touches profoundly on what eats away at the very soul of men—and not necessarily only in our time. And takes up unwittingly the Talmudic idea of the "evil impulse" and how without it, the "good impulse" would not arise. Good & Evil, another of those polar opposites almost impossible to resolve except by severing them into negations of each other. And that doesn't work either, despite the ideologies of religion. […]

George

173

11 MAY 1995

Dear George, very dear friend,

[…] Having just reread your 2 highly charged most recent letters (from March 29 and April 22, respectively) I feel a new wind rising in the mind … Not that I'm up to responding (even to beginning to respond) to these emotional/speculating storms … but I can signal that these are wonderful releases, in which, and through which, you let the voice come from great depth, not often visited, even by you, my dear and passionate friend. Yes I heard you! Yes I resonate sympathetically to what you have made to vibrate … Yes in my own way … as usual … but I heard in your lines the tones of burning concern, even anguish, yet also a kind of resignation in front of the enigma of *homo chaoticus* (a wonderful expression ... yours?). Of course you don't expect me to respond to each turn of thought, to each reference, etc.... You spoke. I listened. I absorbed. I adapted. Eventually an echo will take shape and our great dialogue (which often appears as two huge soliloquies, intertwining at times, distancing themselves from each other at other times, or whatever ...).

You surely, by now have gotten the drift of what your words caused in me ... But let us slow down a bit. I better say that I am happy about the way you've written about the Clarinet Concerto and about the completion of the piano reduction of the orchestra layer. I am curious about what the new piece is like. Can I impose upon you with the request to put into words (if at all feasible) how you went about inventing this piece? What kind of 'language' does it speak? Who is this clarinet? What does the orchestra represent? What kind of relationship exists between the two? But perhaps these are not only 'straightjacket' questions, but, even worse, irrelevant and stupid ones. You play the game then and leave my blind prompting to their justly deserved fate in a trashcan. [...]

MAY 12

Another day ... another evening and I am returning to our conversation ... Where was I above? Yes, the rehearsal score [of *Traces (Tikkun)*]. Before starting to 'reduce' the orchestra I mulled over alternatives. I also looked at the piano-vocal/choral 'version' of *Moses und Aron*, done, I think, by [Schoenberg's pupil Winfried] Zillig [1905–63]. Having sampled it at a few places I saw that he kept all(?) the notes and rendered them in varying sizes, thus giving an idea what to emphasize during rehearsals. This appealed to me (partly because it eliminated the need for deciding what to leave out) and proceeded in the same manner. The resulting score thus represents the orchestra on 2-3-4 even 5+ lines. I've also used different note-head sizes. We'll see how the repetiteur(s) (1–2?) will react to all this.

Now the topic of being Jewish and things related. Who is a Jew? Indeed! In the April '95 issue of *Commentary* (which I'm reading at times in our library) there is a piece on Arthur Ruppin ('An Unsung Jewish Prophet'), about whom before I knew nothing.[6] According to *C[ommentary]* he was a very early Zionist, a contemporary of the young Ben-Gurion in (then) Palestine under Turkish rule. He was a historian, demographer, sociologist, one of the 'founding fathers' of the Hebrew University. According to this article "Ruppin's many books were actually one book continually revised, expanded, updated. ..." The author of the article continues: "R[uppin] starts by trying to define who a Jew is." "On the face of it," he writes, this is "an easy matter to determine"—a Jew is someone "who belongs to the Jewish religion." But then follow all sorts of remarks, comments etc., which call into question the validity of this formulation. Two paragraphs later one reads: "If the Jews had ceased being definable as members of a religious community, were they a race ...?" "Ruppin is not consistent here [either]." "Since no one more than 50 years later can do any better, we should pardon Ruppin for never quite deciding who a Jew is and what the Jews are" (my emphasis). Now, where does this leave one? You and/or I? Well, one could walk away from the question, but can one, does one want to, walk away from this nebulous package of attributes, or whatever (experiences, memories, lived or acquired 2nd, 3rd, Xth hand)? By coming to this time & again, it is quite clear that the topic doesn't leave us at peace. My present contact with it (the most recent ones of a series) would lead me to say this, however tentatively and unsurely: my sense of being also Jewish (I think I have many other 'faces,' as well) resides in a complex web of voluntary (and seemingly gut-engendered) identifications with certain facets of the age-old Jewish experience including the part of it which was/is coterminous with my (and my family's) life, rather lives. This leads to a sense of felt solidarity with an increasing number of people. [...]

Oklahoma City. A tragedy this and its background is terrifyingly ominous. There appear to be groups of armed people who want to exit from your society for whatever reason. People who cannot cope or don't want to accept a prevailing political order, or who are unbalanced enough in whatever mix, who have a need to place themselves under a strict alternative authority, based on a simple enough doctrine, and advocating release-activity which makes the use of power (guns, explosives, etc.) to give the illusion of real power to the powerless a felt necessity. It seems to me a case of blown fuses in a collectivity of people who cannot cope in a society, because they lack understanding, money, influence, and ways & means to influence (due to this lack of understanding) the world around them. Emotion takes over and what results is a flimsy Ersatz of real power in the form of an extreme (simple or violent) program as these individuals go on burning and detonating. I know, I am being simplistic (& perhaps glib/wrong) here, but I sense that these Oklahoma City–type disasters are connected with other societal developments and ills and, which include the all-pervasiveness of TV, the hypes of the 'information highway,' 'virtual reality,' economic dislocations, 'restructurings,' 'downsizings,' loss of status, etc. etc. The powerless (& among those who have given up hope of ever being able to be upwardly mobile) yet sufficiently ego-driven, who yearn, nevertheless, for the right to exercise real power, explode in frustration.

Do these people have traits in common with the suicide commandos of the Islamic Jihad, or the Japanese sarin bombers in the Tokyo subway? What about the killers in Rwanda or in the Balkans, India/Kashmir? Is the anatomy of their violence different? The list seems endless and replays occur. (Are we living in the time of the 3rd Balkan war? After the 1912, 1913 earlier versions? Hopefully 1914–18 will not be replayed, unless a Russian Napoleon/Hitler replaces Yeltsin. Stop me here, please!) Some of this sent me back to Koestler's *The Ghost in the Machine* [1967], in which he expounds (as you no doubt know) the hypothesis that humankind's woes, due to an irresistible urge to kill, maim, fellow intra-species, beings, is caused by a faulty integration of the 3 constituent parts of our nervous system. The earliest layer (he calls it the reptile brain), with its almost automatic springing to action in answering the needs of hunger, survival (fight/flight) and procreation, causes actions which the cerebral cortex (supposedly) is unable to mitigate/civilize. We are a vicious lot it seems, perhaps also a miracle in the Milky Way galaxy, if not even beyond its limits. Silly question. Who will ever know it? Yet, yet ... There is the love on the part of children (some children) ... friendships ... the notion of scientific insight ... esthetic beauty ... mathematical rigour ... Miracles(?) in this vast nothingness, or vast everythingness that is our home, the cosmos ... The possibility of speculating, however hopelessly, about our place in the 'scheme of things' (if there is such a bird ... or is it yet another anthropomorphic dream?) is possibly the greatest puzzle of all. This is how I wanted to bring to a close my *Traces* (*Tikkun*). As to the duality good vs. evil, Nietzsche shook me up a little while ago with his [*On the*] *Genealogy of Morals* [1887]. But by the time I came to this, I was past visiting certain folds of the Lurianic version of the Kabbalah, which (if memory serves) suggest that both good & evil are reciprocal faces of what appear to be in its totality the human. We are both: the good as well as the *sitra ahra* the 'other side,' evil. I tried to put this in notes in *SparkskrapS*, hence the palindromic title. All this is of course but a personal 'turning into metaphor' a deep, and, perhaps, inescapable thought ... as one feels in one's guts both impulses working ... [...]

Istvan

[...]

174

29 MAY 1995

My dear George,

Just a brief word this time ... What prompts this is the still-immediacy of having dashed through (within 24 hours) Shusaku Endo's *Scandal* which you told me to look up. [...] I can see why you wrote to me about it. He is an exceptionally fine writer. The insight, the avoidance of cant, cliché, trendiness, is more than refreshing; it is almost like a breath of clean air in the putrid staleness which is the dominant characteristic of what one gets through the daily paper (ours is called *The Globe and Mail*, which styles itself as Canada's 'national newspaper' ... no less) or our TV. But beyond language, the book's themes: one's *Doppelgänger*, relationship between friends(!), etc. that of a 'stable,' peacefully compatible marriage ... etc. all had relevance. Endo's ability to characterize (but not caricaturize) with a few sentences is impressive. I am especially intrigued by Madame Naruse. I don't quite fathom that monster/angel/woman yet ... As you can see, I'm just as much taken by Endo as you are and am saying 'thank you' for the experience, to you. [...]

Istvan

175

7 JUNE 1995

Dear friend Isty,

[...] I can't tell you how pleased I am to enroll you in one tiny chapter of admirers of Endo. At present Gene is getting her toes wet in his *Deep River* just out.[7] He's remarkable in many ways, not the least of which is his being a Japanese Catholic, apparently a fairly substantial community in Japan but with a history of persecution, etc. But because he is Christian, he brings to bear a special sensitivity to forms of suffering on <u>moral</u> grounds (the very heart & core of *Scandal*). To balance things we've also been reading Amos Oz, the youngish Israeli writer (like Endo, Oz is @ 50–55) who matches Endo for seriousness of attitude toward writing as art, toward human lives and the causes of their suffering, toward the world in which they (Oz & Endo) work. If you are already familiar w[ith] Oz, no need to say further. But if not, in case in a lifetime of preoccupation with work and family you've heard of him but never had a chance to read him like me, then I urge you to read a work like *The Hill of Evil Counsel*.[8] Oz is a true poet with words and of the heart and shares w[ith]

Endo the capacity which you yourself remarked to delineate w[ith] a few sentences a state of being, the feel of a place, etc. […]

Next time I write I'll say a word or two @ the Clarinet Concerto—although I'm not sure I can answer your questions in any way that'll make sense because like everything else I've ever written writing it was mostly a feeling-my-way-in-the-dark. Delighted to hear the reduction of *Tikkun* is done. What are the plans for its performance? Curious, isn't it, how neither of us can let go? Yet in the back of my head is always the thought: time to step aside. […]

George

176

16 JUNE 1995

My dear friend Isty,

Time passes … and we/I lose track of it and things. Always an effort to reorganize, pull inner & outer worlds together. Strange, isn't it; we're always trying to make a whole of things. Why? It would be so much simpler to live in the immediate sensation, small task, passing sensation, just drift with the tide. Temperament—or something more universal? Periodically I remember Chuang-Tzu[9] and his Ten Thousand Things among which we/man/woman are only one thing among myriads yet here in the disintegrating West we hold on ferociously to the made-in-the-image-of-God/Darwinian end of the evolutionary line, in fact that very "purpose" of the creation of life itself, *Homo Sapiens Sapiens*. An old Yiddish saying: "Man tracht und Gott lacht." I like that. It appeals to something deep in me & joins up with old Chuang-Tzu rather than the tradition of the old rabbis who couldn't see the absurdity of man's hubris (even though they were always talking @ walking in the ways of God, in short working on their "humility"), his *chutzpah*. Anyhow, I had not expected to wander off like this from where I started this.

You asked in your last letter @ the Clarinet Concerto. I really don't know how to answer you. I've tried to make something that will be grateful for the soloist to play, put his soul into it, make something beautiful in the air—strange, isn't it, we labor so hard to make air vibrate with the color of our souls—and also to convey the darkness in our hearts. About a third of the way into approx[imately] 26 minutes I let out the gargoyle side of my nature (when I was a boy sitting in class & wandering inside, half an ear on what the teacher was saying, I would draw gargoyles, the kind that grace the old medieval cathedrals, ugly, leering,

brutish, grimacing faces. Don't ask me where they came from ... what was a nice Jewish boy like me doing drawing gargoyles, "Christian" no less?)
 and make a kind of *parodia sacra* (do you know Linda Hutcheon's *A Theory of Parody*?[10] She's at McMaster [University]. Brilliant lady). Mixing up things from my old Chamber Symphony for 9 instruments [1953], Scherzo of Beethoven's Op. 135, the part that hammers away in A major, and the E♭ clar[inet] tune in Berlioz's *Symphonie Fantastique*. I also tip my hat in the direction of Mozart's Clar[inet] Con[certo], very brief & quietly distant. Very little virtuoso-ing. Hate empty display, the kind of Vieuxtemps/Paganini noodling as well as the over-wrought, gratingly strident cadenza-ing of [Alfred] Schnittke [1934–98] (whom I take very seriously even if I like very little of what he does). It all ends with a "*Serenissima*," *ppp*, the heartache stilled but not entirely gone. Now I must simply wait until next winter—end of February—to hear it. [...]

George

177

7 SEPTEMBER 1995

My dear George,

[...] Your letter make[s] me focus on these issues/themes: (1) the electronic revolution in which we live and (2) the minds of our young, as well as (3) how (1) & (2) might impact on, react to, the other, as well as on society as a whole. Let me try to suggest that (1) evidently is a part of (4) a somewhat *nonpareil* money-driven corporate world and one of its offshoots (5) a 'dumbed-down,' brutalized popular culture of which the principal genres are the videos and the rock CDs, especially the most violently sexual ones. I feel that these 5 entities, things, developments, endeavors, events, products, etc. are impacting on each other in a complex, yet simple-in-outline, manner seen at 'certain' levels. It's organizational and 'sales' levels are likely to be complex. The 'as advertised' & 'as sold' are likely to be simple. Obviously what I can put down here on the page will be skeletal and barely indicative of the intensity with which I feel about these matters which increasingly envelop us ... So:

(1) The electronic revolution has been with us, obviously, since a while ... I read recently that the wildfire-like spread of the 1848 revolutions from Paris eastward was made possible by the then new electrical transmission of messages. We never looked back since. [...] The positive applications of the electronic technology today, for me, include the computerized library cataloging/storage/search processes, the direct dialing long-distance phon-

ings, the fax service, the Xerox process and the remarkably easy access to special literatures. […] The computer terminals spit out in minutes miles of abstracts, references to periodicals, etc. etc. […] For all these reasons I am an appreciative user (and a selective and discerning one, I hope) of this technology. But I have drawn my (however ephemeral) line 'in the sand' about other aspects, in reality (practice) and/or in opinion. […]

Now some of the other aspects: I think the CD technology is superior (in sound-reproduction) to the LP technology. Yet both conjured to grievously wound live music, at least on this continent. TV, as practiced, in our environment is a programming disaster, but there are exceptions, fortunately. Allied to the mega-profit corporate machine economy it turns out a steady sewer full of brutal, mindless, sexually exploitative flood of image and sound, which works its insidious black magic on the young, and on those who never grew up. Just take the names of some of these heavy metal and/or punk rockers: The Sex Pistols, The Clash, The Stranglers, The Boomtown Rats, Johnny Rotten, Sid Vicious, and the like … Their examples on unstable minds can be, and at times prove to be, disastrous! […] Of course the deaths of rockers show horrendous examples for our impressionable young: E. Presley, J. Hendrix, J. Joplin, K. Cobain, J. Garcia, just to name a few. And children, probably, ingest this horror, dished out by giant financial interests, corporations, in the guise of 'entertainment,' and 'freedom of information,' 'democratic environment of communication.' Here the potential victimhood of inexperience, normal physical/psychic development (sexual), brutalized/commercialized art(?) and big business merge in a complex interactive mush which pulsates with ferment as a swamp populated by noxious biological organisms from the micro-ones to toothy giant predators, the like of super-reptiles … I see in this swamp the symbiotic co-fermentation of (1) + (2) + (3) + (4) and (5). But that's not all. Like a cancer, the purveyors of electronic forms/ways of doing things make now a grab for more: (6) They try to preempt the education of the young by foisting 'computer literacy' onto school boards, which downgrade humanistic studies because funds go into computer-oriented processes. The art & music teachers are transferred, retrained, 'de-hired,' or not hired in the first place. Band instruments, etc., are not replaced because computers in the classrooms need to be replaced. The 'software' merchants want to set the curriculum now. The choice is set by faceless 'program-designers' who remain out of sight … The medium (i.e., its commercial applicability) does, or soon will, set what will be taught and how it will be taught. The 'interface' gurus will join hands with the program packagers … One is reminded of the potential joys of drowning oneself in information: the disc with the entire *Enc[yclopedia] Britannica* … another with all the pictures of the National Gallery in Washington, the Internet, the World Wide Web (WWW … nice … better than World War …) the Electronic Super Highway, surf, fly along … More & more … faster and faster … don't think just get drunk on the ever-increasing bulk of undigested, unasked for, not-sought-out, information, all thrown at the viewer, who gets mesmerized, hypnotized to the point that, zombie-like, s/he rushes out to buy the next soft- or hardware gizmo […], turning human beings into consumers (programmable supposedly) and *en masse* into human resource. Now this odious expression reduces the individual into a 'thing,' a molecular (perhaps unfeeling?!?) entity in the larger social fabric. As such he/she can be treated (almost) as inanimate matter, like trash, like an obsolete (not worth repairing) appliance which stood just a little bit too long in that corner of the kitchen: an old dishwasher perhaps or a stove … No need for it anymore, because … to the trash-heap with it. Thus the human resource unit (perhaps my neighbour the auto-worker, or the bank teller, or … or … or) gets 'de-hired' … His/her 'place' (or work function) is taken over by one of Dr. Wiener's robots[11] (oh yes: the Italians will still make designer goods, and the French … But not us, because the Chinese … etc.) and he/she becomes redundant. We then acquire worker-elites (i.e., the electronics industry) and worker (former-worker) proletarians. The state will trade much of certain sectors into oblivion, in order that other sectors should flourish, or, at least, survive, a little longer. What will happen to the hordes of the unemployed? Who will be able to buy the (not-exported) products of the still functioning industries? For what kind of world are we educating our children and grandchildren?

These are only some of my questions. The ultimate threat is encapsulated for me by the concept (and its threatened wide(?) application) of the so-called virtual reality. Now does this mean that beyond scientifically & technologically useful applications of this digital capability, one is invited to prefer experiencing the electronically transduced forms of reality (smaller size, 2 dimension instead of 3, poor visual resolution, denatured because it lacks tactility, olfactory potential and is auditorily squeezed into a, say, 40–1,000 Hz bandwidth) to the REAL THING!? Do I (or our young) have to experience our fellow human beings, in all their existential richness, complexity, via electronic mimicking, instead of going out to the forums of our communities to get a feeling of all this throbbing life? I take human contact whenever available & practicable. When the interlocutor is 6,000 miles away (as the lady of the *pensione* in Vienna, who rented a room to us via a transatlantic phone call was) and I need to transact urgently, of course I rejoice in the availability, in the simulacrum, of real communication. I needed only a small fragment of that woman's humanness! And this I was able to tap into via the call! Now, what does all this 'add up' to? The positive and the negative? It adds up to a huge societal challenge: to take the best of the constructive, & to demask the manipulative/exploitative/destructive element by showing its true purpose and its viciously damaging potential and 'works.' I don't expect to call for, to yearn for, to rest hope in, government regulation, in censorship of a public, centralized, kind. […]

I don't know what kind of (self)-regulatory modality is needed, would be compatible with, sane democratic liberties, as distinct [from] a free-for-all, sane and insane … ambitious and greedy … sexually active/healthy and the minimally perverted, etc. etc. It would have to be a societal homeostasis of a very special kind: one which would be based on human understanding by which I mean a broad/deep philosophical/epistemic understanding of the human animal in its full diachronic flow and in all its synchronic multi-facetedness … I know: an impossible hope. Nevertheless here we could envisage a new kind of living/learning (to the grave … in time) society which doesn't need 90+% of its adult members for the purpose of providing food, clothing & shelter for its entirety. Let those who don't produce 'normal' consumer goods and/or services, produce, participate in the flow of, activity which contributes to the establishment and sustenance of an intellectual/aesthetic/moral biosphere based on the never-ceasing celebration of the greatest miracle we are aware of: the reality and existence of the human brain/mind and its not as yet fully realized potential …

If you look at some parts of the text of my *Traces (Tikkun)* you find there echoes of some of the above. I'm confessing to human sexuality's force in the adult/the old in the part entitled "Desert Town" and to the same in the young in the part entitled "The Highdome." Our two young grandsons […] might be already in the grips of pre-puberty, which might suggest that we translate their […] concealing/diverting behaviour into the perception of a complex life force which Kokoschka depicted (remember?) in his *The Dreaming Boys* (1908). We should be (I'm telling myself) understanding and try to transpose their dreams, yearning pains, into our own experience as remembered! […]

But one more word about the depiction of sexual behavior in *Traces (Tikkun)*: in the passage "In the Highdome" a rock concert is in progress … I felt I want to depict its legitimacy for the young, the overall legitimacy of Dionysus … I composed this music 'in stages': first it was a trio of instrumentals: an electronic guitar, a synthesizer and a drum-set, accompanying a *Sprechstimme* voice. Then came added glassy string glides when 'transport' sets in … then the voice was turned into a 75% sung line, rather deep and angular in flow; then a few woodwind runs & tremolos were added … etc., some rap-like, machine gun-like, recitation of text (depicting angular prancing around) remained in the vocal line … What do all these add up to in an overall affect? I think it might add up to an apperception of an older listener/viewer, present at the event who 'takes in' the whole 'happening,' thinking that he understands it, with its 'timeless,' Dionysiac allusions: that of the eternal youth, the forever reappearing nubility (like the 18–19-y[ea]r-old freshmen on our campuses in every September, with their imprinting, bonding and meeting rituals … sights, sounds, costumes & all … sexuality pure and concentrated, ambulating, dancing on the streets and across the grass on the campus … The library is still relatively empty, the beer bottles are already out at 10 a.m. … And the garb is *de rigeur* all over … But in a few days the day-party is over … the engineering freshmen/women wash out the glue from their fake Iroquois hairdos and the purple dye is also off their skins. Classes have begun …)

Traces … I have tried to say so much (in text and through music) in this ca. 35–40-min[ute] work, taking it even as far as the moment of a death, which I conceive here as being our reintegration of the self, reduced to its most elementary particles into the universe. No 'drama' this at the end, no human drama as such. I don't know … What is certain is that the 'human' gives way here to a transformation which takes the procedural 'form' of a merging; this merging, which has no means of carrying over the 'threshold' signs, symbols or signatures of any sort. What only remains is the elementary essence: we become dust, once again, awaiting perhaps in billions of years another cosmic miracle and some of our residue could, just might, once again, be part of a 'life' … But 'human' life? This is ridiculously too unrealistic (i.e., improbable) to expect to happen! The odds are truly astronomically against it. […]

Istvan

[…]

178

18 SEPTEMBER 1995

Dear friend Isty,

Don't know if this will reach you before you take off for Vienna the capital of "Kakania" (according to Robert Musil;[12] &, if I remember rightly, Karl Kraus, Schoenberg's friend & intellectual critic of "the way things were" in old Vienna in the early decades of this glorious century). Your letter of such a sweep and force of statement—both positive and negative (though I sensed more of the latter tilt) really deserves a reply—though not necessarily of the same size & punch. But of course you know how much in agreement we are in re the serious ills and evils of our slide into chaos. Maybe, just maybe our agreement on the general meaning of the technological disaster overtaking world culture may end at the point where it evokes the deepest, even most genetically unconscious predisposition, possibly—if I know you at all after all these years of our friendship—your propensity more to hope in mankind's ability to right itself after great darkness and mine toward the sense of a virtually final catastrophe (moral, spiritual, physical) from which I can't—at least not presently—see mankind surviving its essentially self-destructive drives which have come out fully in our time. Whichever way the next 50 yrs. turn out it can't be good for our children & grandchildren. I don't know what resources they will have to overcome the worst which I sense still lies ahead & in the near future. My deep pessimism is based on, following the old Russian adage, my "well-informed optimism." In that connection the enclosed from the latest *Am[erican] Ac[ademy] of A[rts] & Sc[iences] Bulletin* fits directly into our ongoing "conversation."[13] It would have been even more to the point & truer to present reality esp[ecially] of relations between parents & children if Minow had pointed out the simple chronological fact of several generations of "children" brought up on this fare who became "parents" with their own children etc. etc. and their inability to stand up to & overcome the effects of the sleaze pouring out of TV broadcasters. In other words it is not only successive generations of children who have been corrupted or "stoned" into inability to feel, judge, evaluate & so on. […]

George

179

22 SEPTEMBER 1995

George, dear friend,

The shortest letter ever … Packing's almost done … Things overlooked kept to a minimum (we hope) … Off we go tomorrow to Vienna, via Amsterdam (only 1 hr. waiting time). Guess what I am going to read on the plane … Musil's *The Man w[ithout] Q[ualities]*, which you wrote about. It is the old (1953) translation … I like it … But I should see the new one also. Great writer, Musil. I think his impact on me is almost that of Kafka 100 years ago ... 'Kakania' ... Yes and even more so. Comes at a perfect moment in my own 'archaeological' digs (both historical/general), as a doomed yet also splendidly alive system which went *Kaput* ... [...]

Istvan

NOTES

1 See "1994," note 7.
2 "Indictment (An Old Story)" (1992), unpublished ms., Anhalt Fonds MUS 164/F1,92.
3 Art Spiegelman, *Maus: A Survivor's Tale*, vol. 2, *And Here My Troubles Began* (New York: Pantheon Books, 1986).
4 Abraham Cohen, *Everyman's Talmud*, with an introduction to the new American edition by Boaz Cohen (New York: E.P. Dutton, 1949).
5 Shusako Endo, *Scandal: A Novel*, trans. Van C. Gessel (New York: Dodd, Mead, 1988).
6 Edward Norden, "An Unsung Jewish Prophet," *Commentary* 99/4 (April 1995): 37–43.
7 Shusako Endo, *Deep River*, trans. Van C. Gessel (New York: New Directions, 1994).
8 Amos Oz, *The Hill of Evil Counsel: Three Stories*, trans. Nicholas de Lange in collaboration with the author (New York: Harcourt Brace Jovanovich, 1978).
9 See "1991," note 9.
10 Linda Hutcheon, *A Theory of Parody: The Teachings of Twentieth-Century Art Forms* (New York: Methuen, 1985).
11 See "1984," note 12.
12 Robert Musil (1880–1942); *Der Mann ohne Eigenschaften* first appeared, in three volumes, between 1930 and 1942, and in English translation in 1953–60 and again in 1995.
13 Newton N. Minow and Craig L. LaMay, "Out of the Wasteland, a Jackpot," *Bulletin: The American Academy of Arts and Sciences* 48/7 (April 1995): 19–25; reprinted from the *New York Times Magazine* (4 December 1994). Minow (b. 1926), trained at Northwestern University as a lawyer, was Chair of the Federal Communications Commission under President Kennedy (1961–63). In a landmark 1961 speech he famously referred to American commercial television programming as "a vast wasteland." See also *How Vast the Wasteland Now* (New York: Gannett Foundation Media Center, 1991), and, with Craig L. LaMay, *Abandoned in the Wasteland: Children, Television, and the First Amendment* (New York: Hill and Wang, 1995).

1996

180

5 JANUARY 1996

Dear friend Isty,

[…] Time for me has become something different from what it felt like when I was much younger. In a curious way it has collapsed and the past is far less remote. That is, past times (historically) feel much closer, and at moments more "contemporary." This produces some very odd sensations to say the least. Whatever else it does it increases in me the sense that despite surface changes which are vast—modes of travel, dress, cities, homes, even facial looks, not to speak of technology—we are as much like the ancient Greeks, Romans, Sumerians, Hebrews as they "were" like us. I can readily imagine that such thoughts are for some consoling, for others—especially those who need to feel uniquely themselves—quite depressing. Extrapolations galore can proceed from here …

Isty, I can't remember how many times I have, as I like to put it, "hung up pencil." Meaning, of course, I wasn't going to write any more, or couldn't, or didn't feel the need; on & on. If there's no urgent, pressing need to say something, we should, especially after a lifetime of great effort and often unrelenting pressure from outside and/or inside, accept with grace that state of inner quiescence, a kind of peace with oneself. I say that to you, my dear old friend, as well as myself. Though I confess I am in the process of sketching a 2-piano work for two young friend pianists (married to each other).[1] It goes in spurts. One or two days of hard but enjoyable labor followed by 3 or 4 of stewing & mulling, like resting up for the next round. Winter is in a way conducive to this state because it pushes me in on myself (the very self I wish often enough I could get away from!). So reading is an honorable state of mind. I'm sure after you've "rested up" a bit more something will start nagging at you again. Speaking of reading, have you run across Milan Kundera's *Testaments Betrayed*?[2] Remarkable stuff in certain ways. Talks about music more interestingly than most musicians do but can't say I concur with his tastes (he loves Stravinsky and Janáček). […]

George

181

2–3 FEBRUARY 1996

My dear George,

[…] You are bringing up the end of the millennium … Perhaps some organization that thinks BIG will have the brilliant inspiration to mark this 'event' by commissioning a composer (what about a super-polished minimalist, like John Adams [b. 1947], or a Christian minimalist like Arvo Pärt [b. 1935], etc.) to mark this 'event' with a huge score … (Now, wouldn't it be something ironic if you or I would be approached … What would we do? For one, I would reread some of the parts of the 're-done' (recently) edition of Emil Schürer's majestic multivolume work on the Jews in Jesus' time.[3] (I think the Oxford/Hungarian Judaica scholar, Geza Vermes, is one of the editors. It has fascinating info[rmation] about John of Ghiscala [*sic*], Flavius Josephus[4] and numerous others. These tidbits bring to life that turbulent tale.) Traveling into the past is now one of my favourite pastimes also. To search for meaning in the 'now' one <u>must</u> travel backwards. […]

There is only one more thing to report on … quite a surprise for me … Imagine: exactly a week ago the 'phone rang and what it said was that a 1996 (spring) premiere of my 'new' opera is a distinct possibility! Wow! Ever since the calls went both ways between here & Toronto with a few faxes thrown in for good measure. "Could you send us <u>concise</u>! program notes"? Done. What about the parts? More 'phonings with prospective copyists (2 or more). And today the final fax: I was informed that the premiere IS ON, for late May. Of course, once again, it will be a concert performance *cum* CBC broadcast. BUT, there will be ample rehearsal time and the organizers are looking for the best available performers in Toronto. Exciting! You bet. Now I'm so glad that last spring I made the rehearsal reduction of the full score … […]

Istvan

182

19 FEBRUARY 1996

Dear old friend Isty,

[...] It's here: the week of the 1st perf[ormance]s of my Clarinet Concerto.[5] I'm very grateful for one thing: the weather reports promise rain rather than snow (that would have been a disaster) and rising temperatures. My soloist Anthony Gigliotti (principal clarinet of the Phila[delphia] Orch[estra]) has just gotten over a heavy bronchitis—and just in time. So I've got my fingers (& toes) crossed. I'll hear the work with the orchestra for the 1st time Wed[nesday] afternoon, then the dress rehearsal Thurs[day] a.m. & 1st perf[ormance] Thursday night. I hope it will be more than just another run-through—& depends much on the electricity generated by Tony Gigliotti to his mates in the orchestra and to Wolfgang Sawalisch the conductor who is *Echt Deutsch* and tends to be somewhat too held-together, not so much phlegmatic as not-driven-by-a-daemon. After all not all German conductors are (were) dullards. Certainly not Furtwängler or Tennstedt or Von Karajan. By Saturday night and after Friday's perf[ormance] I hope things will have come together and the players will give off sparks where required and deep quietude and serenity—the last section "*Serenissima*"—where necessary. Then hopefully life can resume its normal, un-dull round. [...]

George

183

28 MARCH 1996

Dear old friend Isty,

Just an interim note in case (as I did until someone gave me a copy) you missed the enclosed piece of "telling it like it is" (or "was"?)[6] This little essay in "isms" & "wasms" a beautiful piece of sardonic thinking on war—exaggerated enthusiasms for false ideas, dead-end directions which virtually deluded 2–3 generations. Of course, "*serialismus*" arose in the age of radical politics (of fascism, nazism, communism) and adopted the same deadly grim ideology of absolute belief or confinement to the gulags & camps (the horrendously real ones; and the equally horrible because soul-damaging philosophic/aesthetic ones) for disloyalty, apostasy, dissent—on & on. Hope preparations for *Traces* advancing well. No dry "Martinos" for me![7]

George

184

20 APRIL 1996

My dear George,

I had before me your 'interim note' from March 28, with the R. Taruskin piece from the March 10 *N[ew] Y[ork] T[imes]*. […] What to make of his diatribe here? I am (feel to be) between a rock and a hard place: having to choose between this Taruskin opus and Milton Babbitt's arrogant dismissal of audiences (some) in the course of the '70s, if I am not mistaken.[8] Neither of them speaks for me! Both are making loud claims and dismiss, wholesale, ideas and people, doing damage in the process. 12-note, and later serial, construction were historical facts, brought about by a complex process of collective thinking. Rather than relating it to totalitarian politics (while not altogether washing out possible connection with these also), I would prefer to think here about a wish to imitate scientific positivism, mathematical rigour, and (with the case of '*Elektronische Musik*') the supposed laws of physics, if not those of psycho-physics. […]

Few are among the composers (searching ones, that is) who were hermetically immune to the series-idea during the period, say 1940–1970. By that time (1970) the realities of a *Moses und Aron* and *Lulu* were parts of our soul-scape. What about today? We're too close to it to see clearly enough. But judging from what my gut tells me (a double guarantee of authenticity reliable enough—with some reservations—for me, for the moment) that we might have, since a little while (say 20 years?) entered a period of eclecticism. And when I am saying this I am not using the term as malodorous *locus* in the mind … Rather, I'm using it in the sense of choosing the 'best' (read: most apposite) of expressive means (and writing 'modes') for a given composition or a part thereof. I chanced very recently on a collection of essays (I'm still reading the book with much learning) about the topic: *The Question of "Eclecticism": Studies in Later Greek Philosophy*.[9] The introduction in it already treats the derivation of 'eclecticism' from *eklegein*, *eklegesthai* meaning to choose, to make a selection. (On p. 4 there is the more telling translation: "… to signify selecting the best from a group of things.") The book promises a sufficiently deep consideration of differing views held about this phenomenon, which we would find reemerging in various fields in the course of intellectual history. Frequently, if perhaps not always, it is put in an opposition to dogmatics. It is, moreover, not difficult to apply the concept to politics also in our times. We have the dogmatics among the North American free traders/neo-Darwinists, as well as among the Muslim clerics in Iran, on the one hand, and those (for ex[ample] in Eastern or Northern Europe) who would like to choose what would serve best the interests of the largest number, and who would rein in the recklessness of the advocates of super capitalism and those of fundamentalism ... Who can assert that today eclecticism is not worth giving a consideration in thought? And for that matter in music also.

With this I am smack at *Traces* (*Tikkun*) which approaches its May 28 premiere. About this I can only say that the prospects are quite positive from the point of view of rehearsal time (ca. 10–12 hrs. for a work that is likely to clock in between 35–40 mins.). The orchestra will be staffed by the best free-lance talent in Toronto; and the youngish Canadian conductor, Kulesha, comes with high credentials. The solo singer is a young baritone, Doug McNaughton [*sic*], who sang "Wozzeck" in Montreal in 1995 to great acclaim.[10] [...]

Istvan

[...]

185

4 JUNE 1996

Dear George,

[...] *Traces*, yes, it had its public appearance on May 28 in the Glenn Gould Studio (a 350-seat beautiful auditorium in the new CBC Broadcast Centre in Toronto's futuristic downtown near the 'Skydome' and the CN Tower). [...] The players were very good to quite okay; the conductor a youngish (42) Canadian (Gary Kulesha) was up to the task: competent, unflappable and a very quick study when this was needed. The youngish (36) lyric baritone, Douglas MacNaughton, is a very fine voice, interpreter and what's important a very intelligent mind, who needed only a single comment here and there to fine-tune the complex multiple character of my 'pluri-drama.' [...] The main problem was with the tempi & dynamics. The former was put 'in place' almost fully, the latter somewhat less as a result of rehearsing in 3(!) different halls of which only the final 1½ hrs. were held in the G[lenn] G[ould] Studio. We opted for a moderate amount of voice amplification which proved to be, I think, a bit much at places (I will ascertain this at the June 9th broadcast). There were the usual grumblings about 'not understanding the text' in the louder passages. (What else is new?) The problem resides, of course, in this simple fact that I had a staged presentation in mind (the orchestra in the

pit). Not what we had: a reduced (less strings) orch[estra] of 40 behind the singer on the same stage! An insoluble situation/problem. But, judging from the comments that reached me so far, the 'burden' of the piece 'came across' clear enough to people with ears & minds. Thus this operatic trio, triad, triptych (not 'trilogy,' definitely) is finally behind me. […]
Istvan

186

13 JUNE 1996

Dear friend Isty,

It is not hard to imagine the deep sense of depletion after so much effort and the hopes and expectations that go into making that effort. Especially at our age. Now is the time when those kinds of efforts require dipping deep into our reserves, our psychic, and what ever physical, capital we still have—which certainly does not anywhere near match what we had 30–40 years ago. Probably the best thing you can do is put your mind elsewhere, on less demanding-of-oneself things. We all have our favorite ways of doing that. I don't know what yours are; but I would imagine some good strolling/walking about where there is lots of greenery and flowers. That's one way for me. Another is reading serious things but that don't require breaking your brains. I find reading & sometimes rereading Milan Kundera very restful & energizing because I respond to his way of seeing things & thinking about them; I esp[ecially] love his ironic, acerbic humor. Recently I read his *Testaments Betrayed*, a long essay which includes some cogent things in re Stravinsky, the brevity of the "modern age" of our century & Str[avinsky]'s uses of the past. He also has a lot of good stuff to say @ Kafka & his friend Max Brod.[11] I just started yesterday to read his latest novel *Slowness*[12] (right, that's the title of it) where two young men, one from the 18th cent[ury] the other from the 20th, meet and discuss "life." Talk @ "uses of the past."

Whatever "consolations" there may be in performances of our music at this stage I personally don't think we should count on them for our private peace of mind. If it comes from anywhere I believe it can only come from doing the work, neither its performance nor its reception. I've had an odd experience with my Clarinet Concerto which will help illustrate my point. The principal clarinetist of the Phila[delphia] Orch[estra] was the soloist & indeed the work was commissioned for him to play. Tony Gigliotti is an excellent clarinetist & good musician, a perfect orchestral player. But no soloist. On top of which he is at least 72/73 and this past season was his last. It turned out as we went into rehearsal w[ith] the orch[estra] that he would not stand and play, he had to sit. Why? Because the weight of the instrument after a while was too much for him, producing—apparently—real physical discomfort. Okay. Fine. One has to accept such conditions. But of course it meant: a) a staired structure upon which he enthroned himself—so in effect he was still sitting in the orchestra, not out front playing his heart out; b) it cast a pall as a result on his movements—he sat like a monolith (he's a big, chesty/stomachy sort of man), i.e., he didn't give an inch in one direction or another, just sat like a stolid lump; c) *enfin*, it affected his playing such that he played as he was accustomed to: like an orchestral player; d) the consequence: the loosenesses, the freedoms I built into the solo part, the brusqueries and burlesqueries all got stodgified and even the quiet-unto-death places were at best a lukewarm almost but never "*pp*" when what I really wanted was something dark, heavy & virtually inaudible. *Magari* ["I wish; if only"], as the Italians say, with a slight shrug of the shoulder, meaning a thousand different subtle things almost inexpressible by word but only by gesture, look—of course. Up to the last of 3 perf[ormance]s I tried all my tact, my sympathetic understanding of his problems, casting irritations & growing angers in apposite tones, tried heroically to get him to loosen up, to go deep into himself (Italian father, Hungarian mother; something's there, no?!?), be wild, be loving, be ironic, be noble, all the "b's" there be. By the last perf[ormance] he had picked up my "vibes" (as kids call our electrical projections) & knew I was deeply dissatisfied. The end result? I have not heard from him since the end of Feb. On the surface it was a great success, for the work, for him, etc. etc. But that success ended a long friendship …

All I'm trying to say is that we cannot nor should we try to draw our inner balance & equilibrium from the world. And yet … if not the world, then what, "God?" I can't accept the Judeo-Christian "god" or "gods" (if indeed they are actually different; or the same with different masks?). I suppose I'm trying to say what we seek is inside in any case, even this "god" that everyone talks @ all the time, prays to, etc., etc., but he never answers. He either is awfully busy elsewhere having decided a) we need to stand on our own two feet; or b) we're not worth bothering about, we're such an unruly lot; or c) he literally is something in us which we project (so he does exist in a way, right?) outward. The big danger, of course, of my line of argument is falling into the bottomless pit of solipsism. So as the "flower *kinder*" used to say, "peace, man, peace." I hope you can restore yourself, make music for yourself (I still like to play Bach,

Brahms, Schubert, Chopin, Beethoven), take Bea & yourself off to places where you can stroll & walk, eat a leisurely lunch—whatever suits you, my dear friend. […]

George

187

[typewritten with handwritten corrections and additions]

1 JULY 1996

My dear George,

Surprise … I'm trying to write this on the typewriter … To get into the 'right' frame of mind, at first, I have reread your content-rich one of June 13th, … about many things, including your advice to me about resetting my 'balance' after the *Traces* experience; your experience with the P[hiladelphia] S[ymphony] O[rchestra]'s retiring clarinetist for whom you composed your Cl[arinet] Concerto: about rereading M. Kundera (no, I haven't read the books you mentioned, but probably, I should …). […] Lots of content, good sense and reaching for the stars as you were reaching for the metaphysical realm, yet another upward-turned glance in the unfathomable … This point brings me to the burden of this page … Isaac Bashevis Singer's quasi-autobiographical text *Love and Exile*,[13] which I am in the process of reading and also the offshoots of the same which helps me to cope with some surprisingly unexpected experiences, bits and pieces, really, which accompanied the 'birth' of the concluding member of this series of works, of 'musics for the stage,' which is a misnomer, barely covering an evidence of wishful thinking on my part, as <u>none</u> of these operas saw the 'light of day' in a staged performance … all received performances 'in concert' … But let me go on dreaming, my dear friend, and refer to them as a 'triptych' of such works. […]

What I'm finding remarkable in this text (book) of Singer's is, once again, the virtuosity of his narrative talent, his candidness about human relationships, mostly (but <u>not</u> exclusively) with women, the 'geography,' 'pace,' and the content of his emotional & intellectual growth, and other related things, and of course, his rooted Jewishness, as a Warsaw-bred offspring of 'Shtetel' Hassidim, which gave him identity, a world outlook, strength and and and … and <u>how true he remained to this heritage all through his writerly life</u>! And, as an outcome: he was accepted, <u>nay celebrated, in this very identity</u> … right through to a Nobel Prize …

Now what I have to do here is to find a sentence, or two, with which to remind you about my Jewish background in Budapest (1919–1945), and how this relates to *Traces*. This I shall follow up with some aspects of the production and reception of the new work in question. Well ... as to Jewish education, apart from a perfunctory *Bar Mitzvah*, I had next to nothing, formally, although I have 'breathed in' a certain amount of Jewish custom at my paternal grandparents' cold-water flat, located in the former ghetto-district of Budapest ... (My father lived there for years after he and my mother divorced.) I paid homage to this in *Simulacrum* ... In short, not only did I remain, while in Budapest, ignorant of the kind of Jewishness Singer celebrates (Cheder, Yeshiva, Talmud, Kabbalah, etc.), but our family's acted-out goal was to live the life of an 'assimilated' Jewish Hungarian family, a hope-driven (though unrealistic) scenario ... But the kind of Budapest Jew we were was a past master in wishful thinking ... In due course it was Hitler & Co. who hammered a measure of 'reality' into our skulls, and if we survived the 'lesson' we could look forward to a new life (although, surprisingly, some 'assimilated' Jews after WW II went right back to their former daydreams ...). That much for my Hungarian-Jewish 'layer' ... In Canada, too, in the first 2 decades there were other priority considerations and I only turned later my face towards a kind of Jewishness I could manage, because of my lack of competence in Hebrew ... But finally it came with *Simulacrum*, and even before that in *Thisness* ... In 1988 it continued with *SparkskrapS* and now *Traces (Tikkun)* which was preceded by my involvement with Robert J. Oppenheimer, a 'detour,' which took up at least 3 years. But now we are in early (Jan.–Feb.) 1996 and, after some dashed hopes, suddenly came the 'call,' telling me that *Traces* is 'on' and the premiere will be in about 4(!) months' time. Wow! Immediately I had to go (and went) into 'high gear.' Soon we auditioned a candidate for the (very taxing) vocal solo part, which required an uninterrupted 'being on' for 40–45 minutes, against a sizable (40–56 strong) orchestra, without the benefit of a pit! And that copying/proofreading of the parts began, too. We also had a publicity/strategy meeting, which also dealt with the publicity 'spin' the work should be given and which groups would be good 'targets' from the point of view of ticket sales. Given the theme, background and the subtext underlying the 'surface' text, the idea arose that Jewish groups should receive a special attention, both in Kingston (it has 2 synagogues) and Toronto with its large, influential and wealthy Jewish population. It was made clear that I will be expected to be active, if not to the extent of actually 'leading' in this endeavor ... I accepted this as a sort of challenge and necessity. It seemed necessary, because I wanted to 'reach' people with this work, perhaps more than ever before ...

Returning home from the strategy session [...] I started making plans. I came up with the idea of a set talk of about an hour's duration, to begin in Kingston, attracting 'opera-lovers,' Queen's U[niversity] colleagues, Jews, others, and to repeat the same in Toronto for similar groups there. In addition, I approached 'print media' in Kingston, Jewish groups both in Kingston and Toronto, leaving the daily papers to be contacted by the publicity person at Soundstreams Canada, with whom I established contact. In addition to the text of the lecture mentioned above, I composed shorter promo-texts, gave interviews to various other publications, too.

I should mention it now that for the past 12, or so, years we are members of a small 'Reform' congregation here in Kingston, which has a membership of about 60 families, but no synagogue building, and only a part-time rabbi who comes here once in every 2 weeks for services and Sunday school teaching. In Toronto I contacted the To[ronto] Jewish Music Society which, after some hesitation, invited me to give my talk for its members in a large Jewish Community Center. Since I missed certain 'calendar' deadlines in Kingston, and since no firm invitation materialized from another organization, I decided to give the Kingston lecture at Queen's, which was very supportive of the endeavor from all points of view. To reach my co-religionists at our little synagogue I sent invitations to all families there. The date of the lecture was set in Kingston, and, eventually, in Toronto and the 'publicity' got underway in this dimension, also. In the Queen's lecture I had an audience of about 30(!) of which about 2/3 were non-Jewish friends and colleagues at Queen's, a number of whom also came to hear *Winthrop* in 1986. I was, of course disappointed by the small number and the scant interest on the part of local Jews! And now that Toronto talk ... As it turned out the audience there was even smaller, barely numbering a dozen ... An apologetic chairman told us subsequently that by an 'oversight' the lecture date coincided with the Day of the Shoah and 'potentially' interested persons (in my 'Jewish' opera) went to attend this or that event of memorial of the Shoah. Perhaps, perhaps not.

[...]

Istvan

188

9 JULY 1996

Dear friend Isty,

What can I say to offer comfort, understanding in your hurt? I find it almost impossible to find a way to express all the contradictions I continue to see & experience in my own life or observe at a near or far remove from anyone else's, esp[ecially] that of a dear friend like you. What am I saying? Only that we each travel alone, we are born & die separately, alone, no matter how many nice stories & myths we invent to help us light up the dark a bit, the "I—Thou" of a Buber, the "God loves you" of the Sunday morning preacher, the "love thy neighbor" of the old rabbinic tradition. I'm trying to say the Jews of Kingston who were also members of your synagogue (I had no idea you & Bea were members of such). I have a built-in antipathy for any institutionalization of religions or spiritual pursuit. [...] The more they socialize the "activity" the further removed they wind up from the hard realities (few want to admit them, believing <u>everything</u> is open to understanding by everyone, a democratization into fatuity & trivialization with corresponding forms of socialized kitsch) and those, as well as the Jews of Toronto, obviously have no interest in the philosophy or metaphysics, let alone psychology, of what they profess to believe. You were offering them a measure of insight into themselves and the life they lead whether as Jews or merely human beings; but clearly the surface of life is much easier to take—i.e., cantorial shows, Shoahs—however gut-wrenching the latter. (I hate the cantorial "crying," since I first heard it in the tiny orthodox *schules* my parents took us to when we were children. To live is to suffer. What then is the crying for?) [...]

Forgive my saying so, Isty, but I think you were thinking too highly of those folks. In your kindness & desire to make them a part, however small, of your world of understanding you <u>over</u>estimated them. I have to tell you I gave up on audiences a very long time ago not out of anything but the realization that they are random, totally anonymous & happenstance onlookers. For me, if anything, all that counts is that I do what I can to realize my idea & if I think of anyone else it is <u>only</u> the performer(s) who loves his instrument and wants to say through it something he is already or becomes convinced of. Real performers care as much @ musical trust as composers do. Even if audiences do too in a kind of generalized, abstract sense, they can only get at it through the projection of the performer(s). Critics? They mean nothing in the final analysis. [...]

George

189

23 JULY 1996

My dear George,

[...] I could not do better in any other way, and take, one by one (some of) your themes and reflect upon them as well as I am able to in this lazy, relaxed afternoon ... You see: I am almost restored to a peaceful existence after the turbulence & tumult of the *Traces* (*Tikkun*) experience. Your advice to get over the 'hurt' ... It was a disappointment, but 'hurt?' Not really the latter, because people who don't convince me about their capability of understanding and who live, agitate, in a different 'world' from that of mine, have only a limited power to touch me, if at all. Only those remarks that come from the depth of a 'parallel' pit of experience qualify for the status of speaking with a command worthy of respect. The first criterion then ought to be a proof of 'I have understood your intent & expression,' followed by (2) 'I think of it this/that way'(3) for this or that reason. Thus, application of intellect/feeling must be complemented by integrity and shared empathy ... The number of 'eligibles,' so defined, is quite, as one would expect, small. But, of course, one tries to ascertain at a premiere: did I say what I set out to say? This is, by far the most relevant information for me.

Our synagogue affiliation (since about 1984) needs to be viewed from 2 angles: (a) the practical-social and (b) the 'spiritual.' First the practical, which preceded the 'other' angle. In 1984 I had to confront the fact of the state of my then 90-year-old mother (who lived with us), whose health & 'personal needs' took a 'turn,' suggesting that she might not 'be around' for many more years. Both Bea & I thought of corollary needs (hospitalization, protracted illness and eventual death, funeral, etc.). It became soon clear that funeral arrangements would have to [be] arranged (or at least thought about) before the 'moment of necessity' ... Kingston has a (larger) Orthodox synagogue and (a smaller) Reform congregation. We joined the latter in 1985. By that time 'Granny' (my mother) was a resident in a chronic-care hospital (the best available in Kingston managed by a religious (Catholic!) order with a medical director who was Jewish(!). My mother was (became) a permanent resident there after suffering a stroke in January, '85. She passed away in October of the same year. She had a Jewish funeral service, led by our synagogue's 'lay' 'spiritual leader,' because our little congregation (of about 50 families) had no rabbi at the time. (Since then we, occasionally, had the services of a part-time rabbi who came for a few days at a time/per month from Montreal.) After Granny's (my mother's) funeral Bea & I had decided to continue our membership for reasons of 'fairness' and (more importantly perhaps) because of a few personal contacts with fellow members (all were colleagues at Queen's & wives) whom we (but Bea mostly) found congenial. […]

So, you see, the little synagogue of ours is a part of this overall pattern. As far as I am concerned I could leave it any day, and the handful of 'friends' in the congregation probably would remain the same … And there is the angle of a kind/degree of social (or societal) sharing in an otherwise overwhelmingly gentile community, in which I have many more collegial ('quasi-friendly' might be an overstatement) relationships, centered around Queen's. But of course my most meaningful bonds are with a few (and ever fewer) circle of friends who live elsewhere.

That ends point no. 1. As far as my interests in things Jewish are concerned this is a totally different story and it has almost no relationship whatever to our congregational affiliation. The roots of this 'interest' 'feed' from these sources: (1) personal memory of a life which was lived with a series of changes in the awareness of 'being Jewish' (what kind of Jew!? was a question which took a very long time to surface in my consciousness); 'traces' acquired in childhood through (2) the Hitler-years, then (3) as a D[isplaced] P[erson] (Jewish!) living/studying in Paris who benefited from (4) a small (but vitally important) stipend from 'L'Union des Étudiants Juifs' in Paris, and 'rescued' from that 'bottleneck' by (5) a H[ebrew I[mmigrant] A[id] S[ociety] worker (Lottie Levinson) who helped me to apply for a Lady Davis Fellowship, tenable in Montreal, which also came with a (temporary) appointment to McGill.[14] In gratitude (& for practical reasons) I dedicated my 1st Symphony (1958) to the Bicentenary of Canadian Jewry, a critical event in my professional life. The first unmistakable 'trace' of 'generalized' Jewish 'statement' (as distinct from 'personal homage' statements, dirges, etc.) became a part of *Thisness* ('Unreason') in which the odious figure of a concentration camp commander appeared in 1985. Since that year almost no work I wrote was free from Jewish allusion. (An exception might be my string quartet movement *Doors … Shadows …*) At about the same time I began reading Jewish history and, after stumbling (literally) on G. Scholem, also about some aspects of Jewish thought. All this I did as an untutored amateur, who, to this day, failed to summon the determination needed for a study of Hebrew. I doubt that I shall ever go as far as that! There are so many topics vying for one's attention … So, I'm continuing with the dabbling in this & that as the fancy strikes me. But finally in *Traces* I succeeded

(I believe) to find the format and expression for 'showing' how I conceive today my 'Jewish' past, present, and also perhaps my foreseeable(!) future. I am very much at peace with that if I can impose this very central & intimate thought on a dear friend: yourself!! But I do it in a whisper, feeling your spiritual closeness to me, George ... the double exclamation marks standing not for sound-volume but for a depth of feeling/emphasis ... Enough of that! [...]

Istvan

190

27 NOVEMBER 1996

My dear George,

[...] My two enclosures: (1) John Beckwith's critique of a book by N. Lebrecht, *When the Music Stops* which our 'national newspaper,' *The Globe and Mail*, reviewed prominently(!) and on the whole approvingly a week earlier;[15] and (2) a brief clipping from p. 1 of today's issue of the *Globe*, with reference to firms 'targeting' (no less!) children, and how the innocent little victims (later called 'consumers in training' with a callous up-front-ness!) 'perform' as trained seals, or Pavlovian dogs.[16] The body of the article has also the gem that children during a 10–12-years-long period (I'm writing from memory) watch 200,000 advertisements on TV! Goebbels, or even Orwell's monsters, were not this brutal and—seemingly—effective, *vide* the huge number of deaths by lung cancer of women(!) who are induced to the habit by atrociously false claims aimed at 'slimness,' 'beauty,' social 'success,' and sexual 'attractiveness' as well as being socially 'with the times.' All these are connected (and much more along these lines!) with what you and I are in the process of lamenting: the seeming demise of serious music from the cultural landscape. I feel this whole issue is so complex that only by putting our finger on all the layers of this sad regression can we begin to see what's happening and what caused this apparently precipitous decline.

I know, what I'm to write now, you know by heart and in the heart. Nevertheless let me relieve myself of some of my frustration, sense of guilt, etc. But, first, some more info[rmation] about the Canadian variety of this awful mess. Item: since about the mid-'80s our successive conservative and (now) liberal governments docilely followed the Thatcher-Reagan-Bush neo-Darwinian libertarian, etc. political/economic policies and subjected our cultural institutions (The Canada Council, the CBC, etc.) to massive (about 30–50% less monies by now, i.e., 1996) budgetary cuts with the result (affecting also the entire education sector) that artists, teachers, orchestras, museums, were forced to seek reprieve/help in the private sector (read: corporations, wealthy 'prominent' citizens, who often were engaged in the higher echelons of these very same corporations, or their wives), and who to minimize expenditures (first), impose management methods from business (second?), and, finally, impose their 'artistic' vision in the selection of artists, programs, etc. (third?), with the result of taking over the entire enterprise, with the 'negligible' exception of not holding a violin in hand ... (After all, they are practical people, who know their limits and also know when to let a hired hand 'realize' their 'vision,' 'dreams,' 'plans,' read ambition.) They can do this with impunity since the gatekeepers of the 'record,' the owners of the daily press and their hirelings (critics, editors, etc.) will not take serious issue with the bosses (owners, publishers, editors-in-chief) who themselves might sit on these very 'lay' boards mentioned before. [...]

The hirelings of the so-called 'chattering' classes cooperate effectively, and with the help of promoters of a new class of linguistic mutations, our conceptual landscape was, and continues to be, subjected to a subtle yet brutal, near subliminal (for those who do not 'deconstruct' these new linguistic horrors) brain washing. Examples: the semantic ballooning of words like: consumer, (human) resource, resource-management, globalization, accountability (who constructs the scales, assigns rank ordering, etc.?) as if it can be taken as proven that the 'thing' lends itself to counting! At our University (Queen's) things are in turmoil: the efficiency (what the hell is this supposed to mean in some disciplines?) boys (and girls) of the Business School are among the loudest demanding changes (pushed by our lay-overseers on the Board of Governors) and supporting the more and more preempting of resources by the propagators of technology within and beyond the university's gates. The issue is no longer how many 'up-to-date' computers should be sitting in every damn office, and in the residence-cubicles of every single student, but ... you can fill the space. Computers are but the latest versions of this mad, accelerating, rush towards the electronic Ersatz of the real thing (i.e., concert music, heard live, museum displays seen in their real glory, etc.). We have been down on the path of this 'Virtual Reality' since: film, TV, recorded music and we all, rather mindlessly, rejoiced in the convenience (plus a few intrinsic interesting aspects of these contraptions) these provided, as ancillary forms, also allowing for the process of democratization to take place. But did I really contemplate that live concerts will be empowered by CDs, and serious music (starved by a lack of audiences due to a starved and reoriented educational system) itself will appear to be irrelevant to today's 'consumer' society? Did I foresee that the process of 'consumerization' demands that the 'market' be simplified, rationalized, and controlled by market-sampling via bar-coding of staples or other like devices, manipulated through advertising processes that keep/hold us by the small hairs from (literally) the cradle to the deathbed (geriatric consumer research, I'm certain, is no fruit of my feverish imagination).

Now this societal-cultural change's 'speed' was rather slow, steady of rate, and not worry- (or concern)-eliciting. The number of people of adequate education/sensibility/tradition (with the capacity of evolution from, say, Beethoven to Mahler, via Wagner or Brahms, etc.) was large enough and they impacted also (if with an ever slowly attenuating effectiveness) on their children's generation, undisturbed by a sea change in aesthetic outlook (which equates a Schubert with, say, Paul McCartney). […] Now, with seeming suddenness: a lurch … from the generation(s) alluded to as the 'baby boomers,' and from them, to the world of the 'twenty-somethings,' on and on to others (let's call them the 'roaring teens,' and the 'prepubescent consumer virtuosi') … Am I a perfect Luddite? Not quite! I had reason to benefit from the 'at the fingertips' rapid availability, via computers, of cancer-research abstracts 2½ years ago when we, in a frantic hurry wanting to know about the most up-to-date research concerning breast cancer, we asked help from reference librarians at Queen's. It was awe-inspiring to find that almost to-the-minute latest information was available to us through computer printouts of abstracts! I am also used to sample our large univ[ersity] library's computerized retrieval system which is truly awesome in its efficiency & speed. But I am resistant to the mindless, i.e., aimless surfing of the 'Internet' with its trivial or useless repertory and/or babble, which includes (in the truest libertarian spirit and money-chasing brazenness) the vast amount of junk-texts, displays, or whatnots, with its 'dumbing down,' or 'corrupting' or 'exploitativeness,' etc. in content, which, admittedly, also is by now beyond any control, by any means (i.e., effective, considered, and comprehensive 'control'). But someone may say this: in the absence of an 'acceptable' ethical standard, framework, or whatever, what/who should set the limits, the parameters, of such control? Isn't this to lead to a totalitarian framework? Possibly … It depends … But not only there isn't the way there is absent the will. Or: things are so completely complexly interdependent that only a sensible *laisser faire* approach is the one that could amount to a practical, sane-enough, course of action. So one hesitates, leans backward, procrastinates, etc. and the Bill Gateses and their multibillionaire colleagues ride on, surf on, unhindered, unconcerned of the common weal, seemingly. (It is difficult to prove that there is an awful conspiracy afoot …) In the meanwhile the apprentice sorcerer of the cybernetic revolution destroys livelihood, i.e., people, by the millions, by 'restructuring,' 'downsizing,' 'rationalizing,' 'globalizing,' 'outsourcing,' etc. without preventing the persistence of the practice of child-labour in India, Bangladesh, Turkey, or wherever else … and in the sweatshops of China's 'new economic' zones … Money concentrates in ever larger amounts in ever fewer hands. The notion of oligarchy is even operational at the level of the working class itself, where the 'aristocrats' are the unionized electrical, electronic, 'high-tech' labourers, and perhaps those in the auto & aviation industries, who maintain (relative) security and wage-levels, while their 'proletarian' brethren in the agricultural-labourer (seasonal) ranks, the textile pieceworkers fall more and more 'downward' in earning levels.

I am writing as if I would know something about these economic-societal moves, but to claim such competence would be a sham. I don't really know these things (and am consequently vulnerable to a well-directed attack) beyond my felt need to walk the world with open eyes, to read 'loaded,' often manipulative, texts with as much critical intelligence that I can bring to apply to it, etc. After all we both are citizens, payers of taxes and the occasional contributors of pennies to charitable purposes for this or that form of Band-Aid for the very poor. But some of the people around must contribute also to the social viability of family members who fell out of the 'life-boat,' i.e., are (temporarily?) unemployed … I could go on, and on, my dear Friend. But enough is written here to sustain in this clumsy way the proposition that the crisis in the world of symphony orchestras (including the greatest ones, like yours in Philadelphia) is but the very tip of a vast cultural-social-economic iceberg, at least in the North American context, aggravated by a lack of adequate private sector involvement. The roots of this malaise go very deep, indeed. What to do? What to say (if anything at all) to a 20-year-old 'aspiring' (for what? propelled by what?) student composer … What justifies a teacher of composition (we both did this also for a salary, a while back) to accept such students for monetary reward when one knows the chances to justify the pain/work for the vast majority, without a hope to arrive to a desired 'plateau'? I, honestly, don't have an answer. Yes, we also were Don Quixotes at a time in the past hoping for the joy of a premiere of a new work which is proving itself to be true. It is one of the greatest of joys. Yes, yes … we know and recall … One lives in the past while one is raging at the present and unsteady on the feet about the future. [...]

Istvan

[...]

191

4 DECEMBER 1996

Dear old Friend Isty,

[...] I must tell you I enjoyed your 2nd letter (27/11/96) immensely—"enjoyed" meaning you were/are splendid in your rage against all the offal the world is producing & wallowing about in—not least starting w[ith] the stink of the human ego. I have always been in a rage vs. the world. Never have I seen a good reason to reconcile myself to the stupidities through which we slog our way in this life. At the same time—mostly, but never 100%, I feel great compassion for my fellow travellers who trod the "dirty streets of London," work in the "satanic mills" (be they institutions, whatever). But you really called the shots. I don't apologize for not being an "expert." In life there are none—we enter the mystery, live it, leave it, never quite knowing what it is or why, whether or whence. The brain/reason is only a tiny light in the vast dark. We live by feel. Unhappily, we mostly guess wrong about almost everything. *C'est la guerre*. [...]

George

192

27 DECEMBER 1996

Dear George, distant/close friend ...

[...] This weekend's issue of our 'National Newspaper's' 'Art'(??) section is, once again, full with evidence that our successive governments (since our festive, 'Centennial' bash of 1967) (save in the super-nationalistic-omphaloskeptic province of Quebec) are doing all they can to belittle, throttle, suffocate, etc. all endeavors in 'homegrown' contemporary art and music. (The printed word is an exception, seemingly. I don't quite know why ...) The power brokers perhaps appreciate, it seems, a well-turned phrase, even if they find the underlying message not in agreement with the politics of the day (increasingly 'right'). What is the news? Yes, the new gladiators are the men/women who are (hold on to your hat, George) our "most prominent sponsorship brokers"! (See the clipping, one of several from today's paper which I could have sent along, if not feeling charitable, and mindful of your digestion.)[17] A Pavarotti and a Bartoli could hold on to a portion of their turf still, but the future is in the hearts(?) and bank accounts of the chairmen of the boards, the brokers, and their ilk. They can repeat *ad nauseam* the banalized amputated Beethoven-limb, or Schubert-limb ... the novelty is on the spectacle & the $$$ take. (In 1995–96 the Can[adian] Opera Co[mpany] brought out Atom Egoyan's *Salome* to considerable acclaim.[18] A.E. is a trendy film-maker, metamorphosed into an opera stage-director ... The music? Let me see? Oh yes, that fellow, what's his name again? Yes, lived in Garmisch ... Strauss, Richard, I think, he was called ...) [...]

Did I write to you of both my latest attempt at penetrating the phenomenological language of the interesting Lithuanian-born, but later Germanized/Francicized, Jew: Emmanuel Levinas?[19] The language can be of Husserlian/Heideggerian complexity, multiplied by a goodly component of Talmudistic-Judaic turn of mind. He is a bit apologetic about his Talmudic texts, but plows ahead fearlessly about his central topic: the relationship between 'being' & 'beings,' on the one hand, and 'the Other' & 'others,' on the other. Herein lies the nub of his contribution. He died recently and a moving necrologue by J. Derrida, in *Critical Inquiry*,[20] sent me back to E.L. for another 'look' ... [...]

Istvan

NOTES

1 *Circles of Fire* (1997), written for the Evan Hirsch/Sally Pinkas Duo.

2 Milan Kundera, *Testaments Betrayed: An Essay in Nine Parts*, trans. Linda Asher (London: Faber, 1995).

3 Emil Schürer, *The History of the Jewish People in the Age of Jesus Christ (175 B.C.–A.D. 135)*, 3 vols., trans. T. Alec Burkill and others; rev. and ed. Geza Vermes & Fergus Millar (Edinburgh: Clark, 1973–87).

4 John of Gischala, a commander of rebel Jewish armies in Galilee during the Jewish revolt against Rome (67–70 C.E.). He fled the victorious Romans south to Jerusalem, gaining control until the destruction of the besieged city and the Temple by the Romans in 70 C.E.; Flavius Josephus (37–ca. 100 C.E.), Jewish historian and soldier whose writings are important sources for the study of early Judaism and Christianity. All that is known of John of Gischala is from Josephus's account (ca. 80–100 C.E.) of the Jewish revolt against Rome.

5 See "1994," note 9.

6 Richard Taruskin, "How Talented Composers Become Useless," *The New York Times*, 10 March 1996.

7 A pun on the name Donald Martino, whose music comes in for some rather harsh criticism in Taruskin's review above. See also "1968," note 7.

8 Anhalt is referring to Babbitt's controversial article "Who Cares If You Listen?" which appeared originally in *High Fidelity*, February 1958, 38–40, 126–27, and which has been reprinted several times in anthologies.

9 John M. Dillon and Anthony A. Long, eds., *The Question of "Eclecticism": Studies in Later Greek Philosophy* (Berkeley: University of California Press, 1988).

10 Gary Kulesha (b. 1954), Canadian composer and conductor; he has conducted several Canadian orchestras, was composer-in-residence with the Kitchener–Waterloo Symphony Orchestra (1988–91), and conducted the premiere of Anhalt's *Traces (Tikkun)*, with baritone Doug MacNaughton as the protagonist, at the Glenn Gould Studio in Toronto on 28 May 1996.

11 Max Brod (1884–1968), prolific Prague-born German-language writer and close friend of Kafka, whose major writings he edited.

12 Milan Kundera, *Slowness: A Novel*, trans. Linda Asher (New York: HarperCollins, 1996).

13 Isaac Bashevis Singer, *Love and Exile: The Early Years—A Memoir* (London: Jonathan Cape, 1985).

14 Lady Henriette Marie Davis (née Meyer) (1875–1963), the first wife (1898–1924) of the prominent Montreal-born Jewish businessman and philanthropist Sir Mortimer Barnett Davis (1866–1928); shortly after the Second World War she founded the Lady Davis Foundation for the purpose of bringing to Canada educated European refugees and helping place them in university positions across the nation. In gratitude, Anhalt dedicated his *Interludium* for strings, timpani, and piano (1949) to her. Lottie Levinson was at the time a representative of the Canadian Jewish Congress in Paris; see Robin Elliott and Gordon E. Smith, eds., *Istvan Anhalt: Pathways and Memory* (Montreal and Kingston: McGill-Queen's University Press, 2001), 24–25.

15 John Beckwith, "And They Shall Have Music ... If They Are Willing to Pay for It," *The Globe and Mail*, 23 November 1996; review of Norman Lebrecht, *When the Music Stops—: Managers, Maestros and the Corporate Murder of Classical Music* (London: Simon & Schuster, 1996).

16 "Firms Target Children, Meeting Told," *The Globe and Mail*, 27 November 1996.

17 Doug Saunders, "No Billboard Too Small as the Arts Go Hunting for Sponsors," *The Globe and Mail*, 28 December 1996.

18 Atom Egoyan (b. 1960), Egyptian-born Armenian-Canadian filmmaker (*Exotica* [1994], *The Sweet Hereafter* [1997]); his production of Strauss's *Salome* for the Canadian Opera Company, which employed live video and film, opened in Toronto in the fall of 1996 and was later mounted in Vancouver (1997) and Houston (1998).

19 Emmanuel Levinas (1906–95), Jewish philosopher and religious thinker who was influenced by Husserl and Heidegger (especially the latter's *Being and Time*); he developed a philosophy based on the notion of personal ethical responsibility for the Other. See, for example, *Totality and Infinity: An Essay on Exteriority* (1961; English trans. 1969) and *Otherwise Than Being: or, Beyond Essence* (1974; English trans. 1981).

20 Jacques Derrida, "Adieu," *Critical Inquiry* 23 (Autumn 1996): 1–10.

1997

193

3 JANUARY 1997

Dear old Friend,

I'm sitting here trying to remember if I sent you the enclosed already.[1] If so, just pass it on to some needy friend or just toss it. Also I have to assume you've already run into this stupid academic game going on in the "humanities" (the very term becomes a farce these days) in which all criteria & standards are jettisoned & the most vapid ridiculous notions are advanced & validated because it is alleged that Eurocentric/Western culture has suppressed, colonialized, subjugated, ignored, whatever … As for "objective reality" all those who disbelieve in its efficacy & existence, let 'em all swim around in the flooded Pacific Northwest & literally test the waters of "reality" vs. their puny outlook. On the other hand I won't go too far to support science & its notions of following "truth" no matter where it leads to & what consequences. Unbridled license in abandoning standards or in pursuing truth are both destructive of <u>ourselves</u>—not the world of nature. She is bigger than all of us! As the winter storms in U.S. (Canada West Coast too?) & Europe demonstrate.

7 JANUARY

I can't remember what interrupted me but I can continue our "conversation." […] Yesterday, our young friends Brian Peterson[2] and his wife Helen Mirkil (very gifted painter) visited and Brian said something I'm still cogitating on: physicists believe there is an "energy field" in the universe—or "is" the universe; and "matter" in all its infinite varieties of large & small forms are merely perturbations of that field. When that "matter" dissolves, disintegrates—dies in other words, it returns to its original state. The theological parallel is of course obvious. Less so is Wordsworth's famous "We come from God trailing clouds of glory" and return to him/it/her/whatever.[3] The gnostics had many "stories" about this; so also the Kabbalists. Even believing that one of these forms of the telling how we came into existence & disappear from it—i.e., are perturbations of the energy field; or come from God & return to him/it/etc.—defeats any effort at logic or reason. A vast & invisible puzzle into which "music" fits as another form of perturbation, an idea which somehow delights me. […]

George

194

12 FEBRUARY 1997

My dear George,

… finally the moment to respond to your Jan. 3 letter … First to pick up your 'threads':

(1) 'Academic' life … I'm glad I'm out of it, given the atmosphere of that of a beleaguered fortress which Queen's shows to some of my colleagues who are 'closer' to its 'heartbeat' than I … The 'tone-givers' appear to be the 'lay board' and the 'business school' … The language of debate, etc. resembles that of the daily paper: "downsizing," "human resources," "repositioning," and the like … It is a language to manipulate with and befuddle opponents of the 'business line' … Enough of this … Wittgenstein's 'language games' apperception was dead on …

(2) Yes, I have followed the 'saga' of Sokal's hoax … How much egg is left on whose faces? That's one question in its aftermath …

(3) Brian Peterson's reference to that 'energy field' strikes a chord here, too. You are, of course, right about the gnostics and some Kabbalists too, in this regard … You may recall the conclusion of *Traces (Tikkun)* 'lands' the piece (i.e., its protagonist) precisely in that *locus* … Apropos *Traces* … I have given a few talks about it here and there … Sometime with a better response than other times … Perhaps I should enclose here the text of my first comment on it, which predated the premiere.[4] […]

Istvan

195

9 MARCH 1997

Dear Isty, old friend,

[…] It has been a busy time with work, business, people. I'm deep into my 2-piano work I call *Circles of Fire*—circles because everything rests on one or another way of treating symmetrical relations, so at times I feel like my head is coming off, fire because symmetry is built into the ferocious, indescribable really, energies which created and continue to sustain the universe and ourselves. The two great mysteries that either enfold each other; or perhaps the greater one, the universe itself, enfolds the smaller one, us. Certainly it is not, cannot be, the other way around. Unless one can accept, i.e., believe the old gnostic belief in "Adam" as the human form of the universe. Harold Bloom writes brilliantly on this in his *Omens of Millennium*, an odd book, analytic/confessional by turn, philosophical/theological.[5] […] There he also writes about the Kabbalah. Which takes me to your *Traces* talk—which you had been good enough to send to me earlier. But it refreshes my memory, perusing it again. One thing I'm in complete agreement with you on, namely that there is no ready answer to our manifold problem; there can't be by the very nature of the universe and our total ignorance of how and what it truly is (Stephen Hawking and the other priests of science who say they know notwithstanding) as well as by the very nature of our total bafflement and confusion about ourselves. I personally think it's a wonderful lesson for those able to learn and absorb it and find out that Sigmund Freud for example no longer holds center stage and that in the many attempts to come to terms with him and what he did accomplish (which is clearly not little even when it turns out he's "wrong" as apparently he often was) people are beginning to describe him more as an "artist," let's say a "poet of the psyche" rather than as a scientist. Fair enough, don't you think? The great danger in the quest for certainty (one of John Dewey's favorite topics)[6] is to be convinced that we have "the answer." This is the, for me, terrible story of every religion I know anything about including Judaism. The human necessity always to be "right," the inability to admit error or fault or flaw. That's what does us in. Hence as I see it the constant turmoil in the world, the readiness to kill over every conceivable kind of difference hardened into dogma or concept. This great thing on which we pride ourselves so much as a species—consciousness—is our greatest flaw and obstacle to self-understanding, apart from God-dogmas and God-concepts. And you see how twisted and paradoxical it gets: even if Lenin was right that "religion was the opiate of the people" (which it clearly is) he was wrong to rob them of whatever it was that comforted them in the face of the ultimate knowledge of death as he was about everything else. My dilemma is that I think I know what is wrong. I've worked very hard to develop my critical faculties—but I'm much less certain about what's "right" and how people should live—even if I decided a long time ago for myself how I should live. So we get back to the bafflements and confusions. What strikes me about the *Tikkun* idea is its marked parallelism with the Greek idea of the one and the many and the ancient Hindu idea of the Fire-God Agni whose "sparks" do exactly what the "sparks" in Kabbalah are purported to do and be. But this doesn't surprise me: there are perhaps only five or six "faces" in the world, five or six "stories" told over and over again, five or six "tunes" in endless variants, five or six "ideas," etc. […]

George

196

16 APRIL 1997

My dear George,

Sometimes it is not the wine that needs maturing, but the drinker who waits for the right moment for the opening of a bottle of vintage wine. So: your generously 'self-probing' letter of March 9, '97 had to wait for this lovely, mellow, quasi-spring afternoon, today, for that indispensable reprise-reading which unlocked not only its 'burdens,' but also its multiple moods as you tried to ease me into a comfortable chair, facing the one in which I 'saw' you in an inclined position … And you talked about your new 2-piano piece, with the sonorous title: *Circles of Fire*, and followed it up with a few intriguing words about its nature. The 'theme' of the 'fire' you returned to later on in the letter, when you brought up references to sparks … And this occurred after you touched down on Freud, Hawking, religion, Bloom, even Lenin at one point … A breathless sweep this … possible only by one who read, absorbed and recalls a lot, in an integrated frame which is an ever-so-complex persona, forever in the making, but which/who has a firm plus! awareness of 'where,' 'whence,' & 'what,' all imbedded in a super-rich soil which sustains new growth in a wonderful combination of the 'will,' the serendipitous, and much much more besides. […]

I think that our respective thinking/feeling about religion are compatible with each other. We belong to a little reformed congregation here in Kingston. It (the membership) came about when I had to think about my mother's declining state of health in 1984. This smallish group (then ca. 40, now ca. 60 families strong) had the (eventually needed) burial plot ... It still has only an occasional access to a rabbi's services, and still has no synagogue. (It meets in sundry, rented, premises, at Queen's U[niversity], or elsewhere.) Bea belongs to some women-groups formed within, and we only attend a service when it's our turn to provide the after-service 'hallah' bread, cookies, and drinks. I don't pray with them, period. The last time I gave a thought to this was when David Flusser[7] (you will recall the name) told me in his home in Jerusalem that I ought to read Franz Rosenzweig's *The Star of Redemption*.[8] (I made 2 attempts at reading the book, and this in the knowledge that he is a highly regarded philosopher, and a man who endured the same illness that Stephen Hawking bears with equally immense fortitude, yet I cannot follow his 'way' to what he terms 'redemption.') But 'religion' is only a word. What does matter [is] what one thinks about one's fleeting presence in a tiny corner of the universe & what happens after one's 'ego-integrity' is at an end and the 'bits and pieces' get ready to falling apart & merging, once again, with the 'rest of the stuff' of the universe. Another wonderful 'sideline' (an odd choice of word this here) is how we are thinking/feeling and how we [are] reaching out to a small number of 'others' who act like supports, mirrors, echo-surfaces, acceptors of our love, friendship, and, at times, receive our indifference or (disguised?) negative affects. We leave behind 'traces' in the process and 'looking back' we see 'lines' and x-dimensional patterns formed by what we did, didn't do, but thought of doing, etc. etc. all in a wonderfully complex whirl ... We are also made up (some would say) of what we recall ... But all this is your territory too, so I won't continue ...

Yes Freud and his ebbing reputation ... I don't know if I ever told you that around 1990 I spent ca. 4 months with the thought that I may (might) write an opera (my 'Jewish' opera) centered on him. The more I read by & on him the less 'appealing' he became. Finally, I dropped the project and I think it was the right thing (for me) to do. After this I spent ca. 2½ years (a much longer time!) on plans, texts, etc. which would have led me to an opera on Robert J. Oppenheimer. This plan also collapsed, but at a much more 'advanced' stage.[9] (You might know that we even visited Los Alamos at the time ...) The upshot/result of both of these 'false starts' is *Traces*, a much shorter (40') piece ... [...]

Istvan

[...]

197

30 JUNE 1997

Dear old friend Isty,

[...] I've been looking forward to this summer as a time to work—but so far nothing more than vague probes. It could be I'm depleted from the large-scale 2-piano work I finished in the late spring. Perhaps I need more time to let the juices gather & flow again. The other very strong reality is that I keep bumping into myself no matter what direction I go in. I've been aware of this for some time—and it makes each new work I've attempted these last years difficult, sometimes beyond words. I marvel at the wonderful unselfconsciousness of Haydn & Mozart who obviously had no particular qualms about saying pretty much the same thing over & over again, only better as each got older (Mozart never got old enough). In our time self-replication is different I think. That is, in the cases of Chagall & Picasso, for ex[ample], they lived to be quite old, into their nineties, and continued to turn out work after work, drawing on a virtual repertoire or catalog of images, gestures, design preferences which they'd built up over many decades. I'm saying they consciously made use of things they'd invented or discovered earlier with apparent delight in the exercise of their powers. Aaron Copland on the other hand told someone who wanted him to write a new work for them—he was 70 at the time, only 70! (and he died at 90!!)—"Thank you, no. I have nothing more to say." Did his "nothing more" mean no "new" ideas or did he mean he'd finished "saying" and wanted to be free of going back down into the mine again looking for gold? Some people do reach the end of their rope—and welcome it. Others don't. At the moment I'm not really sure which it is for me: end of the rope & nothing more to say; no lead in the pencil anymore; or reluctance to go back down into the mine & hope to find a new vein ... The thing is I agreed to write a chamber concerto for guitar and 6 instruments for Eliot Fisk who is a dear friend & fabulous guitarist.[10] Trouble is the guitar is, for me, an almost impossible instrument to write for. In the meantime I'm reading almost exclusively in and about Wm. B. Yeats: his poetry, criticism (chiefly Harold Bloom), biography.[11] What suddenly drew me to Yeats was my discovery of his late poems (he died in 1939 at 74) when he literally rages at old age & is trying to come to terms with death and its inevitability. Death & time are properly speaking the province of the poet. They should be also the province of philosophers—but they found it too difficult & turned to more manageable problems. Yeats is obsessed with these fundaments of human existence & tried unsuccessfully to find "answers" to them in his *A Vision* which is a crazy, mixed-up piece of occultism with brilliant moments of insight. Have you ever tried reading it? I found it utterly baffling until Bloom shed some much-needed light on it for me. Even though I think I understand it better, it is still unpalatable. Or could be because I understand it better ... [...]

George

[...]

198

20 AUGUST 1997

My dear (forever young, but rich-in-years & experience/wisdom) friend, George!

[...] Work. You are yet to tell me about the completed 2-piano piece. Will you do this in your next letter? Please ... Now as to saying 'new' things, to be 'depleted' or only needing to 'recharge' (unhelpful metaphors all) ... The 'standard' of the 'times' is (or can be considered to be) different ... True? False? Irrelevant ? I refuse to take my 'pick' of these ... Some more words ... more sayings (using E. Levinas's distinction between 'the said' and 'saying,' which is another problem, puzzle, for me presently, one, though, which doesn't keep me awake at nights ...).[12] The reality in our mind's, brain's, functioning is where reality is, provided we throw in the 'pragmatic' dimension, also, allowing seeing things working their 'way' through life around us, the Bakhtinian chronotope, really ... Complicated business this. Enough trouble is to cope with it all, and fight through various resistances to a moderate degree of clarity of vision which allows (could allow) one to act with a minimum ballast of self-consciousness. But things are scattered 'on the way' as many stumbling blocks, banana peels, distractions (even destructions of sorts ... at times), but our art (and experience) consist also of the ability to 'sidestep,' 'overcome,' 'transcend,' 'metamorphose' enough of these and drive on toward the/an 'end'-signaling 'double-bar,' which celebrates the fact that yet another work has been 'bagged.' [...]

Yes, I did read Yeats's *A Vision* a few years ago, and I read about it, too. I came to it because of its Kabbalistic elements, and the book as a whole left me perplexed and definitely unedified ... I recall that the overall impression was confusion, and lack of depth in various parts ... (When it comes to the Kabbalah, few can match G. Scholem's virtuosity ... Not even Moshe Idel, whom many consider as the chief wearer of Scholem's mantle at the Hebrew University, now …)[13] So, I read, read, and read still more, and still feel lacking any inside stirrings whatever … I even thought, that with *Traces* I have said my 'final word.' (When you'll see its libretto you'll readily see why this thought wasn't difficult to contemplate … The piece ends with the solo baritone experiencing his physical (including mental) 'dissolution' into 'elementary particles,' the whole process (gradual in words & music) amounting to a 'return' (or 'returning') [of] the self in its elementary particles, to the totality of the universe. (The job demanded that this be done with as little pretentiousness as possible …) An acquaintance told me some weeks after the premiere: 'Now that we have seen, heard, you die in *Traces*, we can look forward to your first posthumous work.' Touché! I thought. He gave me, indeed, a chuckle … But this first 'posthumous' work gave no sign whatever of wanting to emerge from the 'primaeval ooze' … until, that is, I had a Koestlerian experience of 'bi-sociation' (remember this?).[14] Yes I can trace the trajectory of this new idea … In fact, by hindsight, now it seems that recent, earlier, 'vectors' indicated where it might surface to consciousness. Yes, but, I was either too tired, or dumb, not to have been able to 'make' the proper 'connections' … But suddenly, there it was: a new/old (predictable) idea which, if realized in a new work, would carry along an old theme of mine to a larger terrain, to a 'higher' ground, from where I could 'project' with greater clarity some ideas than on earlier instances. (Yes, 'ideas'; without these there is 'no go' for me.) The next step (always an exciting and pleasurable one) was to write a text (yes I heard voices, once more … perhaps stimulated by some truly superb choral singing I heard lately, in the shape of the Danish and Swedish Radio Choirs, 38 voices each and a *nonpareil* virtuosity to boot). This done (took about 10 days, but still subject to changes) I gingerly started looking for/hearing sounds. The whole thing is still very tenuous, and I keep quite a few escape hatches open, just in case I'll feel the need to flee from the project … We'll see … That's all I can (should) say about it at the present time. […]

Istvan

199

18 SEPTEMBER 1997

Dear old Isty,

[…] You want to know something about *Circles of Fire* for 2 pianos. Increasingly I find myself reluctant to talk @ what I'm doing or have done … no good reason, just a kind of abashment (is that a word?) at crowing, tooting the old horn, sounding off, etc. Still, there is really nothing to hide; and to dissipate the veil of obscurity I may have inadvertently (can one really say "advertently"?) thrown around the work, here goes: it's a bit long, approx[imately] 75 minutes, dealt out in 15 sections (or numbers), some quite long, some only seconds. There are two groups of "shorties": a) a set of canonic variations of an initial phrase some 9–10 bars, very chromatic, which follow each other consecutively; b) five "Solemn Refrains" very severe in a kind of layered tonality; self-enclosed units but all five interrelated, coming at fairly wide intervals in the work. Everything is essentially rooted in a symmetrical device, primarily hinging on harmonic symmetries (the enclosed on "polarity" is itself an offshoot of the 900-page book on symmetry/asymmetry that sits in my closet waiting for me to reread it one last time, making changes, etc. before I attempt to interest anyone in publishing it.[15] *Circles of Fire* is the purely musical site which is in no way a "demonstration" or "illustration" of what the book says. It must stand on its own as though what the book attempts to explicate theoretically still remains unknown and the music is simply an outpour of deeply intuitive musical thinking). There are two "oddities" in the work, oddities because they fit no known descriptive categories I'm aware of: a) a kind of "nocturnal" based on melodic and harmonic "agreements" between 2 different pieces of Brahms; in the end it turns out to be mine and Brahms'; b) a piece "*ppp-pppp*" throughout which pits the "Rectus" and "Inversus" of J.S. Bach's Contrapunctus XIII, *Art of Fugue* against each other—so you have occasional moments of tonal discomfiture when E major & C minor briefly "clash" (also B minor vs. F major, delightful things like that); it should sound *sotto voce*, stage-whispered throughout, a strange "fancy" as I hear it. Then there are pieces like "Infinite Ricercar," "Nebulae," "Caprichos" (after Goya) and so on. When I finished writing it months ago I thought I knew what it would sound like *in toto*—now that I'm proofreading its computer-generated score piecemeal (which I tried to get my copyist to look as much like the old Breitkopf and Härtel engraving as possible) I'm no longer sure. And I say to myself, "*che sera, sera*," it's done and out of my hands figuratively & literally. The two young pianists who will be playing it in '98 are first-rate, have been "duoing" it for years: they play a fantastic Bartók 2-piano & perc[ussion] Sonata, Milhaud *Création du monde* (a piece I don't respond to), a big Messiaen 2-piano work (he's a strange bird, that one; esp[ecially] with his "Catholicism"—which I think is a plague on the world in the same way Orthodox Judaism is on Israel and Eastern Orthodox Christianity is on Russia. These days I am more down on "religion" than ever before, both what it says doctrinally in the various defined religions & what it makes people do & say & how they behave as a result. If I were from Mars—which I may well be for all I know—& had to report back "home" after my long visitation "here on Earth" I could sum "humans" up in one simple word: weird. No offense, dear Isty. But the word must stay in my report.) Right now I'm a long way off from finishing proofreading the score and an equally long way off from hearing it in rehearsal. But March/April '98 will see 5 perf[ormance]s & perhaps others to follow. Meanwhile "back at the ranch"—an old novelistic trick—the "man from Mars" is working on a Chamber Concerto for guitar & 6 players. […]

George

200

6 OCTOBER 1997

My dear friend, George,

I better start this by giving my second impression of your eloquent text on 'Polarity in Music: …,' a copy of which you sent me along with your Sept. 18 letter. Your text gives a clear exposition of complex relationships in lucid language comprehensible to a nonprofessional, yet 'thinking,' audience. Beyond this you show your hand/mind on the ongoing pulse of some aspects, recent ones, of our art, alluding to some of the 'how'-s and 'why'-s as you spin forth the tale. All's done in a tight format and clothed in a metaphor-enriched language. No mean feat to bring all this off, but you, once again, succeeded. As I followed your narrative, my inner voice generated comments here and there. Leaving the 'historically-correct'-ness principle in the ditch let me append that to me the relationship between text & musical material (supposedly 'abstract') is a most complex one. Even in such an 'abstract' composer as Palestrina was supposed to have been, you have motet material that amounts to tone-painting, bordering on program music; *vide* his piece on the first Christian martyr, Stephen. The title of the piece, if memory serves, is *Lapidabant Stephanum* and the initial theme depicts the process of stoning.[16] I recall how impressed I was by this when Kodály made us perform it in our class. (I also got a sore throat in the process as I, usually, volunteered to sing, in falsetto, one of the high parts … All took place ca. 60(!) years ago.) Now I come to think (feel) that 'text-setting' is a pretty open-ended process. The central question (for me, again) is given by the multiple aspects of language as actualized by a number of alternative imaginary speakers in a number of possible situations/contexts ... The possibilities, it is easily seen, are manifold.

I am presently, once more aware of this while working on a new, once again 'text-ed,' piece. Before a text finds its 'niche' in the work I have to argue it out with myself what I want to convey with the whole. This involves the 'part' of a 'life' in the 'world' in a 'time point' which is actualized by the music. Through this argument with myself do I come to see my way 'forward.' The outcome, after the last bar has been 'placed,' is that I feel I am no longer the same person as the one who pencilled in an early draft. Another thought is suggested by my current reading of the very interesting book, *The Making of Eastern Europe* by the McGill historian Phillip [*sic*] Longworth, a book well worth reading, at least it is for me, given my background.[17] This is a one-volume 'fly-past' of an enormously convoluted history of conflict, ardent (to the point of burning, literally, one's allegedly implacable enemies) commitment to the elimination of the last enemy soldier, & woman and child (*vide* Bosnia since ca. 1990), fragmentation of small ethnic groups into dozens of factions, lack of perspective, etc. etc., with the vulnerability to the machinations of an *ayatollah*, or a super-salesman of the latest popular craze, McDonald's, Coke, Madonna, etc., the latest in the line of marketable icons. The exposure to some kind, or other, of a type of interior emptiness, a lack of a 'self,' is also present in the Diana funeral frenzy, as well as in the mass bonding that now (clumsily?) threatens our public marketplace by the yet-to-be-divulged ideology of the 'Promise Keepers.'[18] I am vocalizing thus, because I am still sufficiently strongly holding the view that a Mahler, a Schoenberg, Bruckner, even a Bartók is a recipient of context-determined influences. The complex persona, then, is an 'outcome' (what is that to mean?) of the interplay of a mental/genetic self and elements in the moving context-flow. Each one of us can be (ought to be?) seen as the responding entity to this confluence of interiority and exteriority. Moreover (just to muddy it further) what was yesterday an 'exteriority,' through absorption becomes an 'interiority' a (shorter/longer) while later. I feel I am in dialogue with myself while I handle words in a new piece. All this can nicely coexist with the magisterial, 'seen-from-the above,' vision of yours ... The two complement each other ... one makes use of them by moving the 'lens,' by changing the focus ...

Now I'm coming to your letter, in which you do heart-warmingly reconfirm our reciprocal status to each other as soul mates. Indeed so! The new work here progresses as well as can be expected and it appears to be a fairly long one, which will keep me busy for a while. I cannot, should not, enter into details yet. Later, perhaps ... Your 75-minute-long *Circles of Fire* (beautiful title!)—I'm convinced that your via along your night-wanderings in circles takes you to unique and very personal fires—is quite a long stretch. I'm certain that the work eloquently asserts the necessity of its impressive duration. What you wrote about this reads very 'magnetically': these titles (and their succession) amount to a poetry of ideas, genres, forms, etc ... I imagine 'thinking/feeling' pauses in the gaps between the pieces, partly suggested also by the delightfully uneven lengths of the movements. The *ppp* movement intrigues ... *ppp* talk (*vide* Morton Feldman, and more recently in the Ligeti Violin Concerto [1990]) can carry its own aura ... Of course your *ppp* will be totally different ... (I'm yet to write my own *ppp* invention ...) is also enticing ... All in all, I sense that you reached a new plateau with this work for 2 pianos. Hope to hear it one day. [...]

Istvan

201

31 OCTOBER 1997

Dear Friend Isty,

Well, we seem to be poised for takeoff on an exciting, special project: my letters to you in the Nat[iona]l Libr[ary], Ottawa; yours to me already sitting in their appropriate "nest" in Sacher Stiftung, Basel; your colleague Alan Gillmor who's been appraising these documents for the Nat[iona]l Libr[ary]; his evidently very serious interest in making a "book" of our correspondence with, I'm guessing, some kind of running "commentary." So far I haven't heard from him but I'm writing to tell you I've changed my mind from the former rejecting no, *nyet, non* to a genuinely accepting *oui*, yes, of course, why not? I never dreamed that a correspondence such as ours had greater "significance" than a purely personal one; but if Gillmor, who is a scholar, and scholars view everything differently from us strange birds, maybe because they have better close-up and far-distant vision of the "meaning" of things than we do, thinks there's something there of larger value to music & musicians and those who live at least part-time in the exotic world of musical culture, why then I guess we should, each in our own way, encourage him to go ahead. Of course, I'm very interested in his approach and all that. So let's see how it develops. [...]

I'm breathing hard on the end of *Eden: Out of Time and Out of Space* (a slight alteration of a poetic line of Wm. B. Yeats) for chamber ensemble & guitar, cast in the "form" (attitude!) of a "concerto," certainly a "concerted" work. If I'm lucky & actually finish it (Nov.? Dec.?), I shall come up for air! […]

George

PS: The thought struck me that it is certainly very true that over the long years we have opened our hearts & minds to each other; and perhaps in this exceedingly strange age—at least it is for me—for two grown men, adults, survivor sufferers of different if related fates in this day & age to carry on as though this were an earlier time, say, the 19th or 18th cent[ury] and to speak "out loud" in complete sentences their heartfelt thoughts, that is uncommon in the annals of our beknighted generation (benighted? with the "k" it looks better but evokes visions of "white knights" on big chargers bedecked w[ith] banners & symbols of ancient power. Can't be us!). And true enough, I've talked as much toward the last—or latest (better)—stretch of our correspondence about other matters besides music of great importance to us: our families, our search for our past, our obsessions with being Jewish and how we can relate to such an anomaly (but any smallish group by virtue of ethnicity, religion, or belief has always been & must always remain anomalous), our individual proclivity for "truth"—metaphysical, scientific, philosophic. All these are even strengthened in me by my recent reading of Wm. B. Yeats's biography. An amazing man, born 1865 (Mahler & Strauss's generation!), died 1939 at 74, for that time an agèd man. He railed & raged from his 20s on against Death & Time, lived half in and half out of "reality" because of his powerfully driven intuitions of former lives, the mystical, the occult. More than any other great artist of the 20th cent[ury], our time, he sculpted himself, quite literally, shaped & hammered and pounded his feelings/thoughts/visions/sufferings into his poetry. A real phenomenon. Yeats insisted on the supremacy of the artist's imagination over any "temporal" power such as state & church. When I was in my early 20s I tried unsuccessfully to make an opera out of his *[The] King's Threshold* [1904] and the hero of his play, Shanahan. Talk about anomalies! […]

George

202

4 DECEMBER 1997

My dear George, my very special friend,

… with whom we are reciprocally bound into being intimate witnesses to each other's lives, including some of our music thoughts, while being mindful of the need to preserve only intermittent access into our respective 'musical space' ... interior space, that is ... I might be appearing to impose my thoughts on this on you ... Could I be mistaken? Yes? No? Whatever ... I feel (since years) that one should not impose the turbulence of one's soul/mind on the 'other,' while one labours to put musical thoughts on lined paper ... You are, consequently, usually 'frugal' in telling about new works (unless I ask you for detail, which I do, at times ...). A case in point is your new concerted piece for guitar and chamber ensemble entitled (so poetically!) *Eden: Out of Time and Out of Space*. You refer to Yeats in this respect, too, ... as on earlier occasions, also ... You, certainly, have a close & enduring affection, etc., for Y., as you also have for Wordsworth and other greats, too (perhaps), of the literature of poetry in English. I, too, 'visit' some of these texts, but my background & motivations are different from yours ... But I'm losing my 'line' ... why we tell, or not tell, to each other about music-in-the-making ... Although we know (almost for certain) that we would understand only too well what is at hand in individual instances. And that (our closeness/understanding, which made/make our friendship, our brotherliness, possible/inevitable) is the nub ... To share in the intimacy of the nitty-gritty of the 'making-process' might not be compatible with the position/function of a friend/witness/other ... A co-creator is not (cannot be) an 'other' ... He is an alter ego, a *Doppelgänger*, a co-struggler ... Or whatever ... I cannot prove it, not even depict it better ... To be a witness/friend (or a parent, for ex[ample]) one needs to put distance between souls who are so close to each other ... This reminds me (forcibly) of the profound insight of Isaac Luria[19] the great mind of the Kabbalah in the 16th c[entury] in Safed (where he had taught his disciples but for only 2 years, or so ...!) ... when he defined what *Zim-Zum* meant for him. As you might know, this 'notion' referred to one of the strangest acts the unknowable God of the Jews was supposed to have thought about ... If I'm not mistaken, it started with a rabbinical question: If God fills the Universe how could space be found for anything else, first of all for space required for 'man & his/her world'? A logical question, one admits. Luria's answer to this was that God, in his infinite wisdom, generosity, or whatever, decided to shrink himself, thereby providing the required space (*Lebensraum*?) for man and his 'requirements' ... When I first read about this (in one of G. Scholem's books) I thought, what a fanciful, even loony, thought this is ... But years after there came a moment (actually a real-life situation) when I suddenly understood the profound psychological insight in the *Zim-Zum* idea! When applied to human relationships (the 'closer' they are, the more relevant the need for *Zim-Zum* asserts itself) there are situations where a parent, a friend, a teacher, etc., has to stay back from intimacy with the other in order to allow that beloved, esteemed, etc., other to work out undisturbed, uninfluenced, unadvised, etc., what he/she really can live with as a solution to a problem, conundrum, or whatever tight spot it might be …

So, my dear George, this might be at the root of our mutual/reciprocal respect for each other's 'personal space,' especially when it bears on composing, i.e., inventing musical ideas, which would spin on our respective *carmina perpetua* … Speaking about my own *carmen perpetuum* I am going to say, with restraint and frugality (*vide* above … *Zim-Zum* et al. …), two things: (1) In the process of writing my more recent works (*Traces*, for ex[ample]) I came to understand, only now, what I was groping for in writing certain works since 1960, quite consistently. Now I see the 'line'! I see the trace, into which *Traces* had to fit, as a necessary link! And the same is true of the most recent piece, which I just completed in *particel* yesterday. In a nutshell, to keep you informed in a minimal way (again *Zim-Zum* …) the piece is called *Millennial Mall (Lady Diotima's Walk)* … with a genre designation: "A Voice-drama for the Imagination." The text (12 poems in all) is again by yours truly and there is a solo lyric soprano (Diotima) in it, and an equally weighty role for a S.M.A.T. Bar. B. chorus of about 24 voices. I estimate that the piece will take about 50 mins. to perform. It has to do with matters of our day (society), but seen from the vantage of history … the 'new' is really so 'old' that one has trouble finding its roots … There is also a 28–36 piece orchestra which will complement/sustain the vocal lines, suggesting the usual depths and 'spaces' … It is now the last (the concluding?) 'member' of a series of depictions of my apperceptions of 'things' in time … […]

Istvan

203

13 DECEMBER 1997

Dear Brother-in-the-Spirit Isty,

[…] Before I dive into *Zim-Zum*, "Lady Diotima"?—you mean Ulrich's cousin, the very Diotima from Musil's *Man without Qualities*? "Millennial Walk"? You mean the "Millennial Committee" that met & met, and met yet again at Diotima's house to bring on the final peace & reconciliation among the insane Europeans whom not even the God(s) whether of the Catholic or Protestant or Eastern Orthodox not to mention Jewish

Orthodox persuasions could manage to bring about? What a great idea. Am I even warm? Look forward to hearing your response. And as for my seeming shyness/reluctance/backwardness in putting myself forward that's no mystery. First of all, I've always withheld except under extraordinary circumstances. Second, being a long & keen observer of the human species among whom I've moved & with whom I have had "dealings" I've always shied away from self-promoters and hornblowers, and the dangers thereof. It was a long time before I could talk @ my work in public situations. Given certain inner states I still find it extraordinarily difficult. […]

At last on to *Zim-Zum*. It happens I'm in the middle of reading the Torah (in English), trying to get through Numbers at the moment. I find the dry-as-dust recitals of rituals, censuses, instructions on how to sacrifice bulls & rams & other animals for sin expiation (what a crude concept; but must have been "worldwide" considering all the pagans of the time practiced the same—not to mention the Baal-worshippers) unbearably tedious. Worse, what puts me off is the dry, legalish, accounting-mentality (the first empiricists?) of it all. The stories of Jacob, Laban, Leah, Rachel, of Joseph and his brothers—they're great and all too human—but aside from the constant references to "The Lord God" either foreground or background, they are equally lacking in any sense of the spiritual (that which lies outside the realm of our senses & which is wholly awesome & mysterious to them). So it's in the context of that reading & the dissatisfactions they arouse in me that your discussion of *Zim-Zum* falls. Your psychological interpretation of Luria's answer to the rabbis puts me in mind of Wm. Blake's epigram: "He who binds to himself a joy loses it forever."[20] But I agree with your interpretation as applied to the mundane world in which people have to endure & suffer each other, whether through love or hate, is not necessarily to accept either the rabbis' question or Luria's answer. The realms of "discourse" as they call it are literally worlds apart. The rabbis' problem was & remains the Jewish view of Nature, one which "The Lord God" who "created" us gave us "dominion" over the Earth & all its creatures (Genesis)—a horrid, in my poor view, notion which by the stroke of one blow of the axe cut man off from Nature & its mysteries of which—not according to the Jewish view—man is one of, as Chuang-Tzu (one of the founders of Taoism) put it, "10,000 things." The Judaic view is: man is principal actor, fills the foreground virtually completely; everything else goes into or you might say has to be squeezed into the background. So of course the rabbis for whom their one living God fills the Universe had to find a way to ask, how come The Lord God in his Omniscient Omnipotence was able to make room for all the "10,000 things" of Chuang-Tzu (too bad they didn't know @ the Tao). And Luria as you tell me answers, by shrinking himself. Forgive me if I find the notion absurd & ludicrous. It's not only that the ancient Hebrews <u>and</u> the modern Jews had/have no physics, nor do they want it now. It's a bit like the Hassidic Jews in Israel who insist there can be no "State of Israel" without the Messiah—& of course once he comes who needs "Israel"? If "God" is the "substance" of the entire universe then why does he have to expand or contract to allow space for his creations (us included)? Under that understanding of substance he is us & we are him, "we" understood as everything literally in the world including Io, Callisto, Galileo, Europa from the smallest invisible neuron to be highest mountain imaginable. It would have to be this kind of a literal isomorphism to accommodate Luria's literality: if God shrinks himself he must do so <u>physically</u> not metaphorically. Retrogressing from that back to the original question posed by the rabbis reveals how poverty-stricken (literal-mindedness equals such a state) is the view & understanding of <u>what exists universally</u> by robbing it of its total mystery (by "mystery" I simply mean a state of things not comprehensible either by our religion(s) or science(s)). I still am unable to find a shred of reason-to-be-satisfied by the old medieval proofs of the existence of God, of the more appealing because more <u>poetic</u> imagery of Kabbalah, by the theologies of orthodoxies <u>or</u> the <u>theologies</u> of <u>science</u> (including Darwinism). I am & have always been drawn to the <u>non</u>-salvational doctrinal notions of Hinduism (their "Agni," god of universal fire closely resembles Kabbalah "sparks"), Buddhism & feel more at home with Taoist ideas than anything else. This will help you understand some of why I find Yeats so important as a great poet & artist: he refused to be pinned down to any form of rec[eive]d or existent doctrine; kept himself open to the great mysteries of the world & the human personality by "researches" in the occult (a bit dubious to be sure); he "saw" & expressed deeply in convincing language & imagery beyond his limited limitations of time, place, ethnicity et al. We're swimming in Heraclitus's waters! [...]

George

204

26 DECEMBER 1997

My dear George,

[...] You brought up <u>my</u> Lady Diotima ... Well, I plead culpable ... I was stingy with information ... once again ... This I shall remedy now.

My Diotima takes cognizance in a considerable measure of Plato's Diotima as she was made to appear in the *Symposium* in Socrates's words ... She receives a 'star' treatment there. From Musil (I well remember it, dear Friend, that it was you who first drew Musil's *A Man without Qualities* to my attention!) I only borrowed her beauty, subtleness ... etc.... Hölderlin's 'Diotima Poems'[21] came too late into the picture to play a role ... My Diotima is different from these 3 D's. I envisaged her as a psychopomp who will lead a group of 'visitors' daring to enter the 'Millennial Mall.' She will be their guide and will also enact 2 of the 'visits' ('The Scent Shop' and the 'Fashion Show'). At the work's conclusion (Section 12) she will reveal parts of her essence. The work is for mixed choir, lyric soprano solo (Diotima) and an orchestra of about 30–35 players. Without much further ado I'm enclosing a copy of the libretto, which will show you the work's theme, form and character.[22] Just one more comment: the text is maybe at times potentially upsetting for some ... If so ... I accept this ... I felt something had to be said out loudly & unequivocally, yet never without the saving grace of one, or another, kind of beauty. It will be found probing 'below the surface' of some of the most visible manifestations of our (North American) culture ... At times (see the 'Fashion Show') they dip as deep as the Torah (Genesis 6:1–4) ... There are also other echoes from times past ... I don't know how you will respond to it ... If, at all, you will want to respond ... ??

Now on to *Zim-Zum* ... You were brave to have undertaken an integral reading of the Torah. I'm yet to do this, if at all ... We have our personal ways of entering our own Jewishness (if at all relevant ...). It is a problematic exercise as Gershom Scholem, himself, has put it in a text entitled "Judaism," which is a part of the collection *Contemporary Jewish Religious Thought*. His chapter begins:

> Judaism cannot be defined according to its essence, since it has no essence. Judaism cannot therefore be regarded as a closed historical phenomenon whose development and essence came into focus by a finite sequence of historical, philosophical, doctrinal, or dogmatic judgments and statements. Judaism is rather a living entity ... Etc.[23]

To this I must add that I am not foolhardy enough to undertake a defense of the notion of *Zim-Zum* as a cosmological, and/or theosophical notion ... Scholem ventured to do something like this in his (one of his) texts written for one of the ERANOS conferences,[24] held in Ascona (Switzerland] in the 1930s. [...] G.S.'s text on this is available in English in the volume *On the Mystical Shape of the Godhead*.[25] This is heavy going, being theosophy-oriented. [...]

For my own use, I am only drawn to this concept as an early psychological formulation of a way through which to deal with certain difficult interpersonal situations ... Thus I plead guilty to limiting the word's meaning, perhaps, to the point of vulgarization. Yet it pertains to, in my mind, important moments of potential strife and eruption of hostility, if not observed ... That is all ... but still important in my experience.

As to Luria's *sefirotic* system ... it is but one of the models of an abstract symbolization of what (allegedly) the human spirit/soul was thought of consisting of. The 10 *sefirots* (in diverse combinations) were to portray, represent, even 'explain,' perhaps, the anatomy of personality, feelings, affects, propensities, and the like. It was but one (of the several) analogues and antecedents of other such schemes, of which the Freudian 'Id-Ego-Superego' three-some was a more recent reformulation. This is, really, the end of my tiny 'wisdom' of these arcana, which, nevertheless were of help and inspiration to me on occasions. [...]

Istvan

NOTES

1 Paul Boghossian, "What the Sokal Hoax Ought to Teach Us," *Times Literary Supplement*, 13 December 1996.

2 Brian Peterson (b. 1953), a former composition student of Rochberg, is a fine-art photographer and senior curator of the James A. Michener Art Museum in Doylestown, Pennsylvania. See, for example, *Pennsylvania Impressionism*, ed. Brian H. Peterson, with essays by William H. Gerdts, Brian H. Peterson, and Sylvia Yount (Doylestown, PA: James A. Michener Art Museum; Philadelphia: University of Pennsylvania Press, 2002). See also "1994," note 8.

3 "Our birth is but a sleep and a forgetting: / The Soul that rises with us, our life's Star, / Hath had elsewhere its setting, / And cometh from afar: / Not in entire forgetfulness, / And not in utter nakedness, / But trailing clouds of glory do we come / From God, who is our home: / Heaven lies about us in our infancy!" From *Ode: Intimations of Immortality from Recollections of Early Childhood* (1802–4).

4 "On the Way to *Traces*: A Dialogue with the Self," talk given at Harrison-LeCaine Hall, Queen's University, Kingston, 20 March 1996; published in Robin Elliott and Gordon E. Smith, eds., *Istvan Anhalt: Pathways and Memory* (Montreal and Kingston: McGill-Queen's University Press, 2001), 400–11.

5 Harold Bloom, *Omens of Millennium: The Gnosis of Angels, Dreams, and Resurrection* (New York: Riverhead Books, 1996).

6 See, for example, *The Quest for Certainty: A Study of the Relation of Knowledge and Action* (New York: Minton, Balch, 1929).

7 David Flusser (1917–2000), Austrian-born Israeli scholar of Biblical and Rabbinical Judaism and of Christianity. For more than fifty years he lectured in comparative religion at the Hebrew University of Jerusalem.

8 Franz Rosenzweig, *The Star of Redemption*, trans. from the 2nd ed. of 1930 by William W. Hallo (New York: Holt, Rinehart and Winston, 1971).

9 See "1989," note 1.

10 *Eden: Out of Time and Out of Space* (1997–98), chamber concerto for guitar and ensemble (violin, viola, cello, horn, clarinet, and flute), commissioned by the Chamber Music Society of Lincoln Center and Chamber Music Northwest, premiered by Chamber Music Northwest at Reed College, 2 July 1998, Eliot Fisk guitar; Fisk and the Chamber Music Society of Lincoln Center gave the New York premiere at Alice Tully Hall on 15 November 1998.

11 See Bloom, *Yeats* (New York: Oxford University Press, 1970).

12 See "1996," note 19.

13 See "1993," note 9.

14 See "1968," note 13.

15 "Polarity in Music: Symmetry and Asymmetry and Their Consequences," *Proceedings of the American Philosophical Society* 141/2 (June 1997): 169–76; reprinted in *Aesthetics of Survival*, rev. and expanded ed. (2004), 246–52.

16 Palestrina composed two motets of that title, one for four voices (1563) and one for five voices (1569).

17 Philip Longworth, *The Making of Eastern Europe* (London/New York: Macmillan/St. Martin's Press, 1992); 2nd ed., *The Making of Eastern Europe: From Prehistory to Postcommunism* (London/New York: Macmillan/St. Martin's Press, 1997).

18 The Promise Keepers is an evangelical Christian organization, founded in 1990, whose stated goal is to challenge men to "live a life wholly set apart for Almighty God." Its critics view it as authoritarian and patriarchic.

19 See "1988," note 8.

20 "He who binds to himself a joy / Does the winged life destroy; / But he who kisses the joy as it flies / Lives in eternity's sunrise." From *Eternity* (ca. 1793).

21 Plato's Diotima (from *Symposium*), who appears in many of the poems of Friedrich Hölderlin (1770–1843) as well as in his epistolary novel *Hyperion* (1792–99), is a pseudonym for Susette Gontard, the wife of a Frankfurt banker, with whom the poet had a painful platonic affair.

22 The complete libretto of *Millennial Mall (Lady Diotima's Walk)* can be found in Elliott and Smith, eds., *Pathways and Memory* (2001), 445–57; but see "1998," note 5.

23 Arthur A. Cohen and Paul Mendes-Flohr, eds., *Contemporary Jewish Religious Thought: Original Essays on Critical Concepts, Movements, and Beliefs* (New York: Scribner, 1987), 505.

24 ERANOS is a Swiss-based foundation devoted primarily to the work of Carl Jung and its legacy.

25 Gershom Scholem, *On the Mystical Shape of the Godhead: Basic Concepts in the Kabbalah*, trans. Joachim Neugroschel, ed. and rev. according to the 1976 Hebrew edition, with the author's emendations, by Jonathan Chipman (New York: Schocken Books, 1991), 82–87.

1998

205

21 MAY 1998

Dear friend Isty,

[…] It has been fairly hectic, specially the months of March into early April with perf[ormance]s of *Circles of Fire*, the 75' 2-piano work. I'll be joining Sally Pinkas and Evan Hirsch in Cincinnati in a few weeks for another perf[ormance]. (Sally called yesterday to tell me they will do it in Israel this summer at a festival, which pleases me enormously.) After Cinc[innati] I will go to Portland, Oregon for rehearsals & perf[ormance] of *Eden: Out of Time and Out of Space*, a chamber concerto for guitar and 6 players I wrote for Eliot Fisk & which he will repeat in Nov. in N[ew] Y[ork] with the Lincoln Center Chamber Society. All this of course takes its toll physically: I need lots of rest before-during-and-after. […]

What I've enclosed here, Isty, are 2 "sketches" which in another form will probably make their way into my "reflections on the art of composition & other related matters" which is very much on my mind.[1] You yourself are among the very few who have lived and worked in this insane century with a conscious awareness of its Difference and some of the reasons for it. What I want to do, if I can, is "reflect on" the way the events of our time and the aesthetics of the same time are different aspects of, more than likely, a unitary strata of men's minds & soul caught up in dread internal changes which have their outward reflection in external history as it unfolded. My place in all this: simply an individual sufferer who tried to make his way through the hail of bullets & orange/red/black flashes of mortar shells. I see all of it as war: symbolic & actual, which more readily makes understandable why I saw & see things from a totally opposite view from my blind American colleagues who were essentially counterparts of sociological number-crunchers. Also if I can manage it I want to show why the American experience of Modernism in music (& art) is another animal from the European. Not enough has been said on the subject. To me it's extremely important & explains much that has escaped attention. I hope you'll enjoy these sketches & esp[ecially] will join me in ribbing the hell out of Luigi Russolo,[2] the Apostle of Noise and Unprofessionalism (could have been John Cage's grandfather!!) […]

George

206

15 JUNE 1998

My dear George,

Just a few weeks before your 80th birthday is piped in with, I hope, all the smiles, hugs and happy words from family and friends … Let me, let us (since Bea joins me in this), join this joyous assembly celebrating you: You … You … You? Who is this 'you'? Who are all the individual 'You'-s? Self-evident, yet ever so elusive notion this … With others I came to view all our 'you-ness' in terms of human interchange … series of interchanges embedded in the thick layers of memory … And so, my dear friend, you are forever (i.e., as long as the 'I' persists) a very important part of my notion of my 'world' … in fact, you occupy in it a special space … all supported by the memories that bind us together … Memory? Yes … also 'truth' … I have come to believe that the notion of 'truth' being embedded in 'memory' (an old old notion this!) has much to offer … Very recently I learned (serendipitously, of course) that the notion of 'truth' (to the Greeks ca. 8th-c[entury] B.C.E.) *aletheia* was almost synonymous with memory. And what about 'untruth,' lying, deception, trickery, well … this they called (I'm sure you have known it much before I stumbled on it) *lethe*, i.e., darkness, the underworld, forgetfulness … If lying, not-remembering is *lethe*, truth, on the other hand, is its converse: *aletheia*. Simple, isn't it … and also (for me at least) breathtakingly beautiful … All our memories, questings, relating, etc., are, if this holds water, in the service of 'truth' … And what about the old Anglo-Saxon words: 'truth,' 'true,' both related to an old Sanskrit word meaning "tree." Another metaphor-word that one with all its branching and root system … Where [does] all this leave us? In the beautiful garden of metaphors shedding fleeting rays of light on the most elusive notion of all: the mind, our particular 'I'-s and 'You'-s who can in rare instance[s] of my notion of my 'world' ... in fact, you occupy in it a special space ... all supported by the memories that bind us together ... Memory?. Yes ... also 'truth' ... I have come to believe that the notion of 'truth' being embedded in 'memory' (an old-old notion this!) has much to offer ... (Very recently I learned (serendipitously of course) that the notion of 'truth' (to the Greeks *ca.* 8th c. B.C.E.) *aletheia* was almost synonymous with *memory.* And what about 'un-truth', lying, deception, trickery, well ... this they called ('I'm sure you have known it much before I stumbled on it) *lethe* i.e. darkness, the under-world, forget –

Page of a letter from Anhalt to Rochberg (15 June 1998). Paul Sacher Foundation, Basel, Switzerland.

meet (the 'meeting of minds') and when such a meeting of 2 minds (let's call this M2M, if this is not too cute ...) persists over, let's see, 35 years, which you & I managed to sustain, there is a particularly good reason to celebrate ... to celebrate one of the pairs who reached the beautiful threshold of 4 score years and reached it in such a splendid command of mind as yours is quite obviously, both musico-poetically as well as a composer of the thought-filled text …

This brings me to the 2 papers of yours which you sent me along with your May 21 letter. The one in which you 'take on' old Luigi Russolo … well he richly deserved to be singled out as a contributor to our sonically (& foolishly) overloaded world. But, here I must add, without 'absolving' L.R. from what you attribute to him, that I think he is, today, only a 'bit-player,' though a prominent enough one, in the total scene, in which the major players are those who clamor (only partly a figure of speech this) for ever faster transportation (just think of the decibel level of jet planes taking off!) for ever faster individual cars and motorbikes (*vide* the aficionados of the ubiquitous 'formula' races … etc.) and the libido-driven young, yearning to congregate in Woodstock-like Dionysiac festivals by the 100,000s! All that requires amplification, […] filling the air with sound masses of the kind old Luigi could have only dreamt of … But, yes you are right, the futurist lot, Marinetti[3] and his cohorts, were real Pied Pipers dragging the gullible toward euphoria, and thus anaesthetized them while they dragged each other toward destruction … (You, of course, recall the wonderfully horrible painting of one of the Breughels: 'The blind leading the blind'[4] … Well at the head of that line, invisible to the spectator, is a nameless '*meneur*' who misleads, who corrupts for whatever reason …).

Enough of all the above, but this is truth and as such requires remembering …

Your other paper about 'burs' is a telling essay about artistic integrity from which 'originality'(???) might spring … Bravo!

The enclosed is a new ending to my *Millennial Mall* text.[5] In it Diotima lifts her veil and allows us a peak into some of the deeper recesses of her mind/heart … After having been our 'psychopomp' in the course of this dangerous descent (or 'incursion') she proposes elements of an alternate view on life, the self, the lines/bonds that bind 'selves' (like friends, for ex[ample]) together and also suggests hints how to be at peace with the 'nearby' as well as with the 'great beyond' … I offer this, her lines, as a modest present to you, my very dear George, dear friend, on your 80th birthday with the belief that in the years to come more beautiful music will flow from your pen and, your words, too, to come, will continue to nourish and sustain our friendship. […]

Istvan

207

26 JUNE 1998

Dear old Friend Isty,

What a wonderful birthday letter from you on my return from Cincinnati. The love and warmth of it, unbelievably beautiful—for which I thank you with all my heart. Whether it is deserved is another matter; but deserved or not I accept it since it comes from you and is already a sign of the durability of our by now long friendship, those long years in which for both of us much has happened to bring pain and some joy, works produced, life changes, somehow you & Bea, me & Gene able to absorb all the shocks of change, to right ourselves each time and find the strength to go on, to continue.

This Monday I leave for Portland, Oregon to supervise rehearsals and stay for the 1st and 2nd perf[ormance]s July 2/3 & then home of *Eden: Out of Time and Out of Space* which I wrote for Eliot Fisk—more a chamber work than a "concerto" though I do call it a chamber concerto for guitar & 6 instruments (flute, clarinet, horn, vln, vla, c). A quiet work, reflective, introverted. From it one could never deduce the insanity & noise of the "real" world out there where Lady Diotima wanders thru The Mall. After delivering myself (this is back in Cincinnati!) of no uncertain views of the depredations of noise (Luigi Russolo's Cult of Noise *cum* "unprofessionalism") on music and our contemporary culture in general, when it was over one young doomed hopeful came up to me to declare "I think noise is beautiful." (Who am I to tell him he's wrong? Today all "opinions" are valid.) […]

I'm planning to do some resurrection of some early piano music—editing rather than rewriting—don't want to bring anything "up to date"—principally an ancient "2nd piano sonata" which I'd retired permanently (so I thought) but it began knocking on my door—I heard faint cries of "let me out"—we'll see what we shall see.[6] […]

George

208

22 SEPTEMBER 1998

My dear George,

[…] Bea will be 75 come next February, and our little family of 9 plans a 'magnum celebration,' also because of my own milestone, Carol's 45th, and Bea's 60th & my 50th anniversary of arrival in this country, Canada.

Millennial Mall (Lady Diotima's Walk) will be dedicated to Bea, Helen and Carol. But I'm doubtful that I am (shall be) able to complete its near 1,500-bars-long score in the course of the summer of '99. (2 weeks ago I completed the 2nd version—quite detailed this—of the short score and, as in the past, the next stage is the 'final' review and orchestration.) I have fussed with the text until even a few days ago. I'm discovering implications, which managed even until now to remain below the threshold of consciousness, only to be ferreted out through the imperative intervention of a new thought/connection that materialized seemingly from 'nowhere,' but, of course one knows that it is not so … the inner battle of suppression of the deep insight into the self is resistant to revelation, until something says: "stop dissembling," stop averting your glance from a difficult-to-face condition, or ambivalence, or complexity of whatever nature … Something(?) then forces oneself to 'face the music,' literally and metaphorically (or, rather, in the reverse order … these …). As you can gather I am quite engrossed in this enterprise, because it came to me (i.e., the undertaking to tackle this topic) rather (and apparently) so unexpectedly after the writing of *Traces (Tikkun)*. Now all is obvious: I had to face up to the hedonistic, quasi-Greco-Roman, attitude, world's, powerful presence in our own chronotope, and how it coexists with one's (mine!) rather idiosyncratic combination of a monotheistic *cum* cosmic worldview. The cost of this 'amalgamation,' or whatever a good word for it may be, is the feeling of the dual tug of ambivalence … Yes, this might be a way to characterize the cost (price) of the relative inner peace … One other aspect of the attraction *Millennial Mall* has for me is that it has compelled me to see our 'world' (chronotope) in a diachronic way, also. Thus the figure of Aphrodite (I hear that more figurines, statues, to her are extant than the number of all those depicting other goddesses!) surfaces as Diotima, the pyschopomp, & enacts the scene of the 'Scent Shop' & that of the 'Fashion Show.' This can be also seen as tying in with the Bill Clinton/Monica L[ewinsky] saga/soap opera … But I should take back this flippant 'soap-opera' allusion, because I sense some very old, and basic, sentiments (better: 'drives') being re-enacted here … Bea suggests that the world (i.e., man) didn't change since the time of Ishtar even of Innunnu … Monica, the driven huntress, rejected by her beloved, is on the warpath (an Artemis, if she cannot be a triumphant Aphrodite!) and endeavors to betray & crush the male who managed to resist, and eventually, jilt her … Please forgive this amateurish dipping into mythology … but I sense this story is fueled by ever so elemental passions … By the way, Clinton comes through all this very well (at the least: well enough …)

indeed. He appears to us as an appealing human being (fallible according to the Judeo-Christian code, perhaps) one with a very good mind, grace under pressure, self control, + + … Our hypocritical, mediocre prime minister Jean Chrétien, comes off rather poorly in comparison, I must say. Should one dream of 'trading'? What? We can only hope for better political leaders, but, alas, in vain. Our last prime minister of 'quality' was Pierre Trudeau. All those who followed were mediocre, self-serving, ineffectual, silly, in various combinations, with the result of what we are having here now. […]

As you, I'm also 'resurrecting' (rewriting) some older works. My *3 Songs of Love*, originally written for a 3-part *a cappella* women's choir, has 'sprouted' the addition of 2 woodwind (flute, clar[inet]) parts, and the new-old work will be premiered in the coming spring, among other expected developments.[7] All this keeps me happily occupied … although I need more sleep than before. […]

Istvan

209

10 OCTOBER 1998

Dear old friend,

I sent off this a.m. a note to Timothy Maloney, to Alan Gillmor & to yourself—all in connection w[ith] Alan's grand project. This is the first part of a longer letter to try to catch up—before I take off for Boston on Wed. the 14th.[8] My feelings @ that resemble the old cliché "the calm before the storm"—the storm itself, as you can imagine having lived through it yourself many times, occasioned by the rehearsals, the performance—& in this instance add recording sessions, all of it calculable in quanta(?) of nervous energy and their effect upon the glands & hormones. You know the rest. The program itself is a deliberate mix of atonal & tonal & in-between works: *The Cheltenham Concerto* ('58), strictly 12-tone, for 15 players—the title which I now regret only because an "arts center" in Cheltenham, PA, suburb of Phila[delphia], paid me the glorious sum of $50.00 American greenbacks to write it (why memorialize it?); followed by *Cantio Sacra* ('53) a transcription of chorale organ variations of Samuel Scheidt for small orch[estra] (the 1st conductor said it had a real "Brahms sound"); then comes *Black Sounds* (*Sonidos Negros*), title after a phrase of Garcia Lorca, from 1965, non-12-tone but savagely atonal & harsh for 17 brass & winds; ending with my near-tonal monodrama from 1974, *Phaedra*, with text put together by Gene from Rob[er]t

Lowell's "verse translation" of Racine's *Phèdre* for mezzo & orchestra. None of these works which I still like for one reason or another—or think I do right now; maybe I'll change my mind after next week—has been performed for the past 25 to possibly 45 years, unexplainable on the face of it & I think pretty much in most composer's lives "par" for the course. Like all the unpredictables & incalculables in this existence I see these as "givens" of a kind & therefore refuse to take on bitterness over their fate. As to that, I could say the same about almost all my large orchestral works, the 6 symphonies included—none of which have seen the light of day for many years, in some cases counting in decades. The grand exception is the Oct. 16th perf[ormance] of my 5th [Symphony] by Victor Yampolsky with the Northwestern Univ[ersity] Symph[ony] Orch[estra] coming up. He called me, very open, warmhearted, full of enthusiasm last spring to announce he was going to do it. Of course I was pleased & said so. But to be perfectly frank I'd be a hell of a lot more pleased if it were [a] major orch[estra], etc. But as you've probably guessed & know from a long time ago I am not one who believes in manipulating events & destinies. We both know the type—in America they exist in clumps & clusters like grapes on vines but don't make good wine when put through the works. You can't change life habits; so now at the beginning of my 9th decade on this mysterious, unaccountable planet I prefer to continue in my old ways & attitudes.

Speaking of which, what a pleasure, even something resembling a state close to a kind of joy, I have found an intellectual thinker unbelievably close to my essentially dark, pessimistic, realist views of what we humans experience, nay, better put, more often than not <u>inflict</u> on ourselves willfully & with malice aforethought. I am speaking of Isaiah Berlin whom I've heard of most of my life but never bothered to read because the people who generally refer to him rarely convey what he really is saying. I am reading, leapfrog-style, two collections of essays, the first *The Crooked Timber of Humanity* (title comes from a fuller sentence of Kant which goes on to say "from which nothing straight can come") and the second *Russian Thinkers*.[9] In essence Berlin makes powerful arguments for anti-monist answers; the usual fare delivered to mankind, that is, the <u>monist</u> views, by rabbis, priests, theologians, rationalists of all kinds, scientists (but not all), lots of theoretically oriented academics being Berlin's nemesis. His "pluralism" as he calls it viewed vs. the background of monism in all its forms & guises comes off looking quite (and paradoxically) "rational" because he thinks so clearly, writes so succinctly, with a real bite. His essay on "The Apotheosis of the Romantic Will" is almost

works. You can't change life habits;
So now at the beginning of my 9th decade
on this mysterious, unaccountable planet I
prefer to continue in my old ways & attitudes.
Speaking of which, what a pleasure, even
something resembling a state close to a kind
of joy I have found an intellectual
thinker unbelievably close to my essentially
dark, pessimistic, realist views of what we
humans experience, nay, rather put, more
often than not <u>inflict</u> on ourselves
wilfully & with malice aforethought. I
am speaking of Isaiah Berlin whom I've
heard of most of my life but never bothered
to read because the people who generally
refer to him rarely convey what he really
is saying. I am reading, leap-frog style,

Page of a letter from Rochberg to Anhalt (10 October 1998). Library and Archives Canada.

a shock, esp[ecially] if as you read you think of so-called Romantic music as written by a Brahms, a Wagner, or Berlioz … Makes me want to proclaim to the world: "*Ich bin nicht romantisch*" (bad German no doubt, but you get my drift). There is an essay basically on Tolstoy which Berlin calls "The Hedgehog & the Fox." That's a remarkable piece of writing—and therefore thinking. Following a saying of an ancient Greek poet Archilocus, "the fox knows many things, the hedgehog only one," he sets out to "prove" that basically Tolstoy was a fox but yearned desperately to be a hedgehog. He traces out the process of transformation & the contradictions & paradoxes that drove crazy Leo (and drove him crazy). I'm going to have to backtrack to *The Crooked Timber* for the very lengthy essay on Joseph de Maistre, apparently the intellectual founder of Fascism, to get a better grasp of Berlin's telling his reader that Tolstoy was deeply influenced by Maistre(!) I always knew Tolstoy to be uniquely crazy, *pozzo*, *verrückt*, but proto-fascist?—never. So I need to look more deeply. 'Specially as America right now, this very minute, is full of new-style, American-style fascists who are running the impeachment proceedings vs. poor Clinton. As we say, he really blew it.

Next day, Oct. 11, Sunday: starting to get ready to leave Wed. Took out my red toilet articles kit (getting beat up after all these years) and a suitcase. Will start filling them slowly. In these pre-stages of a trip I start feeling pangs of anxiety, apprehension, 'specially now 'cause Gene is not coming w[ith] me but will follow on Saturday. Below this surface tension(?), other feelings brought on by reading the *N[ew] Y[ork] Times*. No good news there; & didn't expect it. More signs all the time of the growing tide of theo-politics, i.e., politics dominated by theology, God-talk, God-fear, God-propitiation gestures. The American variety practiced & put forward by right-wingers & Republican conservatives is pale next to Islamic & Hassidic fundamentalisms, but shares some of the same motivations: reversion to God-dominated, doctrinal religions & theological ways of conducting LIFE. Naturally the same impulse, depending on strength of inner need & compulsion, surfaces & takes on the coloration of each external culture & the history connected w[ith] it. I'm glad to be closer than farther away from the end; that way I will not live and see the coming-into-existence of thoroly hateful forms of living taking over the USA.

MONDAY, OCTOBER 12

Well, I'm half packed. I feel an increasing reluctance to pick myself up and go, to jump into the maelstrom. What I wanted to talk a little about is my reaction to the music which paralleled—in this case you can't say "accompanied"—a fascinating dance by a Japanese woman and her company based on the *Tale of Genji* we saw last week. Hearing the traditional high flutes, the *sho* (a kind of pentatonic cluster in high register played I believe on a panpipes instrument of a kind), *shamisen*, *kotos*, drums, hearing the piercing flutes, harsh-accented string attacks, the melancholy of it all spreading into every nook and cranny of my head and reminded me once again of what I first felt back in 1973–74 when I first began to listen to Japanese traditional music, especially the *shakuhachi*—what a wonderful mournful sound it makes; and what it was I felt all over again is the impersonal or nonpersonal (in Western terms) nature of it. Also its essential slowness—very much like *Noh* drama itself which is wonderfully slow (very hard for most Caucasians to relate to it, but not me I must say); if it's possible to use such a term, this music has a "cosmic" quality, not attached to Earth, earthy feelings and experiences of individuals. It leaves behind all the business of Western historical "style" consciousness: this is classical, this is modern, this is tonal, this is minimal, this is atonal, serial, *ad infinitum*. And all of it having to do with a moment in cultural time (1750s, 1830s, the 1960s) perceived by and projected back through personal refractions. When it's first-rate we can then say "Beethoven" or "Mahler" or "Schoenberg" or what have you; but it's always representative, an echo of an individual ego and soul. Whereas Japanese music manages at its best to sound far removed from the states of individualized feeling and rise to something far more impersonal, as though "the voice of man" is being uttered or the species, "man," is being sounded at its deepest core. And in its presence my own being opens up, feels the tensions of its own life melt away into something larger. What did Freud call it: "oceanic feeling"? Rarely does that occur in Western music. The Adagio of Beethoven's Ninth, yes. The *Tema* of the *Goldberg Variations* of J.S. Bach, yes. And so on. […]

George

NOTES

1 Rochberg, "Talking to Luigi Russolo 85 Years Later" (1998), unpublished ms., and "About Music and *Burs*" (1998), unpublished ms., both in Anhalt Fonds MUS 164/B2,139.

2 Luigi Russolo (1885–1947), Italian artist and composer best remembered for his 1913 "futurist manifesto" *L'arte dei rumori* [The Art of Noises].

3 Filippo Tomasso Marinetti (1876–1944), Egyptian-born Italian writer, one of the chief ideologues of the futurist movement of the early twentieth century.

4 The reference is to *The Parable of the Blind Leading the Blind* (1568), by Pieter Brueghel the Elder (ca. 1525–69).

5 This revised ending is incorporated into the libretto printed in Robin Elliott and Gordon E. Smith, eds., *Istvan Anhalt: Pathways and Memory* (Montreal and

Kingston: McGill-Queen's University Press, 2001), 445–57; see also Anhalt, "About the Libretto of *Millennial Mall (Lady Diotima's Walk)* in ibid., 457–64, esp. 464n1.

6 Rochberg is referring to Sonata No. 2 for Piano (1948, revised 1949) (unpublished), which he revised in 1998 as *Sonata Seria.*

7 *Three Songs of Love* (1951), for SSA chorus, on a text of Walter de la Mare and folk poetry, was revised in 1997, when the parts for flute and clarinet were added.

8 Rochberg's 80th year was celebrated with performances of a number of his works in centres across the United States, from Pennsylvania and New England to Arizona and Oregon. Of special note is the Boston Modern Orchestra Project under the direction of Gilbert Rose, which, under the rubric of "forescore(s) & forward: George Rochberg at eighty," presented, in Boston's Jordan Hall on 17 October 1998, a performance of the *Cheltenham Concerto*, *Cantio Sacra*, *Black Sounds*, and *Phaedra*, with mezzo-soprano Mary Nessinger, preceded by a pre-concert symposium with the composer and moderator Steven Ledbetter.

9 Isaiah Berlin, *The Crooked Timber of Humanity: Chapters in the History of Ideas*, ed. Henry Hardy (London: John Murray, 1990); *Russian Thinkers*, ed. Henry Hardy and Aileen Kelly (London: Hogarth Press, 1978).

1999

210

10 FEBRUARY 1999

George, dear Friend,

The faint dull thud that shook some of the windowpanes in your house on this past Monday (the 8th), which you might have(?) noticed and located as to source coming from a distant northern *locus* ... well ... it possibly was caused by the millstone that fell of[f] my back as I wrote the final note in the full score of *Millennial Mall (Lady Diotima's Walk)*. It was in the late afternoon and Bea just came into my workroom. I asked her to fetch the camera and snap a picture, or two, of the 'event' that came considerably earlier than I hoped for it even in my more optimistic days ... But here it was as the 'end-play' of an accelerating progress; as if 'stuff' penned beforehand would have dictated the still 'outstanding,' i.e., missing, notes. By that time the pattern was familiar and expected: I had to 'operate' on what I thought was the final version of the short score ... Hell, it was! To the end I kept on inventing the stuff as a consequence of yet earlier changes ... But by that time the sleepwalking instinct took over and the 'thing' just appeared to propel itself forward ... I'm convinced you must be chuckling now ... telling me with a smile: "Friend, what else is new?" End of this euphoric account ... Thanks, for bearing with me ... Oh yes ... the 'vital figures' are: 1250 bars, 240 pages of full score for 1 solo soprano, full choir, chamber choir (6 solo voices) and orchestra (2, 2, 2, 2; 2, 2, 2; 2 perc., keyboard, harp and strings (6, 4, 3, 3, 2). Prospects for performance? Nothing definite yet, but some 'nibbles' from Toronto (as usual from the CBC, plus, a fine chorus also in Toronto). The decisive factor will be the approval of a production budget of at least $60,000 plus ca. $20,000 for the copyists. This is big bucks up here right now. The arts being the bottom item on the totem pole of priorities for our present money-crazed, dumbed-down (as to the humanities) government ... But then this comes close to the theme of *Millennial Mall*, and why I was egged on to write it in the first place. [...]

Istvan

211

2 MARCH 1999

My dear Isty,

It's been an up-and-down time & finally I'm able to scratch off a few lines. A more fulsome epistle is waiting to come forth. Lots to talk about. But principally for now, bravo & endless congrats on tenacity, purpose, strength of mind & will to bring your *Millennial Walk* to a conclusion. I hope "they" come up with the money for materials & production. That's the least they can do for an old general like you! Gene & I took in—it's the only way I can put it—*Moses und Aron* of Schoenberg. Saw/heard at the Met[ropolitan] in N[ew] Y[ork]. Orchestra exemplary; Moses chanted remarkably, Aron sang convincingly, the chorus *qua* chorus was really fantastic. But I felt immediately the great & terrible irony: a work composed 1930–32 by a nominal Lutheran who reconverts 1933 to Judaism in the language (German) of the monsters who set about destroying all the Jews (not to mention others) they can, said work performed to great acclaim (at least in N[ew] Y[ork]) long after the horrors of the Holocaust & sung in the very German of Hitler & his version of "Murder Inc." Frankly, it makes me shudder.

I am proofreading my old/new *Sonata Seria* for solo piano, 1948 resurrected & revised 1998. Tying up some loose ends. *3 Elegiac Pieces* for piano next.[1] After that, don't know (the don't know signifies powerful degrees of uncertainty @ 1) whether to take up a new big project; 2) if so, which of 2? That's more or less what the next letter's about. [...]

George

212

19 MARCH 1999

Dear George, dear Friend,

[...] Now with the new work (*M[illennial] M[all] (L[ady] D[iotima]'s W[alk])* complete I'm looking after a backlog of this and that, to make some order on an imaginary 'desk.' I need some emptiness, figuratively, in order to feel the next response to an 'emptiness,' not to dramatize it with words like: "*horror vacui*" ... There is no "*horror vacui*," since memory rushes in and 'floods' the 'empty' spaces ... [...]

Yes *Moses und Aron* ... a very strong, beautifully written work ... The only time we saw/heard it was ca. 6 years ago in the Frankfurt Opera. The orchestra, the chorus, Aron, the setting were superb, and also the Israeli conductor, whose name escapes me now ... The performer of Moses's part was less convincing. His use of the *Sprechstimme* came through as 2nd best to Aron's Italianate *bel canto*. I would like to hear from you a few additional words of the 'Moses' you heard in N[ew] Y[ork]. The very simple staging in Frankfurt consisted of a thrust-forward apron stage area, with a background resembling a medium-high apartment-building façade, with closely spaced rows of windows, in every one of which stood a singer from the choir. The effect was that of the 'tenants' of a large building observing the goings-on 'below' and commenting on it.

Speaking of readings, I managed to 'enter' a few books already. H. Akenson (a Queen's historian)'s book on the Bible and Talmud: *Surpassing Wonder* (I think) is the title.[2] It is a tome, commenting on a vast body of scholarly literature related to the topics. [...] Akenson believes that the Bible is the work of a single super-editor/historian. At one point Akenson makes a bold parallel between the then hegemony of Greek culture, commerce, etc. over the Eastern Mediterranean (+ +) world, way into Anatolia, Syria, Judea, Egypt, Iraq, Iran and beyond, and its clash with 'native' 'local' cultures, and local elites, and the present global thrust of the U.S.A. popular culture/global commerce, which is eliciting similar reaction in certain local elites. [...] Egged on by Akenson I wanted to have a more focused account about the Judaic–Hellenic struggle between say: 350 B.C.E. and 70 C.E. I found it in Martin Hengel's (a Tübingen scholar) book *Judaism and Hellenism*, a detailed and properly footnoted account of this clash of cultures seen from a so-to-say neutral perspective.[3] What Hengel presents about, say, the Hellenic educational system, including the role of the *gymnasia* is truly revealing. By implication the parallels with our North American world are worthy of very serious consideration. (*Vide* Akenson again.) Also this body of study strengthens my then gut feeling which pushed me to undertake the composition of *Millennial Mall*. I think you might find it worth your while to look into parts of M. Hengel's book.

Another find: in a very recent issue of the *T[imes] L[iterary] S[upplement]* there is a lengthy review of the newly appeared correspondence between Martin Heidegger (the man with the post-1945 silence about his Nazi past) and Hannah Arendt his former graduate student/lover in Göttingen before the Nazi period, and his friend again after 1950.[4] The reviewer: George Steiner, no less ... In this review Steiner refers to Heidegger's notion: "*entgegen schweigen*" ... remaining silent 'against,' or 'in the face of something.' Now this set off a loud bell in my head! Wasn't [it] this idea, precisely, that fuelled me as I was conceiving of, and composed, my *Sonance•Resonance (Welche Töne?)*? "*Welche Töne?*" A question relating to the Beethovenian opening: "*O Freunde! Nicht dieses Töne!*" ... The Heideggerian transformation elicits other, 'unanswered,' questions ... Why the silence? Of course in Heidegger's case one is tempted to guess ... With some hope of success ... Other silences might be more difficult to fathom.

Another 'find' is the Bulgarian-born Sephardic writer Elias Canetti. Have you ever had reason to 'check him out'? His autobiographical text (which gives an account of his first 15 years) is a worthwhile read, allowing an insight into the world of an extended wealthy Sephardic family, first in Bulgaria, later in Western Europe.[5] The book (whose title escapes me ... it is back in the library) interestingly parallels the biography of Sir Isaiah Berlin by Michael Ignatieff.[6] Here is the son of a well-to-do Eastern European (Latvian) Ashkenazi family (dynasty) with links to one of the greatest Hassidic rabbis (I think Schneur Zalman,[7] if memory serves well) who ended up in the highest circles in Britain, as one knows ... It is a well-written biography after a 'slow' start. [...]

Istvan

213

31 MARCH 1999

Isty old friend,

[...] Your pointers in the direction of Hellenistic studies reminded me of Arnaldo Momigliano's *Alien Wisdom*, a set of lectures on the relations between the Greeks, Romans, Jews, Celts and Iranians (Persians).[8] Momigliano is an Italian Jew from northern Italy. Chessie did some work with him when she was getting her degree & became friends with him; writes English wonderfully well (just for that his lectures are worth reading); is a tough-minded historian & doesn't play favorites. Seems everybody including the Jews wanted to be able to speak & write Greek but the Greeks weren't interested in anyone else's language or culture. You might find it profitable to read him. The dedication to his mother is very touching. It reads: *Per mia madre presente sempre nel suovigile amore (Torino 1884—campo nazista di sterminio 1943)*. How he escaped the Nazis I have no idea, or for that matter the *Fascisti*. I read a book of his where he talks about the Jews of Italy in the time of Mussolini. I was not satisfied with his treatment of the subject. Which brings me to Heidegger. I'm still unable to separate, as some are, the man from the work. Heidegger became the chancellor or rector of the Univ[ersity] of Freiburg & immediately fired all the Jews on the faculty including I gather one of his best friends. That is truly a man with heart. As for Hannah Arendt: she must have been a serious problem to herself to know what she knew about Heidegger & then to excuse him, explain him away so to speak because she "loved" him still. You must know by now, old friend, I harbor very great doubts about the efficacy & rightness of "the intellectual." More rotten political ideas which have caused the death of millions have been supported by "intellectuals" so-called than is healthy for us to know about. It makes you very suspicious of "high" intelligence. Raymond Aron in France got it right & wouldn't let Sartre & his ilk off the hook vis-à-vis their Stalinism.[9] Robert McNamara[10] is now going around the world mea culpa-ing over how he got us into the Vietnam War, him & his buddies & the "Domino Theory." What were all the "professors" of Germany & Austria & Italy & Spain doing between 1933 (& even earlier) & 1945? Albert Camus if you recall started his *The Rebel* [1951] with: "No means yes." A more succinct statement of the refusal of heartless wrong-headedness I don't know. Camus refused to go along with Sartre. The boys in New York who started up *Partisan Review* & kept it going for years were all Trotskyites: also wrongheaded.[11] I knew a bunch of Trotskyites at age 19–21/22 in college. Brilliant, every one of them. What was wrong with the Soviet Union was that it didn't follow Trotsky but Stalin instead. At 20 I played one summer in the famous "Borscht-belt" at a small hotel "resort" (for middle-class Jewish "capitalists" & their families). The father of the woman who owned it, an old Communist (read Bolshevik) named Sklar, used to try to convince me (every day almost it seemed) that it was better to kill 10,000 anti-Bolsheviks in order to save 10,000,000 Russians, i.e., good, solid, Soviet citizens (whom we found out later from Solzhenitsyn [*The Gulag Archipelago* (1973)] were miserable, besotted by vodka; BUT: God-fearing. So even a writer like him can be & is wrong though somewhere else he seems to be right). Anyhow, I skirmished with Sklar and would never give in—even out of "respect" for the fool's age.

For the present, after reworking an ancient Sonata for piano solo, vintage 1949, into a more satisfactory version as *Sonata Seria* and writing *3 Elegiac Pieces* for piano, the first two also reworkings of old things, I am "resting" from writing music—but not from writing. This week I completed a first draft of the first (presumably) section (or chapter) of a memoir which of course will have autobiographical elements inevitably but whose real subject are the performers who have played my music. That tack allows me to talk about works I've written in nontechnical ways but geared to what I was thinking, why I was, what was going on, why I agreed, why I didn't, even to who said what that might still be worth looking back on & whether it still holds. Also of course I talk about musicians, their stories & attitudes, how they related to my work. I had occasion in this first section to talk about Varèse coming to Stratford in 1960 (remember?) & what he said to me after he heard my *Duo Concertante* which endeared him to me forever. The first section centers around Szell and his doing my Second Symphony which brought with it a flood of memories of the time before the war, our living in New York, the anxieties & fear of that time mixed up with being young & all that goes with being young, at least as I remember it. This is going to be a long haul because there's lots to write about. But then comes the fashioning it into decent English, graspable shape, and subjecting it to hard scrutiny to make sure no narcissism creeps in. By then I should be on my way to 84/85. Publishing? Don't know what lies ahead there. Don't esp[ecially] have "nice" feelings on the subject considering I've drawn a blank with every try to interest a publisher in bringing out a new & revised (amplified) addition of the "old" *Aesthetics of Survival*. And "Chromaticism" still is lying on the shelf, all 900 pages of it. So I'm not sanguine. Nevertheless I will write the memoir so long as health & strength hold out. […]

George

214

14 APRIL 1999

My dear George,

An initial admission to start with: words will fail me as I shall try to give you a feel of my response to hearing this afternoon your 3rd & 4th string quartets[12] … yet try I must … I recalled parts of your 3rd from an earlier hearing, but the opening mo[vemen]t & the finale asserted themselves as a 'first hearing' … I don't know how this response took shape over the years. But this is neither here nor there … What does matter is the sheer daemonic virtuosity of the opening and closing movements of the 3rd. This is great stuff, George, and shows you in all your intensity, integrity and originality. Now, much of the 'lyrical' rest is not less of a 'white-heat' stuff, but the language is thousands of miles/years distant from the 'framing' statements. Your Ukrainian-Jewish forebears (Cernovcy or Kiev perhaps ...), parts of Mahler, Musil's Kakania, via the transposing memory of G.R. (you!), are here singing their hearts out. These are the 2 'transcended' *loci* of your psycho-geography, my eloquent friend, as you kept on pouring out your soul via these 4 strings, which sound (now, in retrospect!) ... how to put it, a Rochbergian cross between several Viennas and several Shtetels of the Pale of Settlement. Wouldn't you have liked to eavesdrop on, say, Schneur Zalman of Liadi's small *schul*? Another Jewish writer whom your music in the 3rd conjured up to me is Joseph Roth. Have you read his *The Radetsky March*?[13] You might want to check it out. The one aspect of your 3rd for which I have not found, as yet, a 'key' (but which I 'hear' as being centrally/essentially you) is the stylistic 'no-man's land' between your 2 dominant stylistic *limens*. But this doesn't prevent me from being all along with you as you sing out your eloquent, moving, lyrical song, dear Friend. Much of the foregoing fits somehow the 4th quartet also, despite the obviously different 'agenda' here. All told: these works will last as partial strong portraits of you, dear friend. [...]

Just 2 more items ... Some people here tried to obtain federal (money) support for bringing out on 3 CD's my 3, performed, operas. (Only the 1st, *La Tourangelle*, exists on LP's.)[14] The outcome so far is negative. To depict the discouraging (political) background is useless here, and bad for the digestion. All this is a phenomenon of the overall dumbing-down process, I cannot resist opining here ... On the other hand, there are some hopeful (or rather hope-inspiring) noises about the feasibility (likelihood?) of a late year 2000 premiere of *Millennial Mall (Lady Diotima's Walk)*. We'll see ... Now let me turn to your most recent letter ...

Momigliano ... Yes I met his name in references in books dealing with the encounter of Judaism and Hellenism. But I haven't as yet tried to read him. Perhaps one day ... Now about the 'Greeks' (a huge container this, of course!) attitude to others ... I am at the Kindergarten level of comprehension of this huge issue. But I have already learned to my surprise that Alexander the Great, after having beaten Darius the 3rd time over, gave evidence of respect, trust, and even (a grudging? or other kind?) of admiration for his erstwhile enemy the Persians. The result: he decided (also, or mainly, for political reasons?) (1) to marry a Persian princess, (2) advise (compel?) 20,000(!) of his Macedonian officers (soldiers?) to marry Persian women, (3) enlisted Persian cavalry in his army, (4) employed Persian palace guards in his own protection. Now, this hasn't gone over very smoothly with his 'own' people, yet he persisted. Now there is a Greek word for this as I've found out: *eunoia*, meaning goodwill, kindness, a gift in token of goodwill. The word *eunomia* means good order, *eunomos* denotes 'under good laws'; *eunoos* denotes 'well-minded, well-disposed, friendly' ... All these indicate the converse of what is behind 'ethnic cleansing,' a process aiming, at horrendous costs, at the attainment of racial, or ethnic, 'purity,' an illusionary thing to begin with. Yesterday it was Bosnia. Today it is Kosovo. I shudder to think what tomorrow might bring. The remedy? That is also an unpalatable bitter pill or worse: NATO attacks. We are not allowed (or should not be allowed) to forget that WW I started in the Balkan powder keg, in Sarajevo. How much further danger must the world endure while parts of Europe still try to cope with the last residues of the Turkish incursion into the Balkans in the 15th century?! (Kosovo's history, according to an Oxbridge historian, reaches back to the 1400s!)[15]

I was interested (very) to read that you had known some fellow students, Trotskyites, in their late teens, early twenties, at the close of the '30s. Aftershocks of the financial collapse in the early years of the decade? Perhaps ... perhaps not. Your picturesque reference to your stint in the "Borsch-belt" (Catskills, perhaps ...) From experience—serendipitous—we learned that the "Borsch-belt" is still a functional reality ... Which is okay. Why shouldn't elderly Jews of modest means go there to eat, loll, play cards, and watch schlocky TV with their brethren/sisters for 2–3 weeks at a go? ... PS: I would love to read a detailed description of young G.R. playing (the piano?) for cold cash in the Borscht-belt, arguing with Sklar and doing/experiencing other things ... before joining the U.S. army to risk his neck to defeat Hitler (which you, dear Friend, managed to do in time!) to contribute positively to my own chances of survival. (Sometimes, then, *in illo tempore*, I thought you might have hurried up a little but this was just a wish ... I did feel that you tried to move east, to liberate me from a minor version of hell, as expeditiously as possible! The outcome speaks (spoke!) volumes in our letters: you made it and I, also, made it. Well, it is time to have put this in writing, dear friend!

I'm delighted that you have undertaken to write a memoir of the nature you described in this letter. It should become a very valuable record and will grow as you allow your recall to flow from the pen onto the page! [...]

Istvan

215

1 MAY 1999

Isty old friend,

Your last letter with so much in it to respond to. I doubt I can to all of it but will do my best after a hellish week of proofreading. The notes get smaller, jiggle around on the staves: Stay put, will you, I have to say sometimes. And too many pages. I'm talking @ the piano-vocal of the old 1974 monodrama *Phaedra* based on Robert Lowell's free-verse of Racine's based on Euripides, an honorable & noble lineage—all put together by Gene—which will see the light of day probably in 2000/2001—utterly ridiculous numbers!! "Y2K problems for computers" you say? How about us ancient ones & our clouding-over brains, like mine? Hah! Simultaneously expecting 2nd proofs of *Three Elegiac Pieces* for piano, last pieces, "last" meaning I don't seriously expect to write any more music. The urge may still be there from time to time—but it will be dreamlike, a dim echo of onetime struggle, a rare victory, a touch now & again of "triumph"—all the real & foolish things that plague the human soul. Shakespeare was 46 when he ret[ire]d to Stratford-on-Avon, a worn-out, sick, disgusted with his fellow man, shell of his former self. He died 6 yrs later, so I've read, exhausted. Verdi between 50 & 70, [who] didn't even have a piano in his house (as he wrote to a friend), took up his pen again & ... "glory" followed. Truth is, in the light of the horrors of reality breaking loose everywhere in the so-called "Anglo-Saxon" world—the U.S., Canada, Britain, plus those in the Slavic world, these thoughts of art & making art are dreams, memories of old dreams, "We are such stuff, etc., etc." On top of all that to see John Turturro as Primo Levi in *The Truce*, a film version of Primo Levi's telling of his crazy nightmare of a journey through the eastern reaches of Poland & Russia before turning westward & southward back to Turin, Italy, is to be reminded of even worse things compounded of human evil and the chaos it produces. Then I reread, esp[ecially] the "Afterword" of Levi's *Reawakening* on which the film's based:[16] no false dramatics, melo- or otherwise; no "Jewish" self-pitying" or "self-glorying" (*à la* the "rememberers" like Elie Wiesel); no nauseating sentimentalizing; no self-righteous finger pointing; no anything of which our species, esp[ecially] here in America, currently reeks—all the "grieving," the "praying," all the revoltingness of adults on both the TV screen & in print—No, Primo Levi is the kind of man who though the world calls a Jew is not a Jew: he is a man, a deeply serious man who can say "If an Auschwitz exists, God does not exist." The time has come for redemptive religion to disappear, Judaism, Christianity, Islamic. People have to cleanse their minds and souls. Sorry to go off on a rant.

Well, turning 80 should have its "rewards." I mean, whoever "they" are in Canada, they should bring out CDs of your operas, absolutely. Selfishly, before I croak, so I can hear them at long last. And your *Millennium Walk* [i.e., *Millennial Mall (Lady Diotima's Walk)*], you out there, whoever "you" are, do it! Two of my favorite poets—Dylan Thomas & Wm. Butler Yeats—because they refused to go "gently into that dark night." […]

George

216

22 MAY 1999

My dear George,

Your May 1 letter was on my mind since weeks, yet I kept postponing this to this moment as I was focusing on the 'must' task of writing the piano-vocal/choral score of *Millennial Mall*, which I think will sprawl over ca. 180–190 pages. (I'm at p. 73 now, which amounts to 37% of the total no. of bars). I really don't like doing this, but have to, just in case the premiere will materialize by the end of next year. (Yes. There is some hope for this happening in Nov. 2000; yes, there were some 'indications,' but nothing certain as yet. The people 'concerned' I had done 'business' before with—they are serious 'pros,' and are loath to commit themselves until they know that the money is there in their budget. No, I do not have a commission for the work (as I did not have one for *Winthrop* and *Traces* either). There is, simply, no money around for this sort of thing, except perhaps with the Canadian Opera Co. With that outfit I had more contacts than I care to recount here. Had ample expression of artistic trust, etc., in what I'm doing and how I do it, musically speaking. Yet, 'they' seem to have troubles with my themes & librettos. I suspect I'm, in 'their' eyes, too 'controversial,' too much, perhaps, willing to poke a finger into some ills or problems in our 'scheme of things' … perhaps those you, also, have made reference to in your most recent letter. […]

My dear friend: I feel that our world is in a state (I'm avoiding more dramatic nouns, such as 'predicament' or 'crisis') of decline of morality, of 'value,' whatever these words may mean today. Yes, I know, Nietzsche visited this theme time & again, especially in his late years. Yet … yet … can one absolve oneself from asking the question, at least? Or are we only animals simply? My answer over the years, in works mainly, is that we should allow for the potentiality that we are not only 'animals,' although this statement would require a thought as to 'what' are animals, if we are not 'they'? My 4 'operas' seem in retrospect, to me, as 'visiting' this very terrain. *La Tourangelle*: female Catholic. *Winthrop*: male Puritan. *Traces*: male, late-20th-c[entury] Jewish. *Millennial Mall*: late-20th-c[entury] North American, hedonistic, neo-pagan picture of the 'social,' with Diotima the ethical (somewhat ambivalently so) pyschopomp as a 'guide.' Will the 'Mall' kill, eventually, my Diotima? I cannot be certain. According to Beate she will prevail. I'm not so sure ... But, anyhow, I have now her portrait, at the least!

And what about the pipe dreams of having the operas issued on CDs? The Canadian Music Centre made an application for funds ... The application was not successful in a Millennial Fund competition, funded by our dumbed-down government. That's all there is to tell. [...]

Istvan

[...]

217

5 OCTOBER 1999

Old friend, dear Isty,

[...] This past Sunday a fine pianist from these parts—Marcantonio Barone—gave the 1st perf[ormance]s of *3 Elegiac Pieces* & *Sonata Seria* and dedicated the perf[ormance] of the latter to Gene on her 80th (Sept. 20!).[17]
[...]

A young British violinist from London whom I met this past summer when he was over here as leader of the Kreutzer Quartet—and very good they are indeed—he sent a new CD of their recording of Roberto Gerhard Quartets No. 1 & 2.[18] I'd never heard a note of his, though I came across his name often in the old days. The music is 12-tone/serial & straight out of the 50s & 60s—but extremely sensitive and finally honed stuff—the Kreutzer (probably none of them over 40!) are very much at home with it—beautiful ensemble playing. Amazing! Just when I'm sure we're going straight down the drain, I'm reminded there are some people—and young ones too—in this crazy world who continue to fight for the good things no matter what—still when I view a scene where a wrestler [Jesse Ventura] is now governor of Minnesota in the same country where an actor became president, another president grew peanuts, still another president was a "crook"—which he loudly denied before the whole world ... The present incumbent is a grave disappointment—oh, he's a great politician to be sure but not much of a *mensch*. I hardly think I can be accused of "pessimism." People use terms loosely anyhow so I pay no attention.

As for reading, in re the Byzantine Empire, Arthur Koestler who believes most European, esp[ecially] Eastern, Jews are descendants of Khazars, a Ural region tribe along with Magyars, Bulgars (and other "—ars" I can't name) says that even before the Khazars converted to Judaism they were already the "fighting arm" of the Byzantine Empire, holding off the Rus on one side & the Arabs on the other. The Khazars decided they wanted neither to be Christian nor Moslem according to Koestler & so elected to become Jewish by conscious choice. It's all in his book *The Thirteenth Tribe*.[19] Have you ever read it? I keep coming back to it because no one else has a plausible theory to why there were over 11,000,000 Jews in Eastern Europe. Certainly not the rabbis. If you have a VCR attachment to your TV, go out and rent the Hungarian film called *Witness*, a wonderful satire on the Hungarian Communist Party with references to the bad old fascist days.[20] Better than [Jaroslav Hašek's] *Good Soldier Schweik* which in certain odd ways it resembles.

[...]

George

218

8 NOVEMBER 1999

My dear George,

[...] About 10 days ago there came a 'phone call out of the blue ... It was someone from the Winnipeg Symphony Orch[estra] asking for scores (I have made a 'rehearsal' score also) of *Millennial Mall*. Things progressed fast after this, and last Monday (the 1st of Nov.) a 'letter of agreement' arrived (with a request of counter-signature on my part) informing me that the orchestra wishes to perform the work's premiere in a pair of concerts on Jan. 28–29, 2000 as the initial event of their annual (or biannual?) 'New Music Festival.' The rest of the news was also fine: the soloist will be the (allegedly) stunning soprano Valdine Anderson, and the chorus the 'Elmer Iseler Singers' of Toronto, by common consent the best professional choir (of 20 singers) in the country.[21] [...]

Istvan

[...]

219

14 NOVEMBER 1999

Isty my friend,

It was good to get your letter with the great news @ the performance plans for your Lady D—'s debut in Winnipeg. [...] January 2000's going to be a banner month, beginning of the new year, century, millennium for us two oldies. I'm referring to the fact that the Boston Symphony with James dePriest conducting will be playing my *Transcendental Variations* for string orchestra (a transcription of the 3rd mov[men]t of the "ancient" 3rd quartet) in the middle of January. So a toast to both of us! As the man said: "We ain't dead yet." And I shall look forward to your *Festschrift*. [...]

George

NOTES

1 *Three Elegiac Pieces* (1998), for piano. No. 1 is a reworking of the slow movement of the First Piano Sonata (1947–48); No. 2 is a complete reworking of the slow movement of a sonatina that was started in 1945; No. 3 is a reworking of ideas taken from *Phaedra* (1973–74).

2 Donald Harman Akenson, *Surpassing Wonder: The Invention of the Bible and the Talmuds* (Montreal: McGill-Queen's University Press, 1998).

3 Martin Hengel, *Judaism and Hellenism: Studies in Their Encounter in Palestine during the Early Hellenistic Period*, 2 vols., trans. John Bowden (London: SACM Press, 1974).

4 George Steiner, "The Magician in Love," *Times Literary Supplement*, 29 January 1999, 3–4; review of *Briefe 1925 bis 1975, und andere Zeugnisse. Hannah Arendt, Martin Heidegger*, ed. Ursula Ludz (Frankfurt am Main: Vittorio Klosterman, 1998).

5 Elias Canetti, *The Tongue Set Free: Remembrance of a European Childhood*, trans. Joachim Neugroschel (New York: Seabury Press, 1979).

6 Michael Ignatieff, *Isaiah Berlin: A Life* (New York: Metropolitan Books, 1998).

7 Schneur Zalman of Liadi (1745–1812), Russian Jewish rabbi, founder of the Chabad-Lubavitch Chassidic Movement, author of *The Tanya* (first printed in 1796), a compilation of Jewish mystical concepts.

8 Arnaldo Momigliano, *Alien Wisdom: The Limits of Hellenization* (Cambridge/New York: Cambridge University Press, 1975).

9 Raymond Aron (pseud. René Avord) (1905–83), French sociologist, historian, and political commentator. Aron rejected those of his contemporaries, among them Sartre, who tended to view Stalinism in an idealistic, romantic light; see, in particular, *The Opium of the Intellectuals* (1955; first English trans. 1957).

10 Robert S. McNamara (b. 1916) American secretary of defence (1961–68) under presidents Kennedy and Johnson.

11 The *Partisan Review*, founded in 1934 by William Phillips and Philip Rahv, began life as a Stalinist organ before veering toward Trotskyism; it ceased publication in 2003.

12 On 31 March 1999 Rochberg had sent Anhalt the CD reissue of the Concord String Quartet's performances of his String Quartets Nos. 3–6, New World Records 80551-2 (1999).
13 Joseph Roth, *The Radetsky March*, trans. Joachim Neugroschel (Woodstock, NY: Overlook Press, 1995).
14 *La Tourangelle*, in *Anthology of Canadian Music/Anthologie de la musique canadienne* (Montreal: Radio Canada International, ACM 22 [1985]).
15 See Noel Malcolm, *Kosovo: A Short History* (London: Macmillan Press, 1998).
16 *The Truce* (1997), Italian-French-Swiss-German-British film, directed by Francesco Rosi and starring John Turturro; based on Primo Levi's autobiography *The Reawakening*, trans. Stuart Woolf (New York: Simon & Schuster, 1995).
17 Marcantonio Barone (b. 1962), American pianist who teaches at Swarthmore College and the Bryn Mawr Conservatory of Music.
18 Roberto Gerhard, String Quartets 1 and 2, Kreutzer Quartet, Metier MSV CD92032 (1999). The leader of this quartet is Peter Sheppard Skærved, who has recently recorded Rochberg's *Caprice Variations* (Metier MSV CD92065 [2003]) and the Violin Concerto, with the Saarbrücken Radio Symphony Orchestra, Christopher Lyndon-Gee, conductor (Naxos 8.559129 [2004]). See also "1994," note 8.
19 Arthur Koestler, *The Thirteenth Tribe: The Khazar Empire and Its Heritage* (London: Hutchinson, 1976).
20 *The Witness (A Tanú)* (1969), a political satire directed by Péter Bacsó.
21 *Millennial Mall (Lady Diotima's Walk)* (1999) was premiered at the Winnipeg New Music Festival on 28–29 January 2000 by the Winnipeg Symphony Orchestra, Bramwell Tovey, conductor, the Elmer Iseler Singers, and Valdine Anderson, soprano. See also "2000," note 1.

2000

220

6 FEBRUARY 2000

My dear George,

This is about a week past the double premiere (Jan. 28–29) of *Millennial Mall (Lady Diotima's Walk)* in Winnipeg and I'm still hovering a few inches above ground. But don't misunderstand this ... I'm too old to fool myself and rarely 'go euphoric' over anything. Yet I was <u>close</u> to this in relation to Valdine Anderson who was my 'Diotima' on this occasion. She is a statuesque, natural blond beauty with fantastic cheekbones and 2 huge dimples to match ... But the real stuff is in her voice & singing. She is a great artist who created the role in a way I could only dream about. (She is a specialist in 'new' music, has perfect pitch, and repertoire experience that includes work with Boulez, Birtwistle, Adès and other European & North American figures.)[1] The choir, the best up here, was the 20-strong Elmer Iseler Singers of Toronto, which had to be amplified (as they were in the back ...) to overcome the less-than-good acoustics of a 2300-seat big hall. They were excellent and negotiated their far from easy part flawlessly. (This is the same choir, with the same coach, Lydia Adams, which performed *Winthrop* in 1986.)[2] The orchestra was the Winnipeg Symphony and the whole under the excellent Bramwell Tovey, a British-born conductor, who conceived this 1-week-long Festival of 'new music' 9 years ago.[3] It has a remarkable community support, thanks to Tovey's talents as a community catalyst, as well as musician.

The piece 'clocked in' at about 55 minutes and the triple vocal levels—solo soprano, 6 soloists chamber choir, and the 'full' choir—worked well. We had some work in balancing the dynamics between the vocal & the instrumental forces. But we managed to do this, especially at the 2nd performance. […]

Istvan

221

18 FEBRUARY 2000

Dear Isty old friend,

[…] I have been plugging away on my memoir. *Finalmente* one chapter, the first, is in its last and honed-down version. I'm trying to bring 2 & 3 to the same state. Slow work, because each version undergoes further corrections and changes until, frankly, I'm heartily sick of them. Meanwhile Chap. 4 (still handwritten form) is waiting its turn before being typed & Chap. 5, already written out, needs to undergo some tough editing & rewriting before I turn it over for typing. […]

The sheer repetitiveness of life is one of the principal reasons I'm dead set against "immortality." Leoš Janáček's *Makropulos Affair* and Virginia Woolf's *Orlando* are also excellent arguments against it. We heard Schoenberg's *Gurrelieder* some weeks ago. For a 26–27-year-old, quite an astonishing feat. But as an echo of old Nordic (Germanic?) legends coupled with Wagnerian Love-Death-Redemption (only Christians & pseudo-Christians long for "redemption") and heavy-handed Germanic efforts at lightness and humor in the 3rd Part, it all proved too much for me. Besides Sch[oenberg] was stuck in the trap of 16/4-v so many times I stopped counting and listening (Part I is especially at fault that way). I added up *Gurrelieder* and *Moses und Aron* & decided Sch[oenberg] really was a German, not a Jew. Phila[delphia] was treated to the "new spirituality" of Górecki's 3rd Symp[hony] a couple of weeks ago.[4] One painfully pathetic slow beat throughout for—what, 40–45 minutes? Oy Vey, Henryk Górecki.

[…]

George

222

19 APRIL 2000

My dear George,

[…] It is good that you undertook writing your memoirs. It also shows braveness … I shall be interested in the story, of course, and also the way you tell it. On my part I had done it (or wrote something resembling a memoir) by a back door, so to say.[5] It went this way. After receiving from the Nat[ional] Lib[rary] of Canada a copy of the lists in the I.A. Fonds that included the names of over 150 respondents with whom I have corresponded over the years, the thought occurred to me that a few comments about them (<u>some</u>, or <u>each</u>, of them) might be useful, or even indispensable, over the years for those brave souls who would want to enter that tangle of thickets ... This started me off into recollecting who is, or was, who ... at times growing into mini-chapters (or not so 'mini') of the cast of protagonists in my life. Having broken the multiple seals of that memory-garden I let my roamings take me as far as they organically spread, each account showing a shape of a relationship which was a picture of its existential self. After these accounts (yes, I wrote about my parents, grandparents ... about everybody on the list) it occurred to me that these 'isolated' accounts do <u>not</u> cover some 'horizontal' (spreading over longer, or long, periods and some interrelationships) themes, such as 'love life,' relationship toward Jewishness, survival, etc. Consequently I added texts related to these and other *canti firmi*. The 'thing' just kept on proliferating as I discovered yet another 'area,' or 'theme' or whatever, that figured in my life. Hence the text kept growing. Then came the addenda about genealogy, and other topics. I kept on with this for a few years (probably not more than 6–7) and for the last 5–7 years I didn't add anything, letting parts of my letters, & other texts, etc. flesh out the picture of a still evolving life. No, I never kept an ongoing diary (perhaps I should have done this ... But it seemed to me that it could prove to be redundant to quite an extent ... So my cop-out found its escape-hatch ...). I am certain that your telling of your *vita* will be vintage G.R. and will give delightful 'AHA' experiences. I'm waiting impatiently ...

[...]

Istvan

223

30 APRIL 2000

Dear Isty, old friend,

[...] I'm fascinated by what you tell me about your memoir—reminiscences of friends, family, colleagues undoubtedly, and perhaps here and there someone you were not esp[ecially] fond of but who played a role in your life. My journals, sporadic, random, fitful as they are, are the record of my mental & psychic journey w[ith] all their aches and pains—probably the reader of them would find them insufferably boring &

repetitive but my defense is two-fold: 1) I was (& still do) writing for myself, no one else, and really simply to relieve pressures, to vent, to curse—when it was required—an unfriendly, hostile world represented not by birds & squirrels but the two-legged, naked ape whom I still retain an ancient love–hate relation to. 2) Therefore, what any hypothetical reader might have to suffer plowing through all this detritus & often poorly expressed, ungrammatical expostulation, bad language showing I was not brought up to be a gentleman & would have resisted like crazy if I had. Having said that, the enclosed 3 chapters will give you a good representation of what I intend, how I go about it, as to substance, ideas, feelings, use of language.[6] I've had immeasurable help from Gene who frequently objects to my long involved sentences & helps me guard against slipping into simple autobiography. Still, some telling of the life story as I lived & remember it is necessary but is not the chief reason for trying to get down in words (much more slippery than sounds/notes) the main story—which is a kind of loosely told compote of the "history" of the time, its aesthetics, its foolishness, its rightness and wrongness, during which I tried to hack out a path for myself and arrive at some understanding of music itself. That's why the emphasis falls on the music I wrote & the people who played it—well and/or not so well.

Fade to Friday nite, April 28, N[ew] Y[ork] Miller Theater (old McMillin) and the two works played by "Sequitur," [a] N[ew] Y[ork] ensemble dedicated to "20th-century" music, *Serenata d'estate* (1955) & Fourth Quartet (1977) representing the "before" & "after" of my break with modernism (as a fantastically rigid set of beliefs imposed by high priests of wrong-headed cults in every case, most fallen by the wayside, one or two still "revered" by those who <u>need</u> the comfort of that kind of belief-system; me, as you know, I claim uncertainty as our lot, uncertainty in the very midst of vast mysteries which neither our perceptions nor our intelligence are strong & large enough to grasp adequately. Which, for me, explains <u>why</u> we hold Bach & Mozart & Beethoven as we do. So I'm home again, ready mentally to push on with the audacious task of writing/rewriting/rewriting the rewritten/and so on … This <u>perhaps</u> will keep me going till I'm in my middle to late 80s, who knows perhaps I may even tip 90. It really is one of the very few reasons why I want & need to get up every day & push the boulder up the hill … Are we not descendants of Sisyphus? I'm also enclosing something not typed up yet on the *Serenata*. I read it at the panel "discussion" preceding the concert Friday nite.[7] As for the memoir chapters, I await your judgement … […]

George

224

23 JUNE 2000

My dear George,

[…] That master of plumbing the soul, R[obert] Musil, comes, just once again, to mind as I'm writing this … (I forgot to record, if memory serves well, in my letters to you that it was you, dear friend, who alerted me, ca. 5 years ago, of the reality of Musil's great book, *The Man without Qualities*, which, as it turned out, has assumed a major significance for me, as you know … I am & will remain grateful to you for this …).[8]

What's new here? You are asking … Life has settled in a 'search' mode since the end of January last … My daily routine includes reading in a very broad way. This included recently George Sand, Musil's recently translated (into English) *Notebooks* (a very worthwhile read!),[9] Walter Benjamin's gargantuan *Arcades Project* (published by Harvard U[niversity] P[ress] in 1999), which was highly praised in a *T[imes] L[iterary] S[upplement]* review[10] … Yes and no … I do see his (Benjamin's) objective … and, in a way, he <u>does</u> manage to grasp, if not 'enough,' then quite a bit of that ingraspable subject: what a world capital ('Paris') <u>is</u> … The book is one that was slated to end up proving itself an unrealisable project … a noble failure if one wants to be a charitable, or 'generous,' reader … There is an uneven 'density-tempo' to this narrative, and the 'quoting-discourse' has a built-in unevenness which (in 'theory') could work well enough, but for me, at least, it did not manage this in a sustained manner … I know … in a huge collage like this the onus is (in part!) on the reader to respond with a suitable <u>reading-modality</u> that would prove to be germane to the way how the author spins his tale … (Perhaps <u>I</u> did not do my bit well enough … Perhaps … but I was <u>not</u> on contract to Benjamin as a reader so, at one point, I've just quit …) […]

Istvan

225

21 JULY 2000

Dear Isty, old friend,

Yesterday afternoon Gene & I and some other people from Dunwoody spent a <u>long</u> 3 hours in an "art" movie house watching the film put together by István Szabó called *Sunshine*, the English for the Hungarian Jewish family called Sonnenschein.[11] Before you attempt it—and frankly I'm not urging you to—try to get hold of the *New York Review of Books* July 20, 2000 issue & read István Deák's piece,[12] rather scholarly, which concentrates mainly on the historical aspects of the lives & fates of Hungarian Jews across the 19th & the 20th century, the 1st WW, the Hitler years, the Fascist & then Communist regimes which in the film I thought were presented in an unclear, jumbled way, mixing documentary films w[ith] the fictional one tracing the dynasty of four generations of Sonnenschein sons, Jews turned Catholics back to Jews at the end of it. It was difficult to decide which Szabó felt was primary & which secondary, the sex life of the sons from one generation to another, but principally one son in each of the generations always played by the same actor, or the historical. Was the foreground the sex life of said actor/son seen against the background of the historical seesaw in the fortunes of Jews or was it vice versa, the sex life—overdrawn, too explicit, too many detailed scenes, etc.—as background to the historical foreground? Whichever Szabó may have had in mind it didn't work for either Gene or me—oddly enough Gene reminded me that the people who were with us had also in their day because of "circumstances" changed their names to Anglo-Saxon ones. In any case there were some labor camp—under the Hungarian Fascist regime—scenes where I couldn't help but think of you. And if you could see the film, that is, it was available to you in Kingston & decided against going, I can't say I'd blame you. I left the theater once again confirmed of the utter monstrousness of the human species—which I'm afraid will ever be present in one form or another because it doesn't sink into our dim consciousness of self, protected by miles-thick coatings of self-love, self-justification, self-glorification, all of it at once. Jonathan Swift may not have been an endearing man but he saw clearly ... Just today in the mail I rec[eive]d a long-awaited copy of *J.S. Bach: Learned Musician* by Christoph Wolff.[13] If it weren't for the utter stupidity of Christianity, old J.S.'s music would have long ago converted me! But nothing will attract me to religious orthodoxy.

If you should find the *N[ew] Y[ork] Review of Books* issue you will also find a quite astonishing piece "Reason in East & West: by Amartya Sen[14] in which a 16th-cent[ury] emperor named Akbar, a Muslim, comes out smelling like a veritable rose & says things that fair take my breath away! I'm still at the 5 lines & 4 spaces, my daily taskmaster. [...]

George

226

9 AUGUST 2000

George, dear friend,

I've just reread your "rich" July 21 letter. No, we haven't as yet seen the sunshine saga as 'told' by that very gifted film-director, István Szabó, whose *Mephisto* and *Colonel Redl*[15] we saw with great interest and sense of enrichment (incidentally, or perhaps not so, in both films the leading roles were played by that incomparable German [*sic*] actor Brandauer, a man perhaps in the same 'class' as the recently deceased Sir Alec Guin[n]ess [1914–2000], another superbly creative stage presence).

Your theme and tale of *Sunshine* is of course an opening of 'locks' on a huge black box of experiences for me. Not only the 2-year-long labour-camp experience in the shovel brigades of the Hungarian Army, which was (1) a semi-prison first, (2) 'full' prison subsequently, and (3) a killing ground in which my best friend and colleague (fellow composer) László Gyopár[16] perished on the first day of what turned into a week-long forced march from Stanislav (then Poland, now Ivano Frankovsk, Russia) to the foot of the eastern slopes of the Carpathian mountains, beginning at the end of July 1944. My survival against heavy odds I regard as a combination of being helped by a few buddies in my hobbling progress and a near miracle that occurred just as we were to undertake a very steep climb to the pass ahead ... It's a long story and elsewhere I've written it up ... Szabó's story also includes, obviously, that of the Hungarian half of Musil's 'Kakania' (or Joseph Roth's 'terrain' in his novel *The Radetsky March*).[17] This part is the tale of my parents' and grandparents' generations which I absorbed as if by 'osmosis' in my childhood. While in Hungary (which I left for good in the end of January '46) I read next to nothing about that history. I had more urgent things to do, obviously, mainly music-related stuff, and also the existential imperative of finding a place (country, city, livelihood, etc.) where I could 'realize' my 'dreams' ... But not until Kingston, after sensing a firm and compatible ground (unthreatening!) under my toes, did I begin to look for clues of my 'background.' This I found 'in spades' in our very honorable university library that contains thousands of volumes of Judaica (thought, theology, history, biographies, etc.). I have stumbled on a vast treasure-trove, as I soon realized. Particularly well documented are the years since 1867, the date of the Austro-Hungarian compromise which saw the birth of the Austro-Hungarian Dual Monarchy. Authors (historians) such as the American McCabb [*sic*] (Colorado U[niversity]) and the Hebrew University's Wistrich are among the noted experts in the period.[18] The greatest expert in the Hungarian Holocaust is R.L. Braham of N.Y.C. whose 2-volume magnum opus *The Politics of Genocide* is a classic in the area of Holocaust Studies.[19] Deák's piece in the *N.Y.R.B.* [*New York Review of Books*] is an excellent condensation of a tortuous tale which Szabó tried (obviously) to compress into 3 hours on the screen, enlivened, as you observe, by torrid sex scenes to lubricate the way to the box office, I surmise ... We shall certainly look for the film's arrival in our backwater town ... But, please, don't try to spare me from painful remembrances ... These are my daily (hourly?) companions, and shall remain so to the end of my days. Like [the mythological giant] Ant[a]eus gaining strength for the continuation of a difficult fight by remaining in touch with the ground, so do I gather further 'breath' for the ongoing struggle as a person, as a writer ... as an everything, I guess ...

Yes, I also 'checked out' A. Sen's interesting text about 'Akbar' in the same issue of the *N.Y.R.B.* As to your 'attraction' to Christ the Jew: you are in excellent company here. Example: the great Oxford U. Judaica scholar, Geza Vermes (yes, another Hungarian Yid ...) just published his 4th(!) book on the Jewish Jesus (or should I say Yeshua). I read the first 3 of these ... & found them very interesting.[20] But to this I could add M. Unamuno's search for the soul of Don Quixote, whom he also sees as a Christ-like figure. (The Miguel de Unamuno book of Cervantes-deconstruction is entitled *Our Lord Don Quixote*.[21] Very moving tale, this ...)

Yet one more word about Szabó, which came my way from another source, at about the same time as your letter. It was contained in a letter from András Szöllösy, a Hungarian composer, still living in Budapest, at age 78.[22] He (a rather sick, home-bound recluse, a fellow student in Kodály's class in the years 1938–41) is a fine man who has shown in deeds that he is aware of the depth of the Hungarian-Jewish tragedy, in 1938–44, and who tried to act accordingly, regrettably, after the fact, as my incomplete records show ... [...]

Istvan

[...]

227

26 AUGUST 2000

Isty, old friend,

[…] Once again, I am impressed by the depth of your knowledge and reading vis-à-vis your family background. But why do you fall into the use of the cliché "Yid"? In the context of the tragic circumstances you recount—of which I only knew the merest surface—that term jars. The only thing against any kind of sick evil hatred of Jews by warped minds (which WE know still inhabit this corrupted earth) as of other racial and ethnic hatreds (still virulent everywhere) is a guarded defense, vigilant watchfulness. We shall never be done with these horrors no matter what new shapes they take in times to come. […]

I've just sketched to the end Chap. VI on my relation to the Concord Quartet & all the works I wrote for them. Only when I see it in typed form will I be able to tell if it's any good. I keep going because it is the only thing I have now that helps me keep my balance. I have no desire to write music. And here in the States they are still battling the battle of serialism vs. tonality. The poison of modernism still is in our veins. […]

George

228

14 SEPTEMBER 2000

My dear George,

[…] Let's put to rest this little 'bump' that popped up on our shared pathway first … I mean, my employment of the "Yiddish" slang word (so identified by my *Webster's International Dictionary*) "Yid." No, I am not hiding behind the mighty defenses of this tome … Knowing well enough that the semantic load of a word in the context of a chronotope might (and often does) mutate from a half-decade to the next one … No defense is needed here, but I simply register what has appeared as an affective dissonance between our respective attitudes related to "Yid" here & now. Now, this I find [to] be of some interest, per se, while willing (even desirous) to abide by your correction which must (and likely does) stem from your different (U.S. vs Canada perhaps, as one axis of comparison?) and superior ear/mind in this matter, in this context. The fact is (I'm trying here to uncover the bottom of my instinctive usage of the word) that what I probably am implying here is an 'in' word, referring to a collective 'us' in which (the term is imagined to be large & accommodating enough) a caftaned Hassid from, say, a 'Jewish' district of New York City and/or a Yeshiva student from Safed in the Galilee, can inhabit, cheek-by-jowl with a 'worldly enough' (once again: what does this collective double expression add up to?) person like you or me, who is hastily perhaps, and in a reductionist way, contrasted with the Safed Hassid. And, yes, one more angle. The word cropped up between intimate friends both Jewish, both deeply, yet uniquely so, in a letter, far from the imaginary ears/eyes of an outsider. In short, it was an 'in expression,' about 'us,' while no one else is within ear-shot ... If the slang is (slightly?) offensive if coming from an 'outsider' it perhaps can be allowed to possess a less grating ring, especially if accompanied by a half-smile and the shade of a chuckle ... ENOUGH! [...]

Istvan

[...]

229

25 SEPTEMBER 2000

Dear old friend Isty,

My metaphysics I've only recently discovered has no teleology. I can't discern an "end"—purposive or otherwise—because it's lost in dense impenetrable fogs and clouds. But oddly, my sense of where we are, where we stem from (but not in the evolutionary sense/meaning), what is the stuff we float and/or swim in—that seems to have taken on a sense, a clarity I wouldn't have nor did I expect. I'll try to describe it simply so as not to obfuscate. It's worth going into and communicating to you because it is coloring all my thoughts and feelings, from the simplest to the most complex.

24 OCTOBER

Yes, a long break occasioned by a whole concatenation of things—but since I started this, all hell's broken out in Israel, too complex and dangerous to know how to guess its outcome. No matter what [Ehud] Barak does—even if he lasts as P.M.—the Palestinians are bound and determined to make war of one kind or another, with stones, molotov cocktails, guns; the Israelis are waking up to the realization that the only way is to seal the Arabs off, geographically, economically & let them fend for themselves, that is, make their own electricity, water, et al. Even so, hawk though I am and have been all along, it bodes ill for Israel. The least of it will be the condemnation of the "world community" so-called, but in fact that has been *sub rosa* since the beginning, so the Israelis can live with it. The U.S. will continue to support them. But to live in a permanent state of war? That will be terrible for the people. But what other way is there, to commit *hara-kiri* to satisfy the beastly Arabs? And the blacks of Africa, themselves no prize, and the French, the Russians, the rest of Europe where anti-Semitism still continues whether there are no Jews or only 2 Jews left? And the utter ridiculousness of the rabbis, 3 or 4 of them standing on a West Bank hill on the border of an Israeli settlement facing the Arab village a couple of kilometers away, saying antique prayers to "ward off evil spirits." And here in America the charade of a presidential election where the population itself is divided into great lumps of illiterates, young and old, obesity rules bodies and minds, those with money to burn concerned only with getting more so that they can carry on in their version/variant of "The Garden of Earthly Delights."

Which takes me back to my beginning. I don't like obscurity or mystification but I have no other way than to describe deep, untraceable root systems, or call them "substrata" (which is how I think of them) in which are locked the scenarios/scripts/image and text preexisting ur-typologies of all varieties of human forms and faces, individual and collective "stories," all of which repeat endlessly in endless variations depending on immediate conditions, circumstances. However different these variant forms may appear to the searching mind or eye contemporary with them, distance and perspective reveal that they are each and all ultimately traceable to the substrata. It is Hegel in reverse. Or borrowing something from the old Platonic Ideas it reverses direction, i.e., instead of looking up to the Inconceivable Heavens of Plato as the Home of Ideas and their Eternal Images, we look, not down, but inward into the depths of the human genome and consciousness sources for the substrata. It borders on the ancient Fate, iron-clad, pre-deterministic outcome, of the old Greeks. The substrata also are the theatrical source for the "fact" and "fiction" of human events, behavior, attitudes et al. In sum, I am positing a set of forever-underlying "great themes" and series of forever-variations, only rarely "beautiful," more often than not ugly, which process has been going on for a very long time and will continue to eternity. Not very encouraging to contemplate. No utopias, no rational solutions, a boiling cauldron always bubbling and sometimes running over. Even religion—every possible shade—is included in the substrata. Not only the ancient & contemporary but those varieties yet to be "born" into the world. Enough, perhaps, even too much. […]

George

230

26 NOVEMBER 2000

My dear George,

I've just reread your Sept./Oct. letter and retraced my recollection of our talk on the 'phone ... These merge with events close by (families, yours, ours), further afield (Israel) (elections, yours, ours) our coping with the time passing and realizing that one cannot ignore an 'end,' or, rather, several aspects/alternatives of ends, personal, historical, political and so on ... ends perhaps channeling into beginnings, early stages of something, or other, the lives of our grandchildren, for ex[ample], in short: life (including genes, but also entities, structures, repertories, etc.) going on after 'our time' draws to a close ... All this resonate[s] with my reading (I seldom read books from cover to cover, I rather 'mine' books for another's 'deep' thoughts, agenda, negotiations with the self, insights, traces of honesty, posturings, etc. which must be—and is—discounted ...). So you see: I'm with you, your themes, concerns, even as our differing temperaments and coping strategies are proving to be (inevitably) different. Yet there is, I feel, a great potential, and actuality, of resonance, i.e., empathy, between the 2 of us, still, and hardly ever interrupted, over our 40-year friendship ... Something to celebrate, which I am doing now in this aside, in this act of pushing pen against paper, drawing this series of wonderful squiggles we call letters, words, as many transparent/expressive messages from here to you ... Yes, my dear friend, there is this affinity between the 2 of us which was, and continues to be, recorded on these pages-full squiggles over the years.

I too revisited a text of Hegel's, i.e., his long introduction (70+ pages) to his *Philosophy of History* (or some such).[23] His language is '*turgidissimo*' ... the man suffocates his text with notions that a few decades after he delivered this in lecture-format (1830–31) became 'outlawed' ... perhaps already by Auguste Comte (and his English friend J.S. Mill ... their correspondence is worth looking into, by the way),[24] and certainly by the turn of the century by the Viennese logical positivists. There is a long passage in this *Philosophy of History* where he writes about men of destiny (<u>my</u> simplified reference) using expressions [such] as " ... all great historical men, whose own particular aims involve those large issues which are the will of the World-Spirit, these may be called Heroes...." What follows is also worth considering ... I <u>smell</u> the scent of a Hitler here, in this 'professorial' (der Herr Professor *à la* Heidegger ...) pronouncement ... While lugging Hegel's tome (tomb?) home I also had with me

Herder's account of world history[25] ... a more *sympatish* attempt in my view ... (Incidentally when Hegel gets around to the people of the Jews, he writes a criticism of monotheism that can be read as (also) anticipating what Mircea Eliade published/wrote a decade, or two, ago in his *History of Religious Ideas* (of which only 2 volumes saw the light of day, if I'm correct ...)[26] (Incidentally, re: Eliade, whom I read extensively while working on sections of *Alternative Voices*, I found out that he was a Rumanian consular official in Portugal during the years of WW II and was known to have harboured some Nazi-type ideas, of the Rumanian variety ...)

Apropos Rumania ... Saul Bellow's *The Dean's December* comes to mind ... a good book ... much superior to his recent *Ravelstein* which I read into[27] ... A rather tired text of an 'academic' philosopher who tries to lure a colleague to accept to be his biographer. I don't know Bellow well ... He does have a personal voice, but he does not make it into the class formed by Proust, Kafka, Joyce and Musil, the great quartet of early 20-c[entury] novelistic letters. Now one reads in Painter's magisterial biography of Proust[28] that he worked on his *opus* almost to the hour of his death ... Musil couldn't part with the 2nd volume of his *Man without Qualities*, etc. This brings me to your thoughts about the 'end of things' ... Yes, this is a timely thought for the likes of us who are 'rich in years' ... I really don't quite trust myself with this, while I am still feeling relatively 'healthy' ... My current ideas about the very last phase of life might not 'hold up' when the going gets really tough ... So when I am reminding you now of the ending of *Traces (Tikkun)*, at least the text of it, and claim that there, in those words, I envisaged my 'end hopes' of an 'end,' in all frankness I have to face up to the possibility that the serenity of that 'scenario's' end might not prove to be feasible during my real end (vs. the imagined end) as it comes. but that's what I still am hoping for ... an end when I shall be able to return all the particles (i.e., material ones) of my body to the totality of the cosmic whole, and at the same time my unique combination of elementary particles in interplay with each other, the result of billions of years of the cosmic drama, a most unlikely event, whose probability ought to have been near 0, will give up its probalistic miracle, and I shall be returning my stuff to the 'whole' ... A nice illusion, but it gave me the ending of *Traces (Tikkun)*, and it was a good experience of having 'found' the musical expression for it. [...]

What can one say about the sad and dangerous situation in Israel? To start with, the non-negotiables: Israel must survive as an independent state. Perhaps a 'federation' with the Palestinians is unfeasible as both ethnicities would demand for themselves the right to unlimited immigration. As it is, the territory is a narrow enough littoral location, with severely limited potable water resources, and I don't see a solution towards a joint (Jewish-Palestinian) entity with equal rights, unless technology and political wisdom could come to the rescue. Now about 'political wisdom' … The lack of this requires consideration of a larger context, that of an Arab/Moslem mass (of near 1 billion) vs. an Israel as a near-eastern Switzerland, i.e., a beach-head of 'Western' (mainly U.S.?) 'modernity' vs. the Arab/Muslim traditional ways (plural) of living … It is necessary, I feel, to see this conflict also in the framework of this, larger, context: The West's need for Arab oil, and whatever control this 'requires' (*vide* the recent Gulf War!) How this larger conflict will play itself out is not shown in my crystal ball of miserably narrow time-range … Where does this leave one? With the imperative of suffering losses, death that is, on both sides, outrage, etc. but keeping overall security in place as much as possible, and wait for the 'larger' forces to play out their complex and dangerous destinies … Yes, this is non-ending.

[…]

Istvan

231

[undated, but postmarked 11 December 2000]

Dear old friend Isty,

[…] I signed the contract for [McGill-]Queen's Univ[ersity] Press & your book which I am eagerly looking forward to. Speaking of books, while I was recovering from my last bout with the dentist I read Michael Frayn's (he, the writer of that brilliant play, *Copenhagen* which focuses on the Bomb, Niels Bohr, Werner Heisenberg, the Second War, the Nazis in positively astonishing ways) new novel *Headlong*.[29] The guts of this spoof of the Brits & their strange ways is the history of Breugel, the painter who followed Bosch, in the late 16th century in the Netherlands under the oppressive rule of the insane Spanish who managed to carry out a horrendous genocide (based on a fanatic Catholic determination with the help of the Inquisition to wipe out the heresy of Protestantism and other forms of "free-thinking"—enter Bruegel and friends) and how Bruegel dealt with all this. Frayn draws historical and theological parallels with Hitler and the Nazis (again in the Netherlands), and makes a particular point of excoriating both historians and art historians for being blind, totally blind. Which sets me going again because after virtually a lifetime of respect for "intellectuals" I have come, with rare exception, to see most of them as obtuse, arrogant, egotistical "scholars" who don't go near the "slums" of history, the depravities and insanities that occur there, over & over *ad nauseam*. That's why I see Frayn as that rare intelligence married to a deep feeling nature which is willing, however horrible, to look the Gorgon in the face. Willing because he's able to look and not turn to stone, to remain fully human. One of the reasons, believe it or not, I regret getting older, is that I don't have the old energy for the old fire of anger which fed my way through this crazy life. Without anger I could not have survived. Nor could I, therefore, have been a Jew who believes in God or a Christian who believes in still more nonsense or ... or ... or ... Hard on the old nerves to be sure but I "see" better after a shot of adrenaline charges through me.

George

NOTES

1 Valdine Anderson (b. 1965), Canadian soprano who has specialized in contemporary music; she has performed Pierre Boulez's *Pli selon Pli* under the composer's direction, collaborated with Sir Harrison Birtwistle, Gavin Bryars, and others, and recorded the role of the Maid in Thomas Adès's opera *Powder Her Face*.

2 The Elmer Iseler Singers, a twenty-voice Toronto-based choir founded by Elmer Iseler in 1979, has been under the direction of Lydia Adams since 1998.

3 Bramwell Tovey (b. 1953), British-born conductor and composer; artistic director of the Winnipeg Symphony Orchestra (1989–2001), where he established a renowned festival of contemporary music.

4 Henryk Górecki's phenomenally popular Symphony No. 3 (*Symphony of Sorrowful Songs*), Op. 36 (1976), catapulted the Polish composer to world-wide renown.

5 "A Weave of Life Lines" (1992), unpublished ms., Anhalt Fonds MUS 164/F1,77–79), and "An Interim Account of My Search for Genealogical Information Pertaining to My Family's Background" (1995), unpublished ms., Anhalt Fonds MUS 164/A,33.

6 Three chapters from Rochberg's ongoing memoirs, *Five Lines and Four Spaces: Reflections on My Music and the Performers Who Played It*, are housed in the Anhalt Fonds MUS 164/13: I. "About Szell and the *Second Symphony*" (1999–); II. "About the *Caprice Variations* (1999–2000–); III. "About Dimitri Mitropoulos and *Night Music*" (1999/2000–).

7 Enclosure: five heavily corrected and edited pages on the first performance of the *Serenata d'estate*, for flute, harp, guitar, violin, viola, and cello, 4 May 1958, New York, "Music in Our Time," Arthur Winograd, conductor.

8 See "1995," note 12.

9 Robert Musil, *Diaries, 1899–1941*, original German version of the *Diaries*, edited by Adolf Frisé; selected, translated, annotated, and with a preface by Philip Payne; edited and with an introduction by Mark Mirsky (New York: Basic Books, 1998).

10 Walter Benjamin, *The Arcades Project*, trans. Howard Eiland and Kevin McLaughlin; prepared on the basis of the German volume edited by Rolf Tiedemann (Cambridge, MA: Belknap Press of Harvard University Press, 1999); George Steiner, "Shops, Sewers, Boredom, Barricades: Walter Benjamin's Mappings of Paris Above and Below Ground," *Times Literary Supplement*, 3 December 1999, 3–4; review of Benjamin, *The Arcades Project*.

11 István Szabó (b. 1938), Hungarian film director and screenwriter; *Sunshine* (1999), starring British actor Ralph Fiennes, is an English-language version of a film that appeared originally in Hungarian (*A Napfény íze*) and as a miniseries for German television (*Ein Hauch von Sonnenschein*).

12 István Deák, "Strangers at Home: *Sunshine* a Film Directed by István Szabó," *New York Review of Books*, 20 July 2000, 30–32.

13 Christoph Wolff, *Johann Sebastian Bach: The Learned Musician* (New York: W.W. Norton, 2000).

14 Amartya Sen, "East and West: The Reach of Reason," *New York Review of Books*, 20 July 2000, 33–38.

15 Szabó's *Mephisto* (1981) and *Colonel Redl* (*Oberst Redl*; *Redl ezredes*) (1985) both starred Austrian actor Klaus Maria Brandauer. *Mephisto*, based on a novel by Thomas Mann's son, Klaus, won an Oscar for best foreign film.

16 See "1992," note 11.

17 Austrian novelist Joseph Roth's *The Radetsky March* (*Radetskymarsch*) (1932) was the basis of a 1995 film directed by Axel Corti and starring Max von Sydow. See also "1999," note 13.

18 See, for example, William O. McCagg, *A History of Hapsburg Jews, 1670–1918* (Bloomington: University of Indiana Press, 1988); *Jewish Nobles and Geniuses in Modern Hungary* (Boulder, CO: East European Quarterly; distributed by Columbia University Press, New York, 1972); and Robert S. Wistrich, *The Jews of Vienna in the Age of Franz Joseph* (Oxford: Oxford University Press for the Littman Library, 1989).

19 Randolph L. Braham, *The Politics of Genocide: The Holocaust in Hungary* (New York: Columbia University Press, 1981; rev. enlarged ed. [New York: Rosenthal Institute for Holocaust Studies Graduate Center, 1993]; condensed ed. [Detroit: Wayne State University Press, 2000]).

20 See Geza Vermes, *Jesus the Jew: A Historian's Reading of the Gospels* (1973), *The Gospel of Jesus the Jew* (1981), *Jesus and the World of Judaism* (1983), *The Religion of Jesus the Jew* (1993), and *The Changing Faces of Jesus* (2001); Vermes has since published *The Authentic Gospel of Jesus* (2003).

21 Miguel de Unamuno, *Our Lord Don Quixote: The Life of Don Quixote and Sancho, With Related Essays*, trans. Anthony Kerrigan, with an introduction by Walter Starkie, 2nd printing with corrections (Princeton, NJ: Princeton University Press, 1976).

22 See "1994," note 5.

23 Georg Wilhelm Friedrich Hegel, *The Philosophy of History*, prefaces by Charles Hegel and the translator, J. Sibree, with a new introduction by C.J. Friedrich (New York: Dover Publications, 1956).

24 *The Correspondence of John Stuart Mill and Auguste Comte*, trans. and ed. Oscar A. Haac, with a foreword by Oscar A. Haac and an introduction by Angèle Kremer-Marietti (New Brunswick, NJ: Transaction Publishers, 1995).

25 Johann Gottfried Herder, *Reflections on the Philosophy of the History of Mankind*, abridged, and with an introduction by Frank E. Manuel (Chicago: University of Chicago Press 1968).

26 Mircea Eliade, *A History of Religious Ideas*, 3 vols. (Chicago: University of Chicago Press, 1978–85).
27 Saul Bellow, *The Dean's December: A Novel* (New York: Harper & Row, 1982); *Ravelstein* (New York: Viking, 2000).
28 George Duncan Painter, *Marcel Proust*, 2 vols. (London: Chatto, 1965).
29 Michael Frayn, *Copenhagen* (London: Methuen, 1998); *Headlong* (London: Faber and Faber, 1999).

PART FIVE

ENVOI (2001–2005)

What better to wish for
you, dear Friend, roam
freely in memory-space
and be at peace.

— Anhalt (May 2005)

Beate and Istvan Anhalt, Kingston, Ontario, October 2000. Photo by Carol Anhalt-Greaves.

2001

232

12 SEPTEMBER 2001

My dear George,

The date on the upper right should have been marked as 11+1/9/2001 for the obvious reason that after 11/9/2001 each day will appear as 11+x/9/2001. One feels that something has changed yesterday that one will not be able to erase from one's consciousness. This being said, what is there to add to what you and I, with countless others, feel and ponder on? I, at least, will need time to place the awful tragedy of yesterday in some kind of a 'frame' the nature of which (if at all!) I cannot guess at and it will take time, much time, for me to feel my way out of this awful, and threatening fog. And then the future ... the consequences, the risks, the acts that are bound to follow ... Awful, awful, tragic, sad, menacing, etc. witches' brew this ... [...]

Istvan

233

23 SEPTEMBER 2001

Dear old friend, Isty,

It's impossible to remember my state of mind. I thought all week to call you, even earlier today, but realized I lacked the energy for a phone conversation—my head is full of the horror of what has befallen us—and the Western world—at one blow, and by fiendishly clever—far cleverer than any of us could ever dream of being ("us" meaning everyone in our gov[ernmen]ts, intellectuals, artists, writers, composers, et al.)—

Islamic minds that twist and turn in the shapes of the calligraphy of Arabic—by contrast the squareness of ancient Hebrew denotes opposite characteristics (no need to spell it out—& no desire). I keep thinking of the Crusades & the "Saracens," the "Moors" of Ferdinand/Isabella's Spain, of Shakespeare's "Othello," of the Ottoman Empire that reached to the very outskirts of Vienna in Haydn, Mozart & Beethoven's time (remember "Turkish Music"—cymbals, bass drum, marches—coffee and croissants?), of the deadly hatred of the old Muslims for the "infidel" Christians—not to mention Jews from whom they "borrowed" the patriarchs Abraham, Isaac & Jacob (who became Israel), the slow, patient coiling of their plan to strike, not just at anything, but at the symbols at the heart of what stands for America to most Americans and most of the world: the financial, capitalistic nerve center of lower Manhattan and the Pentagon, nerve center of our military "might" as some would call it. The human loss which means so much to us means absolutely zero to the crafty twisted mind of bin Laden & his gang of death-dealers. The end of the first stanza of Yeats's "Second Coming" is the very prophecy of the fogbound sated-with-false-dreams & illusions of a fast-asleep-w[ith]-eyes-wide-shut West best represented by America—possibly less so by England & the continental Europeans—though they've been caught napping & off guard too many times themselves—and the fierce hating Moslems in Arabic & non-Arabic lands of the "worst full of passionate intensity" while "the best lack all conviction." I keep thinking of Beethoven and his "*Nicht dieses töne*" followed by his "hymn to the Brotherhood of Man." Was he also full of nonsensical illusions? Truth is, I feel sick at heart and in spirit. Because despite the horror of the shock and the blow, most people here don't comprehend the vastness of the divide and the conflict. And young ones, friends, think that Islam's "intentions" as based on the Koran (a fogbound circuitous piece of mumbo jumbo only surpassed by the Mormon Bible) are "morally" good, peaceful, practicing kindness etc. etc. Since when does a doctrine millions swear by have anything to do with how they act? Never prevented the Hebrews from destroying everyone in sight whom they considered dangerous and could overpower; nor Christians to this very day in Ireland; on and on it goes, the "ideal" belief so-called & the rotten truth coupled with the inability of people with brains to discern the great divide. My young friend, Barry Bobrick (whose last book was on the creation of the English Bible—a very telling story in its own way)[1] said the other day: "I'm afraid they will outsmart us." I think he's right. And *unser* Bush said: "This will be a long campaign"—fulfilling a sense that I've lived with since early maturity: I was born in the last months of WW I, fought in WW II, and will die in the apocalypse of WW III.

[…]

George

234

25 SEPTEMBER 2001

Old friend Isty,

I saw your welcome handwriting on the envelope—our letters have crossed—and I understand more than I can say how you are feeling. Fortunately, none of our young friends or family were directly involved in the horror of 9/11—but a few were indirectly brushed and got away from the area hit very quickly—2 children (in their young adult years, 25+) of close friends here left the Soho area, walked to Brooklyn where their father picked them up 2 days later.

My "problem" is an old chronic one only worsened by the onset of aging—for now I'm functioning again and have to proceed w[ith] care and caution—but bin Laden & his crazed followers don't help much. Tom Friedman, the correspondent who writes for the *N[ew] Y[ork] Times* said today in his op-ed column the combination of "evil, education and suicidal" bent is a frightening one, beyond all or any imagination.[2] I will add it bespeaks a world ahead of such sorry dimensions as to put all past history in the shade. Trying to "figure" it out by any means at our disposal (rationality is beside the point) is beyond any scenario any one can invent or speculate on. All I can tell you is that it proves once again my essential dark assessment of what our species is inherently. You are right when you say 9/11 is a major dividing line, a crucial-beyond-crucial nodal point. Bin Laden is a maniac. But that doesn't make his way of seeing the war ahead "wrong." On the contrary while everyone in the West, including Americans, Europeans and Israelis, shy away from speaking of the coming conflict as a "crusade" or "clash of cultures" and "civilizations," he declared it yesterday, the day before, doesn't matter which, "A Jewish-Christian Crusade against the Islamic World," words to that effect. But note the coupling. Not to be brushed aside as a foolish notion etc. It's what he wants it to be; it justifies his hatred in every way possible. It is *JIHAD* in every sense. And that's what neither the West—nor the Israelis or Jews anywhere—are willing to concede. The ancient hatred which led to the medieval Christian Crusades still burns in Islam. Jews are generally too "optimistic" to even grant such truths.

I must be not all "Jewish." Neither is Ariel Sharon. Keep walking, Isty, shuffling or not. […]

George

235

29 SEPTEMBER 2001

Addendum to 9/25, old friend, nothing "new"—the American and European "intelligence" communities are having some luck—but imagine what it must be like to chase shadows. Ours is a porous culture, more apertures and holes than any Swiss cheese the Swiss ever produced—and these maniacs are possessed by *idées fixes*. A new figure close to bin Laden surfaces—an Egyptian "dissident" whose name I didn't get—like bin Laden, he wants to kill Jews and Christians. That simple. I did a bit of reading in Bulfinch's *Mythology*, last part devoted to Charlemagne.[3] In his introduction Bullfinch gives a thumbnail history of Mohammed, the Prophet of Islam. No sooner had he made his Hegira in 622 (age 40) to Medina (now in Saudi Arabia) than he gathered his followers around him, armed them, and went off and spread (by sword) the Holy Word of Islam across the north of Africa, took most of Spain, and even conquered cities in southern France (also Indus Valley, Persia, etc.). That's where Charles Martel, the grandfather of Charlemagne comes into the picture and cleans them out of France (by Battle of Tours) and pursues them into Spain across the Pyrenees. Etc. etc. (Then, of course, in 1492 Ferdinand and Isabella chase the "Moors" out of Spain—and incidentally send the Jews out too.) The memory of Defeat burns in the hearts and minds of the Defeated (the American South is a fine example). They never forget (same with the Passover remembrance year after year & the telling of the Plagues, etc.). So it is our "good" fortune—those of us living in 2001—to be present at the moment the Defeated all over Islam decide to revenge themselves against the Heathen, the Infidels, then think: What does this have to do with "Time"? Anything? It's as though the Islamic mind brushes Western Time aside and acts when it feels the situation is right for taking the long-awaited revenge. That says more to me about the situation facing Israel all these years than any *Realpolitik* analysis. And how horribly wrong were the Doves. I remember remonstrating with Isaac Stern—you heard he died recently I'm sure—and Isaac was a Dove among Doves—that the Arabs don't know anything about what Jews and Christians might call "reasonable."[4] And however much one dislikes Ariel Sharon personally he was closer to the "truth" than any other Israeli leaders so-called. So we are in the first weeks of a *Jihad* coupled with hi-tech means which the Muslims know how to use and will use again and again. Even destroying the Taliban hold on Afghanistan will not change the larger picture. The ones I feel truly sorry for are the young, the generation of our grandchildren. We're dropping away by the very nature of old age. We see it here almost daily. It again has nothing to do with whether we like it or not. We are root and branch in Nature's inexorable grip and all the writing otherwise won't change it. I accept that. But I am fighting hard to stick around long enough to finish my memoirs—not an autobiography; I couldn't care less—but the story of how & why I wrote as I did in the times I lived through. Incidentally, Isty, did you hear that the maniac Stockhausen left Hamburg in disgrace after his concerts were cancelled because he made a public statement @ 9/11 that it was—"it" being the terrorist attacks—"the greatest work of art ever in the cosmos"![5] […]

George

236

17 OCTOBER 2001

My dear George,

With your Sept. 25 letter arriving today(!) and having also your Sept. 23 one, which came last week(!) I have a picture of your soul/mind before me, keeping company with my mind in a similar turbulence, reaching here and there for causes, precedents, history of what have you, only to come up with more questions and from all this caboodle one derives not a firm point upon [which] to start to imagine a sensible plan/attitude, etc. 'framework,' rationale, upon which one could attempt to build something of a sensible response for oneself as a starter. But as our new realities assert themselves, for a little while at least, one longs to climb out from this viscous, sticky liquid of foreboding, worry (a dull, distant fear for some, for me, too, fleetingly, and I emphasize fleetingly …). Really I am not afraid of that distant madman bin Laden. I have behind me the memory of Hitler with his 1930s rants on the radio, his descent to Auschwitz, his Hungarian henchmen who killed near 480,000 Hungarian Jews; I have before me the hanged killer of our labour battalion who was ready to finish me off at a critical moment in July 1944 on the Polish/Hungarian/Russian front. I looked into his eyes 2 feet away. That was really close. But I was too exhausted then to feel fear. Then came a miracle and 5 huge munitions trucks appeared heading for the nearby pass in the eastern Carpathians and took all the 300 of us over the climb, into relative safety inside Hungary. (There our guards were not authorized to kill those unable to walk.) That was a close call and here I am telling you the tale 57 years after the fact.

But back to our awful situation. What to say? First of all: while remaining with all my deep concerns for our world here (libertarian democracy, amazing achievements in the ease of living for the likes of us, excess for the super rich, wonderful achievements in sundry sciences, great art institutions, many young who continue dreaming great personal scenarios for their lives, gifted young artists, writers, painters, who devote themselves to their inner voices, even if it means a life close to poverty). Yes, we also have the mixed results of 'globalization' ... Is this also, among other facets, a kind of economic/cultural colonization attempt to homogenize a wonderfully pluralistic world? Perhaps? Likely so? Have you read Rohinton Mistry's great Indian saga entitled *A Fine Balance*?[6] It is worth your while to check it out along this theme.

[...]

But back to this bearded monster in Afghanistan. He is the enemy. And I totally identify with the policy of the U.S. in trying to thwart him & his associates, while so rightly shoring up our North American self-defenses. There is only a single North American boat, George! You, and I, with our dear ones, friends, and neighbours are sitting in it. I don't have qualms about this focusing of our minds. I have no trouble with the prudent resolve to go after the person (Bin L[aden]) his henchmen and protectors. This is the imperative first and nth task, until this messy job is done with. After some normalcy(???) will be reestablished in our bailiwick, then we could begin to address the other problems.

First (for me) the problem of Israel/Palestine. (Now a positive feature is the quiescence(?) of Arafat. The man appears to be sitting on a fence, and this could be worse. In my view, when the dust settles, Israel should allow for the establishment of a viable Palestinian state and go all the way with the compromises ... to the limit, which will be still compatible with the ultimate nonnegotiable security of the State of Israel, the home of the survivors of the Holocaust, their children and their grandchildren, together with Jews who came from Mid-Eastern, North-African lands, etc. There should be a meeting-point where the two jurisdictions could coexist and get on with their developments/traditions/statisms/dynamisms, worldliness/religious orientation, and all the other contrasts. Living with differences is the key, it appears to me. How to instill a sense of security telling the parties that my neighbour, former deadly foe, does not contemplate killing me while I, my wife, and my children are asleep.

But the present turmoil would seem to say that this dream of mine is precisely that: a pipe dream. Perhaps so … perhaps for a while longer, perhaps for many years … But one can dream, I must dream! Now the reality seems to be different. All these screaming mobs in Pakistan going through their street-theaters: burning flags, effigies pounded to smithereens, mob leaders (the French call them *meneurs*) work overtime, arms flail in the air. But what one doesn't see is the TV cameras, held by, often, Western cameramen in front of which the mob (500?, 2000?, 5000?, one doesn't know for sure) performs. This is, at the least in part, street theater. And then who are the demonstrators? What is the rest of the neighbourhood doing? How strong is the regime? The law enforcement bodies? The TV images are raw, undigested data. That's all. But behind the footage is the insatiable appetite of our National media, here in North America, for footage, never mind how counter it is to our national, etc., interests. It is viewable footage, to hold the scared viewer, until the next clip of advertisements come on. Sordid business this, all, of course, under the hallowed principle of 'free speech.' One other systemic contradiction some(!?) might say. One is ambivalent. But what's wrong with feeling/being ambivalent? (This is one of the central themes of *Millennial Mall*, of course.)

But once the hard, difficult job of 'neutralizing' the gangster-terrorists is done (it will take some time, I'm certain) then will come the other task. Some people at least will want to question the home front. How did this come about? What, if any, part of the responsibility should we own up to? Here I can only say that you, and I, walked along with open, critical, and, yes, often ambivalent feelings & thoughts about our world here & now. While I am acutely grateful for Canada allowing me in, and giving me a wonderful home for 52 years, it all is compatible with the Canadian near-official attitude that the country is forever improvable. It is a non-ending, ongoing process. Our reality now with its headlong tendencies in certain directions is perhaps not an unprecedented process. Various forces might bring along a new equilibrium. Your Wall Street gives some powerful signals in this instance. But this is beyond my ken. Another thing: our North American/West European (even Central & Eastern European!) junk culture (alongside with Harvard, Yale, etc. and all the Nobel winners) is another, and similarly powerful trend. Awful much moneys are riding here. Young crooners, guitar pickers and drummers are dreaming in Technicolour of the fast/big buck. Young nubile females, males, are in the 10s of 1000s willing to sell their 'bloom years' for fame and glory and lots of cash. But this always seemed to be the case! I stumbled the other day on a short text of Erasmus: *In Praise of Folly* (ca. 1510!).[7] In parts it reads as a description of today's scene here. I also checked out recently Petronius Arbiter's text, *The Satyricon*.[8] It was the edition put together by none other than Oscar Wilde, full of lewd illustrations. That was nearly 2000(!) years ago, under Nero's reign. Petronius, as you surely have known, was one of Nero's cronies, and courtiers. But he also fell out of grace with the emperor and was obliged to commit suicide. End of that story. To sum up: our junk culture was, is, and will continue to barrel on as long as they can enslave young impressionable minds in the thrall of their irrepressible sexual instincts, and their desperate search for easy shortcuts in search of an identity. All the brand-logos, labels, delude the young with the sham promise of 'off-the-shelf' identity. Just hand over the money, kid ... how you got it (begged it, earned it, etc.) we couldn't care less about. Just hand it over in big globs. But why to bad-mouth the kids only? There are 60-year-old 'kids' with much money at hand who also go for popularly labelled goods, like a Mercedes SUV, costing ca. $60,000 Canadian, if not more. Just test-drive it and you have the option to drive it away with your new identity as the owner of this shiny job. But if the guy earned the money? What's wrong with buying this toy? The question leads to another one, it is endless. [...]

Istvan

PS: I also checked out Vol. 1 (of 5) of the U[niversity] of Chicago's *Fundamentalism Project*. Awful read this (one of the editors is Martin Marty), informative, etc. but couldn't read it for long ...[9]

237

13 NOVEMBER 2001

My dear Isty, old friend,

I read your last letter with a sense of how the terrors of the present stir up the years & times of the dangers of our youth. And yesterday's plane crash—accident? Or some other machination at work?[10] It's as though there's a fog, thick beyond description enveloping the world and no one really knows what's really happening or how to deal with it. 1939–1945 was crystal clear once the die was cast—more like the clarity of Mozart (a helluva metaphor!)—but the clouds surrounding events and people on all sides of the unanswerable question gather, deepen, thicken ... my only defense is to get up every day (weekends included) and push on to write a few more pages in the memoir. Chapter 8 revision is done so now there are approximately 400+ typed pages. How many more to go? Not quite sure; but as much again, probably. I'm trying to live up to Wm. B. Yeats's old-age wisdom where he says "he who would sing a lasting song, sings from his marrow bone" (or did he say "write" and not "sing"?).[11] But I will confess there are those times when I'm worn out with the effort to keep ahead of the mortar shells. Strange to find I'm constitutionally in total agreement with Heraclitus and the other Pre-Socratics: existence is war and conflict. "Peace" is simply the pause between necessary cessation to recoup and return to the struggle.[12] (Did I ever tell you how glad I am I never became a "novelist?") […]

George

238

3 DECEMBER 2001

Dear old friend Isty,

This is one of those special times when writing you a letter is a real occasion—because two copies of your book arrived from the press at the end of last week and big congratulations are in order. It's a fine-looking volume, hefty to the hand and handsomely carried out. Inevitably, I turned to the piece I wrote weaving something of ourselves and our lives into a tale which has its own resonance.[13] Believe it or not I had not seen it or read it since after I sent it off back in '94 (seems many ages ago). And after reading it I understood and savored your comments on it in your last letter. Which is to say I enjoyed all over again the fact that you enjoyed it. It will take some time and a number of readings before I can familiarize myself with all that's there—and you have to admit there's a lot. I dipped into Benjamin's discussion and analysis but had some tough sledding with his concepts and dense-packed prose.[14] But that's nothing new for me: I've always found even the most cogent analytic discourse begins to pall. The only exception being on rare, rare occasions rediscovering Donald Tovey and enjoying his English pace and attitudes—breezy and edged or laced with wit, acerbic and otherwise.[15] But perhaps more to the point is what you yourself think @ what someone like Benjamin has to say about your music. The last time someone sent me an analysis of something of mine I said to the author: "I'm sure it's very good and says interesting things—but I have trouble understanding what you're getting at." And so it was, I didn't. What I want to do as soon as I can is start reading <u>your</u> prose pieces. So bravo! Many times over, Isty. It was/is one of those personal events which lifted some of the pressures ever piling higher in re The Weird War as I call it—and over the weekend the horrendous news @ the killings & casualties in Jerusalem and Haifa. I have to restrain myself at this point—but only to say I wouldn't trust the whole Islamic kit & kaboodle of 'em—Arafat is a duplicitous, triplicitous, quadruplicitous lying conniver—and no Arab is to be believed or trusted. Their minds are like their script: twisted & curving in circuitous ways—nothing straight there.

[…]

George

[…]

NOTES

1 Benson Bobrick, *The Making of the English Bible* (London: Weidenfeld and Nicolson, 2001).

2 Thomas L. Friedman, "Foreign Affairs: Terrorism Game Theory," *The New York Times*, 25 September 2001. Friedman is perhaps most widely known for his analysis of globalization, *The Lexus and the Olive Tree* (New York: Farrar, Straus and Giroux, 1999).

3 Thomas Bulfinch, *Mythology: The Age of Fable, The Age of Chivalry, The Legends of Charlemagne* (New York: Crowell, 1970).

4 Isaac Stern, who made the first recording of Rochberg's Violin Concerto (see "1973," note 3), died on 22 September 2001 at age 81.

5 On 16 September 2001, Karlheinz Stockhausen referred to the terrorist attacks in New York City as "the greatest work of art ever." Although he quickly retracted his comments and apologized, concerts of his music scheduled for 18 and 19 September in Hamburg were cancelled; he is said to have left Hamburg "in distress." "Attacks Called Great Art," *The New York Times*, 19 September 2001.

6 Rohinton Mistry, *A Fine Balance* (Toronto: McClelland and Stewart, 1995).

7 *Erasmus In Praise of Folly*, illustrated with many curious cuts, designed, drawn, and etched by Hans Holbein, with portrait, Life of Erasmus, and his epistle addressed to Sir Thomas More (London: Reeves, 1876).

8 *The Satyricon of Petronius Arbiter*, translation attributed to Oscar Wilde, with an introduction by Wilde and illustrations by Alexander King (New York: Privately printed for the Hogarth Press, 1932).

9 Martin E. Marty and R. Scott Appleby, eds., *The Fundamentalism Project*, 5 vols. (Chicago: University of Chicago Press, 1991–95). Vol. 1 is entitled *Fundamentalisms Observed.* A sixth volume, ed. Gabriel A. Almond, R . Scott Appleby, and Emmanuel Sivan, was published in 2002.

10 On 12 November 2001 American Airlines flight 587 crashed minutes after takeoff from New York's Kennedy Airport, killing all 260 people on board as well as several on the ground. The official investigation suggested that "wake turbulence" may have been responsible; although sabotage was not ruled out, all the evidence pointed to mechanical failure.

11 The reference is to the first verse of Yeats's "A Prayer for Old Age" from *A Full Moon in March* (1935): "God guard me from those thoughts men think / In the mind alone; / He that sings a lasting song / Thinks in a marrow-bone."

12 "One must realize that war is common, and justice strife, and that all things come to be through strife and are so ordained." Heraclitus, of Ephesus, *Fragments*, a text and translation with a commentary by T.M. Robinson (Toronto: University of Toronto Press, 1987), 49.

13 See "1994," note 7.

14 William Benjamin, "Alternatives of Voice: Anhalt's Odyssey from Personalized Style to Symbolic Expression," in Robin Elliott and Gordon E. Smith, eds., *Istvan Anhalt: Pathways and Memory* (Montreal and Kingston: McGill-Queen's University Press, 2001), 164–307.

15 Sir Donald Francis Tovey (1875–1940), British pianist, composer, and musicologist, Reid Professor of Music at the University of Edinburgh (1914–40), is best remembered for his multi-volume *Essays in Musical Analysis.*

2002

239

[copy of a FAX sent to Anhalt]

11 JANUARY 2002

Dear Isty, old friend,

I'm sorry not to be able to be with you and Beate, your family and friends on this great day of your book launching, another marker in your long trek capped with recognition of your accomplishments in music which have earned you the love and respect and admiration of so many, myself included. So I greet you on this milestone occasion as a brother-in-spirit and send you warmest wishes and congratulations. […]

George

240

16 JANUARY 2002

My dear George,

This interrupts your exciting work on your memoirs (a future exciting read for me, among other friends & admirers of yours) … just for a minute … I feel an urge to write this little report to you about the book-launch that took place in the Queen's U[niversity] Music Library on Friday last (the 11th) …

It was a lively occasion … about 80–90 people were present (all contributors to the book but you, Robin Elliott who teaches in Dublin, Ireland, and Bill Benjamin who was unable to come from Vancouver—quite a distance & expense—and friends) … Surprise: 30 copies of the book were sold at this event, and I was busy with writing friendly words (names) in the copies. Gordon Smith was the master of ceremonies and he, after thanking sundry contributors to the book & the launch, continued by reading 'messages,' starting with your warm and 'personal' letter to me (a lovely text, my dear Friend, for which I am grateful/thankful to you, as on several similar occasions in the past when our friendship was reinforced by expressions of affection and mutual high regard ever so generously expressed), continuing with others. The event coincided with a display (in glass cupboards, etc. of documentation of my doings (scores, etc.) (see enclosure).[1] Then there was food & drinks (hospitality of the School of Music) with music (2 flutes & keyboard) in the 'background' … After 7 p.m. friends and out-of-town visitors (inc[luding] Alan Gillmor) came to the house where there was more food & wine … The day ended for us at about midnight … It was a fine day. (Helen & Carol were unable to come, but our grandkids came …) Oh yes; there even was a local TV interview in the aft[ernoon] … Quite a full day, one could say …

Istvan

NOTE

1 Enclosed copies of several pages from the Queen's University website announcing "an exhibition in honour of the recent publication of *Istvan Anhalt: Pathways and Memory*," presented by the W.D. Jordan Special Collections & Music Library.

2003

241

14 MARCH 2003

Isty, old friend,

[…] I confess I'm no longer comfortable in this world for so many reasons, the most immediate Bush's push to Empire, spread Democracy to the Moslems in the Middle East as he slowly is squeezing the life out of our "democratic form of government" right here in the States. World Dominion is his goal. And he is as convinced of the righteousness of his ambition as ever Caesar was of his, Napoleon his, Hitler his. If you can, get hold of the latest March issue of *N[ew] Y[ork] Review of Books* and Norman Mailer's piece "Only in America."[1] The man is a veritable old-time shaman. He sees into the immediate and far future. My own insights rec[eive]d more than full corroboration from his articulation of meanings and intentions inherent in Bush's attitudes & actions. Whatever the future it looks mighty grim—and culturally, too. The values we believe in (still, I'm sure) are being pushed to the far periphery. I don't know @ Canada, but the good ol' USA is physically obese (a revolting sight), fat in body as well as mind. Ignorance (and love of) rules alongside of pursuit of pleasures, unreality, cheap sensation, bad art, music, movies, theater, et al. The inevitable disintegration of the slow slide down the drain that started not long after WW II ended. And as for the Europeans—France, Germany, Russia, others—they've had more than their fill of war & death and horrors going back centuries. I don't blame them for wanting to lead the quiet life and whenever possible to die in bed. The old lust for glory, *la gloire*, finished there—but not here with Bush & Co. It's a replay of old Rome but bigger, much, much bigger. […]

George

242

2 JULY 2003

Dear Old Friend Isty,

Amazing enuf to be turning 85—but bordering on the unreal that the Sacher Archives in Basel should have made me such a grand present!* Strangest of all, the *Caprice Variations* which I wrote as a lark seems to have caught the fancy of so many fiddlers.[2] Anyway, even as life seems (as now) somehow a constant amazement, the "real" world takes on more and more the look of too dark a forest where strange rites and rituals are being performed by still stranger creatures. Against such a background music remains the magic shield—though there seem to be tremors out there vis-à-vis the orchestra world: one grand corporate mess; bankruptcies, facing financial disasters etc. […]

George

*Enclosed with this letter page 42 of the fair copy of *Caprice Variations* for unaccompanied violin (1970) held by the Paul Sacher Foundation in Basel.

243

11 SEPTEMBER 2003

Dear Old Friend Isty,

Bea's garden so beautiful—a touch of beauty in a terrible world—a difficult summer for me—brief (though still too long) stay in hospital in Aug.—much better now—gathering strength for a few things—cataract removal, etc. The CD enclosed is first of two Naxos has released.[3] Bless diversity! […]

George

244

1 OCTOBER 2003

My dear George,

The sounds of your music on the CD you've sent me are still in my ear/mind as I'm writing this … *Black Sounds* is truly powerful and masterly so … The sounds (and colorfully 'black' they are) and the angular articulation of the 'discourse' unite convincingly! Yes, I 'hear' the homage to Varèse, the splendid old/young man we both met in Stratford in

1960 … I still have the sounds of his *Déserts* in my ear … But your piece is very much G.R.! It is an anguished/raw cry from the heart …

The *Cantio Sacra* transcription is a soothing contrast … much to the point in this context … *Phaedra* (from 1973–4, if I'm not mistaken) is also a powerful work. The late baroque gestures ('hints' only here) are welded together with the expertly conceived 'raw' sounds in it to create the character of this savage female who seduced Racine, before compelling you to give her voice in such a convincing way. Another *réussite*, evident to responsive ears/minds … Once again <u>bravo</u>!

Of the 2 CDs here enclosed (both are real-time concert performances) *Sonance•Resonance (Welche Töne?)* dates from 1989 (it was premiered by the Toronto Symphony [Günther Herbig conductor] in Sept. 1989).[4] *Millennial Mall (Lady Diotima's Walk)* was done by the Winnipeg Symphony, the Elmer Iseler Singers, and Valdine Anderson is the soprano solo; it was premiered in Jan. 2000 in Winnipeg.[5] The CD is a copy of that performance. […]

The enclosed program booklet of the Kingston Symphony has info[rmation] about a new piece of mine: *The Tents of Abraham*.[6] 'People' (members of our family, friends & others) asked me, from time to time, what I think of the awful situation existing between the Israelis and Palestinians … Looking for a *terminus ab quo* that <u>could</u> be relevant here, I've ended up with the time of Abraham … The outcome of all this is the new piece, quite likely my 'rounding-out' statement about wanderers/searchers … a 'role' and 'type' I have known only too well … […]

Istvan

245

10 NOVEMBER 2003

Dear Old Friend Isty,

I hardly know where to begin. But certainly my warm thanks for your CDs. You're going to have to forgive me but I've had no time to renew old acquaintance yet. All of October was preoccupied with hospital and gallstone removals endoscopically (weird stuff, all of it!) and during recuperating period working like mad on putting together the mss. for the revised and expanded edition of the old 1984 *Aesthetics of Survival* which is scheduled to come out next fall in paperback. Gave me a chance to remove pieces I found had lost their lustre and replace 6 pieces I'd wearied of with things I wrote (& some publ[ished] in journals here & there) <u>following</u> 1984 which still "ring" for me. The oddity of which I'm very fond in the "new" group is a 1957 piece, an imaginary dialogue that takes place in the great Beyond between Stravinsky and Schoenberg I call "My Dear Igor." So here in early Nov[ember] I'm feeling a bit more like my old self. […] I shall enjoy Doing Nothing—or, at the very least, very little, for a while. Sheer luxury. Only problem there is I become too aware of the wretched state of the world of human beings. Bush & Co. are Robbing Us Blind. It's all a replay of the old Roosevelt (Teddy) Era of the Robber Barons stealing everything in Broad Daylight & getting away with it. Meanwhile he struts about like the braggart stupid fool he is acting as though he knows what he's doing in Iraq (which he & his military clearly do not know what's up), treating the rest of the other nations like Dolts (but then again I'm not too impressed w[ith] France, Germany, Italy, et al. either). A Fine Stupid Mess, our First Great Emperor of the Great American Empire based on Hot Air and Technology and very sad indeed at all the illness among the people here and among our friends. I find all too little to comfort me except Gene who was (and remains) the greatest trouper during my nightmare period. […]

George

NOTES

1 Norman Mailer, "Only in America," *New York Review of Books*, 27 March 2003, 49–53.
2 See "1999," note 18.
3 In 2002 Naxos released a recording of *Black Sounds*, *Cantio Sacra*, and *Phaedra* performed by the Boston Modern Orchestra Project under the direction of Gilbert Rose (Naxos 8.559120), and, in 2003, Symphony No. 5, *Black Sounds*, and the *Transcendental Variations* performed by the Saarbrücken Radio Symphony Orchestra, Christopher Lyndon-Gee, conductor. Naxos has since released a recording of the Violin Concerto and the Second Symphony (with *Imago Mundi*) (see "1994," note 8) and the First Symphony, Naxos 8.559214 (2007), all with the same forces.
4 See "1989," note 5.
5 See "1999," note 21.
6 *The Tents of Abraham* (2003), an orchestral piece in five movements, was premiered by the Kingston Symphony Orchestra, Glen Fast, conductor, at Grant Hall, Queen's University, on 11 January 2004. This piece received a Juno award in 2005 in the "best classical composition" category.

2004

246

19 FEBRUARY 2004

My dear George,

[…] I better not get into politics, war, terror, and the like. I still read the papers & watch the evening news … The world is changing in some ways … I guess. I also watch with indifference the machinations related to technology, dumbed-down entertainment … yet I would be churlish not to acknowledge that there are noticeable positive features in my professional life. (The personal dimension, within family and a few friends, is, of course, of a kind which must, & does, require gratitude …) The enclosed [program note for *The Tents of Abraham*] tells of some of these … Yes, there was the premiere of a new orchestral piece (my first in multiple movements) on Jan. 11th last: *The Tents of Abraham*. It 'clocked in' at 37 minutes, my longest orchestral work. I guess I need not tell you why I thought of writing a piece with this title … The response was such that I could believe that I reached a few 'ears' … […]

Istvan

247

26 FEBRUARY 2004

My dear Isty,

[…] Strange lot we humans. I see TV pictures of Israel, then the walls built to keep the Palestinians out (Frost said somewhere in one of his poems: "fences make good neighbors"),[1] then I read the program about your *Tents of Abraham* as your idealistic "picture" in music of

Abraham's "offspring" living in peace side by side. A dream picture. Perhaps a myth to be realized in some as yet unknown future. But whatever the hope, the ideal in the dream, Abraham or no-Abraham, the reality stares us in the face: human beings are essentially a dysfunctional species, the naked ape who makes war on his own kind and most other kinds. Years ago I wrote a work for baritone & small orchestra (or large ensemble) for Testimonium, a celebration of Jerusalem. I called it *Mizmur l'Piyus: Sacred Song of Reconciliation* [1970]. I believed the myth, the dream then—but unhappily am no longer able to. For the Jews of Israel to survive in the midst of barbarians such as the Arabs are (Ishmael somewhere in the Bible is referred to as the "wild man of the Desert")[2]—survival being what is at issue, not borders, territory, hegemony, those are merely tools (political) to an end—they have no recourse after what has been the demonstrated fact of Arab unwillingness to accept that Jews live, are alive in their midst, and that they (the Arabs) are determined one way or another to destroy them. I pointed out to an American mathematician friend who lives in Israel with his family and works at the Weizman Institute that if you find vermin in your house, you stamp them out. Poor man, he was visibly shocked at my remark. If I were to suddenly turn into a historian or cultural/political commentator I would plan to write a book "explaining" the title: "The Great Unravelling." Signs and portents, the central core of which may be traced physically to the Middle East, abound on all sides. As it is, I have quite enuf to do seeing my old *Aesthetics of Survival* through to the fall release of its revised paperback edition. Also trying to find a publisher for my memoirs. If I'm lucky, that will encourage me to write the last chapter. […]

George

248

19 MARCH 2004

My dear George,

[…] The premiere of the *T[ents] of A[braham]* piece was quite an experience and this, with the routine work (proofreading of the parts, interaction with an excellent conductor, rehearsals …), took quite a bit out of me, but after our 3-week stay in the south of Portugal, with its slow life (good eating, walks around town & on a fabulous beach, etc.), with good 'reads'—the daily *Frankfurter Allgemeine Zeitung*, with its superb 'Feuilleton' section, and 3 fine books: a Galileo biography by James Reston Jr., Saramago's *The Cave* (S[aramago] is a great novelist!) and parts of a Mercator biography (by??)—I got back to 'normal' whatever that means.[3]

Now I ought to turn to your reaction to the 'Abraham' piece. I must say candidly that I am at a loss about how I should go about it ... As a starter we could agree in our deep commitment to our Jewish personae ... This is 'non-negotiable.' "We' as individual Jews must survive, and this 'survival' today is inconceivable without the peaceful existence of Israel. Where, we, individual Jews, might fail to be in agreement with each other, might reside in how the security of the existence of individual Jews (wherever they reside), and how the security of the existence of the State of Israel, are best achieved. (Both hinge, of course, in the relationship between Jew and non-Jew!) The idea of (1) writing this "Abraham' piece and (2) the way I tried to present the 'story,' are both derived from fairly deep considerations that might only correspond in part with the way you see this tale both in its own epoch, as well as diachronically, including our own days. To dig into this via correspondence is a daunting task which I, for one, am reluctant to undertake. In my case, I don't see it as being my 'task' ('duty'), or whatever, to try to sway you from your 'interpretation.' We relate to this whole mountain of stories, both of us, in our individual ways, and SO BE IT! (Just one detail: you are correct in pointing out the 'character-snap-shot' of Ishmael in Genesis ... To have included in this piece a 'clear' reference to it, would have made my 'approach,' as expressed in the dedication, not feasible. So: I have remained silent about it, although the music in m[o]v[men]t 4 ["The Two Sons (Boys' Games)"] depicts the drama in the games these two half-brothers are playing ...

All the above is 'framed' today in the almost daily atrocities one reads about and the 'injection' of films such as Mel Gibson's 'retelling'(??) of the Christ story [*The Passion of the Christ* (2004)] into this already overheated public situation. Enuf! As you have written. Indeed!

[...]

Istvan

NOTES

1 The proverb "Good fences make good neighbors" is quoted twice in Frost's poem "Mending Wall" from *North of Boston* (1914).

2 See Genesis 16.12 and 21.20–21.

3 James Reston, Jr., *Galileo: A Life* (New York: Harper Collins, 1994.); José Saramago, *The Cave*, trans. Margaret Jull Costa (London: Harvill, 2002); Nicholas Crane, *Mercator: The Man Who Mapped the Planet* (London: Weidenfeld and Nicolson, 2002).

2005

249

20 APRIL 2005

Dear old Friend, Isty,

I've been plugging away at reading our letters and stopped a few moments ago at page 234. My assistant (or secretary—whichever comes closest to her enormous range of help to me) Beverly Holmes[1] called to say she was bringing chapters from the (by now) old "treatise" on Chromaticism this morning & would be a little delayed. Not quite but almost simultaneously I have been proofreading treatise stuff and our voluminous correspondence, trying to get as much done as aging energy and capacity to focus allow so that things will be in "progress" while I'm being "fixed up" for a few more "miles" of living. I'm wanting to complete everything I can before the last "act." I came across references—copious ones I must say—to something I wrote back in '85/86: "Iconography of the Mind: Inward Seeing and Iconic Thinking."[2] Your comments were amazingly detailed—but would you believe, I'd completely forgotten @ the paper? I'm asking Alan Gillmor to arrange if he can—don't want to bother you, only if it is necessary—to have a Xerox sent me from your archives. Curious how you keep urging me to be more personal. (My reticence of course is a lifelong shield.) I now begin to understand Alan G.'s excitement over discovering our correspondence. So here he is working like mad!! […]

George

250

5 MAY 2005

My dear George,

Your March 29th letter came with this morning's mail, following our long telephone talk about the volume to contain our correspondence (it promises to be quite a 'dense' text). There is still a considerable amount of work to be done by A. Gillmor, as we agreed, and proofreading, etc. chores by the 2 of us. But with a bit of luck we'll all manage to accomplish our share of this … (NB: I am very heartened to know that we share similar positive views concerning Alan G.!)

Your words about health matters, doctors, and other aspects of the normal(?!?) process of accumulating years, leave me with such a load of conflicting thoughts and feelings (this is the important domain!) that I cannot even begin to put them into (adequate … apposite …) expressions … I can only wish for us all that our aging should be slow, stress-free, etc. and we should (we … all …) should have the mind/'heart' to bear what must be faced … however hard a job it is. You and I know that we are able to 'share' in a multidimensional way, thoughts and feelings. Please let me, us, share in your reality and I promise to keep on having for you the same feelings of friendship and yes(!) LOVE, too, as always! Your (also) aging friend, still (also) in love with music.

Istvan

251

[undated but postmarked 21 May 2005]

Dear Friends,

Thanks so much for your warm wishes & lovely card. I read it to George this evening & could tell he took real pleasure in most of the news. Please thank Alan G. for me; his card was most kind & George has enjoyed their "telephone" friendship. […]

I purposely leave my words about George for last. I am extremely worried about him. At the point when he should be getting stronger each day he grows weaker & tho the surgery was a success there's something else to deal with which more testing should reveal. As soon as the news is better I'll be in touch again.

Meantime my best to all the family & love to you, Bea & to Isty. Keep well & continue to make this world beautiful with your presence.

Gene

252

26 MAY 2005

Dear Gene, dear George, both of you at least doubly dear!

Thank you for the latest note. We are with the two of you both in heart and mind … But, of course, this is hardly news … Dear Friends: make it sure that you work fully on getting better, reaching a *niveau* of well-being with which, we, all octogenarians, can be in peace with! (Long time ago I jettisoned unrealistic levels of perfection re: health … as my walking turned to ambling, and my ca. 8 hrs/day sleep allocation grew to 9–10 (in installments). I came to be with peace (in peace) within what asserted itself as my spontaneous reality … What matters now (the latest novelty is that due to macular degeneration I cannot read (with my left eye …) is to adjust to the daily *niveau* of reality (somatic that is) which is my lot and maintain a degree of inner peace. I don't know how it is with you, George, dear buddy of mine … sometimes I feel like listening to an old recording of a piece of mine, but lately I just sit, with eyes closed and find myself roaming across vast expanses of the past on a contraption(??) that puts into the shade the fastest & most versatile magic carpet (or its technological derivative) … I flit here and there in memory-space, totally on the wings of the mind, ignoring all other physiological givens … I find this absolutely wonderful, and specially stressless, since I don't expect any suggestion to materialize, that would require a 'travelogue,' i.e., subsequent work, that is … It is all pleasure and no obligation, without anyone watching over with an expectation or another … i.e., I'm free to roam … What better to wish for you, dear Friend, roam freely in memory-space and be at peace, and take your medication as prescribed … A big hug for 2 unique friends … from …

Istvan

NOTES

1 Beverly Holmes (b. 1943), MM (Syracuse University), first met Rochberg when they both worked at Theodore Presser, Rochberg as Director of Publications and Holmes in the Department of Performance Promotion; she served as Rochberg's administrative assistant from May 2000 until his death.

2 See "1985," note 33.

INDEX

www.ingramcontent.com/pod-product-compliance
Lightning Source LLC
Chambersburg PA
CBHW070732120726
47910CB00001B/76
9781554584734